THE COMMUNITY

An Introduction to a Social System

IRWIN T. SANDERS

PROFESSOR OF SOCIOLOGY
UNIVERSITY OF KENTUCKY
AND RESEARCH DIRECTOR
ASSOCIATES FOR INTERNATIONAL RESEARCH, INC.

THE RONALD PRESS COMPANY · NEW YORK

2

Library of Congress Catalog Card Number: 58–5854

PRINTED IN THE UNITED STATES OF AMERICA

To

my wife

PREFACE

This is a book about community life, designed primarily as a textbook for undergraduate courses. It treats the generic characteristics found in all communities, whether large or small, industrial or rural, at home or abroad. At the same time, account is taken of the differences among communities due to size, type of occupation, and cultural heritage. Since the book has been written for those with only an introductory background in sociology, the main stress is upon orientation and the general conceptual framework.

Although attention is given first to a series of social traits, the ultimate objective is to tie these together so that the student can view the community as a social system made up of human relationships. Such relationships are seen as organized around important clusterings or focuses which can be thought of as particular systems conveniently named *local government, education, the family, religion,* and the like. Not only can each such system be studied independently, but each can also be related to all other systems to show the part it plays in the total community.

Wide use is made of basic sociological concepts. These are introduced not for their own sake but because they are needed in the discussion of community life. An effort has been made to place these throughout the book as they are required and in such a way as to permit the explanation of the more complex concepts in terms of simpler concepts which have been already introduced.

Each chapter contains at the end a list of references cited in the text. These publications are also suggested as outside reading. Articles mentioned have purposely been chosen from the standard sociological journals which are apt to be found in most college and university libraries; articles in less-well-known periodicals and in foreign journals have thus been omitted, although some of the ideas from such sources occasionally have found their way into the textual material. Cases cited are chiefly from the United States, although an occasional reference to communities abroad is used to illustrate some important point.

Special acknowledgment should be given to colleagues who have rendered friendly criticism, though, of course, without assuming responsibility for the content of this work. These are Willis A. Sutton, Jr., A. Lee Coleman, and Thomas R. Ford. Mention should also be made of the help of L. E. Griswold in many technical details, the typing by Louise Midkiff, Ruth Armknecht, and Joanna Johnson, and especially the editorial assistance of my wife.

This textbook, like other textbooks, is a compilation of what others have done and of what the author himself has observed and tested in his years as a student of social phenomena. It is written in the belief that a good textbook should stimulate thought even more than it should try to provide definitive answers, that it should open vistas without necessarily drawing in all the details of the scenery, and that it should also give the reader central themes around which his own personal observations can be meaningfully organized. It is hoped that anyone who uses this book will thus see the community—any community he selects—in a new light and that he will be aware of the necessity for proper application of the scientific spirit and method before making broad generalizations. It is also hoped that he will feel challenged to pursue, through further inquiry and study on his own, many interesting topics only partially treated here.

IRWIN T. SANDERS

Cambridge, Massachusetts
January, 1958

CONTENTS

CONTENTS

PART III

Community Action

INTRODUCTION

Different people have different reasons for studying the community. The candidate for public office is often a keen observer of his community because he knows that his election depends upon how well he recognizes and identifies himself with the majority opinion on public issues. The businessman tries to find out what types of product will be in greatest demand a few months hence and to plan accordingly, while the school administrator, though seeking to exercise educational leadership, must nevertheless be aware of community expectations as far as the school system is concerned.

Personal Reasons. Many people study the community to get answers to those questions which are intimately connected with their own immediate welfare. Their definite personal interest reveals itself in many ways, such as in the parents' concern about inadequate recreational facilities for children or in the city councilman's concern about the shrinking tax base as economic values in the central part of the city decline. Certainly, there can be no more legitimate reason than that of personal involvement as a motive for community study, an assumption implicit in every chapter of this book.

Reasons of the Social Scientist. The social scientist is also interested in community study, for he finds in the community a comprehensible social universe. The family and many kinds of social groups deserve special study, but they do not represent the wholeness of life found in the community as defined and used in this book. And the total American society is much too large and complex for the average person to try to fathom. To be sure, describing Little Rock, Arkansas, as a community is difficult, but not nearly so unmanageable a feat as the delineation of the whole of American society. However, when hundreds of communities have been analyzed and the findings put together, those interested should be able to come up with many generalizations about American society itself. Furthermore, the components of a community can be identified and studied and then related to each other. Then what was found to have been true in 1950 can be measured against what holds true in 1960; thus the change over the decade can be traced, and after explanations

hange have been worked out, tentative predictions for 1970
possible (11).*

scientists also study the community because it is almost
a universal social form found wherever human beings live. There
are wide variations, to be sure, but everywhere people strive toward
a common basis for meeting common needs; this is the essence of
community life. But more than that, men learn in communities.

Although the family circle is one of the most important educational agencies, the community also is an influential training ground.
Even the family itself is greatly affected by the type of community
in which it is located. We need only to compare a farm family of a
generation ago with an urban family of today to note how changes
outside the family—that is, within the community—alter family relationships.

Children, even at an early age, move outside the home in their
play contacts and learn much from neighbors and others whom they
meet. Johnny may come home with a black eye and earnestly explain to his mother:

"Timmy hit me in the eye because I saw a picture of the Pope and
laughed at the funny kind of clothes that he wears."

"But," the mother adds, "you know that Timmy is a Catholic and
that you shouldn't say things like that."

"Yes, I knew that Timmy was a Catholic, but I didn't know the
Pope was."

Here, then, is a simple illustration of how one learns through a
play group, school associates, and elsewhere in the community many
lessons that might never be taught at home. A fuller treatment of
this learning process will be given in Chapter 10, which describes
socialization, not in the economic sense of government ownership
but in the sense of preparing individuals for full-scale participation
in society by inculcating in them the basic social values and teaching them to play the roles that others about them expect them to
play (4, 14).

Social scientists are also interested in the processes by which local
people are able to solve, in part at least, their local problems. One
of the most encouraging signs on the social scene is the growing
awareness by action-minded people that preliminary study of their
community is a requisite to successful planning. The rewards of
success are great and they fully justify the extra effort of preliminary
study, for they are shared not only by the members of the community who have experienced the satisfaction derived from doing some-

* Figures in parentheses in the text throughout the book, such as (11) above, refer
by number to the publications listed at the end of each chapter.

thing together but also by those who were wise enough to make the project a community one rather than a narrow one-group affair. But there is the other side that needs to be recognized.

Almost every American community has a social graveyard of unsuccessful community projects. The epitaphs on these community tombstones show with what high hopes these projects came into being and how disillusioning was their death. In one community an organization decides that there is a great need for a community swimming pool. The members of this group move into action. They start raising money, telling others of their plans, and seem to enjoy basking in the limelight of directing a community project. Before they have gotten very far, however, people begin to ask, "Do we really need a swimming pool more than a ball field?" "Can we afford such a costly investment for use only a small part of the year?" "Who do these people think they are that they can tell us what we are to do and not to do?" As the questions increase, the contributions lag; as the contributions lag, the early enthusiasm wanes; as the enthusiasm wanes, the leaders find business and domestic affairs more pressing and devote less and less time to the swimming pool project. A month goes by and nothing happens; two months go by without a committee meeting. Finally, the organization abandons the swimming pool project and gets the permission of the contributors to use the money collected for some other purpose. The former leaders now assert, "You'll never catch me trying to help out this community again." And, indeed, what appears to be ingratitude is hard to bear. But if a leader has studied the community and learned how communities can best go about accomplishing such a project, he knows that the community is not ungrateful. Rather, its members have resented the way the project has been organized and conducted. They want to be in on the planning; they want to participate in the decisions if they are supposed to contribute and benefit.

Despite such failures the positive achievements must not be minimized. As social science knowledge is applied to such efforts, the likelihood of success increases and, at the same time, social science hypotheses are put to the test—a step necessary in the development of any science. In adding up the total effect of all these accomplishments at the local level—most of them undertaken quite apart from governmental initiative or control—one gets a sense of the power that there is in the American way of life. Some of this energy can be wasted by haste or ignorance of what the community really wants; it can be effectively multiplied when based on a sound knowledge of local conditions.

To be realistic, however, one must recognize that the improvement of many local conditions calls for cooperation with public and private agencies outside the community. Even the funds provided from these sources go farther and meet local needs better when there is real citizen participation in planning for the expenditure of these funds. Consequently, a knowledge of the local community is helpful in either case: that in which outside resources are tapped or that in which the local people try to achieve some goal by the use of their own local resources.

Reasons of the Social Philosopher. Americans are *doers;* they like action. When they are aware of a problem, they want "to do something about it." In these days of baffling international tensions most individuals do not feel that they can play any significant part in restoring world order at the global level; many do feel, however, that they can do something about the improvement of their own local community. In this they are on solid ground, for the community is an area well adapted both spatially and socially for substantial achievement by interested citizens. This is one reason for learning more about the nature of community life (1, 13).

The fundamental philosophy on which rests the American governmental structure calls for rule by the people. This means that the people make decisions about those who are to represent them and from time to time even make decisions about specific issues, particularly those of a statewide or community-wide scope. Those who study our political life stress the importance of this decision-making by ordinary people if our democracy is to endure and grow stronger. When people turn over to others the responsibility for controlling all of their affairs and express little interest in what is done and how it is done, then the democratic way of life is jeopardized (12).

The social philosopher asks: "Is there a paternalistic power structure that settles all issues for others in the community without involving them? Is there general apathy toward trying to improve local conditions? Or, are matters of public concern hotly debated by many people and final conclusions reached after a fairly wide airing of the points involved?"

Obviously, the intricate points of foreign policy cannot all be determined simply in the local community, but the implementation of any such policy fundamentally rests upon the support a national administration receives when it requests funds, campaigns for votes, or seeks well-trained personnel from the electorate. An uninformed or misinformed public, a lack of interest, a widespread apathy, can jeopardize what national officials consider to be a sound policy as much as can countermeasures by countries who may feel hostile toward the United States. If this is so, one asks, what are the ways in which people living in Muskogee, Oklahoma, can understand the meaning of and express their concern about questions which must ultimately be decided at the state or national level? One assumption frequently made, which needs periodic re-examination, holds that democracy is stronger where most of the people have the desire and the opportunity to make decisions on matters involving their welfare; it is weaker, on the other hand, where a few people make decisions for all the rest, whom they have not even consulted.

To the extent that community participation is tied in with national security and survival, the community becomes a major focus of interest for those engaged in public affairs. An important development along this line has occurred within the past few years in that branch of our government now called the International Cooperation Administration, which is charged with the responsibility of assisting underdeveloped countries to build up strong defenses against a potential military threat by forming a sound and stable economic base. Five years ago not many American officials connected with this agency recognized the importance of the people who were being served as human beings. The emphasis instead was upon techniques of agricultural production, of highway construction, of industrial management, of improved health standards—all on the implicit assumption that modern techniques bring benefits to those exposed to them. Within the past few years Americans have had some rude awakenings which have made them realize that technology alone does not solve problems nor does it even create friends. Many administrators are learning that people are more important than techniques. Consequently, many of the men responsible for directing the ICA programs in the various countries are now asking that *community development specialists* be attached to their offices to help coordinate the program so that the ordinary people of the country have some voice in, and understanding of, what is being done. They use the trite but expressive statement that they are trying to get the aid down to the grass-roots level and to involve the local community and not just the central governmental officials in the nation's capital (19).

One can chronicle in much greater detail the intense interest the world over in what is currently being called community development. Chambers of commerce, private utility companies, educational administrators, women's clubs, and the like are promoting study of the American community and community development; American

interests abroad—whether governmental or private foundations—
likewise see that the community is an important focus for their activities. Furthermore, many foreign governments are requesting,
through the United Nations and other agencies, the assistance of
community development specialists in their search for answers to
their age-old problems (17). Only time will tell whether the expectation is greater than these specialists can fulfill, but there is no denying the importance being attached to the local community throughout the world today.

Ways of Studying the Community

There are at least three levels at which people can study the community (2, 3, 6, 15). The first is social science research. In this case
professionally trained personnel employ the latest scientific methods
to analyze the underlying social structure and basic processes of a
community. They know what statistical sources to tap, how to select
a representative sample of informants, how to make up question-
naires and conduct interviews, how to analyze newspapers and
other available documents, and particularly how to tabulate and
classify the data collected and draw up the findings (5, 8, 21). This
approach usually is called "research in depth," since no effort is
spared to do as complete a job as possible. The costs usually run
into thousands of dollars, but the findings may result in savings to
community leaders of much more than the original expenditure. Or,
even if the local community does not expect specific benefits, the
research adds important knowledge to the related social science
fields. Only such research, often repeated, can test adequately the
various hypotheses on which the theoretical analysis of community
life depends (3, 7). Many of the statements in this book are based on
studies of this sort.

A second means of studying the community is through a reconnaissance approach or through a self-survey. In the first of these,
social scientists conduct a preliminary study to arrive at a profile of
many important social traits of the community (16). In the self-
survey, a group of local citizens, often with the assistance of an outside consultant, examines various aspects of the community, frequently concentrating on problem areas and trying to work out
possible solutions to these problems (9, 20). Such intermediate research, though not conclusively testing hypotheses about the community, does give considerable help in formulating such hypotheses
for later testing by research in depth.

A third way to study the community is by means of personal observation and individual interpretation. This is the method stressed

in this book, for two reasons. First, those doing basic research need much fuller preparation than any one textbook can provide and they have to learn many lessons in actual field experience; those wishing to make reconnaissance studies or self-surveys can do so as a team and can work out their plans jointly with the help of specially prepared guides. Second, the individual student who has no opportunity for training in research methods or even in a class-sponsored community survey must still live in a community and try to act as an intelligent, observant resident of that community (10). Through the years he can do much to study his community. But to do this most effectively several things will be necessary.

When a new driver is being trained, his teacher first insists that he learn a specialized vocabulary which includes such words as "hand brake," "accelerator," "gear shift," "starter," "fuel tank," and "carburetor." Likewise, if one wishes to analyze a community, he needs a special vocabulary to describe the kind of social phenomena he will see. Such a vocabulary is the first requirement and one which this book should help the student to meet.

Another requirement, sometimes difficult to fulfill, is objectivity. This means putting oneself in the place of other people instead of looking at every matter merely from a personal vantage point. What are the reasons for the behavior of certain groups? Why do some people like and some dislike certain cliques or groups to which the individual observer might belong? In other words, one should try to view the community through the eyes of others; he should try to see what is often called their "definition of the situation."

A further necessity is to check one's observations with those of others. There is no reason to be afraid to talk about the community, even analytically, with those who seem to have its welfare at heart. Should there be disagreement, those involved can decide on ways of getting more facts to clarify the actual situation. Frequently, of course, there is no one simple explanation to account for a failure—say, a Community Chest Drive—or a success—of the Woman's Club Follies, for example. But discussion and questioning can help one get a clearer picture.

Intelligent reading can also be of great assistance in learning about community behavior. Accounts of other communities, whether fictional or real, frequently suggest dimensions of local life which had not previously been observed.

These as well as other suggestions on how to study the community make sense only if one has first taken a thoroughgoing, systematic look at the essential traits of local communities. Such a study is the chief purpose of the chapters which follow.

References and Suggested Readings

1. ALINSKY, SAUL D. *Reveille for Radicals.* Chicago: University of Chicago Press, 1946.
2. ARENSBERG, CONRAD M. "The Community-Study Method," *The American Journal of Sociology,* LX (September, 1954), 109–24.
3. BENNETT, JOHN W. "The Study of Cultures: A Survey of Technique and Methodology in Field Work," *American Sociological Review,* XIII (December, 1948), 672–89.
4. BROWNELL, BAKER. *The Human Community.* New York: Harper & Brothers, 1950.
5. DOBY, JOHN T. (ed.) *An Introduction to Social Research.* Harrisburg: Stackpole Co., 1954.
6. HOLLINGSHEAD, A. B. "Community Research: Development and Present Condition," *American Sociological Review,* XIII (April, 1948), 136–46.
7. ———. *Elmtown's Youth.* New York: John Wiley & Sons, Inc., 1949.
8. JAHODA, MARIE, DEUTSCH, MORTON, and COOK, STEWART. *Research Methods in Social Relations.* New York: The Dryden Press, Inc., 1951.
9. KIMBALL, SOLON T., and PEARSALL, MARION. *The Talladega Story: A Study in Community Process.* University, Ala.: University of Alabama Press, 1954.
10. LAMB, ROBERT K. "Suggestions for a Study of Your Hometown," *Human Organization,* XI (Summer, 1952), 29–32.
11. LYND, ROBERT S., and HELEN M. *Middletown.* New York: Harcourt, Brace & Company, 1937.
12. POSTON, RICHARD W. *Democracy Is You.* New York: Harper & Brothers, 1953.
13. ———. *Small Town Renaissance.* New York: Harper & Brothers, 1950.
14. REDFIELD, ROBERT. *The Little Community.* Chicago: University of Chicago Press, 1955.
15. REISS, ALBERT J. "Some Logical and Methodological Problems in Community Research," *Social Forces,* XXXIII (October, 1954), 51–64.
16. SANDERS, IRWIN T. *Preparing a Community Profile: The Methodology of a Social Reconnaissance.* Lexington: University of Kentucky, Bureau of Community Service, 1952.
17. United Nations, *Series on Community Organization and Development.* Consists of country monographs, regional studies, and bulletins dealing with principles of community organization published over a period of time.
18. United States, Federal Security Agency, *An Approach to Community Development.* Washington, D.C.: International Unit, Social Security Administration, 1952.
19. United States, International Cooperation Administration, *Community Development Bulletin,* No. 1 (January, 1956), Community Development Division.
20. WARREN, ROLAND L. *Studying Your Community.* New York: Russell Sage Foundation, 1955.
21. YOUNG, PAULINE. *Scientific Social Surveys and Research.* 3d ed. Englewood Cliffs, N.J.: Prentice-Hall, Inc., 1956.

PART I

The Social Traits of the Community

INTRODUCTION TO PART ONE

The first ten chapters of this volume serve as an introduction to various aspects of community life. Each one describes some general topic from a particular vantage point, which is shifted before the next general topic is treated. The community is a place; it consists of people; it provides jobs and services; it has a communication network; it has a past living on in traditions and values; it contains social layers; its people express themselves through groups; it is an arena of interaction; it experiences social change; and it has a system of controls to enforce a reasonable degree of conformity to its traditions and values. Through such a treatment the richness of the social life of a community as well as some of the systematic ways of looking at this life become apparent. These ten chapters also introduce the terminology and provide much of the background out of which a more thoroughgoing sociological approach can be derived in Chapter 11, which presents a simple but comprehensive theoretical scheme in relation to which all possible kinds of social data about the community can be fitted and put into some logical order. Chapter 11 introduces the reader to social systems analysis.

Those who already have a grounding in sociology or an interest in social theory may prefer to read Chapter 11 first; others may prefer to take each chapter as it comes and, through the process of acquiring whatever new information it contains, develop a more mature, detailed, and well-rounded picture of what goes on in one's home town.

Chapter 1

THE COMMUNITY AS A PLACE

One of the most noticeable characteristics of a community is its physical appearance. A community sprawled out on an extensive plain presents a different picture from one huddled in the cove of a mountain or one overlooking a slowly moving river. Frequently, in moments of homesickness, one longs for the physical aspects of the home town almost as much as for the people left behind.

What man does to the natural setting also is reflected in the physical appearance. Busy, belching factory chimneys or stately public buildings, run-down residential areas or a beautiful park system, well-kept business establishments or cluttered up secondhand car graveyards—all tell a story of what life in that community must be like. An approach to a community by railroad is usually less attractive than one by highway, since the former shows a side of the city that the highway frequently avoids. Because people are conscious of the community as a place, there are many beautification projects undertaken by civic clubs; there is much local pride in a new school building handsomely proportioned and well landscaped; there is a tendency to show off a new factory built on modern, efficient, attractive lines.

Students of the community, however, need to look more deeply into this matter of the community as a *place* and can conveniently do so under a threefold topical division: (1) the community as a settlement pattern, (2) the competition for space within a community, (3) and the establishment of the boundaries of a community.

THE COMMUNITY AS A SETTLEMENT PATTERN

Much study has been devoted to the question of man's adjustment to his physical surroundings through cultural adaptation. One of these adaptations is the settlement pattern. But before discussing this topic, it is necessary to clarify two very important terms. One is the physical environment, usually called the *habitat*, which consists of location, shape, and size as well as surface features, climate, and natural resources.

The second term to be defined is *culture*. In contrast to habitat which is natural, culture is man-made. It is the accumulation of things, ideas, and social arrangements which a given people has invented or borrowed from other people. All of these different culture traits are woven together into a way of life which is passed on as a social heritage to each succeeding generation. Thus, the lay of the land around any community is natural; what man does to this physical setting becomes a part of his culture, since he uses his tools and draws upon his ideas of technology or even his sense of what is beautiful or utilitarian.

This is why the community as a settlement pattern is an important illustration of man's adjustment to his physical surroundings, or habitat, through the use of his culture, or social heritage. Although most of this book is devoted to a discussion of those topics which might be called *sociocultural*, at this point brief attention will be paid to some of the physical aspects of the community as they are reflected in social life.

Location. It is interesting to speculate about the reason for the location of any particular community. The reasons advanced by residents of the community may correspond to the facts or they may be very fanciful indeed. Some Greek villagers, in explaining why their village was located where it was, told the story of a conflict which had broken out among the people of their former village many years before at a village dance. There had been an argument and violence had ensued. The spirits of those killed were soon thought to haunt the village, so the elders decided to change its location. They took three large pieces of meat, placed each piece at what appeared to be a favorable location, and selected the spot where the meat stayed fresh the longest in the belief that it would prove the most healthful place to live. Again, in a Bulgarian mountain village people believed that their community had been located on its present site three or four hundred years previously because one day a peasant widow living on the plain below missed her sow who was about to bear young. Finally, after a long, tiresome search, Baba Draganna, the widow, found the sow and her litter far up on the mountainside. According to the story, she was unable to carry all the animals back to her home below and decided to build a hut up there. Because she liked the water as well as the protection from passing armies which this location afforded, she persuaded others to join her. And today in this village the people say that the church stands on the exact spot where Baba Draganna found her sow, and they call the village Dragalevtsy, in honor of this enterprising woman.

For most American communities we do not have to look for legends to account for the location, nor do we, for that matter, have to rely upon them in the case of the Balkan villages. For this particular Bulgarian village of Baba Draganna represents what the geographers would consider an excellent adjustment: an adequate water supply (both a spring and a small river that turns the water wheels of the mills), proximity to the forest and upland pastures above, and easy access to the cultivated land below.

Some communities come into being and develop because of location on some important waterway or seacoast harbor. Others grow up because there are important mineral resources to be exploited; others because a rich farming area needs a set of services which only some expanding settlement can provide. Resort communities owe much to their scenic surroundings or to the development of some mineral springs, a sandy beach, or mountain paths.

Thus to understand a particular community, it is important to know why people located it where they did and whether or not the same factors still afford it advantages today.

Shape. The shape of a community is directly influenced by its physical surroundings. Anyone who has flown over Charleston, West Virginia, is at once aware of the limitations set by its topography and understands why a whole mountain top had to be leveled off in order to create a place for an airport. True enough, today man does move his residential areas up and down the slopes of the hills, but the main part of most towns in rugged terrain tends to be in whatever level land can be found along a river bottom. And the community tends to stretch along this bottom as far as it can before it spreads out to the hills. These variations in shape can best be understood through the various diagrams shown in Figure 1 (9).[1]

Size. Perhaps the first question we ask about any community is "How big is it?" Usually we expect an answer in terms of the number of people rather than in terms of square miles. The communities considered in this book vary in size from the small, self-subsistent, relatively isolated settlements to the subdivisions of the great metropolitan areas of our country.

[1] Figures in parentheses in the text, such as (9) above, refer by number to the publications listed at the end of the chapter.

LINEAL

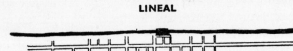

GRIDIRON

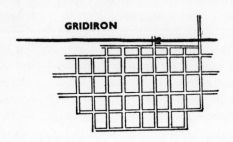

RADIAL

SPIDER WEB

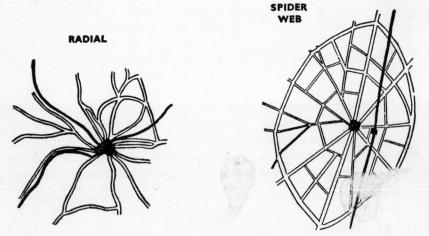

From PEP (Political and Economic Planning), *Report on the Location of Industry* (London: PEP, 1939), p. 157.

FIG. 1. Examples of town patterns.

The size of a community has much to do with the kind of inter-action people have (19, 21). The larger the community, the smaller the proportion of people known to the individual member and the greater the tendency toward anonymity and impersonal relations. Also, the individual's contacts tend to center around professional, occupational, or other social groupings rather than upon the immediate neighborhood in which one lives. The larger the community, the greater the likelihood of availability of a wide variety of services, the richer the so-called "cultural offerings," and the higher the degree of educational and economic specialization. These rather obvious facts are what might be called a function of size, which explains why people so often ask "How large is your community?"

Since we do not ordinarily think of the size of a settlement in terms of area but rather in terms of people, the matter of population density becomes important. Communities with a large population per square mile differ in some social respects from those with relatively few people per square mile. For example, in the latter case, part-time farming may be important because a man can hold down a job in a factory or in a business and at the same time, with the help of members of his family, run a small farm to supplement his weekly wages. On the other hand, in a very densely populated area, even vegetable gardens are out of the question, and the growth of a single plant may take on much meaning, as shown in the novel *A Tree Grows in Brooklyn*. Thus where density is high, the man-made environment (culture) is very influential and even at times overpowering; where density is low there is more opportunity for interaction with the natural environment (habitat).

Communication and Transportation Routes. In the discussion of location above, mention has already been made of the importance of riverways and highways. A sketch of a settlement pattern is incomplete without some discussion of its means or routes of communication with other centers. If the only way out of a community is by way of a rickety bridge, then outside contacts are discouraged much more than in the case of a community at the crossroads of several highways leading in different directions and serving as arteries for the inflow of goods, ideas, and guests. What such roads mean can be illustrated by the case of India, where a great many villages cannot be reached by modern transportation. They are not accessible to trucks, and hence everything has to be carried in on the backs of animals or human beings. If a community's level of living is limited to material which can be carried on a donkey, the chances of rapid technological change are not very great.[2] But donkeys are a rarity even in the most isolated American communities, most of which are increasingly being linked through highways with larger centers. The description of such connections is an important part of the treatment of the community as a settlement pattern.

COMPETITION FOR SPACE WITHIN A COMMUNITY

In most communities a premium is placed upon good location by those living in that community. Where the community is small, the population sparse, and plenty of land available, this competition for space is not pronounced. But as business centers develop here and there, as some areas are known as good residential areas and others as poor residential areas, then location becomes an important factor in community life. After observing this process long enough, one will notice that there are at least two types of competition: that existing among various possible uses of the land for industrial, commercial, institutional, and residential purposes and that existing among individuals looking for desirable sites on which to locate their homes. Each will be taken up in turn, after which their connection with the field of human ecology will be indicated.

Competition with Respect to Land Use. In a growing community this competition is at work every day. Consider, for instance, the area set aside for industry. Usually, people do not want to build nice homes in the neighborhood of a factory. In the past, a factory has meant smoke, noise, and often ugly piles of materials, railroad sidings, and shifting property values. However, an industrialist who is building a factory wants it near enough to transportation and to utilities to make its operation efficient. It must also be accessible to its workers; before the day of the automobile this meant the factory had to be within walking distance of the workers. Furthermore, the industrialist also wants his plant located near other factories whose products are linked to his own output and is often prepared to go to great lengths to get his firm situated to best advantage. At the same time, however, he finds himself in competition with those who, for

[2] A few years ago a prominent American consulting engineer suggested to an Asian government that it ought to give up the idea of building at prohibitive cost a road network over the whole land. He pointed out how unpredictable the rivers were and how difficult and expensive it would be to construct bridges so strong that they would not be washed away by the periodic floods. His solution was quite modern—too modern for his audience. He suggested that the national government build small airports all over the country and serve the transportation needs of the people through the use of small planes and helicopters. The government officials thought this an impractical suggestion and asked him to delete it from his report. They wanted to follow the conventional approach of having autobuses before airbuses.

example, oppose his location near a river (where he can empty industrial waste) because they think that area might better be used as a park or a residential area. Both sides deserve a fair hearing, and some accommodation can probably be worked out in the general interests of the community.

Although such competition exists, most communities feel that factories are a great asset, or they would not try so hard as they do to persuade companies to locate in their midst. Nevertheless, the arrival of industry means greater competition for space within any community.

Commerce, too, has its preferred points at which businessmen like to be located. It is a maxim of retail business that one does best at a location where the greatest possible number of people pass by daily. As there are only a few places in a city where the maximum is reached, competition for these spots is intense. As business grows, it spreads out from the main center, involving side streets in its expansion, and even moves out to set up suburban centers. This spread brings it into conflict with residents in the areas being invaded.

The use of land for institutional purposes introduces a further competitive element. A university, a state mental hospital, church plants, and a municipal park are all illustrations of institutions which take up part of the area of a community. Some of the institutions may occupy sites desperately wanted by industry or business and yet they remain adamant when requested to move or to give up some of their grounds. These institutions themselves may even be expanding, as in the case of churches which buy up surrounding residences for use in the church school program. A case in point is one church which owns a row of four small houses, in each of which it houses a different Sunday school department. Even universities feel forced to expand at the expense of residential areas and also at times to buy out business and industrial firms in order to get more land contiguous to the central campus. The larger the amount of nontaxable institutional land in the central area, the lower the tax return from that area. Thus institutional competition often involves not only a competition for mere space but also a competition for sites on which others would pay taxes but on which public institutions would not.

Competition between residential areas themselves is likewise keen in a growing community. Some of those living in what might be called downtown residential areas may protect their values by walling off outside invasion and may preserve many of the advantages of a central location with a rather high residential tone. Others desiring good location give up the struggle, sell out, perhaps at a loss, and move to the suburbs, where they hope to set up legal safeguards through zoning to guarantee them the type of exclusiveness they think in keeping with their social status in the community.

Those at a lower economic position take the poorer accommodations available, frequently having to overcrowd to pay for the higher charges being made. Even so, eventually they are told that they must move, for their dwelling is to be razed for a filling station, a new bank building, or a supermarket.

Thus we can see that as far as land use is concerned the community is very active. Here in a physical sense one can observe at work the competition which is part and parcel of the community as a place. The control of this competition by means of planning and zoning will be taken up in Chapter 19.

Competition Between Individuals for Residential Sites. It is interesting to observe the questions asked of a newcomer by the settled members of a community. The oldtimer out of courtesy tries to make the newcomer feel at home but at the same time seeks to size up what this stranger is like. Questions run something like this: Are you a native of this state? How large a family do you have? What kind of work do you do? Have you found a house yet? Where are you living? What church do you attend?

On and on the polite questions come, each answer filling in details about the newcomer. Frequently the location of the home has much to do—in the minds of many people, at least—with the degree to which one is accepted in certain circles.

Thus we can say that there is a social selection at work in this competition for residential space. As people rise economically they often want to rise socially; they say that they want to give greater advantages to their children, so they try to move to a better address. They find sometimes that money alone is not sufficient to assure their being welcomed in some seemingly desirable area to which they want to go. An instance of this occurred in the 1930's when a rich bootlegger who had bought a fine house on the parkway in a large southern city was about to move into his new home. The neighbors, greatly disturbed by the prospect of having such a person so close, made it clear in unmistakable terms that this bootlegger would not be welcome. As a result he sold the house shortly afterward at a loss, thereby revealing the part that social considerations frequently play in residence shifts of this sort.

A further factor, perhaps the basic one, is that of cost. One can afford only so much in the way of rent or of payments on a mortgage. The better areas tend to be purposely priced high in order to give them a greater prestige value; one pays for the location or address as well as for the accommodations. But the reverse does not hold true at the other end of the economic scale. The poorest people, competing as they do for shelter itself, frequently have to pay proportionately higher for their meager accommodations than those better off financially. Thus poverty begets poverty.

This becomes especially evident where there is segregation, whether it be racial, as in the case of the Negro, or cultural, as in the case of immigrants with differing language and social patterns. They are hemmed in, as it were, and are not allowed to expand into areas where their presence may be thought by the dominant group to lower the property values. As their numbers grow, the living space does not grow proportionately, and the competition becomes even more severe. This gives rise to many social problems and brings into existence both private and public welfare agencies, among which the public housing program is one of the clearest examples.

We find, therefore, that not only is there competition within a community as to the various uses to which the available space will be put (industrial, commercial, institutional, and residential) but also there is serious competition within the residential areas themselves, where economic, racial, and social factors all play a considerable part.

THE STUDY OF HUMAN ECOLOGY

This impersonal competition for space discussed in the preceding pages is really part of the subject matter of ecology, which is the field of study dealing with the spatial distribution of man and his institutions.[3] There are numerous textbooks and special studies that give comprehensive treatment to this subject, for it has become an important area of research in its own right (11, 17). For example, electric and telephone companies in metropolitan areas have large staffs of social scientists who study population and residential trends so that they can decide today whether to put in large or small cables to take care of the anticipated business ten years from today. They need to estimate the outcome of this competition for space which is currently taking place.

Some leading religious denominations also employ sociologists with ecological interests to try to predict where the chief population centers will be a few years hence. On the basis of such predictions

---

[3] Other aspects of ecology, such as specialization of labor and symbiosis, will be taken up in Chapter 3, which deals with jobs and services. Dispersion and the urban fringe are discussed in Chapter 2.

denominational leaders plan the location of new chapels in the expectation of eventually developing self-supporting churches there.

What does this all mean? It illustrates the significance of the study of the community as a place for a proper understanding of the social world about each individual.

The ecologists have set forth certain patterns which they think a city might be expected to follow in its development. The sociologists at the University of Chicago, the first to give serious, sustained attention to these spatial patterns, have listed several ecological processes which explain much of the competitive behavior described above. These processes are five in number:

1. *Concentration*—the tendency toward marked population density in certain geographic areas.
2. *Centralization*—while concentration deals with density of populations and social institutions in a given area, centralization denotes the tendency of basic types of institutional services to locate at focal points of transportation and communication (centers of activity).
3. *Segregation*—the tendency of like units to form a cluster is called segregation. This can be applied to business and industry; most often it is used with reference to clustering of well-defined population types.
4. *Invasion*—the process by which new types of institutions or population groups gradually penetrate an area already occupied and displace its institutions or population groups.
5. *Succession*—if invasion results in complete displacement, succession has occurred, for succession means a complete change in population type or use of the land.

R. M. Hurd in 1911 and E. W. Burgess later on (4) set forth the theory of concentric zones as shown in Figure 2.

Due to geographic and other factors no city expands in such perfect circles but, according to the theory of Hurd and Burgess, some cities do tend to approximate this general scheme.

Another theory seeking to account for the ecological structure of the city is called the sector theory (see B in Figure 2). Homer Hoyt is one of its chief advocates (10). He held that the city moves out along main transportation routes or at points where its spread meets no resistance. Thus the expansion is not in general waves as the concentric zone theory would indicate but in radii moving out from the center.

For cities which have more than one nucleus, or center, the multi-nuclear theory is proposed (C in Figure 2). Two formerly separate towns may merge by growth into one built-up area, while the center

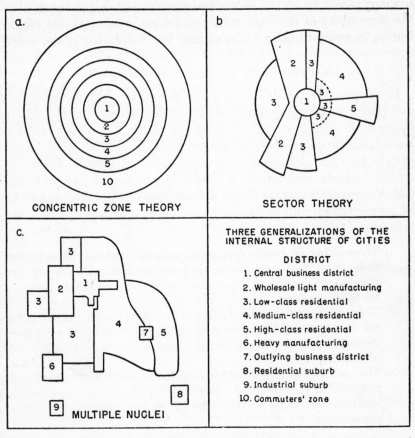

From Chauncy D. Harris and Edward L. Ullman, "The Nature of Cities," *Annals of the American Academy of Political and Social Science*, 242 (November, 1945), 12.

FIG. 2. Three theories about the growth of cities.

of each maintains much importance (7). Or different nuclei related to specialized commercial or industrial activities may develop, and each may become a center for expansion of its type of land use.

When these theories are used in the study of particular cities it becomes clear that no one of them wholly explains why the city grew as it did, but each can afford insights which would otherwise probably be overlooked. Furthermore, some sociologists, such as Walter Firey, hold that sentiment and symbolism tend to operate to keep the land-use pattern from developing as some of the ecological theories would have expected (2, 6). Thus, one of the much-discussed areas in sociology today continues to be the relative importance of the impersonal ecological forces and processes (8, 14) as opposed to the importance of the local value system and existing social organization in accounting for types of land use within the community.[4]

DETERMINATION OF COMMUNITY BOUNDARIES

If a community exists in space one should be able to map it and describe it in physical terms as the ecologists successfully do. In doing so, it is fairly easy to start with a center, but what about the boundaries or edges of the community? This question leads immediately into the definition of a community, at least as far as its spatial features are concerned. The only practical definition is one which recognizes that no single delimitation of the community will be appropriate for all purposes. Three considerations must be taken into account:

1. Those living in smaller settlement units will not only be a part of their small local community but for certain purposes will be counted as part of a larger community by individuals planning for those purposes.
2. There are many segmental ways of looking at a community: from the standpoint of business, of planning and zoning, of a religious denomination, of a school board, of newspaper circulation, of hospital areas, etc.
3. The sociological community, which is described in this book, corresponds to some kind of a combination of many segmental communities and might therefore be called the over-all or combined community.

A major question then becomes that of putting these segmental approaches into one over-all community pattern. This leads first to the problem of how small or how large a community can be.

Variations According to Sufficiency and Type. 1. The isolated, relatively self-sufficient rural community. The first condition a community must meet is that it have a relative degree of self-sufficiency. That is, it must provide people with many of their basic needs. By this criterion, an isolated rural village where people grow all of their own food, spin their own cloth, make their own shoes, build their houses themselves, and provide for religion and education is a community in that people have a set of services to share in common.

---

[4] For two of the best though somewhat divergent statements of the ecological position see A. H. Hawley, *Human Ecology: A Theory of Community Structure* (New York: The Ronald Press Co., 1950) and J. E. Quinn, *Human Ecology* (Englewood Cliffs, N.J.: Prentice-Hall, Inc., 1950).

By the same measure, in mountainous areas of the United States an isolated settlement which two generations ago had little dealings with the outside world would be considered a community even though it numbered not more than ten or fifteen households.

2. *The town-country community.* With the coming of roads and the opening up of means of communication, rural communities no longer remain isolated. The people there become more involved in the ways of the town where they bank, see a movie, get a part for the tractor, attend a function at the consolidated school, pay taxes, and get United States Department of Agriculture checks. When this happens their community expands to include the town. Their immediate settlement takes on more of the characteristics of a neighborhood, with its insufficient services, and becomes part of the outreaching community of the town. Thus most rural people in the United States today, even though they may or may not live in recognizable neighborhood units, are a part of the larger community of some town upon whose services they have become dependent. This means that people who live in these towns can correctly think of their community as extending far beyond the city limits to the rural people who identify themselves with this town as a chief shopping or recreation center. This can be called the town-country community in contrast to the isolated, self-subsistent rural community.

3. *The urban community.*[5] Moving up the scale of size one finds cities, medium-sized and large, which attract into their orbit the surrounding town-country communities. The size of these constellations, including the center and the hinterland, is particularly impressive in the case of the biggest cities. These may be considered communities for planning purposes but usually are more correctly referred to as trade areas. Nevertheless, persons living at some distance from this urban center may identify themselves not only with the town in which they live but also with this urban center and really feel a sense of identification with both places. For example, many residents of small county seat towns in the vicinity of a center of fifty thousand people, while not denying their affiliation with their home town, would think of themselves as members of the larger community to which they go for the concert and lecture series, for the athletic contests, or for visits with close relatives settled there, for a luncheon party at the best city hotel for some young bride-to-be, and often for jobs. There is a general tendency for one's primary loyalty to belong to the smallest, most immediate grouping, but

[5] The U.S. Bureau of the Census classifies as urban those places of 2500 inhabitants and above incorporated as cities, boroughs, towns, and villages. Obviously towns close to this figure are really part of the town-country community.

there is no reason why one cannot also belong to expanding concentric circles of association.

4. *The metropolitan subcommunity.* In the case of metropolitan aggregations, however, there is occasionally a very interesting development. In contrast to this movement of identification from the small to the large unit many newcomers to a metropolitan area, while developing an identification with the over-all symbol, such as Chicago, also put down their roots in the immediate locality in which they live. The result is that some of them become very much attached to and feel a part of what is really a subcommunity of the big metropolitan areas. For example, a study made of recreation in Chicago in 1937 lists the seventy-five communities used as a basis for planning in the Chicago area (22). These are sufficiently well defined to be mapped; each has its own name which people throughout the area recognize, and many of them have their own local groups through which to act in achieving common purposes. One of the questions now being explored more intensively is this problem of attachment to smaller subareas of the city. Much research done quite a few years ago seemed to indicate that city people, because they tended to associate with acquaintances from all over the city, had little loyalty to the immediate locality in which they lived. Some more recent studies indicate that even in the metropolitan area the locality grouping may still have considerable significance.

Methods of Mapping Communities. If, then, there are communities varying from the isolated, self-subsistent rural type to that found in a highly urban environment, how does one know where to begin in locating boundaries? Will there not be so much overlapping that any mapping will be so complicated as to be useless?

There is a simple answer to this problem. Before doing any mapping decide what the community focus is to be. Remember that one can work at different levels of identification but must set up criteria before starting to map. If these criteria are clear, then the map will be clear. Figure 3 will illustrate this point.

Notice that in the area shown in Figure 3 there are three centers of over one hundred thousand within eighty to one hundred miles of each other. These are identified by the Roman numerals I, II, III. In addition there are twenty towns ranging from three thousand to twenty-five thousand in population scattered at varying intervals from the large centers and from each other. These towns are shown by the letters A through T. Around each of these towns are several hamlets or rural neighborhoods, each with its own identity and name, but each so insufficient in services that the people visit some

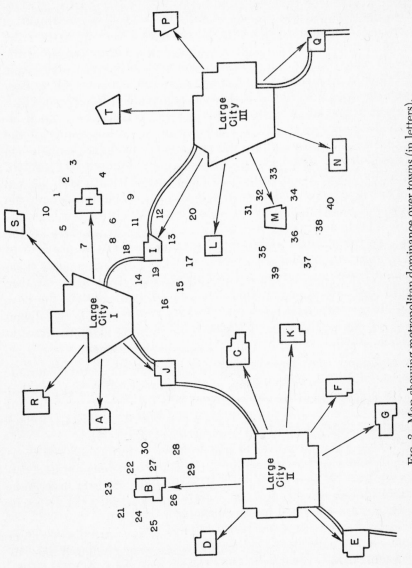

Fig. 3. Map showing metropolitan dominance over towns (in letters).

nearby town to fulfill many of their economic and social needs. For four of the towns these neighborhoods have been drawn in, numbered from 1 up to 40.

There is no question but that the three large centers (I–III) exert great significance over the area because of the metropolitan newspapers published there, the radio and TV broadcasts, and certain kinds of facilities which they alone can afford to those demanding them (5). Some examples of these are "cultural" (drama companies with Broadway casts, concerts by prominent artists or musical organizations) or medical (some world-renowned specialist is located there). Also, women wishing the latest styles in dresses or fur shops may visit the large center. Businessmen and industrialists may look to these centers for scarce items or machine parts that they need in a hurry. This illustrates how such large centers really exercise metropolitan dominance[6] over the area although they touch people living at some distance only in terms of one or two interests (3, 23). The people who live at a distance of fifty miles or more get most of their needs from and give most of their attention to the smaller towns of which they are a part. On the other hand, those living close to and working in the large centers have a multipurpose identification with that center and may develop a feeling that it is their community. Even in such a case the suburbanite is likely to think in community terms of the locality where he lives, where his children go to school, where he pays his taxes, and where he finds his golfing partners rather than in terms of the place where he works.

In the determination of boundaries of social identification, a sample of the population shown in the area on Figure 3 can be asked to indicate with which of the three larger centers (I, II, or III) each feels most closely identified because of trade, newspaper, or other contacts. While the areas drawn for I, II, and III, respectively, are trade rather than community areas, even as such they have much social significance.

By the same method the smaller places designated by letters can be considered as centers in their own right. People living in the area can be asked to tell with which one of the above centers they feel most closely identified. The answers may name the one closest to the person's home but need not necessarily do so. Considerations other than mere geographical nearness, such as previous ties, ethnic

---

[6] For information on metropolitan dominance see the chapter of that title in Rupert B. Vance and Nicholas J. Demerath, *The Urban South* (Chapel Hill: University of North Carolina Press, 1954). Also see Don J. Bogue, *The Structure of the Metropolitan Community: A Study of Dominance and Subdominance* (Ann Arbor: University of Michigan Press, 1949).

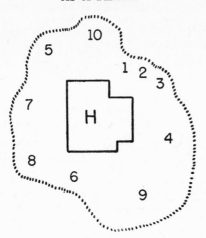

FIG. 4. Map showing community H as obtained by identification method.

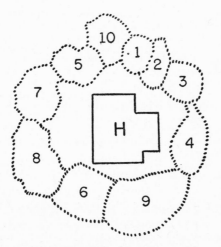

FIG. 5. Map showing community H as obtained by neighborhood
cluster method.

relationships, or convenience of transportation, may affect the bonds
one feels for a given center. When these responses are in, then lines
can be drawn around the area most closely identified with each center,
recognizing that there will be some areas which cannot be assigned
to any community center, because people living close together in
these areas have quite different ideas about the desirability of the
competing centers (see Figure 4). Such areas should be left un-
attached. This method of determining community boundaries where
individuals living outside the city limits of a town are asked to choose

between two or more possible centers can be called the *identification method* (16).

Referring again to Figure 3, we see there are forty numbered hamlets or small localities, each with its own name and self-consciousness. But for purposes of the investigation they may not be considered sufficiently large to be called communities. The term "neighborhood" may be more appropriate (1, 12). A community map may be drawn up by determining to which center most of the people in each neighborhood feel most closely attached. Then the whole neighborhood may be attached to that larger place instead of connecting only individuals as done in the identification method. This second method is called the *neighborhood cluster method* (see Figure 5) and seems to work well where the rural neighborhood is an easily recognizable unit (15, 20). This method has the advantage of attaching an already existing social unit (the neighborhood) to the larger unit (the community) and provides a ready-made social mechanism for participation by members of the neighborhood in community affairs. Each neighborhood can be asked to select representatives for the purpose of planning community-wide programs in which its people are involved. On some occasions the neighborhood will still remain the functional unit through which some problem is approached; at other times the wider community is needed. But still this local community, even though the center numbers well up into the thousands, is dependent upon the larger centers of metropolitan dominance.

This discussion began with three observations about the definition of community in space and indicated that, depending upon the criteria of what people have in common, there are various types of communities from the standpoint of size. Indeed, for this reason, people may belong to two communities if definitions of a community vary. But it was also noted that by using only one criterion, such as newspaper circulation, one found a trade area rather than a social unit adapted to common action. The fact that some people in New Haven, Connecticut, may read *The New York Times* is no sure sign that they feel themselves a part of New York City. Or, if high school attendance areas are the sole criterion for drawing up community boundaries, again a segmental picture emerges which may or may not correspond to the sociological community, which is really a composite of many economic services and social factors.

From this discussion of the community as a *place* it should be apparent that unless a person takes these spatial factors into account he misses much of the rich detail of community life and can certainly err in his guesses about future growth and economic possibility. Later on, in Part Three, Chapter 19, on physical planning and zoning, there will be a further consideration of some of the practical problems of space. Meanwhile, people should be aware of the contributions made to the understanding of community life by those sociologists working in the field of human ecology.

References and Suggested Readings

1. ALEXANDER, FRANK D. "The Problem of Locality-Group Classification," *Rural Sociology*, XVII (September, 1952), 236–44.
2. ALIHAN, M. A. *Social Ecology: A Critical Analysis*. New York: Columbia University Press, 1938.
3. BOGUE, DON J. *The Structure of the Metropolitan Community: A Study of Dominance and Subdominance*. Ann Arbor: University of Michigan Press, 1949.
4. BURGESS, ERNEST W. "The Growth of the City," in Park, Burgess, and McKenzie, *The City*. Chicago: University of Chicago Press, 1925.
5. DEFLEUR, MELVIN L., and CROSBY, JOHN. "Analyzing Metropolitan Dominance," *Social Forces*, XXXV (October, 1956), 68–75.
6. FIREY, WALTER. "Sentiment and Symbolism as Ecological Variables," *American Sociological Review*, X (April, 1945), 140–48.
7. HARRIS, C. D., and ULLMAN, L. "The Nature of Cities," *The Annals of the American Academy of Political and Social Science*, 242 (November, 1945).
8. HAWLEY, A. H. *Human Ecology: A Theory of Community Structure*. New York: The Ronald Press Co., 1950.
9. HAWTHORN, HARRY B. and AUDREY E. "The Shape of a City," *Sociology and Social Research*, XXXIII (November, 1948), 89–91.
10. HOYT, HOMER. *The Structure and Growth of Residential Neighborhoods in American Cities*. Washington, D.C.: Government Printing Office, 1939.
11. MARTIN, WALTER T. "Ecological Change in Satellite Rural Areas," *American Sociological Review*, XXII (April, 1957), 165–73.
12. MELVIN, BRUCE L. "The Rural Neighborhood Concept," *Rural Sociology*, XIX (December, 1954), 371–76.
13. Political and Economic Planning, *Report on the Location of Industry in Great Britain* (London, 1939).
14. QUINN, J. E. *Human Ecology*. Englewood Cliffs, N.J.: Prentice-Hall, Inc., 1950.
15. SANDERS, IRWIN T. and ENSMINGER, D. *Alabama Rural Communities: A Study of Chilton County*. Montevallo: Alabama College Bulletin (July, 1940).
16. SANDERSON, DWIGHT. *Rural Sociology and Rural Social Organization*. New York: John Wiley & Sons, Inc., 1942, ch. 13.
17. SCHMID, CALVIN F. "Generalizations Concerning the Ecology of the American City," *American Sociological Review*, XV (April, 1950), 264–81.
18. SCHNORE, LEO F. "The Growth of Metropolitan Suburbs," *American Sociological Review*, XXII (April, 1957), 165–73.
19. SCHNORE, LEO F., and VARLEY, DAVID W. "Some Concomitants of Metropolitan Size," *American Sociological Review*, XX (August, 1955), 408–14.
20. SLOCUM, WALTER L., and CASE, HERMAN M. "Are Neighborhoods Meaningful Social Groups Throughout Rural America," *Rural Sociology*, XVIII (March, 1953), 52–59.
21. TERRIEN, FREDERIC W., and MILLS, DONALD L. "The Effect of Changing Size Upon the Internal Structure of Organizations," *American Sociological Review*, XX (February, 1955), 11–13.
22. TODD, J. ARTHUR. *The Chicago Recreation Survey*. Chicago: Chicago Recreation Commission, 1937, vol. IV.
23. VANCE, RUPERT B., and DEMERATH, NICHOLAS J. *The Urban South*. Chapel Hill: University of North Carolina Press, 1954.

Chapter 2

THE PEOPLE

Some interesting facts about a community come to light when people are viewed as a population rather than as personalities. The study of population is called *demography* and deals with the birth and death rates, the movement and distribution of the people, and other variables such as age, sex, occupation, religion, educational attainment, and the like. In other words, just as one can measure and map the physical layout of the city, so one can measure and characterize the various population categories found in the community. To one untrained in statistics and cautious of figures, such study may at first seem puzzling, but these statistics come alive when interpreted in terms of their significance to the community.

GROWTH AND DECLINE IN COMMUNITY POPULATION

Total Numbers over a Period of Time. Even in a period when our national population is steadily increasing each year, there are many American communities that lose more people than they gain over a five- or ten-year span. What does it feel like to live in a community where numbers are declining? What prospects lie in store for the businessman, the professional person, or the property owner? The least one can say is that the people in such a community must adjust to this changing situation, thereby altering in part, at least, their customary manner of approaching their problems. Some in the community may respond to the fact of population decline by thinking this loss a social evil in itself and may propose what they consider satisfactory ways of reversing the trend and setting the community back on the path of growth. Others may not view the population decline with such alarm but may urge that people accept the trend of events and stress quality of living rather than quantity of community residents. Nevertheless, new businesses are not apt to locate in a community faced with continuing population loss, and young people are likely to set their sights on goals outside such a community.

Rapid growth brings its problems, too. One of the best documented studies is that of Willow Run, just outside Detroit, Michigan, where thousands of newcomers arrived during World War II to work in the bomber plant (4). Almost half (forty-eight per cent) of these were recruited in the states of Kentucky, Tennessee, Alabama, and Mississippi, and they made an impact on this northern community not only by sheer weight of numbers but by the type of cultural patterns which they brought with them. Here increase led to social disorganization, since under wartime conditions assimilation into the prewar community was practically impossible, and no adequate provision had been made to help these new arrivals develop a sense of community.

A minimal approach to the study of the people of a community is that of determining their shift in numbers through the years. If the place is incorporated, then the figures of United States census, taken every ten years, will tell the story; if the community is unincorporated, then perhaps county or township figures will have to be used or a special effort made to have the numbers totaled for the magisterial districts most closely approximating the community boundaries. For cities of over 50,000 population, special census tracts are drawn up to assist in comparing the numbers in one part of the city with those elsewhere. In using the figures for a given city one must determine whether reference is merely to the incorporated area called the "central city," which does not include all of the surrounding built-up area, or whether the figures include the metropolitan area lying around the central city.

Table 1 shows what happened in the way of population growth to a number of American cities (11).

Usually, however, people are interested in knowing about the increase in the whole metropolitan area, which includes the suburbs as well as the central city. In Atlanta, Georgia, for instance, less than half (49.3 per cent) of those in its metropolitan area lived in the central city in 1950. Furthermore, while the central city grew only 9.6 per cent between 1940 and 1950, the whole metropolitan area grew 29.7 per cent. By contrast, the central city of New Orleans, Louisiana, includes 83.2 per cent of those in the metropolitan area whose growth was 24.1 per cent, compared with the 15.3 per cent for the central city shown in Table 1.

TABLE 1

RATES OF GROWTH FOR SELECTED CENTRAL CITIES, 1940–1950

City	Rate of Growth (per cent)	City	Rate of Growth (per cent)
Atlanta	9.6	Los Angeles	31.0
Baltimore	10.5	Minneapolis	6.0
Boston	4.0	Nashville	4.1
Buffalo	0.7	New Orleans	15.3
Chicago	6.6	Philadelphia	7.3
Cincinnati	10.6	Pittsburgh	0.8
Cleveland	4.2	Portland	22.3
Columbus	22.8	San Francisco	22.2
Dayton	15.7	Seattle	27.0
Denver	29.0	St. Louis	5.3
Hartford	6.7	Washington	21.0
Indianapolis	10.4		

Source: Richard W. Redick, "Population Growth and Distribution in Central Cities, 1940–1950," *American Sociological Review*, XXI (February, 1956), 39.

Bases for the Increase or Decrease. The population numbers for a particular community depend upon three factors: natural increase or decrease, migration, and annexation. Each of these will be examined in turn.

Natural increase or decrease. In order to be able to compare the same community at different periods or to compare two communities, birth and death *rates* must be used rather than statistics of the actual number of births and deaths. A birth rate shows the number of live births per thousand people in a given year; a death rate shows the number of deaths per thousand people for a particular year. These are called "crude" rates, since they take into account everyone in the community, whether children or octogenarians. In the state of Washington (12), for instance, the crude birth rate in the early 1920's was around 18.0; by the early 1930's it had declined to about 14.0. At the present time it is over 24.0, almost identical with the rate for the country as a whole. Death rates in the state of Washington have always been low in comparison with the country as a whole. In 1910 the crude death rate per one thousand population was 10.0; in 1920, 11.1; in 1930, 10.6; in 1940, 11.4; and in 1950, 9.8. When this last figure of 9.8 is subtracted from the birth rate of 24.0, it provides the rate of natural increase, namely 14.2.

These figures for the state of Washington are given to show how community leaders in any state can see to what degree their community compares with the state average and with the nearby communities. When one town differs significantly from such averages the search for an explanation may lead to some important findings about the community. County or state public health officials are often in a position to provide these statistics and can advise as to how they should and should not be interpreted. For example, infants born in a city hospital to women who come from an area outside the city should not be counted as a part of the natural increase of that city any more than should the deaths of nonresidents brought to the hospitals from outside the city. This is why some well-informed person needs to interpret what population statistics do and do not show, particularly when these are based on a single city or small community.

A better index of fertility, or the actual rate at which a group reproduces itself, is the *net reproduction rate*. This assumes that there is no migration either into or out of the area being studied, that an index of 100 will signify the population in its present size, and that anything over 100 represents an increase. For example, in a clear and interesting analysis of the people of Mississippi (8) the net reproduction rate for that state is given at 175 for 1950. This compares with 145 for the whole United States.

Migration. In America today there is considerable movement from one community to another as well as within a community. Indeed, nearly 25 million Americans, or 17.1 per cent of those one year of age and over, lived in a different house on April 1, 1950, than on April 1, 1949. Another fact of importance is the failure of large cities in the past to reproduce themselves; that is, the birth rate of those living there has not been high enough to offset the death rate, although there is recent evidence of a trend now toward a full replacement ratio. Nevertheless, if a city is to grow, newcomers must be attracted. As is evident from the figures already given in Table 1, cities are increasing in size, indicating that these newcomers are being attracted in quantities larger than needed simply to make up for the difference in births and deaths.

Three questions about migrants are of special interest: (1) Where do these migrants come from? (2) What are their characteristics? (3) Why do they move? Warren S. Thompson gives the following answers (15).

1. *Whence the urban migrant?* Before 1900 two main internal movements were of importance. The first was the east-to-west migration. People were rapidly settling west of the Appalachians, and they have been continuing this trend toward the Pacific even in our own day. The second shift was from the country to the city. By 1880 the urban population outnumbered the rural.

Since 1900 four main movements can be described. The first of these is from the South to the North, involving both white and Negro workers. Since the South had a higher birth rate and fewer economic opportunities, migration began during World War I, declined during 1930–40 and was resumed during World War II. The second covers regional shifts, such as that between large cities in different parts of the country. Frequently people move between communities of the same general character. The third movement is a continuation of the shift from rural communities to urban centers. The farm population is now less than one-sixth of the total U. S. population and can no longer provide for large regional shifts. The fourth trend is the suburban one, which is a centrifugal movement in metropolitan areas from the central city to the area surrounding it.

2. *What are the characteristics of the migrants?* As far as hereditary qualities go, the migrants are a fairly good cross section of the community from which they come. Also, men move more than women. For example, within a state 101 men move to every 100 females; between contiguous states 103 men; between noncontiguous states 110 men. The farther the move, the greater is the proportion of males involved.

Migrants are most commonly found in the 15-to-34 age group. In general, migrants are better educated than the nonmigrants among whom they settle, a fact contradictory to the general impression. Of course, this does not refer to migratory farm workers, since they do not settle down; but it does refer to the newcomers (the migrants) who seek to become definite members of the community.

This characteristic of education ties in with the fact that those occupations requiring most training are more mobile. White-collar workers move more than hand workers, and the higher the social status of the white-collar workers, the more mobile they are.

3. *Why do people move?* The "push and pull" theory of migration attempts to answer this question. Mere dissatisfaction with one's situation is not in itself a cause for migration as a rule; it usually is accompanied by some presumed alternative. The migrant may have heard that there is a good job waiting or may have received letters from a friend telling of the great opportunities in a new place. In any case, there must be a desire to change or to improve one's present situation. At times, the "pull," as one begins to contrast it with one's opportunities in the home community. becomes the irritant that leads to dissatisfaction, which in turn, forms the "push." In other words, the migrant may have been quite satisfied until he learned of these possibilities elsewhere.

Professor W. A. Anderson of Cornell University, in his study of *How Much Do New Yorkers Move?*, found among other things that New York people were residentially more stable than those in the rest of the United States; that the rural nonfarm population of New York state moved most and the urban population least; that two out of every three persons who shifted residences in the year did so within the same county; and that migrants into the state comprised 11 per cent of those moving. In concluding his study, Professor Anderson writes:

Planning and operating the life of the community is affected decidedly by stability or lack of stability in a population. Schools, churches, voluntary organizations, public utilities, use of land, development of services, to name a few, are all related to population shifting. . . .

Change of residence creates new problems for individuals and families, too. To establish new friendships and neighborhood contacts, to reorient self to different community characteristics and values, to find and adjust to new work or working conditions, are often all involved.[1]

Annexation. Cities also increase the number of their inhabitants by annexing the territory lying adjacent to the city. Thus people who live just outside the city limits and who were considered as rural nonfarm people by the census takers may immediately after annexation become classified as urban people even though their place of residence is unchanged. Indeed, one student of this problem, Selz C. Mayo, claimed in the early 1940's that 30 per cent of the total increase in urban population growth could be accounted for by annexation (extension of urban boundaries) and by the change in census classification from rural to urban of smaller places that exceeded the 2500 persons figure needed to rank a community as urban (10). Mayo also thinks that growth by natural increase and migration may be overstressed in our analysis of urban populations. It is interesting to note in this connection that the number of urban places in the United States in 1930 was 3165; in 1940, 3464; but in 1950, 4284. The shift between 1940 and 1950 is therefore quite startling.

Certainly anyone using the population figures for a given area such as a community must be sure that the figures all relate to the same geographic base and that what seems to be growth is not merely the accretion of new territories together with their residents.

POPULATION COMPOSITION OF THE COMMUNITY

Only when the total numbers of a community are broken down into special groupings does the true importance of population analy-

[1] W. A. Anderson, *How Much Do New Yorkers Move?* (Mimeograph Bulletin No. 45, Department of Rural Sociology, Cornell University, Agricultural Experiment Station, May, 1955, p. 5.)

sis become evident. There are many possible ways of making these divisions, and some may prove more useful than others (9).

Sex Ratio. One important fact to know about a community is the sex ratio, the number of men to each 100 women. Washington, D. C., and other cities in the East where large numbers of secretaries and office workers are needed contain more women than men and thus represent a poor place for a young woman to go in search of a husband. Wars tend to lower the sex ratio, as does the migration from a community by men in search of work. On the other hand, in areas being newly settled, where single men initially comprise the bulk of the population, the sex ratio is very high and a "man's society" tends to develop. Figure 6 on age, sex, and marital status shows on close examination that women outnumber the men in the urban population in every age group beginning with the fifteen- to nineteen-year-old category. But men outnumber the women in almost every age group of the rural-farm population

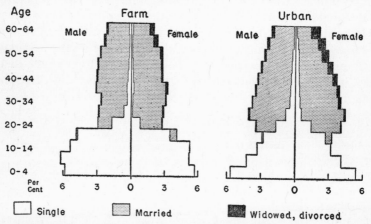

Source: Bureau of the Census and Bureau of Agricultural Economics.

FIG. 6. Age, sex, and marital status of farm and urban population, 1951.

In a discussion of some of the sociological factors involved in an unequal sex ratio, Hans von Hentig reminds us that, at the time of birth, there is a sex ratio of about 105 male babies to 100 females in the white population and that an equilibrium is reached in the early adult years, only to be soon turned into a female surplus "by nervous wear and tear, occupational diseases, accidents, homicide, and suicide."[2] In 1850 the sex ratio for the United States was 104.3 but by

[2] Hans von Hentig, "The Sex Ratio: A Brief Discussion Based on United States Census Figures," *Social Forces,* XXX (May, 1952), 443–44.

1950 it had become 98.1, indicating a surplus of females. Von Hentig has indicated some of the peculiar features of the frontier, where there were many more men than women, before he turns to the present situation:

Even before the Census figures told us that the United States had entered the category of countries suffering from a female surplus (or enjoying it), a change had taken place in mores and manners of the American woman. It started after the first World War, gave the woman equal political rights, freed her from many conventions, and produced the career woman. The evolution was accompanied by a distinct effort to appeal to the man by cosmetics, perfumes carrying significant names, and tempting dresses. Quite obviously there is an intensified endeavor in winning the attention of the male. Not seldom a certain aggressiveness has succeeded in getting the approval of public opinion. If girls do not propose officially they "propose" by their make-up, the situations to which they betake themselves nonchalantly, the choice of subjects they talk about, and the encouragement, or non-resistance, they offer to male advances. We suggest that the explanation is that these changed attitudes express the aggravated competitive state of affairs. Who does not outsparkle and outbrave the rival will be left on the shelf and the shelf is large when there are many more women than men.[3]

The observations and conclusion of this European observer of American life may or may not be accurate for the community which a particular person knows best, but it does suggest a cause-effect relationship between the sex ratio and selected social phenomena.

Age Composition. Age composition is determined by dividing up the population into age groupings based on five-year intervals. For example, to know how many youngsters there are under five, how many between five and nine years, how many ten to fourteen, and so forth, helps in predicting the structure of the population five or ten years hence. By comparing the oldest age groups with the youngest, for example, the businessman knows whether to deal in wheel chairs or baby buggies, the community whether to open a rest home or a children's nursery, or whether to put a croquet court in the park for the old people or add more slides for the young. Also, planning for the educational needs of the children can only be done in terms of the age distribution. The case of Duluth, Minnesota (16), illustrates the applicability of such findings.

Duluth voted a $3,000,000 bond issue in 1948–49, for example, and the buildings planned with those funds were to be completed by the spring of 1954. By 1956, Duluth will have this bond issue completely paid. It is already evident, however, according to a recent report by Duluth's Superintendent of Schools, that the continued high birth rate in that city makes it necessary

[3] *Ibid.*, pp. 446–47.

to reappraise needs for the future. There are already 300 *more* pupils in
Duluth junior high schools than there were in 1950, and within three more
years there will be an *additional* 500 children. . . . Therefore, in 1954 Duluth
voted an additional bond issue of $6,000,000 with plans to finance the new
buildings over a ten-year period.[4]

Communities differ markedly in the proportion of people of working age. As Figure 6 shows, there is a tendency for the rural communities, which have many children and old people, to lose those
inhabitants in the productive age group to other areas. This means
that rural communities must educate the young and care for the old
without the benefit of the relatively larger working force found in
the cities. Such demographic facts are obviously of great importance.
For example, such facts might be used by advocates of an equalization educational fund within a given state providing for an allocation
of school money on the basis of need and not merely on the basis of
where the taxes are collected, since cities tend to benefit from the
work of those who have been educated elsewhere before their migration to the cities.

Race Composition. People in a local community are often unaware
of the real distribution of the people by race. On one occasion the
leading residents of a community, assuming that the facts corre-
sponded with their prejudices, complained about the high crime rate
among a racial minority living in their midst. A careful check of the
record of arrests and of the racial composition showed that actually
those in the minority grouping were responsible for a smaller proportion of arrests than their share of the population. Generalizations
about any minority group are all too commonly based on prejudice
rather than fact and need to be checked against the statistical record
to assess the true situation.

When large numbers of two or more races live side by side each
race tends to develop its own subcommunity, each with its own institutions and social outlets. But despite these discernible differences
all inhabitants of a particular area defined as a community, no matter
of what race, can be considered as members of that general community and are apt to feel that they should be taken into account
when any community-wide program is being formulated. Failure on
the part of any race to recognize its dependence on the other results
in various manifestations of social disorganization. Thus knowledge
of the percentage of each race in the total population of the community is basic to any discussion of full community participation by
each race.

[4] *Minnesota Trends: A Report to the People* (University of Minnesota: Social Science
Research Center of the Graduate School, 1954), p. 49.

One changing aspect of American community life is the redistribution of the Negro population. One study summarizes it as follows:

In 1950, 10 per cent of the United States population was Negro and the Negroes are unequally distributed among the states. The heaviest concentrations are in the South, although much less so than formerly. In 1950, 68 per cent of all Negroes in the United States lived in the three southern census divisions: South Atlantic, East South Central, and West South Central. Industrial employment, however, has attracted many Negroes to cities outside the southern region. In 1950 there were 23 states, and the District of Columbia, which had over 100,000 Negroes each. Together, they included 95 per cent of all Negroes. . . . If West Virginia is considered in the South, 15 of the 23 states are southern and 8 are not. The latter contain over one-fourth (about 27 per cent) of all Negroes in the United States. New York alone contains more Negroes than all but five of the southern states. The other nonsouthern states are: Illinois, Pennsylvania, Ohio, California, Michigan, Missouri, and Indiana. Within these states the Negro population is concentrated in such cities as New York, Chicago, and Detroit. In the South the Negro population is more evenly distributed on farms and small towns, as well as in cities.[5]

The three aspects of composition discussed thus far—sex, age, and race—are based on biological characteristics which cannot be changed. Cultural definitions surrounding them or their distribution within a community may change, but people cannot change their sex, age, or race. Women, who at one stage of a country's history were looked upon as chattel subservient to men, may attain a position in society where they control far more than half of the wealth of the nation, as they do today in the United States. Young people, who should be seen and not heard according to earlier traditions, may now be given an important place in the scheme of things. Furthermore, life expectancy has increased to the point that many people will live throughout more of the human life span, although the life span itself has not basically changed. Likewise, attitudes toward race which developed in an earlier day may undergo marked modification with the passing of time. Thus, clearly the cultural aspects of population composition are subject to change. Some of these aspects are treated briefly in the paragraphs which follow.

Marital Status. A greater proportion of American people are married than ever before. Demographic factors such as a more nearly equal sex ratio and an increased life expectancy may account for much of this change but not for all of it. Furthermore, the young people in many American communities marry at an earlier age than formerly. This has a direct effect upon the interest the young people

[5] Morton B. King, Jr., and others, *Mississippi's People, 1950* (University of Mississippi Sociological Study Series, No. 5, Oxford: 1955), 74–75.

take in the welfare of the community in which they have settled. (See Figure 6 for comparisons of marital status between farm and urban people.) A study of the changes in marital status through the years can reveal community characteristics which might not otherwise be apparent—a case in point would be the effect of such trends on the fertility pattern.

Nationality and Language. Due to the assimilative character of American society, most of those who enter the United States as immigrants acquire American citizenship and try to outdo others in becoming "good Americans." The older people find it hard, however, to master English and may feel more comfortable when using their mother-tongue. They may also want to maintain some reminders of their former life; hence they patronize delicatessen stores where they can buy the type of food to which they are accustomed. They may even want to provide elementary schools where their children can be taught their parents' native language as well as English.

Unquestionably, these ethnic divisions, when they exist, play a great part in community life, particularly where minority groups entertain traditional prejudices toward those of other nationalities who have also emigrated to the same American community. Furthermore, factions tend to arise within these ethnic groups as the immigrants try to adjust to political and economic changes occurring in the "home country." It is not simply that an Armenian-American may be suspicious of the Swedish-American ethnic group in his community; he may be even more at odds with another Armenian-American group.

If a person is to understand the importance of such groups, he must first determine their size. When he has learned from the census or other figures the kinds of nationality and language groups in his community, as well as their relative size, he can then see the total population of his community in a clearer light.

Religious Groupings. In some communities religious divisions assume great significance. Knowing the relative size of each major religious grouping aids in understanding the type of problems which may periodically recur. It is important to know, for example, how representative the Ministerial Association is of the whole community or to what degree the Federated Church Women speak for all the churches of the town. To what extent do the Knights of Columbus speak for the Catholic men? What organizations represent the divisions of the Jewish people, divided as they frequently are into Orthodox, Conservative, and Reformed congregations?

Communities vary in the extent of church affiliation. In some, church-going is customary and even a matter of social pressure; in other communities, there is much less emphasis upon formalized religious activity. Some churches serve as social centers as well as places of worship, a fact which may show up in higher affiliation statistics. In using the figures from a religious census it is important to remember that some religious bodies count as adherents the entire family when the head of the family is a communicant; other bodies count only those individuals who after reaching maturity voluntarily choose to join as official members of the body.

Educational Composition. For many purposes it is useful to have a general idea of the number of college graduates or high school graduates in the community. Such data provide still another way of viewing the population. In certain communities where college graduates are proportionately high, it is very likely that there will be considerable support for such organizations as the American Association of University Women, the League of Women Voters, or discussion groups among the men, such as the Torch Club. Such figures help one understand the point of view certain segments of the population take toward the type of school program that will be most enthusiastically supported by the community. Likewise, industrialists seeking a location for a plant are apt to give preference to a community where their highly trained technical staff members will find congenial associates of a comparable educational level.

Rural-urban Distribution. When the community boundaries have been drawn up as described in the previous chapter, it may well be that both rural and urban people will be included. This is especially true when one realizes that those who live outside incorporated settlements of twenty-five hundred people or more are counted as rural. In other words, people who live just beyond the city limits and whose houses are connected with city sewer systems are classified as rural rather than urban. As a matter of fact, between April, 1940, and April, 1950, the rural population of metropolitan counties increased by 41 per cent, whereas the rural population of nonmetropolitan counties decreased by 2 per cent. The United States Bureau of the Census, however, in order to take care of this anomalous situation, has set up a threefold division of rural residents: *the nonfarm,* who like the person just beyond the city limits does no farming; *the part-time farmer,* who derives a certain proportion of his income from farming and the rest from some other economic activity; and *the full-time farmer,* for whom farming is a full-time undertaking.

The term "the urban fringe" has been widely used to describe the nonfarm person and even the part-time farmer who have settled near the cities in what was ten or twenty years ago open countryside (2, 3,

13, 17). It has been called a new social frontier and is described as follows by Solon T. Kimball:

> The tide is an irresistible one. It sweeps in and through old communities. It engulfs farm after farm, breaking up rural neighborhoods that have had decades of stability. It turns quiet little villages, which have preserved their numbers and institutions for many decades, into places having problems that those who have spent their lives there find they are unable to understand or cope with.[6]

Professor Kimball then goes on to describe one of these fringe communities in southeastern Michigan. He found that farm land was being withdrawn from productive purposes to provide space for people to live and that the number of farmers was diminishing both relatively and absolutely as they retired or died and were not replaced.

He also noted that the village community showed much greater resistance to the invasion of outsiders. Those who supplied professional or retail services actually improved their economic lot because of the larger number to which they catered. The old religious, fraternal, and social groups continued their activities with relatively little disturbance. Only the school system with its overflow of children from the newcomer families found itself inadequate to meet the new problems.

In this fringe community the population was relatively young and heterogeneous. These newcomers plus the grown children of the "oldtimers" succeeded through two-community-wide organizations (The Mothers' Club and the Civic Club) to help the community face its problems.

This account of what has happened in Lambertville, as this community is called, is reminiscent of many accounts of the frontier. This study shows the usefulness of looking at the people of the community in terms of urban, nonfarm rural, part-time farm, and full-time farm categories. Each of these groupings may have certain unique problems worthy of special study.

Occupational Distribution. A listing of the occupational distribution of the members of the community is indicative of many local characteristics. Together with racial, religious, educational, and similar aspects of population composition, it is useful in presenting an over-all demographic picture. With these figures it is possible to trace changes in community patterns—to see, for instance, to what extent the occupational distribution has changed through the years.

---

[6] *The New Social Frontier: The Fringe* (East Lansing: Michigan State College, Special Bulletin 360, June 1949), p. 5.

Because a community has certain demographic characteristics, it tends to attract those to whom such traits are appealing. Young parents are attracted to communities where there are many other young parents concerned about similar problems; those of a given ethnic background may be drawn to areas where others with comparable backgrounds reside. And so it goes. Statistics help reveal the groupings, and knowledge of the groupings, in turn, affords insight into the patterns of living in a particular community. One example will point this up. In the following description of an area in Los Angeles consisting of nine neighborhoods, notice what the figures, most of them on population composition, reveal:

. . . Of the total population of the Los Angeles area, 1.3 per cent lives in this social area.

Out of each 1,000 wage earners in these neighborhoods, 629 are in the craftsman, operative, or laborer category. This represents a higher proportion of workers at this low occupational level than in any other area throughout the region. For each 1,000 persons living in these neighborhoods, 595 have had no more than grade school education. The average rent per capita for the population in these neighborhoods is $4.46. It is this combination of low income as reflected by rent, low level of schooling, and a high proportion of its residents working at the lower occupational levels that qualifies this area as one of low social rank.

These are the neighborhoods of large families. For each 1,000 women between the ages of 15 and 44, there are 460 children under the age of five. . . .

This area has one of the highest sex ratios of any of the nine areas. It is 107, as compared with the ratio for the county of 97. In other words, there are 107 men for each 100 women in these neighborhoods. This proportion of men is characteristic of populations at the low urban and social levels.

The breakdown of age groups in these neighborhoods shows that 51 per cent of the population is in the productive age span of 15-50. As might be expected in an area with a high fertility index, there is an extraordinarily high percentage of the total population under the age of 15, in this case 30 per cent. This high proportion of children in a total population structure is also typical of a society in which both economic level and level of urbanization are low. . . . Persons over the age of 50 represent only 17 per cent of the total population of these neighborhoods.

Among the segregated groups in these neighborhoods, the Mexicans predominate. . . . The smallest representation is that of the Russian-Jewish group. . . . The distribution of the other three minority groups is as follows: 1.9 per cent of the city's Orientals, 1.4 per cent of its Negroes, and 1.9 per cent of its Italians.[7]

How Healthy Are the People?

The people of a community are more than an aggregation as measured by numbers and viewed in terms of composition. They are

[7] Eshref Shevky and Molly Lewin, *Your Neighborhood: A Social Profile of Los Angeles* (Los Angeles: The Haynes Foundation, 1949), pp. 13–14.

human beings who have to carry on their daily duties as best they can. In other words, students of population are interested in selected *qualitative* as well as quantitative characteristics of the people of any community. Since poor health is one of the greatest drains upon the community's human resources, it should be viewed in community as well as in individual terms, in terms of the extent to which illness disrupts social relationships at home, at work, and in other organizational activities. A sick person in the home sets up a chain reaction which not only affects his relationships with members of his immediate family but also frequently changes the contacts between these family members and other people. The economic burdens of illness are well known: they mean loss of earning power as well as the out-of-pocket expenses for medical services and drugs.

The *morbidity rate*, or incidence of illness, may or may not be available for the local community, depending upon the kind of statistical service that the local health authorities have set up. The task is complicated by the fact that such statistics must be gathered from physicians who may be too busy to fill out complicated reports. Often, however, the information for the more serious types of illness can be obtained from hospital sources. Perhaps the only really satisfactory way of getting relatively accurate information on such matters is to conduct a special investigation within the community itself. A careful sample of the population may be questioned about symptoms of ailments they now have or the illnesses suffered within the home during a given period. Results obtained can first be checked with local medical authorities for interpretation and then issued as a picture of the health conditions of the community. These findings would provide valuable data on community health patterns (5, 6).

To summarize, a community is lived in by people who can be counted, studied in terms of the various groupings to which they belong, and understood in the light of the problems that demographic trends reveal. Demographic trends represent only one aspect of the community but when added to the knowledge of the community as a place or the community as the provider of jobs and services, they provide a necessary background against which to view the intense social activity of which community life consists.

References and Suggested Readings

1. Anderson, W. A. *How Much Do New Yorkers Move?* Ithaca: Cornell University Agricultural Experiment Station, Rural Sociology Mim. Bull. No. 45 (May, 1955).
2. ———. *Social Change and an Urban Fringe Area: Ithaca, New York, A Case Illustration.* Ithaca: Cornell University Agricultural Experiment Station, Rural Sociology Publication 35 (February, 1953).
3. Blizzard, S. W., and Anderson, W. F., II. *Problems in Rural-Urban Fringe Re-*

search: Conceptualization and Delineation. State College: Pennsylvania State College Agricultural Experiment Station, Progress Report No. 89 (November, 1952).

4. CARR, L. J., and STERMER, J. E. *Willow Run: A Study of Industrialization and Cultural Inadequacy*. New York: Harper & Brothers, 1952.

5. HOFFER, CHARLES R., and JANE, CLARENCE. *Health Needs and Health Care in Two Selected Michigan Communities*. East Lansing: Michigan State College Agricultural Experiment Station, Special Bulletin 377 (June, 1952).

6. KAUFMAN, HAROLD F., and MORSE, WARREN W. *Illness in Rural Missouri*. Columbia: University of Missouri Agricultural Experiment Station, Research Bulletin 391 (August, 1945).

7. KIMBALL, SOLON T. *The New Social Frontier: The Fringe*. East Lansing: Michigan State College Agricultural Experiment Station, Special Bulletin 360 (June, 1949).

8. KING, MORTON B., JR., PEDERSEN, HARALD A., and BURRUS, JOHN N. *Mississippi's People, 1950*. "University of Mississippi Sociological Study Series," No. 5, 1955.

9. LINTON, RALPH. "Age and Sex Categories," *American Sociological Review*, VII (October, 1942), 589–603.

10. MAYO, SELZ C. "Two Factors in Urban Population Growth," *Social Forces*, XXII (October, 1943), 80–81.

11. REDICK, RICHARD W. "Population Growth and Distribution in Central Cities, 1940–1950," *American Sociological Review*, XXI (February, 1956), 38–43.

12. SCHMID, CALVIN F., DORNBUSCH, SANFORD M., and MILLER, VINCENT A. *Population Growth and Distribution: State of Washington*. Seattle: Washington State Census Board, 1955.

13. SHELDON, HENRY D. "Changes in the Rural Population, 1940 to 1950," *Rural Sociology*, XVII (June, 1952), 118–26.

14. SHEVKY, ESHREF, and LEWIN, MOLLY. *Your Neighborhood: A Social Profile of Los Angeles*. Los Angeles: The Haynes Foundation, 1949.

15. THOMPSON, WARREN S. *Population Problems* (4th ed.). New York: McGraw-Hill Book Co., Inc., 1953, ch. 14.

16. University of Minnesota, Social Science Research Center of the Graduate School, *Minnesota Trends: A Report to the People*, 1954.

17. WHETTEN, NATHAN L., and associates. *Windsor: A Highly Developed Agricultural Area* (Bulletin 212, October, 1936); *Norwich: An Industrial Part-Time Farming Area* (Bulletin 226, May, 1938); *Wilton: A Rural Town Near Metropolitan New York* (Bulletin 230, February, 1939) (Storrs: Connecticut State College Agricultural Experiment Station).

Chapter 3

THE COMMUNITY AS A JOB AND SERVICE CENTER

THE ECONOMIC STRUCTURE IN ITS SOCIAL ASPECTS

Not only can a community be viewed as a *place* and as a *collection of people;* it is also a *service center* for those people. At the same time, it is the place where most of the adults desiring a job can earn a livelihood unless, of course, the community is of the suburban type, where the job holders make the daily trip back and forth to the metropolitan center. But even in the suburbs the stress continues to be on the provision of adequate services.

The use of these services depends, of course, upon the financial ability to pay for them, which goes back to the level of employment, the average wages and salaries received, and the degree of occupational specialization found in the community. To understand this economic structure and its social overtones, before dealing with the various types of services, one can look at a particular city such as Oshkosh, Wisconsin, described so fully by John W. Alexander, who writes:

A city is like a living organism. It has a shape and a form—a skeleton, so to speak, of streets, city limits, blocks and buildings. But a city is more than that. A city has life. It has people circulating in, through, and around those features which constitute its skeleton. Without people Oshkosh would be dead. To be sure, the streets would still be there; the factories, the stores, the schools, the parks would all be in their same location. Perhaps from the air, it would still look like Oshkosh. But it would not be Oshkosh. It is the people who make the city. They constitute the life that ebbs and flows through the inanimate framework.

Life flows through a city primarily because people cannot procure all the things they need within the bounds of their own property. They must "go to work" to earn money for purchasing the things they need. They "go to the store" to spend that money. They "go to school" to learn about life and things.

38

They seek relaxation by going to the park, or to the library or other places for recreation.

A city is a group of people on the go. The one most important factor lubricating such complex activity is *money*. This medium of exchange frees a man from growing all his own food and making all his own clothes and equipment, or from the wasteful and time-consuming necessity of barter. Every citizen in a city is engaged in some form of economic activity, either earning money, or investing money, or spending money, or perhaps all three.

A city then is an economic organism through which the life blood of commerce, money, is continually circulating. The flow is an endless cycle. The factory worker receives his pay check which goes to the landlord for rent, to the grocer for food, to the clothier for clothes, to an auto dealer for a car. These businessmen in turn use that money to make purchases from others to satisfy their own needs. Much of the money goes right back to the factory in payment for goods which the businessmen have purchased in wholesale lots. And so it goes, a continuous flow of money is the life blood of a city's economy.[1]

This flow of money, this specialization of labor, this social interaction leads to the formation of groups which in turn are linked to other groups. In a sense the economy which we usually think of in terms of impersonal factors is also based on social factors. Like the family, it is made up of people in relationship to each other. Without such predictable, relatively permanent relationships a complex economy could not operate; people would not know what roles were expected of them in a given business situation. Later on, in Chapter 13, attention will be given to the kinds of social organizations which comprise the economy; here only some of the facets of the economy, such as jobs and services, will be taken up. This analysis is facilitated by asking such questions as the following: What is the source of money that flows through the community? What do the people of this community do for a living? What are the other facts about the economy of the community? This will be our present approach to the study of the economic structure.

THE COMMUNITY AS A JOB CENTER

The chances are that a person will already have some idea of the active labor force if he has done a good job of analyzing *the people* of the community. He may know, for instance, how many out of the total population are employed in some form of activity for which they receive financial remuneration. They constitute the *active labor force*. The remaining people are the *dependents* who participate in the city's economic activities by helping to spend the dollars which the labor force earns. In Oshkosh, the Wisconsin city serving as our case study, out of forty-three thousand citizens, about sixteen thou-

[1] John W. Alexander, *The Economic Life of Oshkosh* (Madison: University of Wisconsin Bureau of Community Development, Vol. 5, Nos. 1 and 2, 1955), 23–24.

sand are employed and about twenty-seven thousand are dependents. For detailed studies, the active labor force is sometimes broken down by sex and age categories.

Major Categories of Employment. One way of studying the employment picture of a community is to notice in what type of establishment people work. This also gives some idea of the major economic concentration, if one exists, in the community. Table 2, in rounded numbers, gives the major categories of employment and the number found in each for Oshkosh.

TABLE 2

OSHKOSH EMPLOYMENT, 1950

Employment Classification	Number of Employees	Per Cent of Total
MANUFACTURING	8,200	51
Metals	3,100	19
Woods	2,800	17
Textiles	1,300	8
Foods	450	3
Others	550	4
CONSTRUCTION	500	3
COMMERCE	5,500	35
Services	2,800	18
Retail trade	2,400	15
Wholesale trade	300	2
TRANSPORTATION	300	2
PUBLIC EMPLOYMENT	1,300	8
OTHERS	200	1
TOTALS	16,000	100

Source: John W. Alexander, *The Economic Life of Oshkosh* (Madison: University of Wisconsin Bureau of Community Development, Vol. 5, Nos. 1 and 2, 1955), 26.

From Table 2 it is apparent that Oshkosh is basically an industrial community. About half the workers are employed in manufacturing. The ninety-six factories which constitute the industrial structure of Oshkosh vary in size, and employment ranges from a minimum of one to a maximum of nearly 1500 employees.

Construction, in which 3 per cent of the working population is engaged, may be classed as a specialized form of manufacturing. In general, it includes the manufacture of "on-the-spot" structures—schools, churches, factories, houses, bridges, roads, etc.—using raw materials plus labor and equipment. The essential difference between construction and manufacturing is the *location* of the activity.

Commerce falls into two general types of activities—*services* and *trade.* The service activities are difficult to analyze for two reasons:

first, they encompass an extreme diversity, and second, they comprise a multitude of small firms or individual operators. The diversification includes doctors, dentists, maids, cobblers, barbers, insurance salesmen, bankers, lawyers, musicians, accountants, advertising specialists, automobile servicemen, and employees of certain business firms, such as theaters, laundries, dry cleaners, hotels, and bowling alleys. People in the services make up 18 per cent of the total working force of Oshkosh.

Trade includes those engaged in selling a wide variety of goods. Food stores and drinking places are not only the most numerous but the most widely scattered. About 17 per cent of the work force is engaged in trade, the large majority being in retail trade.

Transportation is a particular type of commercial service—the moving or transporting of goods or people from one place to another where they are wanted. It involves 2 per cent of those who work.

The term "public employment," as used in Table 2, applies to all types of economic activities which are operated by the public or a segment of the public primarily for nonprofit-making purposes. This includes government and religious organizations. The city government (including teachers, firemen, policemen, etc.), the county government, the state government, and the federal government make use of 1280 employees living and working in Oshkosh. The forty-five churches in the area supply approximately 130 jobs.

Although it does not figure prominently in the Oshkosh study, agriculture is directly related to the business life of many American communities. Indeed, for many purposes it is useful, as already pointed out, to think of the larger community as extending into the countryside and encompassing those who identify themselves with the central part of the community. This means that one must keep in mind the distinctions between the nonfarm rural person, the part-time farmer, and the full-time farmer. Any agricultural extension agent, who is a member of the staff of the state agricultural college and whose office is in the county seat of the county where he works, can help one understand these occupational groupings in his own county, for he, too, is interested in following the shifts, particularly in watching the urban fringe develop with its predominance of nonfarm or part-time rural people.

In any employment classification it is difficult to avoid overlapping titles, since some positions could be listed in two or more occupational categories. Hence it is highly important to define the precise basis of the classification used so that students of the community in later years can use a similar classification for determining occupational shifts in making comparative studies. To illustrate, a man working at a filling station is in retail trade in that he is selling commodities such as gas and oil. On the other hand, garage repairmen can be classified as being in a service rather than a trade, since their particular mechanical skill is the service they have to offer. To understand this economic aspect of community life, therefore, one should make use of the kind of classification that will give the best picture of jobs in a given community. At the same time, care must be taken to describe the basis on which certain positions are classified among the main categories.

Another way of describing what the people do for a living is to list the actual occupations which people pursue, which also shows some of the chief economic characteristics of the community. One of the more complete listings is found in the United States Census volumes dealing with population. These volumes contain tables devoted to a description of a state-by-state, county-by-county, and even city-by-city distribution of occupations.

Far removed from Oshkosh and its industrial picture lies San Luis, a town in Guatemala. This is chiefly a farming area inhabited by thirty-five hundred people, of whom twenty-five hundred are identified as Indian and the remaining thousand as Ladinos, a people of white ancestry with an orientation toward Spanish culture. The

TABLE 3

OCCUPATIONAL CLASSIFICATION OF ALL ABLE-BODIED MALES, AGE 18 TO 60,
IN MUNICIPIO OF SAN LUIS, GUATEMALA, 1942

Classification	Number	Per Cent
Jornaleros	1,341	87.3
Landowners	100	6.5
Devoted to agriculture	63	
Devoted to commerce	37	
Skilled and Semi-skilled workers*	94	6.2
Masons	9	
Woodworkers	19	
Carpenters	15	
Tailors	3	
Ironworkers	12	
Barbers	4	
Stone workers	12	
Roofers	6	
Slaughterers	3	
Shoemakers	1	
Marimba players	1	
Monthly contractors	1	
Total	1,535	100.0

* These workers total 96 instead of 94, probably indicating overlapping employment.
Source: Melvin M. Tumin, *Caste in Peasant Society* (Princeton: Princeton University Press, 1952).

great majority of those engaged in agriculture own so little land that their official job classification is *jornalero,* or day worker or wage hand. In 1942 in the *municipio,* of which the town of San Luis is a part, there were 1535 able-bodied males between the ages of eighteen and sixty, of whom 1341, or 87 per cent, were listed as *jornaleros,* as shown in Table 3.

In addition to those listed in Table 3 there are many other part-time or full-time occupations in San Luis not considered the primary source of income by those pursuing them. For instance, a *jornalero* may be so listed on the official register but may raise bees during his spare time. Some of these supplementary occupations include:

Dressmaker	Baker
Musician	Candlemaker
Tile and adobe maker	Rope and lasso maker
Saddlemaker	Pension and dining-room keeper
Horse trainer	Dairy-product manufacturer
Bee raiser	Diviner
Midwife	Storekeeper
Curer	Writer of documents
Bonesetter	Pharmacist
Masseur	Practical doctor
School teacher	Telegraph officer
Military and civil official	Soapmaker
Water-supply tender	Policeman
Veterinarian	Religious leader
Lime worker	Hatmaker
Pottery worker	Wizard
Animal castrator	Fish-net manufacturer

Symbiotic Relationships. Symbiosis is the name given to this development of specialized socioeconomic groupings and the interdependence which thus comes into being (9). These groupings which are discrete, each with its own tasks and occupational complex, do not frequently interact as equal social partners in a common undertaking. The symbiotic significance lies in their difference and in their separateness as well as in the unique contribution each makes so that others might benefit from what they have to offer.

What the people do for a living in any community, as these illustrations indicate, is dependent upon a number of factors (15). For one thing, the resources available either locally or through cheap transportation have much to do with the development of handicrafts, the location of industry, or the type of agriculture practiced. Another factor is the level of technology in the culture of which the community is a part. Complex machines may replace the cobbler who made shoes by hand; tractors and other machines may replace the gangs of field hands who chopped cotton. In a small university town such as Gainesville, Florida, the occupational distribution is skewed in favor of the white-collar worker (23); in a port city such as San Francisco, the stevedore or dock worker is important; in a resort town such as Las Vegas, popular entertainers are at a premium.

Division of labor, or the tendency of people to specialize in one task at which they can become expert, is found in nonindustrial communities as well as in the highly industrial ones. Some tasks carry more prestige and are taken over by those in the upper statuses with greater power; other tasks are considered "inferior" and are performed by those having the least advantages. Emile Durkheim, a prominent French sociologist, argues that this division of labor, since it made people dependent upon each other, actually led to social solidarity which would not exist if everyone were self-sufficient in an economic sense (18). One advantage of studying the job classification and the numbers employed in each job is the picture one gains of the interdependence on which community life is based. In a town like San Luis, referred to above, life goes on because the veterinarian can be called if an animal is sick, a curer if a human being is sick. Others will make the saddles, the pottery, or the dairy products and sell them to those busy with different activities.

Level of Employment and Measures for Dealing with Unemployment. A man may be classified as a bricklayer (construction) or a woman as a sales person (services), but if they do not have fairly regular employment this classification reveals available skills rather than the true employment picture. Throughout the whole United States, the federal government working with the state employment commissions tries to keep in touch with the levels of employment in a given community. The purpose of these state commissions is to assist those without a job to find a permanent position and to remove them from the compensation rolls. (The jobless are entitled to such compensation for a period that varies from state to state ranging from 16 weeks in the case of Florida to 30 weeks in the case of Pennsylvania.) These employment agencies, one of which is described in Chapter 13, usually issue brief reports on the current job picture, specifying the shortages and surpluses of workers in various job categories.

Anyone wishing to understand the economy of his community should know whether it experiences cyclical periods of unemployment. For example, can an unskilled worker get a job only when there is much farm work to be done or many roads to be built? Can he obtain work in a factory which processes farm produce such as tobacco only during a few months of the year? Is surplus agricultural labor brought into the community at peak harvesting periods, and, if so, what are the social needs of this migrant labor and what can the community do to meet them?

Organized labor and the management of some of the larger corporations are trying to ease the uncertainty of unemployment by such schemes as the guaranteed annual wage. Since all industries are not in a position to work out such provisions with their employees, the community may well inquire as to the cushion which workers and their families have when the breadwinners are temporarily or even permanently laid off. Fluctuations in the business cycle have obvious and pronounced community effects (7, 11).

A study of many communities through the years has shown that every community has its own employment and unemployment cycle and that people there recognize the effect of a slack period and try to adjust to it. Recognizing the nature of this employment pattern and determining whether it reflects an inevitable or a remediable situation affords greater insight into the community as a place where people seek jobs in order to earn the money needed to buy goods and services.

The Community as a Service Center

Adequacy of Services. Even though the head of a family is able to find a job in a community, he may not feel that it is the kind of place in which he wants to rear his children. His pay may be good and he may enjoy his job, but the community setting may be either so unattractive or afford so few advantages that he will refuse the job out of consideration for his children. Or, to put it another way, some communities have a drawing power over a large area which others, just as fortunate from the standpoint of geographic location, do not seem to have. One explanation for this is the difference in the adequacy of services each community provides.

What are the tests of adequate services? One measure might be the satisfaction of the local people with what they have. Complacency or contentment with things as they are would indicate adequacy in this sense; local dissatisfaction would imply inadequacy. This is certainly one test that should not be overlooked, for the attitude of residents toward their community is of unusual importance in determining the way in which that community will develop. Frequently, however, one finds that a minority is discontented, but a majority is inclined to let things go on as they are. A few propose building a new hospital, but the majority contend that the existing hospital is good enough and that a new hospital would cost too much money. When such a difference of opinion exists, a local public opinion poll will not furnish a good description of adequacy. However, there is a second kind of test which may prove useful here, namely, objective indices which have been set up as standards of adequacy for American communities in general (2).

There are objective indices, for instance, as to the number of different kinds of business services which population centers of a certain size can support (6, 8, 16). There are indices also with respect to the adequacy of recreational facilities, hospital and medical care, educational level, governmental efficiency, housing standards, support of religious bodies, and available transportation. To be sure, most of these indices are worked out for the larger communities, but those interested in understanding a community of any size can frequently develop indices applicable to that community with the help of some person professionally trained in the special field being investigated.

A third type of adequacy test, and one of the most practical, is a comparison of the community being studied with similar nearby communities in respect to measurable items (12, 14, 19). For example, is the local tax rate in a given community higher or lower than that of other nearby communities of similar size and type? How do the communities compare in unemployment figures, retail trade, bank deposits, and tax assessment? Such factual comparison furnishes a better basis for action than if the comparison were with some ideal, objective index set up by professional practitioners interested in advancing research in some specialized aspect of the field (21).

The purpose of this discussion of adequacy of services is to indicate that the community has an added economic dimension. It is more than a place where people have jobs; it is also a collection of services available to those who participate in the life of the community. Some types of services can be briefly mentioned simply to indicate how important they are to local residents even though people usually take them for granted as long as they provide adequately for local needs.[2]

Types of Services. Business services. One way to view business services is to ask what basic and necessary commodities are available locally at reasonable prices. Does one have to drive to the next

---

[2] Here the stress will be upon *facilities,* since separate chapters later on will describe economy, government, recreation, health and welfare, education, and religion as particular social systems within the community.

larger center to buy Johnny his wardrobe for his freshman year at college? If Aunt Jane, who dotes on ripe olives, is coming to visit should she be asked to bring her own ripe olives, or can they be purchased locally? Are there lawyers, insurance salesmen, and real estate agents in the community, or is it necessary to go elsewhere to have a will made, take out theft insurance, or obtain help in selling a house? Can local architects and builders construct the kind of house a wife has envisoned for her family after six months of brooding over many issues of the house-and-garden magazines? Can watches, toasters, and sewing machines be repaired locally, or must they be sent back to the factory?

Of course, the people of any community will tend to demand those services and commodities which they have been taught to demand. One plane passenger regaled a stranger all the way between Cincinnati and New York on the good work a dog psychiatrist was doing with an eleven-year-old cocker spaniel that had developed a feeling of insecurity in the presence of three other dogs in the mistress' entourage. Such a person will need to stay close to a large city which can provide enough people like herself and enough dogs like her cocker spaniel to give full-time employment to a dog psychiatrist. No medium-sized city will be adequate for his needs. Yet, it is fair to look at any community in terms of the adequacy of its business services, realizing that the quantity and type of service is a function of population, size, wealth, and local expectations.

Communities also differ in the way that salespeople treat the customer, although mass merchandising is today reducing these differences. Furthermore, people vary in the expectations that they bring with them when they go shopping.

A study made by Gregory P. Stone on Chicago's Northwest Side showed that among the housewives shopping in that area there were really four types of shoppers as follows:

The *economic consumer* . . . This type of shopper expressed a sense of responsibility for her household purchasing duties: she was extremely sensitive to price, quality, and assortment of merchandise, all of which entered into the calculus of her behavior on the market. She was interested in shopping. Clerical personnel and the store were for her, merely the instruments of her purchase of goods . . . The quality she demanded of a "good" clerk was efficiency.

The *personalizing consumer*. This type of consumer shopped "where they know my name." It was important that she shop at *her* store rather than "public" stores. Strong personal attachments were formed with store personnel, and this personal relationship, often approaching intimacy, was crucial to her patronage of a store . . . Her conception of a "good" clerk was one who treated her in a personal, relatively intimate manner.

The *ethical consumer*. This type of shopper shopped where she "ought" to.

She was willing to sacrifice lower prices or a wider selection of goods "to help the little guy out" or because "the chain store has no heart or soul." Consequently, strong attachments were sometimes formed with personnel and store owners or with "stores" in the abstract . . . Since store personnel did not enter in primarily as instrumentalities but rather with reference to other, more ultimate ends, she had no clear conception of a "good" clerk.

The *apathetic consumer*. This type of consumer shopped because she "had" to. Shopping for her was an onerous task. She shopped "to get it over with." Ideally, the criterion of convenient location was crucial to her selection of a store, as opposed to price, quality of goods, relationships with store personnel, or ethics. She was not interested in shopping and minimized her expenditure of effort in purchasing goods. Experiences in stores were not sufficiently important to leave any lasting impression on her. She knew few of the personnel and had no notion of a "good" clerk.[3]

Of the 124 housewives interviewed, 41 were of the economic type, 35 the personalizing, 22 the ethical, 21 the apathetic, and 5 the indeterminate type. After giving the social traits of these four main types, the writer takes up the matter of identification of the shoppers with the area where they shopped. He found that a significantly larger proportion of personalizing consumers had established subjective identifications with the Northwest Side without or with little apparent basis (such as long residence, location of friends, etc.) than had consumers of the other three types taken together. Certainly, for these personalizing housewives their shopping experience had much to do with their feeling of community identification.

With the rapid suburbanization which has been occurring a number of economic shifts have been under way as well. Leo F. Schnore, in his study of suburban life, has described two types of metropolitan suburbs: one is the industrial suburb and the other the residential suburb. His characterization of the two types shows the basic differences in the economic services offered:

In general, the *industrial suburbs* are employing centers, attracting workers from other parts of the metropolitan area. As might be expected, they tend to be concentrated in the heavily industrialized areas of the northeastern and north-central regions. They appear relatively more frequently in the areas with the smaller central cities, but they are themselves larger than other suburbs. Industrial centers also tend to be older than other subcenters. Although they appear throughout the entire metropolitan area, they are more frequently found beyond the limits of the densely settled urban core. As distance from the central city increases, in fact, suburbs of the industrial type are found with relatively greater frequency. Finally, these industrial centers are typically characterized by low rents.[4]

[3] Gregory P. Stone, "City Shoppers and Urban Identification: Observations on the Social Psychology of City Life," *American Journal of Sociology*, LX (July, 1954), 39–40. Coypright, 1954, by the University of Chicago.

[4] Leo F. Schnore, "The Functions of Metropolitan Suburbs," *American Journal of Sociology*, LXI (March, 1956), p. 458.

Residential suburbs, on the other hand, have local retail trade as the dominant economic activity; they are found in the metropolitan areas of all regions of the United States, and tend to appear more frequently as the size of the central city increases, although they are themselves smaller than the average. This type includes more of the recently incorporated subcenters and few of them lie outside the densely urbanized area or farther than thirty miles from the central city. In these residential suburbs, rents are above average.

Recreational services. These should be viewed in a three-fold way: (1) the commercial; (2) the public or governmental; and (3) the outlets provided by schools, churches, business concerns (for their employees), and other private sources. Many communities rely almost entirely upon the businessman to provide the recreational outlets for their residents. The motion picture theater, the bowling alley, television and radio, professional sports, and even adventure magazines and serious works of literature are tied in closely with the commercial aspects of our economic system. Frequently, some local business will arise in response to a fashion or a craze but will fade just as quickly when the enthusiasm is spent. A history of the commercial recreational outlets from taverns to roller skating rinks would show how many different kinds of recreational tastes can be satisfied in the community through commercial channels.

Most communities have some type of public recreation program. The park system and its sponsored activities, the roadside tables and picnic grounds, and the staging of many sports by local public recreation leaders testify to the part that local as well as state and national governments play in helping citizens to find constructive use for their leisure time. In addition to these, there are many recreational programs sponsored by religious or school groups, fraternal orders, socially minded civic clubs, or small neighborhood groups. The complaint by many people today is not that they wish they had something to do but rather that they have difficulty in deciding how to spend a free evening. In the case of a family one child may wish to go to a movie, the mother may prefer to stay at home and watch a favorite television program, an older son may want to go to a driving range and practice golf shots, while the father may really want to watch the lady wrestlers billed for a match in the local arena for that evening.

If young people in particular think it necessary to go outside the community for amusement, they may be illustrating the adage that the grass is always greener in the other fellow's yard, or they may simply be indicating that recreational facilities, especially the type enjoyed by young people, are lacking in that community (17, 24).

Medical and hospital services. Certainly people cannot consider their community adequate as a service center if it does not meet their basic health needs. Ordinarily, a satisfactory evaluation can be made in terms of the number of doctors per one thousand people or the number of hospital beds available.[5] However, those familiar with small communities, where the doctor shortage is usually most acute, know that the number of doctors tells only part of the story. Satisfaction with medical services is related to the personality, training, and even age of the doctors in that community. The same holds true of dentists and other practitioners in the medical field. In the American system, health service is a qualitative and not just a quantitative problem (4, 14).

Behind those in private practice there is a corps of public health specialists whose job it is to prevent illness from occurring and to step into the breach in case of epidemics. Too few citizens are aware of the many services that the better public health departments render. Not only do they collect vital statistics, but they inspect dairies and restaurants, aid in mosquito control, enforce quarantines, and at the same time render assistance to needy patients who, in the public interest, require various kinds of inoculation or preventive treatment. A full inquiry into community medical services would include a chronicling of what the public health officials are and are not doing. Good hospital service and competent medical care tend to go together; they exist only when a first-rate medical tradition develops to attract the more promising physicians, surgeons, hospital managers, and well-trained nurses.

Educational services. Ever since America was settled by refugees from Europe in the early seventeenth century, the school has been at the heart of the community life. At first, it existed to teach the children how to read so they could study the Bible. Later its utilitarian purpose was emphasized, since it produced more versatile and efficient workers. And at the same time, in the developing political philosophy of our country, education came to be thought of as a bulwark of democracy. Today, in our complex society, the test of educational services is not one simply of having a sufficiently large, attractive plant—difficult as that is to provide in the face of growing enrollments: the test must relate to what goes on in the school building as far as basic learning, character development, and preparation for citizenship are concerned. Some community leaders rate their

[5] In 1955 there were 4.2 general hospital beds per 1000 population, which is approaching the figure of 4.5 per 1000 traditionally considered a standard measure of need. The Mountain states averaged highest with 4.9 and the East South Central the lowest with 3.2 beds per 1000 people.

school system by the win–loss record of the high school basketball team; others more wisely look at the later records of those who have gone on to college.

More and more adults are becoming interested in adult education courses and expect some local agency or the state university to assist them in obtaining these courses. Businessmen, doctors, housewives, and mechanics study public speaking, photography, American history, or international relations in order to become more proficient in their occupation or hobby or to satisfy their intellectual curiosity about what is going on in the world.

Transportation services. People like to be able to move themselves and their goods in and out of a community with considerable ease, whether by train, plane, bus, truck, or private automobile. The connections provided and the frequency of service are important to many types of people, including those who have out-of-town relatives who would come for weekend visits if travel schedules permitted, those responsible for shipping merchandise, and those arranging dates for a concert and lecture series. What demands are not being met? How many trains and buses run half- or even quarter-full as losing propositions for the transportation companies who may therefore be seeking to curtail travel facilities on valid economic grounds? Factory location as well as cultural contacts is usually tied in with type, quality, and frequency of transportation services, a further illustration that the community is a service center.

Governmental services. Not the least among local services are those provided by the government, whether county, town, or municipal. There is much paperwork to modern living, and many of these documents cross government counters—birth certificates, passport applications, marriage licenses, stock transactions, deeds for a house, wills, car registrations, and hunting licenses. In addition, many welfare programs are publicly financed (3, 4, 5). Clean streets, law and order (10, 14), easy traffic flow and adequate parking, planning and zoning, and receptions for visiting dignitaries—these are all aspects of government in action.

There are many other services of a religious, aesthetic, and cultural character which might be mentioned to round out an inventory of the kinds of provisions most local communities make for their members. A brief study of such services—which may range from buying a washing machine to having an appendix removed—makes us aware of the complexity of an American community from this one standpoint alone. It also emphasizes the extent of interdependence of its members.

Availability of These Services to the Whole Community. Even when the indices seem to show that services are adequate, all the people of the community may not be able to share in their benefits. Certain limitations on availability often exist. What, then, are these limitations?

Residence or location. A playground or swimming pool may be located at one edge of town and consequently not within easy reach of those living in other parts of the community. The distance involved is itself a deterrent, for it means that the only way many children can take advantage of these opportunities is to be taken there by their parents, a limitation all too acute in many families.

Income. Another limiting factor is that of cost. The community may have services available to those who can afford them, but only a small proportion of the people may be able to pay for some of these services. Here again, recreation is a good example. Golf may be limited to members of the country club where there are no public golf links; hospital services may tend to be limited to those who can pay in advance or those who have hospital insurance. The better schools may have so many incidental costs in addition to tuition that only those from higher income families can afford to attend. To be sure, there will always be economic differentiation in any workable economic system, but a person should understand the nature of this differentiation in the community he is studying, particularly with respect to the utilization of the services provided by the community. Nor is this differentiation always what one might expect. In some types of services, for example, provisions for the care of the poor are such that they are better provided for than the middle income groups who have to pay the costs yet have insufficient savings or earnings.

Race. Throughout the nation certain facilities are closed to members of particular races. In the South such restrictions have been supported by legislative measures and local ordinances passed by the dominant white group; in other parts of the country where no such legal barriers exist there are often social barriers which also discriminate. On the West Coast the Japanese and Chinese face hurdles because of their race. In many areas there exist really two communities, the white and the Negro, with symbiotic relationships between them. One community cannot be understood without an understanding of the other or of the degree to which both communities are moving toward one community, at least as far as utilization of a community's services is concerned.

Religion. There are barriers to some community services on the basis of religion, though they are often secondary to the residence and income factors mentioned above. Where the services are public services, this discrimination with respect to religion is kept at a minimum, but this is not the case where the services are privately owned and operated. The problem becomes particularly acute in resort communities where there is an attempt made to accept guests only from one particular faith, be it Jewish, Protestant, or Catholic. To see to what extent the services of a community are available to all of the people one should find out whether religious discrimination exists.

GENERAL ECONOMIC TRENDS

The economic situation in a community, be it Oshkosh, Wisconsin, or San Luis, Guatemala, never remains static for long, since the dynamic nature of capitalism is based on anticipated change. The marketing area of a given place is either expanding or contracting, the payrolls are increasing or decreasing, bank deposits are going up or going down. As we have seen, some of this is seasonal and much of it is linked with impersonal economic forces operating on a national and international level rather than only within the community. Yet anyone inquiring objectively into the economic welfare of a community should be able to discern the long-term trends under way. Many of these are directly related to the jobs and services previously discussed.

The county agricultural extension agent, as mentioned previously, can tell what the relative importance of farming is at a given time compared with what it was a few years back and what it might be in the future. It may be that in the present community fewer farmers are raising more food and feeding more people while also producing important industrial crops such as cotton, soybeans, or tobacco.

The utility companies know what has been happening in industrial expansion and are making carefully calculated plans for future developments. Mortgage companies keep a close eye on changing property values and tendencies toward undersupply or oversupply of housing.

One useful indicator of the confidence people have in the local economic situation is the proportion of young people raised in a town who plan to settle down there after completing their schooling. The mere fact of settling down is a vote of confidence in the economic future as well as a testimony to a sufficient variety of jobs to satisfy the occupational ambitions of those starting their careers.

To one trained in economics or in business forecasting, there are many other more reliable indices to be used in gauging a community's economy. To the ordinary citizen, however, his community in the economic sense is not a mass of statistics but rather a place which he judges in terms of the type and steadiness of employment, the type and availability of services, and the general outlook of the people toward the future.

REFERENCES AND SUGGESTED READINGS

1. ALEXANDER, JOHN W. *The Economic Life of Oshkosh.* Madison: University of Wisconsin, Bureau of Community Development, Parts 1 and 2, 1955.
2. BAUR, EDWARD JACKSON. "Statistical Indexes of the Social Aspects of Communities," *Social Forces,* XXXIII (October, 1954), 64–75.
3. BLACK, BERTRAM J. *Our Welfare Needs: A Study of New York City . . .* New York: The Greater New York Fund, 1949.
4. BUELL, BRADLEY. *Community Planning for Human Services.* New York: Columbia University Press, 1952.
5. Community Chests and Councils of America, Inc. *Social Breakdown: An Outline for Procedures for Compiling Social Data,* Bulletin 137 (May, 1948).
6. DUNCAN, OTIS DUDLEY. "Urbanization and Retail Specialization," *Social Forces,* XXX (March, 1952), 267–71.
7. GORDON, ROBERT AARON. *Business Fluctuations.* New York: Harper & Brothers, 1952.
8. HAWLEY, AMOS H. "An Ecological Study of Urban Service Institutions," *American Sociological Review,* VI (October, 1941), 629–39.
9. ———. *Human Ecology.* New York: The Ronald Press Co., 1950, chs. 3 and 12.
10. MACNEIL, DOUGLAS H. "The Vulnerability Index: An Account of Experimentation in Predicting a Community's Crime Rate," *Survey Midmonthly* (January, 1948), 3–6.
11. MITCHELL, WESLEY. *What Happens During Business Cycles.* New York: National Bureau of Economic Research, 1951.
12. OLDS, EDWARD B. *How Does Your City Rate? Comparison of 57 Metropolitan Areas . . .* St. Louis: Social Planning Council of St. Louis and St. Louis County, 1952.
13. PORTERFIELD, AUSTIN L. "Rank of the States in Professional Leadership and Social Well-Being," *Social Forces,* XXV (March, 1947), 303–9.
14. PORTERFIELD, AUSTIN L., and TALBERT, ROBERT H. *Crime, Suicide, and Social Well-Being in Your State and City.* Fort Worth: Leo Potishman Foundation, 1948.
15. PRICE, PAUL H. "Economic Problems," ch. 10 in T. Lynn Smith, *Social Problems.* New York: The Thomas Crowell Co., 1955.
16. SCHETTLER, CLARENCE. "Relation of City Size to Economic Services," *American Sociological Review,* VIII (February, 1943), 60–62.
17. SHAW, CLIFFORD R., and MCKAY, HENRY D. *Social Factors in Juvenile Delinquency* (Publications of the National Commission on Law Observance and Enforcement, No. 13, Vol. II). Washington, D.C.: Government Printing Office, 1931.
18. SIMPSON, GEORGE. *Emile Durkheim on the Division of Labor in Society.* New York: The Macmillan Co., 1933.
19. THORNDIKE, EDWARD L. *Your City.* New York: Harcourt, Brace & Company, 1939.
20. TUMIN, MELVIN M. *Caste in a Peasant Society.* Princeton: Princeton University Press, 1952.
21. United States Bureau of the Census, *County and City Data Book,* 1952. Washington, D.C.: Government Printing Office, 1953.

22. United States Bureau of the Census, *A Report of the Seventeenth Decennial Census of the United States:* Census of Population, 1950 (Washington, D.C.: Government Printing Office. Vol. I. Number of Inhabitants, 1952; Vol. II. Characteristics of the Population, 1953).
23. University of Florida, Bureau of Economic and Business Research, *Economic Survey of the Community of Gainesville, Florida, 1950.* Community Economic Surveys No. 1.
24. Welfare Council of Metropolitan Los Angeles, Research Department, *Youth Project Yardstick: Measuring Youth Services Needs.* Special Report Series No. 36, 1953.
25. WHITE, VIRGINIA KANN. *Measuring Social Need.* Cleveland: Press of Western Reserve University, 1951.

Chapter 4

THE COMMUNICATION NETWORK

For any modern community to come into existence, ways of communication must develop. This involves not only the transportation of people and goods, but also the interchange of ideas and information. People not only need to come together in physical proximity, but they must have enough common knowledge and background to be able to talk intelligibly and meaningfully to each other when they are together. Furthermore, communities must also possess methods of disseminating news quickly in an emergency as well as methods which provide for the normal percolation of facts about less pressing everyday affairs.

An unusual and certainly not a typical example today of how the people of a community learn what is going on is that of Huntington, Texas, as reported in the following news item:

People at Huntington, Texas are not clamoring for a dial telephone system —not so long as Mrs. Beulah King is on the job as "central"—for they get far more service from the manual telephone she operates than they would from one they had to dial.

Huntington is a town of 1,000 in Angelina County. To "central" those 1,000 inhabitants are reduced to 250 phone numbers which she knows from memory.

Beulah King is really the heart of the town; she knows everybody—those she cannot recognize by sight, she knows by their voice—and residents tell her where they are going, when they will return, and give her countless messages to relay. She is called upon to report fires, announce births, make emergency calls and on many occasions her initiative and resourcefulness have saved lives.

A typical example was the case of the young hunter who was lost in the woods near Huntington. Beulah King called the volunteer fire station and asked them to sound the alarm whistle.

When curious residents called in, she told them what the trouble was and soon everybody was tramping through the woods looking for the youth. He was found at 1:00 A.M. unharmed.

"I knew they were going to do it," says Mrs. King. "When that fire whistle blows, everyone with a phone wants to know what is going on."

But Beulah King does much more than connect people with the right numbers. She has established a set of signals with bus drivers. They transmit them to her by blowing their horns as they pass. For example, three blasts mean for Mrs. King to call Lufking depot and tell the agent to hold the Houston bus for a passenger from Huntington. One blast means to do the same thing for the New Orleans bus . . .[1]

COMMUNICATION AND TRANSPORTATION

Not often is a single person like Mrs. King so intimately connected with both the media of communication and the operation of a transportation system, such as the bus company. In most communities they can be looked at separately, as was done in the previous chapter in which transportation was discussed as one of the important services which add to or detract from a sense of community pride. These same facilities, however, may be viewed from the standpoint of the ease with which people are brought together for intimate social contact or for large mass meetings. Where people share in such activities, they are apt to develop a deeper sense of the larger community than if they remain at home in their small neighborhoods. Communities differ greatly in the ease of access to downtown events or the ease with which merchandise can be delivered to one's door. Time spent in travel, together with the comfort and general atmosphere of this travel, has a direct bearing upon social participation, which is central to community life.

In any community, also, some points are more accessible than others. Far too often, community leaders who themselves rely almost exclusively on private automobile transportation, when selecting some meeting site, fail to take into account the convenience or inconvenience of public transportation. Or, someone with an assured parking spot at the place of meeting may be unaware of the difficulties others encounter in trying to park their vehicles before the meeting begins. This whole problem of the movement of people into, out of, and within the community is discussed more fully in Chapter 19, on physical planning and zoning, but deserves passing mention here, since transportation does have a decided influence upon communication, especially as used in the sense of physical circulation of people and things throughout the community.

An awareness of the growth of transportation facilities also gives one an insight into the historical development of the community. Gist and Halbert point out this connection between urban growth and available transportation:

During the early period of urban growth in this country, water routes were the major form of long-distance transportation. The middle of the nineteenth

[1] *Christian Science Monitor*, June 8, 1956.

century marked the beginning of an era of railway transportation which provided an impetus to the development of cities not reached by water. After 1910 the automobile and motor truck became important factors in city growth. The passenger automobile has not only increased the size of the local trading areas of both large and small cities, but has brought them into closer relationship with urban centers. The effect on the commercial life of the metropolis has been especially significant, since automobile and motor-truck transportation has tended to attract purchasers from outside the city, thereby stimulating trade and making possible the employment of more workers.[2]

The airplane has more effect upon the development of the large centers since cargo and passenger planes tend to overfly the smaller communities.

THE INFORMAL COMMUNICATION NETWORK

When a person turns from trains and trucks, automobiles and airplanes to the human element in communication, he finds that there are frequently well-defined systems of transmitting news through informal contacts. Although not actually visible, these chains of human relationships are just as real as the electric cables from which the city buses draw their current.

Baker Brownell in his discussion of "Communicability and the Community" indicates that communication arises from the fact that people are many and different and still establish contact with one another:

Communication is also a function of the identification of people with one another. In this is the substance of community. Men behave not only as if they were separate; they behave also as if they were identified with one another . . . Through communication we confirm the basic unity of our common life and try to convert it into intelligent or at least successful action. By means, either direct or indirect, we identify our experience with another's. We try to live together in a fairly coherent world, share in its values and bring about mutual cooperation . . .

Through communication we enter more fully into the knowing and assimilating process of living. We identify our experience more fully with that of another thing . . .[3]

Informal Patterns of Communication. This process of communication is the action of mind upon mind, although Professor Brownell would rightly claim that man can commune with Nature or with an orderly arrangement of wood and stone, as represented in a beautiful cathedral. Basically, however, human interaction builds the human community.

---

[2] Noel P. Gist and L. A. Halbert, *Urban Society* (New York: The Thomas Crowell Co., 1956), p. 63.

[3] Baker Brownell, *The Human Community: Its Philosophy and Practice for a Time of Crisis* (New York: Harper & Brothers, 1950), pp. 240–41.

Communication in the sociological sense is more than movement; it is more than the existence of media of interaction. Indeed, it is basically an exchange of ideas between people (13). To communicate is to interact mentally with another person. It may be by a physical gesture, such as a wink, a smile, a frown, the raising of a hand, or it may be by verbal gestures. Furthermore, these gestures must be meaningful to both parties (9, 20).

The opposite of communication is isolation, a phenomenon which those who deal with the mentally ill describe as being all too common in modern life. It is mental rather than spatial isolation, for the isolate may be *near* other people all of the time but seldom has or takes the opportunity of communicating with others (9, 16). In some groups any member may tend to be an isolate if he does not know the other people very well or is uninformed about the topics being discussed, but when this isolation extends to all groups of which he is a part, then life takes on a drab appearance. The basis of community life, therefore, is communication through which people interact or exchange ideas. People who do this only to a slight degree do not share in the sense of community, although they get a certain vicarious pleasure out of communication of others whom they observe. This sense of isolation is discussed in several of the best-selling books of the past few years, such as David Riesman's *The Lonely Crowd*, Margaret Wood's *Paths of Loneliness* and Erich Fromm's *Escape to Freedom*.

Communication, in the sense of sharing ideas, is synonymous with the term "social interaction" and is more completely considered in Chapter 8. As will be seen, there are recurring patterns of interaction which can be identified and studied and which give an insight into the social structure as well as into the prevailing social processes of a community.

One method of describing these informal patterns is that of sociometry, which follows the procedure of asking people to name others with whom they would prefer to be associated for different kinds of activities. When these choices are charted, one can learn a great deal about the interaction among those involved. For example, if a bit of important information starts circulating quickly within an area of the city, through what existing formal channels is this information apt to flow? Does an informal communication network exist and, if so, what is it like?

To answer this question, during World War II every housewife in several widely separated blocks of a medium-sized city was asked: "If you were to get together with three women in this block (defined as both sides of the street) and discuss how you could help in the war effort, which three women would you choose?" When the replies had been collected, sociograms were constructed by letting a different number represent each woman and drawing lines between those who had been chosen and the person making the choice (17). The sociogram on page 61 shows that a genuine informal structure existed.

Figure 7 shows which women in a single block were chosen and which were not chosen with reference to the specific activity of helping in the war effort. From every square, each of which represents a housewife interviewed, three lines go to other squares. These show the three women named by that particular woman. The women most frequently named have most lines going to their square; women who named each other are shown by a small mark at the middle of the line connecting them (such as 21–23).

Such a sociogram shows much about the communication network for this particular area. If number 13 and 25 were well-informed about some issue, they could pass the word with authority (for they are accepted) to a great many others. These two *leaders* need not contact all the women personally but could use *subleaders* (such as 3, 4, 8, 24, and 29) to get the word to those with whom they are connected. Special attention would have to be given to a few *isolates* who are newcomers or who, as in the case of one practical nurse, feel they are too busy to visit with the other women. This sociogram furnishes, for this block at least, a ready supply of useful information that can be tapped by those wishing to inform the whole community about something of interest to them.

The gossip chain. Numerous other studies of large collections of people, whether in factories, in universities, on the police force, or as sports enthusiasts, would reveal similar clusters of people who are interrelated as part of a large "gossip chain" that stretches through much of the community. Some of those in this chain get many details of a news story from the formal media, but as the story spreads, it becomes more personalized, frequently more vivid and even altered in its essentials.

These informal channels operate wherever social cliques gather and wherever conversation becomes free and easy and intimate. Word gets passed around at filling stations in the short period while the gas tank is being filled, at the courthouse where hangers-on congregate to learn what is new, at the feed store where farmers gather to discuss crops or politics, at the union hall, on the job, or in the beauty parlor or barber shop where no formal pattern of conversation is determined in advance.

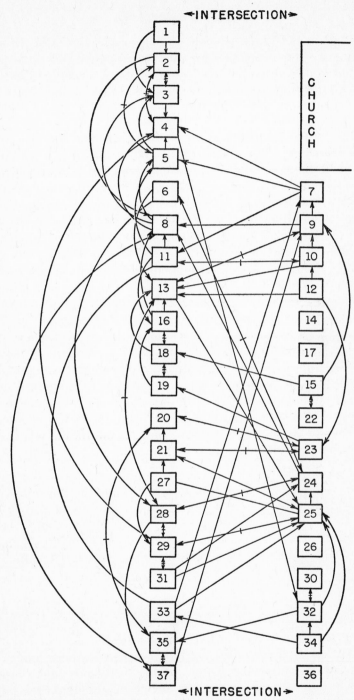

Source: Irwin T. Sanders, "The Use of Block Leaders in Effective Community Mobilization," *Sociometry*, XII (November, 1949), 267.

FIG. 7. Sociogram of acquaintance and visiting patterns in an urban block.

The gossip chain operates at most recreational functions—at the bridge club, the church supper, the after-theater party or during a golf game. Topics may relate to events as well as to personalities. They may range from the cause of a recent fire to the behavior of the minister's wife. Men just as much as women are part of this informal system of communication, which deals not only with matters in the day's headlines but with affairs that could never be printed or broadcast without fear of libel suits.

To understand then how people communicate with each other in a given community, one needs to be aware of more than the bus, streetcar, or subway system. One also needs a familiarity with the formal media of spreading news and ideas as well as with those informal means which any community develops long before it is fully equipped with telephone, press, radio, and television (14). "Word sure gets around!" is the surprised statement that people often make when they discover just how rapidly segments of the community can learn of something that has just occurred.

Rumor. The role of rumor in this whole process of informal communication deserves careful study. For a well-documented case we turn to the account by Warren Peterson and Noel Gist of what happened in a community as an aftermath of an unsolved crime involving the rape and murder of a fifteen-year-old baby sitter. These authors define rumor as "an unverified account or explanation of events, circulating from person to person and pertaining to an object, event or issue of public concern."[4] They also point out that rumor "opinion" differs from other forms of public opinion in that it is not verified through customary channels. "A social setting conducive to rumor occurs when a public is interested and concerned about a past or anticipated event, when authoritative information and explanation are lacking and when social controls relevant to the situation are external to most members of the public."[5]

Peterson and Gist indicate that people who were never interested in nor informed about the situation were drawn into the informal discussion of the murder which had occurred. They observed: "As persons move from one discussion group to another, speculation tends to be passed as rumor; and rumor comes to be represented as fact, often supported by citing supposedly authoritative sources. Typically, the rumor public is more emotional than other publics."[6]

---

[4] Warren A. Peterson and Noel P. Gist, "Rumor and Public Opinion," *American Journal of Sociology*, LVII (September, 1951), 159. Copyright, 1951, by the University of Chicago.

[5] *Ibid.*, p. 160.

[6] *Ibid.*, p. 162.

In the beginning, the opinion about the event is unstructured with many differing views being expressed. "The communication of rumor tends to reduce the divergence in attitudes and to produce a common definition of the situation and a common feeling or mood. Rumor is one means by which a collectivity, albeit a temporary and unstable collectivity, emerges from an aggregate."[7]

The central theme of a set of rumors which circulated for three or four days about this crime was that Mr. X, the baby sitter's employer, had left a party which he and his wife were attending, returned home, entered the house, committed the crime, and subsequently returned to the party after changing his clothes. According to Peterson and Gist,

The numerous variations which developed from this central theme indicate interpretation, speculation and creative imagination on the part of the public in the direction of coordinating the story with previous conceptions of the murder, of attributing stereotyped sex-criminal characteristics to Mr. X, of constructing a basis for sympathizing with his wife, of supplying authentic verification and of generally molding a sensational account.[8]

Other types of rumors, such as those which precede race riots or a run on a bank, although ephemeral in character, have grave community consequences, since the misinformation and doubts which are spread are never fully counteracted by correct stories of what actually occurred (11).

Differences in Perceptions of and Knowledge About the Community. In the day-to-day activities of the community, however, facts about matters other than rumor need to be taken into account. For example, who talks to whom about specific community problems and projects? In a Mississippi town of five thousand population called Bakerville by A. Alexander Fanelli in his report, an effort was made to distinguish between the traits of those who report a variety of communication contacts and those who report few or no contacts (3). Those who are the high communicators (that is, talk to three or more *different* persons about community problems), as would be expected, are more strongly identified with the community than the low communicators; they are more apt to be active participants in community affairs. Furthermore, the high communicators are likely to perceive the community in a different way than the low communicators; they are more apt to understand what the community "really is." In Bakerville, which is split into many factions, the high communicators are more likely to admit the existence of these groups and factions than the low communicators; they are

[7] *Ibid.*, p. 160.
[8] *Ibid.*, p. 162.

more likely to report the blocking of attempts to get new industry, and they are less likely to give a high rating to Bakerville's community spirit. According to Fanelli, this study illustrates the value of communication as a "reality-checking" mechanism in interpersonal relations, since the more extensive one's communications contacts, the more objective is the perception one has of community affairs.

Gresham M. Sykes in a study of Plainfield, New Jersey, a city of well over forty thousand and not far from New York City, tries to find out "the social location" of the knowledge about this community. He thinks of social location in terms of status, occupational role, ethnic group, and position in the power structure. In other words, do people in some statuses know more about the community than others in different statuses who live in the same community? Since many people from Plainfield commute to New York City, Sykes found it necessary to draw a distinction between *local* statuses (characterized by long residence, home ownership, work located in Plainfield, children in local schools, and geographical immobility) and *nonlocal* statuses (where the opposites of the above characteristics hold true).[9]

After a thorough analysis in terms of this two-fold typology (local and nonlocal), Sykes has this to say:

A high level of community knowledge would seem to be associated with a cluster of statuses which have, as the common element, orientation toward the community. "Local" individuals possessing such statuses are, in a certain sense, truly members of the community. They live there; they work there; their goals and interests are intertwined with those of the community itself. Such individuals apparently are tied to the community by a multitude of bonds, and it is this cohesion which provides both the means of obtaining knowledge and the motivation to do so.[10]

Another way of stating the last sentence is to indicate that those with a community-orientation are more apt to be integral parts of the informal patterns of communication which transmit information about local affairs, a fact which is "circularly self-enforcing," according to Sykes. His data suggest that the person oriented away from the community has a low level of knowledge about the community, even though he may be well-educated and have a high income.

[9] In drawing this distinction, Sykes follows a similar one drawn by Robert K. Merton in a study of a town called "Rovere." There Merton found two types of individuals exercising differential influence, one of which he calls "locals" and the other "cosmopolitans." See Robert K. Merton, "Patterns of Influence," *Communications Research 1948–1949*, Paul F. Lazarsfeld and Frank N. Stanton (eds.) (New York: Harper & Brothers, 1949), pp. 180–219.

[10] Gresham M. Sykes, "The Differential Distribution of Community Knowledge," *Social Forces*, XXIX (May, 1951), 382.

The information gained from studies such as these raises some serious questions about the functioning of local democratic processes when so many people in a community are so poorly informed, and even so little concerned, about what actually transpires there. Fundamental to the understanding of this problem is the knowledge of ways in which people gain their information about affairs, both within and without the community. This study of the dissemination of news and ideas, a form of cultural diffusion, has been greatly intensified in recent years, with some interesting results. The process is dependent, however, not only upon the informal channels just described, but also upon the formal media, to which we now turn.

THE FORMAL CHANNELS OF COMMUNICATION

The best way to list the existing channels of communication in one's home town is to ask a series of questions about the channels which would be used in the case of certain events.

Suppose the largest department store is having its big annual sale, and its manager wants to be sure the people know what bargains are available. What means of communication would he employ to inform prospective customers of the sale?

Suppose a foreign plane, probably carrying a bomb, has been sighted a few hundred miles away, headed in the direction of the home town. What defense organization, if any, would swing into action?

Suppose the community is shifting from standard to daylight time in the early hours of Sunday morning. How would people be notified so that they would not arrive at church or at other engagements the next day an hour behind schedule?

Suppose that snowfall is so heavy that the school buses cannot run, and the schools are to be closed temporarily. How would parents whose children attend school find out?

Suppose some deadline is fast approaching by which time people are to buy new automobile licenses, pay property taxes, register to vote, or contribute to the community chest. What means are there in the home town to inform people of these deadlines?

Answering these and other questions like them shows which media would be employed—the postal system, billboards, newspapers, television and radio, sirens. The size of the community may affect the choice of media, but basically the same approaches will be tried. The successful advertising man's dream is the development of some channel of communication more effective than that of his competitor. In 1955, $8,750,000,000 were spent on advertising in the United States, which shows the confidence businessmen and others have in these formal channels of communication. The shift in how part of the advertising dollar has been spent between 1946 and 1954 is shown in Figure 8. It is noticeable that radio and magazines have shown relatively little increase.

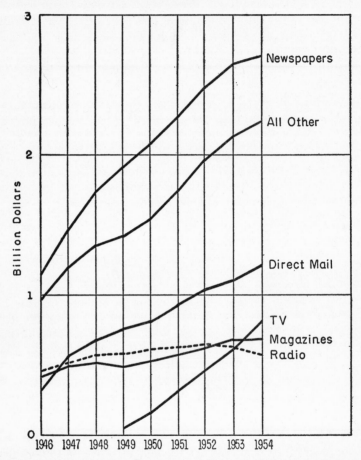

Source: Cleveland Trust Company Business Bulletin, 37 (January 16, 1956).

FIG. 8. Annual volume of advertising by media, 1946–54.

The Press. The printed word continues to be a powerful means of communicating information and ideas (5). Often people choose to read those papers and publications which continually tell them what they want to read. Very few community members purposely read materials which are designed to present points of view different from their own. But this reinforcement of sentiments can serve a useful community function in that people are enabled to make up their minds more assuredly with the support of such media. Of course, different segments of the community may read different papers and different magazines, thus moving in different climates of public opinion, but such variations in points of view are not necessarily divisive forces within a community where processes have been worked out whereby differences can be publicly aired and a decision reached through the ballot or some other method of widespread expression.

Rose Hum Lee has this to say about the urban press in American society:

The urban press is the most important medium of communication. A variety of material is included: (1) daily newspapers, (2) special interest organs, (3) periodicals, (4) sensationalized features, and (5) community papers. Large cities offer a wide variety of newspapers, but they all may be owned and operated by one management or by a chain. The trend is toward more mergers, resulting in the standardization of content, news gathering, release and distribution. Circulation has climbed, although the number of independent papers has decreased.

The Negro press is a growing institution and is the greatest single force uniting the members of the group. From a crusading, race-conscious organ, it has become an educational medium. The Negro press is seeking to improve race relations.

The immigrant press has existed longer than the Negro press but has dwindled in importance as native-borns increased. However, the persistence of immigrant papers is due to the role they play in holding the members of a subculture together and aiding in the assimilation process.[11]

Television. The increasing popularity of one of the newer media, television, has changed some of the American's living arrangements. Since 1948 a New York advertising firm, Cunningham and Walsh, has been studying the television audience of New Brunswick, New Jersey, a town of 39,800, located thirty miles southwest of New York City. Some of the findings of this seven-volume *Videotown* series have been summarized in *Agrisearch,* published by the National Project in Agricultural Communications (10).

About nine out of ten television sets can be expected to be tuned in for about four hours every weekday evening.

Normally, 67 to 75 per cent of the members of television families will view television for about two hours a week during an average weekday evening.

The average television fan spends about twelve hours a week watching television on weekday evenings.

Monday through Friday, husbands and wives spend the most evening time watching television (13+ hours); children under ten the least (7.7 hours); while teenage children and young adults occupy a middle position with ten to twelve hours.

[11] Rose Hum Lee, *The City: Urbanism and Urbanization in Major World Regions* (Philadelphia: J. B. Lippincott Company, 1955), p. 433.

Television owners who buy sets some time after television becomes available are less devoted to television than the earlier buyers.

Members of television families adjust home routines to allow for television and for other leisure-time activities.

Visiting and entertaining friends decreases in television homes.

When a television set is brought into a home, movie attendance and magazine reading drop at first, then increase.

Housewives are the most avid daytime and evening television fans.

Except for weekday mornings, radio listening tends to decrease initially in television homes and then to increase.

Factors other than upkeep costs explain why the lower-class families own relatively fewer television sets.

Studies such as this, showing who is likely to be reached at what time of day and on what days, might be very valuable to community leaders in using spot announcements in support of some local undertaking.

Social Significance of Mass Media. These formal channels of communication, such as television, radio, and the press are owned and managed, for the most part, by private business corporations. To make use of these channels, one usually has to pay for the space or time used, except for certain public service programs, on which community events may be publicized without cost. Since the controlling voice is that of the manager or owner of these media, it is always important in any community to know how these powerful means of communication are controlled (23). Where there is a monopoly of the press or of the press and radio combined, those in charge of these media have an even greater obligation to see that various points of view, each representative of responsible groups of citizens, be given publicity. What at first passes for communication, if continually one-sided in emphasis, can become indoctrination and can stultify over-all community development (18). Social scientists, without necessarily trying to say what the correct point of view on any issue should be, are interested in knowing to what extent and by what means competitive opinions may be voiced (1).

The social significance of access to different communication media in modern American society is clearly shown by Harry Estill Moore in his review of mass communication in the South, a region where the people do not have and, therefore, do not use the media of mass communication to the extent they are used by other citizens of the nation. He comments:

... It is through communication, on varied levels, that social interaction takes place. The content of communication makes up the mass of information and ideas which arouse the sentiments and emotions and intellectual activities through which the person and the group find self-expression. The nature of the resulting interaction depends upon the nature of the content of communications received.

In a situation in which communication is sluggish and limited in content, there is a lack of stimulation and food for thought which results in a relatively static society, dependent upon traditional concepts, ideas, stereotypes and prejudices which too often do not mirror changed and changing relationships with the accuracy required for realistic understanding and action. . . .

Prejudices and stereotypes tend to disappear as free and efficient communication brings more, and more recent, evidence. This does not mean that antagonisms and differences evaporate with adequate knowledge, as is sometimes naïvely assumed. But it does mean that such antagonisms become based on rational considerations and are logically supported, when they remain, rather than being upheld by nothing more than rumor, myth or superstition. The problem of social well-being, then, would seem to be largely one of keeping clear the channels of communication, of making accessible to the people the materials out of which intelligent opinions are formed and on which intelligent action must be based.[12]

DIFFUSION OF IDEAS AND INFORMATION

A great deal of research in the diffusion process, as the spread of information might be called, is being conducted by rural sociologists (2, 22). They are concerned with helping to find ways of transmitting the scientific facts gained by research in our agricultural experiment stations to the farmer for whom this research is supposedly done and who must apply the findings if the research is to prove economically justifiable.

TABLE 4

COMMUNICATION IN DIFFUSION OF INFORMATION TO FARMERS

Diffusion Stage	Order of Importance of Sources
1. Awareness 2. Interest	a. Mass media b. Agricultural agencies c. Neighbors and friends d. Agricultural salesmen
3. Trial 4. Acceptance	a. Neighbors and friends b. Agricultural agencies c. Mass media d. Agricultural salesmen

Source: Adapted from Agrisearch (October, 1955).

[12] Harry Estill Moore, "Mass Communication in the South," Social Forces, XXIX (May, 1951), 375.

Table 4 is useful in analyzing the diffusion process. On the left it shows the stages through which diffusion of information or the spread of a new practice goes. First, people become aware of the new practice, then they become interested; after this, they are ready to try it and accept it if it works. On the right are listed the sources of information about the new practice in their order of importance.

The findings shown here indicate that awareness and interest are stimulated most importantly by the formal channels, including farm journals, bulletins from the experiment station, and other media. The findings also show that for the trial and acceptance stage to be reached, the informal channels, including the gossip chain, are most important, with the mass media ranking much lower here.

THE LARGER COMMUNICATION STRUCTURE

If a community is to remain a part of a larger society, it must be in touch with what is going on elsewhere in that society. Even the internal system of communication, which we have just discussed, depends for many of its features upon media operating outside even the largest centers. Not even New York is self-sufficient, since it, more than smaller places, is subjected to a daily barrage of new ideas and fresh information because of its worldwide contacts. The ordinary citizen today travels more often and over greater distances than formerly. The number of Americans traveling abroad has also substantially increased. Through such travel members of the community absorb new ideas from the world outside their community. Television, with its advertising appeals, comes very intimately into the living room. Movies are imported into the community from Hollywood, and the nationally circulated magazines arrive in large bundles from outside distribution points. Such an obvious fact need not be belabored, but the results of such extensive outside communication should be noted.

First, mass communication is leading to standardization of our material life. People in New England want ranch-type houses. People in the Southwest put up prefabricated Cape Cod cottages. A supermarket in California is not too unlike one in Georgia: the same brands are on display and packaged in much the same way. Each home town is intimately involved because of the dynamic nature of the capitalistic economy. In an industrialized society, mass production is necessary to take advantage of the heavy investment in capital equipment; accompanying mass production must be mass distribution or getting products to every potential customer; but mass production depends upon mass advertising, which leads to the development of and heavy support of mass media.

But in addition to the standardization of material life, the *social organizational* aspects of community life are being standardized. A Rotarian from Shreveport, Louisiana, should feel at home in a club in Boise, Idaho—so standardized is his membership role. The same holds true for the numerous other local religious, civic, welfare, educational, and cultural organizations which have national affiliations, since the central office of each is trying to get the local groups to follow certain programs of action to emphasize the same creed and ritual and to send in adequate financial support.

Finally, through the numerous contacts with the larger society, whether through informational, media, travel, or national organizational affiliation, Americans are moving toward uniformity in thought patterns and social values. Often local ideas are made to appear provincial or parochial if they differ very much from what seems to be an emerging national pattern. In some areas of life, such as politics and religion, we "agree to disagree," but there is a general likelihood that those who wear the same label, even in these areas, may grow more alike with increased communication. However, communication within the community may prove integrative or disintegrative. The same holds true for communication within our society at large, which puts an east Tennessee mountain community in touch with the ideas of the rural Mississippi community or with the speeches made in Philadelphia, Pennsylvania. The rallying points may be around significant differences rather than common purposes, which emphasizes again the need for wisdom on the part of those connected with the system of communication within the community and among the communities throughout America.

REFERENCES AND SUGGESTED READINGS

1. BERELSON, BARNARD, and JANOWITZ, MORRIS (eds.) *Reader in Public Opinion and Communication*, enlarged edition. Chicago: Free Press, 1953.
2. COLEMAN, A. LEE, and MARSH, C. PAUL. "Differential Communication Among Farmers In a Kentucky County," *Rural Sociology*, XX (June, 1955), 93–101.
3. FANELLI, A. ALEXANDER. "Extensiveness of Communication Contacts and Perceptions of the Community," *American Sociological Review*, XXI (August, 1956), 439–45.
4. HULETT, J. E., JR. "Estimating the Net Effect of a Commercial Motion Picture Upon the Trend of Local Public Opinion," *American Sociological Review*, XIV (April, 1949), 263–75.
5. JANOWITZ, M. *The Urban Community Press: An Empirical Study of Metropolitan Integration.* Chicago: Free Press, 1952.
6. KATZ, ELIHU, and LAZARSFELD, PAUL F. *Personal Influence: The Part Played by People in the Flow of Mass Communications.* Chicago: Free Press, 1955.
7. KLAPPER, JOSEPH T. *The Effects of Mass Media.* New York: Columbia University, Bureau of Applied Social Research, 1949.
8. KOHN, M. L., and CLAUSEN, J. A. "Social Isolation and Schizophrenia," *American Sociological Review*, XX (June, 1955), 265–73.

9. MEAD, GEORGE HERBERT. *Mind, Self and Society*. Chicago: University of Chicago Press, 1934.
10. Michigan State University, National Project In Agricultural Communications, *Agrisearch*, I (July–August, 1955; October, 1955).
11. ODUM, HOWARD WASHINGTON. *Race and Rumors of Race*. Chapel Hill: University of North Carolina Press, 1943.
12. PARK, ROBERT EZRA. *Society: Collective Behavior, News and Opinion, Sociology and Modern Society*. Chicago: Free Press, 1955.
13. RATNER, JOSEPH (ed.) *Intelligence in the Modern World: John Dewey's Philosophy*. New York: Random House, Inc., 1939. See pp. 385–400 on "Communication and Communal Living."
14. RILEY, MATILDA WHITE, and FLOWERMAN, SAMUEL H. "Group Relations as a Variable in Communication Research," *American Sociological Review*, XVI (April, 1951), 174–80.
15. ROSE, ARNOLD M. "Communication and Participation in a Small City as Viewed by Its Leaders," *International Journal of Opinion and Attitude Research*, V (1951), 367–90.
16. RUESCH, JURGEN, and BATESON, GREGORY. *Communication, the Social Matrix of Psychiatry*. New York: W. W. Norton & Company, 1951.
17. SANDERS, IRWIN T. "The Use of Block Leaders in Effective Community Mobilization," *Sociometry*, XII (November, 1949), 265–75.
18. SCHRAMM, WILBUR, and RILEY, JOHN W., JR. "Communication in the Sovietized State, as Demonstrated in Korea," *American Sociological Review*, XVI (December, 1951), 757–66.
19. SOROKIN, PITIRIM A. *Society, Culture and Personality*. New York: Harper & Brothers, 1947.
20. STRAUSS, ANSELM (ed.) *The Social Psychology of George Herbert Mead*. Chicago: University of Chicago Press, 1956.
21. SYKES, GRESHAM M. "The Differential Distribution of Community Knowledge," *Social Forces*, XXIX (May, 1951), 376–82.
22. WILKENING, EUGENE A. "Roles of Communicating Agents in Technological Change in Agriculture," *Social Forces*, XXXIV (May, 1956), 361–67.
23. WIRTH, LOUIS. "Consensus and Mass Communication," *American Sociological Review*, XIII (February, 1948), 1–15.

Chapter 5

TRADITIONS AND VALUES

In western New Mexico, two communities, composed of people with a similar cultural background and living in the same general ecological setting, reveal striking social differences which can only be explained satisfactorily by the fact that each group brought different traditions to its new settlement. The communities, each numbering about 250 people, are forty miles apart, and both villages have subsistence patterns based upon combinations of farming and livestock raising.

"Rimrock," one of these communities, was settled by Mormon missionaries in the 1870's as an outpost for the conversion of the Indians; these early settlers were "called" by the church and sent by the church authorities. Today the church is the central core of the village. "Homestead," the other community, was settled by migrants from the South Plains area of western Texas and Oklahoma in the early 1930's; it was a part of the Okie movement described in Steinbeck's *Grapes of Wrath*. Each farm unit is operated by a nuclear family, consisting of father, mother, and unmarried children, and the many different denominations show religious factionalism.

Evon Z. Vogt and Thomas F. O'Dea, in comparing the differences in value orientations found in Rimrock and Homestead (both fictitious names for the real communities studied), took four examples of possible community action and showed how each community responded differently (8). When land became scarce, the people of Rimrock borrowed money from a church welfare plan agency, bought some land, and instead of breaking the plot up into individually owned units, kept the parcel as a bloc and put it under the control of a cooperative called Rimrock Land and Cattle Company. On the other hand, in 1934 the people of Homestead had the opportunity of acquiring additional land through the Federal Security Administration. This land would have been managed cooperatively by a board of directors selected by the community. The scheme collapsed because it soon became clear that each family expected to acquire its own private holdings on the range and that a cooperative would not work in that community.

A second illustration was the graveling of the village streets. As late as 1950 the streets of both communities were in bad repair. In that summer a construction company brought much large equipment into the area to build and gravel a section of the state highway. In Rimrock, the villagers, acting through their church organization, decided to take advantage of the presence of these machines, had meetings of representatives from almost every family, and voted that each family would donate $20 to a fund to get the job done. In Homestead the construction company offered to gravel the streets of the center if the residents would contribute enough funds for the purpose. This community plan was rejected by the local people, and an alternative plan was followed. Each of the operators of several of the service institutions independently hired the construction company truck drivers to haul a few loads of gravel to be placed in front of his own place of business, thus leaving the rest of the village streets a sea of mud in rainy weather.

The construction of a high school gymnasium was the third instance. Residents of both communities were told that the funds for materials and for certain skilled labor would be provided from state school appropriations provided the local residents would contribute the labor for construction. In spite of some difficulties the people of Rimrock completed their project by arranging that each able-bodied man contribute at least fifty hours of labor or $50, the latter to be used to hire outside laborers. The homesteaders of the second community were willing to work on the gymnasium only if they were paid a dollar an hour. At this rate, the funds were soon exhausted and construction stopped. Today a partially completed gymnasium and stacks of some ten thousand adobe bricks disintegrating slowly with the rains, stand as monuments to the individualism of the homesteaders.

The two communities show differences, too, in their dances. The Mormons have always considered dancing to be an important form of recreation, and almost every Friday evening they hold a dance in the village church house. These dances are family affairs and are opened and closed with prayer. On the whole, these Rimrock dances are peaceful, although at the dances held in the local school there has been some evidence of drinking (quite contrary to Mormon rules), and at times fighting has resulted from the presence of non-villagers. The village dances in Homestead are also important focal points for community activity. These affairs take place several times a year in the school house and are always well attended. They often end in fist fights because of tensions between rival families.

These illustrations show definitely that the people of Rimrock, the Mormon village, respond to group problems as a group and that cooperation has become second nature to them. It has become a part of the institutionalized structure of expectations, reinforced by religious conviction and social control. On the other hand, in Homestead, the researchers found that the strong commitment to an individualistic value orientation has resulted in a social system in which interpersonal relations are strongly colored by a kind of factionalism and in which persons and groups become related to one another in a competitive, feuding relationship.

THE HISTORICAL PERSPECTIVE

This study in contrasts between Rimrock and Homestead indicates the importance of knowing the historical development of any community. At least three major questions can be asked in this regard.

1. *Who were the first settlers?* Many local landmarks may be named for these otherwise forgotten founders who gave more than their names to the community. The chances are that they also brought with them important traditions and a value orientation which they tried to implant in the new settlement. Thus, in describing the first settlers, it is not enough to know their names and occupations; we must also try to understand their convictions, their reasons for moving to the new place, and the kinds of community they hoped would evolve.

The interplay between history and the traditions and values of a community is strikingly described in Horace Miner's account of Hardin County, Iowa, in which he states:

The westward moving wave of settlers spilling across the Mississippi and flooding over the wild western prairies, reached central Iowa in the middle of the past century. Contrary to present popular belief and the explicit statements of the hardy pioneers themselves, the spirit which motivated this surge to the West was not the desire "to found a home" in the traditional sense, but rather a yearning to "get ahead," to better one's situation. Security was left, not sought. *The drive for progress at the expense of the safe and friendly traditional ways continues to the present.*[1] (Italics added.)

After pointing out that willingness to do hard work was a cardinal virtue and telling of the areas from which the new settlers came, Miner adds the following comments.

[1] Horace Miner, *Culture and Agriculture. An Anthropological Study of a Corn Belt County* (Ann Arbor: University of Michigan Press, 1949), p. 8.

Possibly the most striking aspect of this early settlement period is the rapidity with which these pioneers duplicated the formally organized social environment which they had left. They wanted to progress materially, but in a world like that in which they had grown up. . . . Only five years after the first settler came to the region, the county had two established churches and two schools, county officials were selected and a court of law was operative, and a doctor had been practicing for three years. The next two years saw the formation of an agricultural society and the establishment of a newspaper, a sawmill, and a store. Life began to take on its old context—the frontier was giving way before the progressive drive of the settlers.[2]

The above is all the more remarkable when it is remembered that the people were still living in log cabins or sod-covered "three-faced camps," that life was not only primitive but precarious and was full of hard work with small financial remuneration. As life grew more secure through the years, some of the basic drives remained and some new values were added, but much of what one sees today in Hardin County, Iowa, can only be understood in terms of its early days.

Cities of all sizes, just as truly as the settlements of Hardin County, have certain dominant values which the people stress. Some of these have been passed down from early times and help give that particular city its uniqueness. The value orientation of Cincinnati, Ohio, differs in many ways from that of Memphis, Tennessee, although both are river ports. An important part of the explanation for these differences lies in the social characteristics and cultural backgrounds of the settlers who founded each place. In this sense history lives on most dramatically.

2. *What shifts in traditions have been caused by newcomers?* This is a second question to ask in tracing a community's historical development. Many communities have experienced such an influx of people from outside that local traditions have been greatly modified. In many instances these newcomers have brought culture patterns originally acquired in Southern or Northern or Central Europe. These periods of influx are easy to trace, as is the attempt made by the older families to protect their traditions against those of the newcomers. Internal migration, as already pointed out, is characteristic of the United States. Many southern people are moving from hill farms of limited opportunity to better paying jobs in the North. They, too, bring a type of culture which differs considerably from the more urban pattern of those with whom they settle. The community is never the same after such an influx because to keep it going as a social system its people must adjust their cultural differences and work out some way of getting along together. The prob-

[2] *Ibid.*, pp. 9–10.

lem of the "second generation" child is not so much one of language or of having a different-sounding name: the problem for him is trying to live up to the traditions of his family circle and at the same time trying to abide by the traditions of the wider community which he sees illustrated at school, on the ball field, or at work.

3. *What community crises have influenced the traditions?* Such crises may have been of several sorts (2). For instance, economic disruption such as the closing down of a factory around which the life of the community is centered may have been connected with a subsequent shift in value orientations. Until that time, people may have come to believe that the owners of the factory were responsible for their welfare. They may have accepted a paternalistic tradition according to which they let the factory owners take the lead in almost all matters and willingly and even gratefully received the benefits handed down from above. But with the closing of the factory, this paternalistic tradition may have given way to one of strong self-assertion. The workers may not show appreciation for what was done in the past but may instead feel deeply wronged. They may now readily embrace labor unions which promise to fight in their behalf. Hence, when the factory reopens under the same or a different management the tradition of paternalism is no longer accepted. People no longer want to live in company houses; they want to own their own homes. They no longer want churches and recreational facilities provided by the factory; rather they demand higher wages so they can obtain these advantages and services where and when they like.

Prolonged economic crises can change the traditions of independence, on which the people in a community had prided themselves, to one of dependence upon others. Within a relatively short period of time those who had not liked the idea of accepting government checks or "relief handouts" may have come to feel that they should be protected against almost any kind of vicissitude and may actually take pride in gaining every advantage they can from unemployment compensation or other measures designed to help them in emergency situations.

Crises can be social as well as economic. For instance, political or religious events may have caused deep community cleavages with attendant shifts in value orientation. Problems of school desegregation may bring some of the accepted values of the past into the hot glare of public debate, leading to the discard of some values and the reinforcement of others. The thorough study of the historical development of any community would include a description of all types of major crises and an effort to evaluate the social effects of these crises, not only in terms of changed social relationships but also in terms of what has happened to the traditions and value orientation of the people.

CUSTOMS, MORES, TRADITIONS, AND VALUES

Although it is easy to recognize that communities have different traditions and ways of doing things, it is not easy to describe just what these are without a precise vocabulary. These terms or concepts stand for observable or verifiable social facts. For example, in the previous section, the terms "traditions" and "values" may seemingly have been used interchangeably, but do they really stand for the same thing? Does a tradition differ from a custom? If so, how? Clarifying these differences will provide mental tools for social analysis.

Customs. A custom is a folkway, a behavior pattern; it is something people do. The word *people* is important here because a single act by a single individual does not create a custom. An eccentric man may like to wear some unusual headgear in cold weather, but in so doing he is not following a custom. However, if in summertime men generally go bareheaded or wear straw hats, these can be considered customs. In other words, a custom is an accepted behavior pattern for people occupying certain statuses in the community. In this sense, custom is like a social role that people perform at a given time and place. As E. A. Ross has pointed out, the customs are carried by tradition and lodged in the group and are not the mere random personal activities of the individual.

Communities differ markedly in such customary behavior (3). For instance, it may be customary in one place for people to speak to strangers; elsewhere, parents may stress to their children the importance of not even smiling at strangers. Customs connected with Halloween, such as the popular "trick or treat," or the custom of shooting off firecrackers on the Fourth of July, are simple illustrations.

Customs are as widespread as group behavior. In some communities it is customary for young people of certain social classes to marry in a church and not in the home, for the family to go on a Sunday afternoon drive, for women to run the P.-T.A., or for bus drivers to stop and wait for a passenger hurrying down the street. It is customary to serve turkey at Thanksgiving, and according to the meat packers' advertising campaigns, today ham is the customary meat for Easter dinner. Obviously, the individual who follows a custom without giving it second thought is relieved of the responsibility of deciding just what he is supposed to do; those who originated, and passed on, and taught the individual the specific behavior pattern made the decision for him. Customs therefore save much decision-making "wear and tear."

Mores. Some customs, however, are sacred. People must not treat them lightly. Humorists may poke slight fun at them, but most people still take them quite seriously. Such obligatory customs are called *mores,* a term first used in this connection by William Graham Sumner in his classic work, *Folkways,* published in 1906. Examples of mores for most communities would be the following: a couple wishing to live together as husband and wife must go through an officially recognized marriage ceremony; a father must support his minor children; an employer must pay wages to those who have earned them; a citizen must pay taxes. The list could be extended indefinitely and would include some items which have been embodied in laws and other items which are supported by the informal sanctions of the community. In addition to these practices which must be observed there are certain things that must not be done lest they threaten the welfare of the group. Such prohibitions are often termed *taboos.* They are mores in reverse. Both have the sense of compulsion or punishment connected with them.

Traditions. Customs and mores are traditional in that they have been handed down from the past by word of mouth and by example. Traditions such as Christmas, a pride in having good schools, the patriotism shown by a given community in time of national need or the hospitality shown to newcomers are all more than a set of customs or behavior patterns; they also involve an explanation of why these traditions are important and must be preserved. Explanations derived from such a distant past that their origins cannot be readily explained or which rely upon unscientific formulas are usually called *myths,* although modern man does not feel complimented if some of his sacred explanations are termed "mythological." Therefore, to understand the richness of community life it is necessary not only to observe what people do but also to listen to their explanations for their behavior.

Values and Value Orientations. Obviously, no individual, no group, no community, can possess all that it might want to possess nor achieve all that it might want to achieve. Therefore, possible goals have to be ranked in some order of importance, and available energy and resources spent in pursuing those goals considered most important. *Values* are those things or achievements which the community considers good, and therefore to be sought, thereby implying that the opposites of these are bad, and consequently to be rejected. From the study of Rimrock it was clear that cooperation was a value, whereas in Homestead individualism was a value ranked higher than cooperation. But these things and achievements do not exist as separate entities. They are part of what has been called value orientations. As defined by Clyde Kluckhohn, *value orientations* are those views of the world, often implicitly held, which define the *meaning* of human life or the "life situation of man" and thereby provide the context in which day-to-day problems are solved (4). Just as customs are what the people do and traditions are the explanations people have for doing specific things, so value orientations are the ways people look at life in general. For instance, American agricultural technologists who are trying to help Asian people increase their farm production are frequently nonplussed at the reluctance of the peasants to follow suggestions based on scientific research. They keep telling the peasants, "If you would treat your ground this way and use this kind of seed, you could increase your crop by a third." This appeal may fall on deaf ears, since the peasant is not always interested in increasing his crop; his concern is not with how much he can grow on a given piece of land but rather with how little he needs to grow to take care of his family and to sell in order to get money for taxes. His value orientation is toward minimum rather than maximum production, and he has a different set of assumptions from the American technician whose whole professional career has been spent in helping people maximize their efforts.

Understanding the Value Orientations of a Community

Types of Value Orientations. Without clear-cut categories for the analysis of value orientations the whole concept remains vague and difficult to describe for any particular community. Figure 9, prepared by Florence R. Kluckhohn, gives an excellent way of sorting out and classifying what can be learned about the value orientations for any locality.

Figure 9 deals with what Florence Kluckhohn considers to be the five problems crucial to all human groups. The first category takes up the question of the character of innate human nature (human nature orientation). As the three columns show, it can be viewed as essentially *evil*, as *neutral* (a mixture of good and evil), or as *good*. Likewise in each case it may be considered mutable, that is, subject to change, or immutable. The Puritans stressed the point that human nature was basically evil but perfectible, and

Innate human nature	Evil (mutable-immutable)	Neutral $\begin{cases} \text{mixture of} \\ \text{good and evil} \end{cases}$ (mutable-immutable)	Good (mutable-immutable)
Man's relation to nature and supernature	Subjugation to nature	Harmony with nature	Mastery over nature
Time focus	Past	Present	Future
Modality of human activity	Being	Being-in-becoming	Doing
Modality of man's relationship to other men	Lineal	Collateral	Individualistic

Source: Florence R. Kluckhohn, *Dominant and Variant Value Orientations.* Unpublished manuscript. The explanation of this figure paraphrases or directly quotes this manuscript.

Note: Since each of the orientations is considered to be independently variable, the arrangement in columns of sets of orientations is only the accidental result of this particular diagram. All combinations are considered to be possible. For example, a doing activity orientation may be combined with a mastery-over-nature position and individualism, as it is in dominant American culture, or, as one finds in Navaho Indian culture, it may be in combination with a first order harmony-with-nature position and collaterality.

FIG. 9. Ranges of variability in value orientations.

many American communities seem to hold to this as a dominant value. In other communities where the Puritan tradition is weak or has never been present, the orientation is toward the belief that human nature is a mixture of good and evil. In daily life, this human nature orientation lies behind any community's approach to such matters as juvenile delinquency or reformation of the adult offender. If human nature is thought to be essentially evil, it follows that "bad people" must be constrained and confined, and the emphasis is one of "protecting society" rather than of rehabilitating the criminal. If human nature is considered essentially good, as would be the case in certain communities with strong Quaker or Friends' Society traditions, the problem is chiefly one of finding what influences led the individual astray and of seeking to correct those influences so that the good in the person can really shine forth.

The second orientation is that between man-nature (including the supernatural). The Spanish-American communities of the Southwest illustrate the *subjugation-to-nature* orientation. Many people there believe that there is little that man can do to help himself against the wrath of storms or the scourge of illness. A person says fatalistically, "If it is the Lord's will that I die, I shall die," and may even refuse the services of a doctor because of this attitude. The *harmony-*

with-nature approach sees no real separation between man, nature, and supernature and is illustrated by the Navaho Indians or by the traditional orientation of the Chinese peasant. Most American communities, however, stress the *mastery-over-nature* orientation and, as Florence Kluckhohn points out, believe that "the Lord helps those who help themselves." People put up flood walls to control a stream, span the river with bridges, tunnel through mountains, air-condition homes, and conduct surveys to be sure that they are fully utilizing local natural resources.

The *time* orientation represents a third range of variations. All communities have some concern with the *past,* the *present,* and the *future,* but they differ in the importance accorded to each. Where most of the people of a community stress the past, they tend to be complacent and take pride in what their ancestors have done more than in what they have done themselves. They tend to resist change, and stress conformity almost as an end in itself. Most American communities, however, are future-oriented. Civic clubs, women's groups, and many church organizations work untiringly to make the community "bigger and better." People think in terms of their children's future and plan accordingly; they have hopes of improving not only their material status but their social status as well. Change is viewed as inevitable and desirable.

A fourth dimension of value orientation is *activity.* As explained by Florence Kluckhohn, in the *being* orientation the preference is for the kind of activity which is a spontaneous expression of what is conceived to be "given" in the human personality. Mexican society illustrates the *being* orientation in its widely ramified patterning of fiesta activities, which though spontaneous, are nevertheless restrained by definite codes of conduct. The *being-in-becoming* orientation emphasizes the kind of activity which has as its goal the development of all aspects of the self as an integrated whole. This is illustrated in the writings of those such as Erich Fromm who try to get people to accept the total personality and eliminate the split between "reason" and "nature." The *doing* orientation, so common to American life, has as a distinguishing feature the demand for the kind of activity which results in accomplishments that are measurable by standards conceived to be external to the acting individual. "Getting things done" and "let's *do* something about it" are stock American phrases.

The *relational* orientation, the last to be considered here, has three subdivisions: the lineal, the collateral, and the individualistic. These three are present in some form in all systems of human relations but receive different emphases from community to community.

When the lineal principle predominates, there is stress upon age and generational differences and upon cultural continuity. Social patterns in the community are set by traditions, groups such as the family are more important than the individual, and young people tend to follow the occupations of their fathers. Many of the more isolated rural communities which are strongly family-centered are of this type. *Collateral* relationships are those based not on lineage (father-son) but on laterally extended relationships such as sibling (brother-brother, brother-sister, sister-sister) ties. The stress here is upon the goals and welfare of this laterally extended group, which is always moderately independent of other similar groups. When applied to communities, this principle would result in strong influence of peer groups upon individuals growing up and the desire for the approval of one's contemporaries more than the approval of one's elders. In an *individualistic* orientation a man need not remain in a fixed position and need not so often bow his head in acceptance of a dominating authority. As Florence Kluckhohn points out, he is much more free to be like everyone else. When the individualistic principle is dominant, individual goals have primacy over the goals of specific collateral or lineal groups. At the same time, each individual's responsibility to the total society and his place in it are in terms of goals (and roles) which are defined and structured as *autonomous* ones in the sense of being independent of particular lineal or collateral groupings.

One of the major contributions made by Florence Kluckhohn and those working with her has been the clarification of the importance of variant value orientations. In other words, as soon as the dominant values as outlined in Figure 9 have been determined for any community, it is also important to determine the variant value orientations, because social change is definitely related to shifting value orientations. Values which at one time may have been simply variant may later on become dominant. The key to understanding these variations lies not only in deciding which of the divisions (such as *being* or *doing*) under any orientation (such as *activity*) apply to a given community but in finding out the order of importance given by the people of a local community to the possible orientations. Studies show that some major groupings in the community will rate some orientations at the top, while other groupings may place a different orientation there. This reveals that there are variant value orientations which must be taken into account. For example, Florence Kluckhohn sets forth the following hypothesis (which relates to one of the matters discussed in connection with the arrival of newcomers to a community in an earlier section of this chapter): *"The rate and degree of assimilation of any ethnic group to dominant American culture will depend in large part upon the degree of goodness of fit of the group's own rank ordering of value orientations with that of the dominant culture."*[3]

Getting Information About Value Orientations. By now two points should be quite clear: first, that understanding the value orientations is necessary if one is to understand a community; second, that communities differ with respect to their value orientations (7). The problem facing anyone seeking to learn more about his community is one of methodology: how does a person approach the problem of defining the value system of some community in which he is interested (1)? If one goes into a new community to teach school, to start a business, or to be a city manager, how can these values be determined? First of all, since the community is a part of the larger American society it can be assumed that, unless it is quite isolated, it will have many of the traits of the total society (6, 9). It will play up as values (though it may not always put them into practice) certain parts of the American creed—individual rights and responsibilities, economic opportunity, justice before the law, a government responsive to the people, and a number of other themes which Americans believe. Yet, as the newcomer goes around the community he may be sharply aware of certain countervalues. He may hear a leading citizen say, "The trouble with this community is that we have too much democracy!" Or a person who gives an inspirational address on the Declaration of Independence before a local group may say that he does not want any children from the lower classes attending the same school as his child. The inquiring observer will usually have to put together the various statements he hears. He can, through discreet discussion with others, find out if these statements reflect the opinions of only a few individuals or whether they are generally accepted as true or desirable. By using the categories offered by Florence Kluckhohn he can type the community, tentatively at least, for each of the five orientations and also discover those groupings with variant orientations.

Community values are frequently embodied in the constitutions of different organizations. Reading several of these, particularly those that are local in inspiration, will bring to light items which the writers of these documents considered important. Or, simply asking acquaintances "What do the people of this community want most out of life?" will provide further information to use in forming judgments.

[3] Florence R. Kluckhohn, *Dominant and Variant Value Orientations.* Unpublished manuscript.

One of the newcomer's clues, however, will be to find out which persons in the community enjoy the highest prestige and then determine the bases of this prestige. The chances are that this analysis will bring one face to face with some of the dominant value orientations, since the people who are at the top are most apt to possess those things or traits which the local people accept as most desirable. Thus, the value system is tied in with the social layers of the community, the topic to be treated next.

REFERENCES AND SUGGESTED READINGS

1. BECKER, HOWARD. "Looking at Values and Value-Systems," in Irwin T. Sanders (ed.), *Societies Around the World*. New York: The Dryden Press, Inc., 1956, Shorter Edition, pp. 378–98.
2. BERNARD, JESSIE. *American Community Behavior*. New York: The Dryden Press, Inc., 1949, chs. 22–25.
3. KINNEMAN, JOHN A. *The Community in American Society*. New York: Appleton-Century-Crofts, Inc., 1947, chs. 9–11.
4. KLUCKHOHN, CLYDE. "Values and Value-Orientations in the Theory of Action: an Exploration in Definition and Classification," in Talcott Parsons and E. A. Shils (eds.), *Toward a General Theory of Action*, Cambridge: Harvard University Press, 1951.
5. MINER, HORACE. *Culture and Agriculture: An Anthropological Study of a Corn Belt County*. Ann Arbor: University of Michigan Press, 1949, ch. 2.
6. MYRDAL, GUNNAR. *An American Dilemma: The Negro Problem and Modern Democracy*. New York: Harper & Brothers, 1944, ch. 1.
7. RYAN, BRYCE. "The Ceylonese Village and the New Value System," *Rural Sociology*, XVII (March, 1952), pp. 9–28.
8. VOGT, EVON Z., and O'DEA, THOMAS F. "A Comparative Study of the Role of Values in Social Action in Two Southwestern Communities," *American Sociological Review*, XVIII (December, 1953), pp. 645–54.
9. WILLIAMS, ROBIN M. *American Society*. New York: Alfred H. Knopf, Inc., 1951, ch. 11.

Chapter 6

SOCIAL LAYERS

In every community we find some people holding higher rank than others. If inherited wealth and family background are dominant values, then those who have this wealth and background are placed at the top; those whose income is irregular and meager will be placed near the bottom, as will those whose families do not enjoy a favorable reputation in the community. Should other types of values be prized, then the people would be ranked in terms of those (14, 21, 28).

THE FACT OF STRATIFICATION

Stratification is the term which describes this social expression of inequality and carries with it the image of strata or layers such as one would see in the rock walls along a highway cut through a mountain. A *social stratum* is actually a grouping of people of similar social rank—having functions, accomplishments, and possessions of similar value (21). Tied in with the idea of stratum or rank is that of *status,* or position, within the social structure. As Harold F. Kaufman has remarked, "One's community status is a composite of the statuses in the various groups in which he participates and of the evaluations of his personal qualities, accomplishments and possessions."[1] It is obvious that in the smaller primary community, where people know each other quite well, there will be considerable agreement about the community status of each individual. In the metropolis, where people are not nearly so well known to each other, the concept of community status is more difficult to define. Kaufman gives three reasons for the greater difficulty (21). First, there is a lack of status equilibrium in the metropolis, which is another way of saying that an individual's characteristics will not have similar value and will not be consistent (congruous) with each other with respect

[1] Harold F. Kaufman, "An Approach to the Study of Urban Stratification," *American Sociological Review,* XVII (August, 1952), p. 431.

86

to rank—for example, the underworld operator who resides in the exclusive residential district. When incongruity in status becomes the rule rather than the exception the conception of community rank tends to lose its scientific usefulness. Second, there is differential perception of status in the urban world. The person being ranked will not only differ with observers concerning his status, but the observers will also disagree among themselves depending on the stratum to which they belong. Third, whereas in the small, primary community the individual is the unit which is ranked, in the metropolis it is formal positions, such as occupation or organizational memberships and possessions.

Social *classes*, the customary way of referring to the status levels, are traditionally accepted as the upper, middle, and lower, although sometimes each of these has been divided into two groupings. A *caste* system is one in which those in an inferior status level are prohibited in various ways from moving upward. They are not allowed to marry into an upper level (endogamy), cannot practice vertical mobility (or the movement from the lower status level to the higher by educational, occupational, or other attainment), and are segregated.

These definitions—stratification, status, class, and caste—are necessary for any useful discussion of the social ranking present in a community.

One way to clarify these terms is to look at the diagrams various writers have used in an effort to depict the kinds of social layers

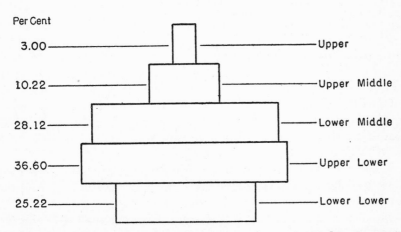

See W. Lloyd Warner and Paul S. Lunt, *The Social Life of a Modern Community* (New Haven: Yale University Press, 1941), p. 88.

FIG. 10. Class structure of "Yankee City" as presented by W. Lloyd Warner and associates.

they observed in different communities. W. Lloyd Warner and his associates, who have pioneered in this area (37), prefer to work with the fivefold division of lower-upper, upper-middle, lower-middle, upper-lower, and lower-lower. Few communities have an upper-upper class. The class structure of "Yankee City" as they present it is shown in Figure 10.

In a study of "Georgia Town," Mozell C. Hill and Bevode C. Mc-Call found the distribution set forth in Figure 11 (16):

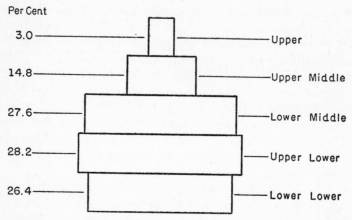

Per Cent

3.0 ——————————————————— Upper

14.8 ——————————————————— Upper Middle

27.6 ——————————————————— Lower Middle

28.2 ——————————————————— Upper Lower

26.4 ——————————————————— Lower Lower

Source: Mozell C. Hill and Bevode C. McCall, "Social Stratification in 'Georgia Town,'" *American Sociological Review*, 15 (December, 1950), 724.

FIG. 11. Class structure of "Georgia Town."

Figures 10 and 11 describe the total community without making any distinctions on the basis of racial or ethnic lines. If whites and Negroes are considered as separate social groupings, "Georgia Town" would have the caste-class structure shown in Figure 12, with the vertical line denoting the caste barrier (16):

W. Lloyd Warner employed a different type diagram to show the caste-class structure of a Mississippi community which he calls "Old City." This is illustrated in Figure 13.

Figures 11 and 12 show that within each caste there are class lines, although the lower caste has a much larger proportion of the total lower class members of the community (22).

But a word of warning is necessary. These figures give the impression that the status arrangements for communities are so hard and fast that they are easily identified. Without denying the fact of stratification, one can recognize certain basic problems in the study of social classes in American society. First, there is the problem of

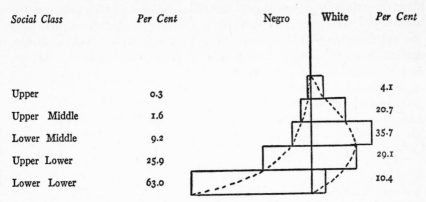

Social Class	Per Cent	Negro	White	Per Cent
Upper	0.3			4.1
Upper Middle	1.6			20.7
Lower Middle	9.2			35.7
Upper Lower	25.9			29.1
Lower Lower	63.0			10.4

Source: Mozell C. Hill and Bevode C. McCall, "Social Stratification in 'Georgia Town," *American Sociological Review,* 15 (December, 1950), 725.

FIG. 12. Relation between the caste-class structures of "Georgia Town."

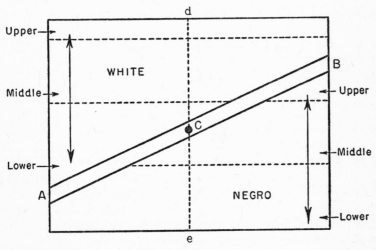

Source: W. Lloyd Warner in the "Introduction" to Allison Davis and Burleigh Gardner, *Deep South* (Chicago: University of Chicago Press, 1941), p. 10.

FIG. 13. Relation between the caste-class structure of "Old City."

the number of strata to be found in a given community. For example, the great majority of the American people when asked to choose between the upper, middle, and lower classes say that they belong to the middle class. On the other hand, when they are asked to choose between upper, middle, working, and lower classes more than half in many communities identify themselves with the working class. In a California community Thomas E. Lasswell found that fifty-six persons interviewed as an area sample failed to agree on the number of strata existing in that community, with the number suggested ranging from one to seven and with no one number being agreed upon by more than 17 per cent of the respondents (23). Some studies of stratification, such as that conducted by Neal Gross, in Minneapolis, Minnesota, (11) indicate that very different results are obtained if people are given an open-end question in which no specified classes are suggested. Table 5 shows the distribution of respondents when given a free choice (Question 1); when confronted with the upper, middle, worker, and lower class option (Question 2); and then with the upper, middle, and lower class choice (Question 3).

TABLE 5

A COMPARISON OF CLASS IDENTIFICATIONS BY RESPONDENTS IN
FOUR RENTAL AREAS OF MINNEAPOLIS*

Class Designations	Question 1 (Open-End)	Question 2 (U-M-W-L)	Question 3 (U-M-L)
	(Per Cent)		
Upper class	1	2	5
Middle class	31	42	76
Working class	11	45	—
Lower class	3	3	10
No classes	14	1	2
Don't know	20	2	4
Other class responses	15	5	3
No response	5	—	—

* Based on a sample of 935 respondents.

Source: Neal Gross, "Social Class Identification in the Urban Community," *American Sociological Review*, XVIII (August, 1953), 402.

A second problem is the fact that in many communities a considerable number of families are not identified with any particular social stratum. It seems that there are well-defined layers at the top and at the bottom but that in the middle ranks the situation is quite fluid. In a study made by Gregory P. Stone and William H. Form of a Michigan city, which they labeled "Vansburg," it was found that a sizable segment of the population had no adequate "status reputation" (35). This was due perhaps to the large number of truckers in the male population who, because they are away from home so much, are not well known to other members of the community. But many communities have some such contributing factor that makes any easy cataloging of residents by rank a complicated undertaking.

A third problem arises in those communities where there may be two or three competing status systems. In Vansburg, for instance, "cosmopolites" who are managerial personnel connected with national manufacturers have come from outlying metropolitan and large urban centers and do not accept the conventional symbols or the norms of status held by the members of the community prior to their arrival (35). They, of course, do not fit into the older status scheme.

IDENTIFYING THE SOCIAL LAYERS

There are two quite different approaches to the identification of social classes. One makes use of certain objective indices such as type of house, dwelling area, occupation, and source of income in ascribing a class position to individuals. This has been the method developed by W. Lloyd Warner and his associates and worked out as an Index of Status Characteristics (I.S.C.) (38). Supplementing this I.S.C. is the subjective evaluation of a person by his associates to get at what might be called his social reputation. This Evaluated Participation (E.P.) is determined by the individual's social acceptability in formal organizations and informal cliques—as judged by others and not by himself (13, 38).

A second approach is that which makes use of an individual's subjective awareness of his position in a class structure. It seeks to discover the individual's feelings of identification and on this basis to assign him to the rank to which he thinks he belongs. This is the approach employed by Richard Centers (3). The two methods have been compared by John L. Haer as follows:

> The approaches of Warner and Centers, then, differ with regard to the units of stratification, indices employed, and general orientation. Warner focuses on communities taken singly, Centers on diffuse publics which may be nation-wide in scope; Warner obtains a ranking of individuals in terms of a composite of objective socio-economic symbols, Centers in terms of verbal designations of affiliation; Warner perceives social classes as a function of disparities in objective status symbols, Centers as a product of the subjective aspirations or interests of large aggregates distinguished by their relationship to the means of production and political structure.[2]

Haer also conducted a study to find out if the two approaches measure the same thing. He found that the two agree quite well in the case of high position. Disparities develop, however, with differences in size and heterogeneity of the cities; also, cities varied in the perceptual differences in the evaluation of status characteristics.

[2] John L. Haer, "A Comparative Study of the Classification Techniques of Warner and Centers," *American Sociological Review*, XX (December, 1955), 690.

Many adaptations of these two approaches have been made. A. B. Hollingshead has made use of the objective scale, having constructed an Index of Social Position which he has applied to New Haven, Connecticut (19). He uses ecological area of residence, occupation, and education as the items for his index. What is particularly interesting is the series of five classes which he delineates for New Haven:

Class I. This stratum is composed of wealthy families whose wealth is often inherited and whose heads are leaders in the community's business and professional pursuits. Its members live in those areas of the community generally regarded as "the best"; the adults are college graduates, usually from famous private institutions, and almost all gentile families are listed in the New Haven *Social Directory*, but few Jewish families are listed. In brief, these people occupy positions of high social prestige.

Class II. Adults in this stratum are almost all college graduates; the males occupy high managerial positions, many are engaged in the lesser ranking professions. These families are well-to-do, but there is no substantial inherited or acquired wealth. Its members live in the "better" residential areas; about one-half of these families belong to lesser ranking private clubs, but only 5 per cent of Class II families are listed in the New Haven *Social Directory*.

Class III. This stratum includes the vast majority of small proprietors, white-collar office and sales workers, and a considerable number of skilled manual workers. Adults are predominantly high school graduates, but a considerable percentage have attended business schools and small colleges for a year or two. They live in "good" residential areas; less than 5 per cent belong to private clubs, but they are not included in the *Social Directory*. Their social life tends to be concentrated in the family, the church, and the lodge.

Class IV. This stratum consists predominantly of semi-skilled factory workers. Its adult members have finished the elementary grades, but the older people have not completed high school. However, adults under thirty-five have generally graduated from high school. Its members comprise almost one-half of the community; and their residences are scattered over wide areas. Social life is centered in the family, the neighborhood, the labor union, and public places.

Class V. Occupationally, Class V adults are overwhelmingly semi-skilled factory hands and unskilled laborers. Educationally most adults have not completed the elementary grades. The families are concentrated in the "tenement" and "cold-water flat" areas of New Haven. Only a small minority belong to organized community institutions. Their social life takes place in the family flat, on the street, or in neighborhood social agencies.[3]

Further light on class behavior is given in a study of Evanston, Illinois, by Leonard Reissman, who divides his informants into high and low classes (31). These two divisions contrast with Hollingshead's five, although Reissman used occupation, income, and education as objective indices to assign his ranks. He found that the higher class (which he equates with the middle class) showed a

---

[3] August B. Hollingshead and Frederick C. Redlick, "Social Stratification and Psychiatric Disorders," *American Sociological Review*, XVIII (April, 1953), 165–66.

higher degree of participation and involvement in the community. As one would expect, individuals in this class read more books and magazines, attend church more frequently, belong to more organizations, and more often hold office in those organizations. They tend to dominate the organizational activity, the intellectual life, and the leadership of the community. Also this class is more realistic in its aspirations and knows just what steps to take to move upward. The lower class, on the other hand, shows a startling lack of ideals in this matter. Not only are they less active in the life of the community but they are also more willing to sacrifice their personal views to take advantage of an opportunity for upward mobility. They seem unwilling to become involved in community affairs, a point of considerable political importance.

Enough reference has now been made to actual studies of community class systems to reveal the wide differences in methods employed by those conducting these studies. Those differences are often due to variations in definitions of social class (9, 10). The state of knowledge is such at the present time that no one definition will suit everyone. The best a person can hope to do is to make sure that in trying to describe the stratification within a given community he makes clear which approach to the problem he is employing. Before discussing a class system there must be some agreement on a preliminary definition.

Vertical Social Mobility

Social mobility, as used by Pitirim A. Sorokin who wrote the first book on this subject, means "the transition of an individual from one social position to another" (34). Vertical social mobility, the movement from one class position to another, downwards as well as upwards, is an important aspect of American life and is closely connected with the democratic system. One can frequently hear people discuss social mobility, perhaps without realizing it, when they characterize mutual acquaintances. Carson McGuire has selected the following comments to describe the types of mobility orientation in Jonesville:

The Climber: "He's really getting along in the world." "Oh! She made a good marriage and finally got out of that mess at home."
The Strainer: "He's really trying to get ahead—but I don't think he's got what it takes." "She's doing her best to get in . . ."
The Static (non-mobile): "Like father, like son." "She's a nice, quiet person like her mother." "He'll follow in his father's footsteps." "She's not much interested in things—stays at home."
The Clinger: "He's trying to follow in his father's footsteps but he's not doing

so well." "Her folks didn't leave much—she's going to have a hard time." "They're just managing to hang on."

The Decliner: "Just a backslider." "She dropped out of things—we never see her anymore." "The family's hit the skids—the kids are delinquent." "Maladjusted." "Alcoholic."[4]

Just as there are different types of mobility orientation, so there are special channels through which mobility may be effected. Harold F. Kaufman has described these channels as follows:

Major channels of mobility are occupation and the job, entrepreneurship, education, formal associations and marriage. Most studies of mobility have used as an index either the change in occupation or in years of schooling from one generation to the succeeding one. Demographic conditions which set the stage for rapid mobility are (1) the upper occupational groups do not replace themselves and (2) the great reservoir of rural youth together with the continuing expansion in industrial employment. . . .

The absence or closure of channels which facilitate upward movement might be considered as obstructive of mobility. Some major barriers would be: (1) lack of continuous economic expansion, especially in industrial employment; (2) restriction of membership in professional, business, and workers groups on any basis except competence; and (3) limitation of educational opportunities and other aids to acquiring the knowledge and skills necessary for higher ranks. If the channels for vertical mobility are absent and if a large number of people possess a strong desire for improved status, they either greatly modify their aims, or tensions are created which threaten the social order.[5]

Many social scientists have tried to find out if the channels described above remain open or if a "closed" class system is developing in America in which vertical social mobility would be more difficult than in the past. Here, as in so many matters of a complex sort, there are at least two schools of thought. Some writers think that the stratification lines are becoming more rigid (6, 38); others feel that, despite rigidity in some channels, vertical social mobility still continues to operate with considerable force (27, 32). Brief consideration will be given each of these points of view.

A. B. Hollingshead, whose New Haven study has been previously mentioned, discerns decreased mobility both in his research in New Haven and in a middle-western community studied in the 1940's. While readily admitting that data for the United States as a whole are still inconclusive, he points out that during the past two generations in the New Haven community, highly stratified parallel social structures have evolved that compartmentalize the social life of its inhabitants (18). He believes that the rigidity in the status structure

4 Carson McGuire, "Social Stratification and Mobility Patterns," *American Sociological Review,* XV (April, 1950), 200.

5 Harold F. Kaufman, "An Approach to the Study of Urban Stratification," *American Sociological Review,* XVII (August, 1952), 436–37.

is reinforced by (1) the tight occupational structure and (2) the association of ethnic origin with occupational pursuits. He also thinks
that the community's religious, educational, marital, and leisure-
time institutions serve as bulwarks to the existing status structure.

In his study of the middle-western community which he calls
Elmtown, Hollingshead finds that social mobility, either upward or
downward, has been confined to a relatively small percentage of
individuals in each class (17). In addition, he notes that this mobility
has occurred with greater frequency in the upper than in the lower
portions of the social structure.

Further support for the view that America is moving toward a
closed class system is provided by J. O. Hertzler who, after reviewing the related studies (which will not be mentioned here), cites a
number of reasons why he thinks social mobility is declining (15):

1. The original position of the individual's family. In brief, the race
   up the social staircase does not start at the bottom or on the same
   step for all; many have a family head start which cannot be over-
   taken.
2. Ethnic group membership. Many minority group members have
   "two strikes against them before they come up to bat."
3. Curtailment of immigration. The effect of immigration prior to
   World War I was to fill up the bottom to the point that the older
   arrivals were almost forced up the ladder. Immigration today is
   selective and includes better-educated arrivals; this has tended to
   crowd somewhat the upper educational levels and create "less
   room at the top" for American middle and lower class young folks.
4. Shifts in urban-rural and education-oriented fertility differentials.
   Earlier the upper classes did not replace themselves biologically,
   thus creating a vacuum in the higher social layers that tended to
   suck up persons from the lower classes to fill the vacancies. Especially since World War II all classes seem to be reversing the
   long-term trend and are having increasingly large numbers of
   children.
5. Restraining factors in the economic ladder. It is harder now for an
   individual to launch out in a business of his own today because of
   complexity and increased costs; industrial workers are tied to a
   craft and can move horizontally from plant to plant but not easily
   upward; American business leaders are being increasingly recruited
   from the upper ranks of society; the professions are more closed
   to lower class persons; and, finally, the labor unions of the workers
   themselves are a fixing factor of growing importance since a
   worker's security and advancement is tied in with his union.
6. Gaps and blocks in the operation of the educational conveyor belt.
   Many factors cause lower class children to drop out of school before those of other classes.

7. The reduction of the vertical mobility "drive." Many people prefer
certainty and fixity in some stratum of a more or less rigidly stratified society to the opportunity for success offered by a fluid, laissez-
faire, competitive society.

Hertzler stresses this last point especially and links the growing
complacency concerning status and role with popular unwillingness
to endure the strains of competition in our complex society. He
indicates that, in general, there is evidence that the American
Dream is becoming less real for many people.

In contrast to this view of declining social mobility, many writers
see numerous channels still open to those who would improve their
status. Stuart Adams, in his study of the origins of business leaders,
questions the hypothesis that American business leaders are increasingly coming from the higher classes and points out that while there
was a hardening of the business occupational structure as a result
of the Depression, afterward those of lower origins were able to
move upward (2). Many of the studies made of this problem, according to Adams, may reflect the peculiarities of the Depression
Decade and not be typical of the present or of the long-term trend.
The same author, in his study of lawyers, finds a decreasing stratification of this profession in the sense that entrance from any lower
occupational stratum has become easier in recent decades (1).

A study of the Oakland, California, labor market, conducted by
Seymour M. Lipset and Reinhard Bendix, indicates that Americans
are still a very mobile people, regardless of long-run trends, and
that it is possible, within rough limits, to differentiate careers which
reflect a great deal of mobility and those which do not (25). While
cautioning the reader against accepting their findings as typical of
communities quite different from rapidly expanding Oakland, the
writers do find that the opportunity and the desire to enter small
business may still be a major goal of American wage earners. They
see self-employment as one of the few positions of higher status
attainable to manual workers. That most of those who try it apparently fail does not change the fact that they do try. In other
words, social mobility means the chance to fall as well as to rise in
the socioeconomic scale.

Gideon Sjoberg, in his effort to answer the question as to whether
or not social classes in America are becoming more rigid, supplies
an answer quite different from that of Hertzler, quoted at length
above. Sjoberg also goes through an impressive number of studies
and articles related to this question and comes up with the following
five conclusions.

1. Although a number of social forces have been conducive to a more rigid and differentiated class system, others possibly more significant have counteracted this process. Thus, in many respects the class system is less well-defined than it was a half-century ago, particularly in the urban community. There is, for example, a less observable élite . . .

2. As a result of the re-distribution of selected highly valued prestige criteria, people's notions about class lines have in all probability become confused . . . For example, although certain traditionally middle-class persons may retain some status by virtue of their "white-collar" employment, in terms of monetary achievements they have lost status to many industrial workers . . .

3. The idea of class mobility as set forth by many sociologists requires careful scrutiny. For example, studying social climbing solely in terms of occupation may produce very misleading results. Changes in income, personal attributes, and the power held by individuals are also meaningful.

4. Debunking the American belief in a relatively "classless" society may be carried too far . . . During the present century the traditional lower classes have been acquiring some of the highly valued objective criteria of class differentiation at the expense of some members of the traditional upper and middle classes who have been losing theirs . . .

5. The world as a whole is presently undergoing the greatest social upheaval it has yet experienced; the American social structure, including class itself, will in all likelihood be subjected to further strains. Under these conditions the growth of a rigid and clearly differentiated class system in the United States is not a reasonable expectation.[6]

As a final comment on this controversial topic it may be helpful to cite the observations of Ely Chinoy who seeks to prove neither one side nor the other. Rather, he shows how particular studies have been variously interpreted, and how difficulties of terminology continue to plague those who work in this field. He also indicates that the mere fact of changes in channels for mobility does not necessarily indicate more or less mobility. Chinoy reaches the unsatisfactory but perhaps the only sound conclusion to the effect that the answer to what is happening to social mobility in American society must await more detailed studies which not only build upon research already done but which also seek to test precise hypotheses concerning the impact of changing institutions, social organization, and demographic characteristics upon the rate of mobility (4).

CASTE AND SUBCOMMUNITIES

Community studies, particularly in the southern states, have customarily treated the social differentiation between Negroes and whites as a caste-like arrangement (7, 8, 16, 29). There Negroes and whites are prohibited by state laws from intermarrying and are segregated on the basis of residence and frequently by occupational

[6] Gideon Sjoberg, "Are Social Classes in America Becoming More Rigid?" *American Sociological Review*, XVI (December, 1951), 783.

status. Negroes are not permitted to enter the white class system as fully participating members. Whether one calls this caste or not (5, 30) the net effect is to create a separate Negro community which exists side by side with a white community, with the two in a symbiotic relationship. Thus in most southern communities with any large Negro population, the Negroes have their own social institutions, their own leadership, and their own value orientation, which may or may not correspond fairly closely with that of the dominant white group. Usually the white community leaders think that they understand the Negro subcommunity, but the chances are that they are badly informed about such matters. For example, the Negro leaders whom the white people meet may be considered nominal rather than real leaders by the Negroes. Or the white leaders who seek to interpret the aspirations of the Negro people may do so quite incorrectly. This means that in a biracial situation it is important to apply the same methods toward understanding the Negro community as are applied to the white community with the added task of describing how the two are functionally related to each other.

Where the caste-like character is less prominent, such as in northern states whose laws make no distinction on the basis of race, there are still biracial aspects to be studied in an over-all view of the community. This is borne out by a study made by Frank F. Lee of race relations in Branford, Connecticut, a small industrial, vacation, and suburban town of just over ten thousand people, situated ten miles east of New Haven (24). Although this town differs from many others in New England as well as in other sections of the country, its white and Negro people do not participate as members of the same community. First, approximately three fifths of the Negro population (who make up from 1.5 to 2 per cent of the total) live in a semisegregated area within one or two blocks of the railroad and the major industries. Buying or renting homes for Negroes is practically impossible elsewhere. A proposed public housing project was rejected by the Town Meeting for fear that Negroes would become tenants. Secondly, there is a good deal of job discrimination against the Negroes. Those with skills greater than required for unskilled or semiskilled work usually have to go outside Branford to find jobs. Where Negroes are employed, however, they are treated equally with whites up to and possibly including the supervisory ranks. In the third place, religious activities show almost complete separation of the races. Adult social activities of all types include little joint Negro-white participation; interracial social contacts exist only on the most superficial level. Only two formal organizations, the Chamber of Commerce and the Town Band, have Negro members. On the adolescent level, Negroes participate with whites in three social activities: the American Legion Baseball Club, the Boy Scouts, and the Junior Musical Arts Society. There is some discrimination in use of public facilities, with the most discrimination being shown in barber shops and bars and the least in stores and professional services. Aside from voting, Negroes do not participate in any aspect of politics and government, probably because of Negro lack of interest. The school system was found to be the "freest" area of behavior, although the possibility of Negro teachers being hired is neither clear nor promising. As Lee noted:

> The Negro therefore lives in a somewhat separate world: he inhabits certain sections of town; he has his own church and social activities; and he is barred from most of the private clubs and organizations and from many public facilities. At the same time he works with whites (although usually on a lower level), and is allowed to participate on an equal basis in the school system.[7]

Here is an example of stratification on a racial basis. Although there are numerous forces in America today creating changes in such a status system (to be discussed in Chapter 9), anyone who would understand Branford or any other community with a similar arrangement should know how this racial subcommunity operates as well as in what respects it is and is not integrated into the larger community of which it is supposedly a part.

SIGNIFICANCE OF SOCIAL LAYERS

To one who is professionally engaged in the study of society, the theoretical problems connected with the analysis of social stratification have great meaning. If they can be answered by thoroughgoing research many aspects of society become clear, and the knowledge of how communities are structured is advanced. For most people, however, social classes are quite a personal thing. They may dismiss the talk of social climbing as nonsense, or they may say that they are perfectly content with things as they are. Yet, even while disclaiming any interest in social class, they are apt to be aware of the attitudes of others who they think occupy the same stratum as themselves. If they are ambitious for themselves or for their children, they begin to think about how their situation can be improved, often through forming relationships with those who are in a more preferred position in their particular community. The choice of a school, the selection of a job or even of clothes, may have a class tinge which they would not readily admit or even understand.

[7] Frank F. Lee, "The Race Relations Pattern by Areas of Behavior in a Small New England Town," *American Sociological Review*, XIX (April, 1954), 143.

For the intelligent layman as well as for the sociologist, a knowledge of how the class system works in any community—assuming it is definite enough to be delineated—helps one understand the behavior of other people. Mrs. Smith may be friendly with both Mrs. Jones and Mrs. Brown but soon discerns that these two women are not very comfortable with each other because of social distinctions. Mrs. Brown may be trying to "cultivate" Mrs. Jones, who may be trying to keep Mrs. Brown at a distance. Through a knowledge of the patterns of stratification one can understand the clique structure and know why some people feel intimate and others do not. A highly urbanized community may lack some of the social class traits characteristic of the smaller community from which some neighbor has come. Indeed, such traits may seem "small townish" to his new urban acquaintances and therefore need to be modified. This is only another way of saying that the social layers, along with place, jobs and services, and all the rest constitute just one more dimension of community life. In themselves alone they do not constitute the community, although some people are inclined to stress them. They must be seen in perspective.

A final significant detail deserves mention. For a community undertaking to be truly representative of the community, people from all social strata must be involved. This means more than simply getting representation from all of the organizations, or more than a wide geographical distribution. It means trying in some way to identify the social layers and being sure that spokesmen whom the people in a given layer trust represent them. Few if any community projects ever succeed in doing this fully; yet it is a consideration to be taken into account when something of community-wide interest is proposed, be it a school bond issue or the development of a total recreation program. It also means seeing that channels of opportunity are open to capable young people who, without some economic or other support, could not rise to the extent of their capabilities. The American Dream must be realized on the community level —the "home town" level—if it is realized at all.

REFERENCES AND SUGGESTED READINGS

1. ADAMS, STUART. "Regional Differences in Vertical Mobility in a High-Status Occupation," *American Sociological Review*, XV (April, 1950), 228–35.
2. ———. "Trends in Occupational Origins of Business Leaders," *American Sociological Review*, XIX (October, 1954), 541–48.
3. CENTERS, RICHARD. *The Psychology of Social Class*. Princeton: Princeton University Press, 1949.
4. CHINOY, ELY. "Social Mobility Trends in the United States," *American Sociological Review*, XX (April, 1955), 180–86.

5. Cox, Oliver C. *Caste, Class and Race.* Garden City: Doubleday & Company, Inc., 1948.

6. Davidson, P. E., and Anderson, H. D. *Occupational Mobility in an American Community.* Stanford: Stanford University Press, 1937.

7. Davis, Allison, and Gardner, Burleigh. *Deep South.* Chicago: University of Chicago Press, 1941.

8. Dollard, John. *Caste and Class in a Southern Town.* New Haven: Yale University Press, 1937.

9. Gordon, Milton M. "Social Class in American Sociology," *The American Journal of Sociology,* LV (November, 1949), 262–68.

10. Gross, Llewellyn. "The Use of Class Concepts in Sociological Research," *The American Journal of Sociology,* LIV (March, 1949), 409–21.

11. Gross, Neal. "Social Class Identification in the Urban Community," *American Sociological Review,* XVIII (August, 1953), 398–404.

12. Haer, John L. "A Comparative Study of the Classification Techniques of Warner and Centers," *American Sociological Review,* XX (December, 1955), 689–92.

13. Hatt, Paul K. "Stratification in the Mass Society," *American Sociological Review,* XV (April, 1950), 216–22.

14. Hawthorn, Harry B., and Engle, Audrey. "Stratification in a Latin American City," *Social Forces,* XXVII (October, 1948), 19–29.

15. Hertzler, J. O., "Some Tendencies Toward a Closed Class System in the United States," *Social Forces,* XXX (March, 1952), 313–23.

16. Hill, Mozell C., and McCall, Bevode C. "Social Stratification in 'Georgia Town,'" *American Sociological Review,* XV (December, 1950), 721–29.

17. Hollingshead, August B. "Class and Kinship in a Middle Western Community," *American Sociological Review,* XIV (August, 1949), 469–75.

18. ———. "Trends in Social Stratification: A Case Study," *American Sociological Review,* XVII (December, 1952), 679-86.

19. Hollingshead, August B., and Redlick, Frederick C. "Social Stratification and Psychiatric Disorders," *American Sociological Review,* XVIII (April, 1953), 163–69.

20. Kahl, Joseph A., and Davis, James A. "A Comparison of Indexes of Socio-Economic Status," *American Sociological Review,* XX (June, 1955), 317–25.

21. Kaufman, Harold F. "An Approach to the Study of Urban Stratification," *American Sociological Review,* XVII (August, 1952), 430–37.

22. King, Charles E. "The Process of Social Stratification Among an Urban Southern Minority Population," *Social Forces,* XXXI (May, 1953), 352–55.

23. Lasswell, Thomas E. "A Study of Social Stratification Using an Area Sample of Raters," *American Sociological Review,* XIX (June, 1954), 310–13.

24. Lee, Frank F. "The Race Relations Pattern by Areas of Behavior in a Small New England Town," *American Sociological Review,* XIX (April, 1954), 138–43.

25. Lipset, S. M., and Bendix, R. "Social Mobility and Occupational Career Patterns," *American Journal of Sociology,* LVII (January and March, 1952), 366–74, 494–504.

26. McGuire, Carson. "Social Stratification and Mobility Patterns," *American Sociological Review,* XV (April, 1950), 195–204.

27. Mills, C. Wright. *White Collar: The American Middle Classes.* New York: Oxford University Press, 1951.

28. Montague, Joel B., Jr. "Some Aspects of Class, Status, and Power Relations in England," *Social Forces,* XXX (December, 1951), 134–40.

29. Myrdal, Gunnar. *An American Dilemma: The Negro Problem and Modern Democracy.* New York: Harper & Brothers, 1944.

30. Pohlmann, Edward W. "Semantic Aspects of the Controversy over Negro-White Caste in the United States," *Social Forces,* XXX (May, 1952), 416–19.

31. Reissman, Leonard. "Class, Leisure and Social Participation," *American Sociological Review,* XIX (February, 1954), 76–84.

32. ROGOFF, NATALIE. *Recent Trends in Occupational Mobility*. Chicago: Free Press, 1953.

33. SJOBERG. "Are Social Classes in America Becoming More Rigid?" *American Sociological Review*, XVI (December, 1951), 775–83.

34. SOROKIN, PITIRIM A. *Social Mobility*. New York: Harper & Brothers, 1927.

35. STONE, GREGORY P., and FORM, WILLIAM H. "Instabilities in Status: The Problem of Hierarchy in the Community Study of Status Arrangements," *American Sociological Review*, XVIII (April, 1953), 149–62.

36. WARNER, W. LLOYD AND ASSOCIATES. *Democracy in Jonesville*. New York: Harper & Brothers, 1949.

37. WARNER, W. LLOYD, and LUNT, PAUL S. *The Social Life of a Modern Community*. New Haven: Yale University Press, 1946.

38. WARNER, W. LLOYD; MEEKER, MARCHIA; and EELLS, KENNETH. *Social Class in America*. Chicago: Science Research Associates, 1949.

Chapter 7

GROUPS WITHIN THE COMMUNITY

In a very real sense, community life is group life. Seldom, however, does a whole community come together in one place to take action or to enjoy some spectacle. Most of the time, the residents associate with each other in numbers totaling only a few people at a time, though now and then larger aggregations (such as a movie audience) may form about events or matters of considerable general interest. Thus an individual, even though he is a bona fide member of the community, associates with a comparatively small proportion of those making up the total community. The larger the community, the smaller is this proportion.

THE STUDY OF THE SOCIAL GROUP

The study of the social group is just as specialized as the study of the community. Indeed, in 1954, Fred L. Strodtbeck and A. Paul Hare listed 1407 books and articles published from 1900 through 1953 which dealt with small group research (23). Many more have been published since then. It is, therefore, impossible to summarize here all that social scientists have learned about social groups, but it is possible to indicate some of the relationships which exist between social groups and the over-all community of which the social groups are a part.

This partial survey is especially necessary since so much emphasis is given to the development of groups and associations in American society. Group work is one of the major areas of the social welfare field; group therapy is a subject of great interest to psychiatrists and psychologists; and concern with a person's group relations runs through many industrial companies as well as many educational systems (9). Frequent use is made of the sociogram, such as Figure 7 in Chapter 4, to find out the preferences of individuals for others in the group and to plan personnel policy accordingly. This is a technique of sociometry, the scientific method of studying interpersonal relations, worked out by J. L. Moreno, which has had much influence both in the United States and abroad (18). Also influential is the group dynamics movement, begun largely under the leadership of Kurt Lewin (14). Howard V. Perlmutter points out that "group dynamics" has been used in three senses:

1. A program of action research which leads to solution of such problems as changing food habits, increasing participation in discussion.
2. Style of conducting discussion so as to facilitate interaction and the arriving at consensus through role-playing and the "buzz group" of six people who thrash through a problem and report their deliberations back to the main group.
3. A theoretical scheme subject to empirical tests involving such researchable problems as group cohesiveness and communication in groups.

The whole interest in group dynamics has led to a better understanding of and emphasis upon democratic leadership in groups.

The interaction-process approach of Robert Bales has also led to the development of important research in the small group (3). This method classifies behavior act by act, as it occurs in small face-to-face groups trying to solve some problem. The resultant data are analyzed to obtain indices descriptive of group process and of factors influencing that process.

Quite apart from this scientific interest in the study of the small group is the simple fact that people within a community move from group to group judging their community by the kind of group experiences they have. The involvement of any individual in the group life of his community will become clear if one views the individual in terms of his status-role.

The Status-Role Bundle

The Daily Routine. Mr. Ezra Smith, devoted husband and father of five young children, has risen according to schedule, shaved, dressed, breakfasted, and gone over the day's details with his wife. He then backs his car out of the garage of his modest home and is soon lost in the line of traffic of others headed for work. He parks his car behind the shoe store where he is a salesman and goes in for a brief staff session with the manager before the doors are opened to customers. Here he becomes the employee from the standpoint of the manager and a salesman in the eyes of the customers.

At lunchtime he goes to the Lions Club, where he is an officer and where he visits informally with many of his friends. On the way back to his store he stops at a car dealer's showroom to look over a low-priced car which he is thinking of buying. The rest of the afternoon he spends at the store. Occasionally this routine is interrupted when he arranges with the manager to be away for jury duty, to serve on the board of a crippled children's home, to go to the dentist, or to take care of some business affairs of the veteran's organization of which he is a member.

After work he finds life varied enough. Some nights he goes to "pack meetings" with a son who is a cub scout; occasionally he accompanies his wife to a P.-T.A. meeting or to a church supper. On other evenings he gathers with some of his friends at the veterans' club for card games or takes others in his family to the drive-in theater or watches television with neighbors, or goes to a night baseball game in a large city sixty miles away, or attends an evening course in salesmanship sponsored by the extension division of the local college.

During his vacation period he introduces further variety into his life, taking a trip by car to visit his relatives in another state or going to a state forest with his family for a camping trip or simply staying at home and doing some much-needed repair work around the house.

Even this brief inquiry into the private life of Mr. Smith is sufficient to indicate several interesting things. First, during his waking hours Mr. Smith moves from one status to another. He is husband, father, motorist, salesman, customer, club member, scout leader, student, and vacationist as well as a man, an adult, and a member of the middle class. Secondly, each status he assumes carries with it certain roles or behavior patterns which he considers normal and which others around him expect him to perform. As a shoe salesman he is not supposed to play "This little pig went to market, this little pig stayed at home . . ." on the toes of his customers, although as a father he does this at the insistence of the baby; as a motorist he is supposed to obey the traffic signals; as an adult he is supposed to "put away childish things" and "act his age." Many of these roles have little to do with the unique traits of Mr. Smith as an individual but have been passed down to him and to others in his community as customs and mores. They constitute learned behavior, but the community has had a hand in deciding what is and what is not to be learned.

A third consideration is the fact that Mr. Smith performs most of these roles in the presence of other people; he communicates and interacts with them. What he does and how he does it is closely tied in with his idea of his status and his understanding of what is an appropriate series of roles for that status; he is guided by the response of other people in deciding whether he has initiated the expected role or not, and, if what he is doing seems to be displeasing, he can change his behavior accordingly. His own idea of what a father should do may differ from his wife's idea of what a father should do in a given situation; as he starts to discipline a child, perhaps as his own father disciplined him, his wife may say, with a glance: "You are not treating this child right. Don't you remember what Gesell, the writer on childhood and the teens, said?" and thus cause him to alter his role. Even though his own status as father gets confused from time to time with that of the dutiful husband, he still remains a father; it is the roles and the role expectations that change and not that particular status.

This combination of status and accompanying roles has been called "the status-role bundle" by Talcott Parsons. From one standpoint a community may be looked at as a gigantic collection of statuses—"rich man, poor man, beggar man, thief . . ."—and each new generation inherits these statuses and adds some new ones. The fact that these statuses and roles persist in time apart from the personality of any one individual or collection of individuals gives a community a predictability; one can anticipate in general how a policeman directing traffic will act no matter which officer is on duty a particular day at a particular spot. Obviously, each individual has some leeway in playing these roles; what we call his personality may seem better adapted for some kinds of role-playing than others, and he is urged or guided into those positions where he can best perform.

The term *social relationship* is useful in describing the bond between two interacting persons. Each has a status vis-à-vis the other, and each supposedly acts in keeping with the role expectations which accompany that status. This means that a social relationship has both static and dynamic (role-playing) aspects. As pointed out in the previous chapter, *social values* assist in ranking statuses as higher or lower, more or less important; *norms*, on the other hand, set the limits within which roles must be played. A school teacher can discipline a child, but community norms tell what he may or may not do in carrying out the discipline. He will probably not be allowed to whip the child with a birch rod, but he may send the child home with the request that the parents seriously consider such a step. The norms are a great deal like the rules covering the game of football in that they tell what a player may and may not do (4).

With this discussion of Mr. Smith and the status-role bundle and the concepts of value, norm, and social relationship, the way has been paved for a definition of a social group.

THE NATURE OF A SOCIAL GROUP

The Group as a Set of Social Relationships. One of the simplest ways of looking at a social group in a community is to make use of the term *social relationship* just defined above and to describe a group as *a set of social relationships organized around a common interest.* This means that two or more people are in communication with each other, each conscious of the other's status and each expecting certain culturally defined roles within the limits set by accepted norms. The fact that these relationships are organized means that there is some arrangement of statuses into leadership and followership terms; the organization may be of a temporary, transitory sort, a way of getting along for the time being, or it may have a continuity or even a permanence to it. Organization also carries with it the consciousness of belonging in the sense that each individual participating in the group sees where he fits into the total setting; he identifies himself with the symbols of the group and reacts with pride or embarrassment to the fact of membership in the group according to the status of the group in the community. As already pointed out above, organization implies mutually acceptable values and norms so that the role-playing can be meaningful. Finally, organization of the social relationships, when fully worked out, means a division of function within the group: leaders (or officers) know what their responsibilities are, and members know theirs.

In addition to these features of organization there is a common interest which acts as a sort of social cement for the group. If the interest is fleeting, then the group is of short duration; if the interest is deep and abiding, then the group persists through time, should other conditions permit.

But no set of social relationships (group) is completely self-determining and self-sufficient; it must interact with other groups, or plurality patterns, as they are often called. Frequently, many of the main characteristics of a group become evident only as it becomes involved with other groups in the community. As a matter of fact, it has become increasingly popular to think of the group as a social system, especially since the appearance in 1950 of George C. Homans' book *The Human Group* (12). This in no way contradicts the main points of the working definition given above, but it does look at the group from a slightly different perspective.

The Group as a Social System. Any social unit that is a continuing, going concern, that has its own identity, and that can be separated —at least for purposes of analysis—from other units can be viewed as a social system. This means that there is some systematic arrangement of the parts of the unit as well as interdependence among these parts. According to Homans a group has a boundary, not hard and fast but outside which lies the group's environment (physical, technical, social). The group possesses an *external system,* so-called because it is conditioned by the environment, and an *internal system,* which is an expression of the sentiments developed by the members of the group toward one another in the course of their life together. The group as a total system is characterized by the interplay between the *external* and *internal* systems.

As a result of the study of five cases, widely spaced geographically and quite different in content, Homans concludes that there are three behavior elements which need to be described if one is to explain the workings of a group. These are sentiment, activity, and interaction. *Sentiments* refer to the internal states of the human body. These range from fear, hunger, and thirst to such complicated psychological states as liking or disliking for individuals and approval or disapproval of their actions. *Activity* is, as the term implies, what people do. It covers not only what people do in the physical environment with implements but what they do with other persons.

Interaction occurs when one man's act follows or is stimulated by some act of another. For example, two men at opposite ends of a saw, sawing a log, are interacting, for the pull of one man on the saw is followed by the pull of the other. Sawing is the activity.

To understand how a group tries to solve the problems of the environment through its external system, one must study the interdependence of each of the above three behavior elements upon the other. The sentiments in the beginning may serve as motivating forces to call forth certain activities; these activities on the part of those involved lead to interaction, which in turn leads to other activities and other sentiments. Interaction calls for the development of a scheme of communication in the group as well as some kind of an organization, with leaders and followers. To summarize, a satisfactory group description would call for a statement of the sentiments or the feelings on the part of the group members and a listing of the activities of the group and the patterns of interaction that followed. This description would also require one to trace how changes in any one of the three elements, such as sentiment, affected the other elements, such as activity or interaction. Finally, in completing this account of the external system one would have to relate group behavior to environmental forces.

This, however, would be only part of the task. There remains the internal system. Here one would show how the mutual dependence of sentiments and interaction would lead to what Homans advances as a hypothesis: an increase of interaction between persons is accompanied by an increase of sentiments of liking among them. There is also mutual interdependence between activity and interaction in that a great deal of social activity (dances and parties are examples) is enjoyed less for the sake of the activity itself, which may be trivial, than for the possibilities of social interaction. Activities of the internal system tend to become standardized, and norms of behavior are adopted or invented by the group. Thus by looking at the group first with reference to its relation to its environment and then with reference to the developments among the group members themselves, Homans moves toward a description of the group as a social system. By methodical use of the three behavior elements he takes up such important topics as differentiation within the group, leadership, social control, and social conflict and sets forth some basic hypotheses.

To try in such a brief space to summarize the main points of Homans' work is unsatisfactory at best. Yet, even this much calls attention to the fact that a group is a social system, that anyone trying to describe such a system needs to employ a special set of terms such as that used by Homans, and that the study of any group— whether a church choir, a bowling league, or a committee in charge of a youth center—is really a complex affair but one subject to certain generalizations which students of the social group are gradually formulating and testing through careful research.

All groups, whether viewed as social systems or not, have certain common characteristics, chief among them being the presence of social interaction (1). On the other hand, they have a wide range of differences, too. These differences can best be accounted for if a distinction is made between the informal, primary group and the formal, secondary group.

Informal Groups and the Community

In a simple society represented by the rural villages of Europe and Asia life goes along chiefly on a face-to-face basis without the help of numerous formally organized groups (associations) to mediate in behalf of the individual. The family, the kin group, the neighborhood, and the play groups are definitely structured in that they possess recognized statuses to be respected or accepted; yet the groups are not set up in the same way and for the purpose that the numerous societies and clubs of a modern American city come into existence. A description of one such community will illustrate the importance of the informal groups.

Informal Groups in Pelpola, Ceylon. Pelpola is an agricultural village of four hundred households situated in the lush lowlands thirty-five miles from the city of Colombo, the capital of Ceylon, a member of the British Commonwealth just south of India. Although the majority of its households depend upon paddy (rice) cultivation as their primary economic activity, the more prosperous ones own small rubber holdings, while the poor supplement agricultural income by labor in the nearby absentee-owned rubber estates. Within the village there are no telephones, although mail service, a school, temples, and retail traders are present. The village boasts four radios. About fifteen newspapers are delivered daily, a number of them to retail shopkeepers.

Most of the people of Pelpola are closely interrelated by blood, are members of the "cultivators' caste," and live in homes set in small highland gardens, seldom more than a quarter of an acre in extent. Given such a setting, what connections does one find between the informal or primary group and the community?

Bryce Ryan provides some answers to this question (20). The strongest unit of social life is the patriarchal marital family, whose household is typically both a production and a consumption unit. In addition to the immediate family household, the kinship group is very important. The vast majority of household heads live in physical proximity to their siblings, many of whom are also married householders, although wives are more frequently isolated from their blood kin. As a matter of fact, the multiplicity of daily contacts with kin is so great that its statistical expression would be extremely difficult.

A third type of a primary group which looms in importance is the neighborhood. In the intimate circles of those who chat and gossip together—Pelpola's most frequent form of interhousehold social life —43 per cent of the household heads specified groups composed exclusively of relatives, while 89 per cent described groups composed exclusively of neighbors, many of whom were also kinsmen. The significance of the neighborhood within village life does not detract from earlier observations as to the importance of kin. Kin tend to be represented within the neighborhood, and in many instances blood and "in-law" relationship is, no doubt, fundamental to the bonds of personal intimacy. The neighborhood appears, however, to be the most critical boundary of personal interaction.

For the vast majority of villagers, it is the chatting in the village lanes and similar unspecialized forms of interaction that encompass the adult individual's primary social life outside the home. Participation in the few secondary or special-interest groups is limited. Less than a fourth of the household heads attend a cinema, and even of the literates only 37 per cent are regular newspaper readers. Insofar as the evidence goes, the kinship and neighborhood bases of intimate social life are entirely congruent and harmonious with the village special-interest group. It is quite possible that kinship and neighborhood cliques are the nuclei upon which successful interest groups are organized.

Thus, Pelpola maintains a strong primary group life on the basis of the neighborhood and kinship, neither of which seems threatened by the coming in of special-interest groups. But what of the American city? Do informal groups exist there too?

Informal Groups in the American City. One study of Lansing, Michigan, indicates that there is much local intimacy in a middle-sized city (22). The investigators asked a sample of 573 people to give the location of their three "best friends." Only 15 per cent did not report as many as three and only 4.5 per cent reported none. All the rest indicated that they had these intimate associates and could tell where they lived. Whereas in Pelpola, the Ceylonese village, the neighborhood was the chief basis for intimacy, in Lansing most of the friends named lived outside the neighborhood of the person interviewed. This means that the city is a place where the person finds it possible to develop a sense of intimacy, both city-wide and locality based.

However, an analysis in terms of degree of intimacy of the friendships that are locality based shows that the highest intimacy scores of Lansing residents are found in areas of high socioeconomic position. Also, local intimacy develops as a result of residential stability. According to those making this study, there are two reasons why greater local intimacy will be found in high-income areas than in middle and lower economic areas: first, low economic groupings are more often subject to economic pressures demanding changes of residence than are high economic groupings; second, low economic groupings occupy a greater share of the city's space and have more spatial alternatives for moving. As a consequence, friendships in this stratum tend to be dispersed more widely through the city's space than friendships among urbanites in higher strata. The Lansing study concludes: "Thus, urban social integration is contributed to by the fact that urbanites derive social satisfaction from informal relationships both within and outside of their local areas of residence. Spatial mobility makes for city-wide ties; stability makes for local area ties; and most urban residents have both."[1]

A study of New Haven, Connecticut, which concentrated upon the patterns of voluntary association of working-class families there, showed that three-fifths of the men and four-fifths of the women and children in the families studied did not participate at all in formally organized associations (10). However, there was widespread informal contact of three types:

1. Acquaintanceship and friendship. According to Floyd Dotson, who reported on the study, the acquaintanceship category is large but vague. It embraces people known in childhood, former neighbors, and fellow workers. Such contacts may give a superficial sense of broad participation, but their role in day-to-day activities is a marginal one. Since organized social life must rest upon a firmer basis than acquaintanceship provides, the loosest type of informal, voluntary association which can be profitably recognized is the friendship group. The study showed that the majority of working-class husbands and wives did have friends outside their own families and relatives, but *two-fifths did not*. (In Lansing, Michigan, the study covered all occupational groups and not just working-class families.)

2. Kin cliques. Dotson defines a clique as "a psychologically intimate relationship which involves frequent and regular interaction." In New Haven, which is a relatively stable community, family and kin groups played an unusually important role in providing for the companionship and recreational needs of the persons interviewed. Even the two-fifths who had no friends did have relatives in the community, for until recently, working-class families have been typically large, thus providing a large enough social circle to make possible a self-sufficient social life.

3. Nonkin cliques. Such cliques, founded upon neighborhood propinquity, are nearly universal among children and adolescents. As noted above, strong adult cliques of nonrelated persons are less common than those among kindred, but they nevertheless appear in appreciable numbers. A note of particular interest is the fact that although most of these adolescent cliques break down and disappear with the coming of adulthood and marriage, most adult clique re-

[1] Joel Smith, William H. Form, and Gregory P. Stone, "Local Intimacy in a Middle-Sized City," *The American Journal of Sociology*, LX (November, 1954), 284.

lationships found in this study could be traced back to childhood and adolescence.

Neighborliness in the Town or City. Most neighborhood visiting patterns arise spontaneously as people meet casually over the back fence or as the person next door drops in to call. In many parts of a community such patterns may be rare, and in such a case an effort may be made to *organize* a neighborhood club. But the very fact that it has to be organized consciously, frequently by an outsider, means that it takes on the character of the formal or secondary association and seldom captures the spontaneity of the informal neighborliness pattern.

In one approach to the informal locality group, Peter H. Mann considers neighborliness as a twofold concept (15). On the one hand, there is what he calls "manifest neighborliness." This is characterized by overt forms of social relationships, such as mutual visiting in the home and going out for purposes of pleasure. On the other hand, there is what he terms "latent neighborliness," which is characterized by favorable attitudes to neighbors which result in positive action when a need arises, especially in times of crisis or emergency (17). After a study of two British housing projects, in which he tested out his ideas of neighborliness, Mann concluded:

> This paper has stressed the importance of latent neighborliness as the basis of social solidarity and how a high degree of manifest neighborliness can be mistakenly taken to be indicative of social solidarity for all the inhabitants of a neighborhood. At times sociologists overestimate the significance of manifest forms of action, while the underlying attitudes are neglected. The modern neighborhood is not a functional unit in the older sense of the isolated agricultural village. In many cases all the people have in common is the fact that they happen to live near to one another. Community centers, clubs, and other such groups cater largely to special interests; they rarely attract the whole population of a neighborhood. Nevertheless, if, at first visit, a neighborhood appears to be sleepy and apathetic, with absolutely nothing happening at all, this is no reason for thinking that the inhabitants lack neighborliness. If the observer can go below the surface to discover the latent neighborliness, he may well find a very definite attitude expressive of social cohesion. In the modern urban neighborhood this may well be the most important factor of all.[2]

Further Observations About Informal Groups. The informal group in every society comes about spontaneously and in a comparatively unplanned fashion. It continues as long as people follow some traditional behavior pattern or pursue some common interest; it lasts as long as it continues to provide the satisfactions that its members expect from it. In the formal group, on the other hand, much atten-

---

[2] Peter H. Mann, "The Concept of Neighborliness," *American Journal of Sociology,* LX (September, 1954), 168.

tion is frequently focused on qualifications for membership, rights and duties of the officers, and a program involving the membership.

In the case of the family, individuals decide to marry and set up a home—certainly a very permanent arrangement—yet, the way this is done, the factors taken into account, differ from those involved in organizing a Rotary Club or a chapter of the Daughters of the American Revolution. Furthermore, the family is a primary group in that its members tend to know each other as whole personalities, whereas in the formal associations people are often known to others simply in terms of their membership roles in the particular association. They may never see each other, for instance, except at a meeting.

In recreational pursuits the contrast between the formal and informal types is evident. A group of children living near each other may gather on a vacant lot after school for a ball game, kite flying, or bicycle races. No adult may be present, and more time may be spent arguing over rules than playing the game; yet, this is an informal, primary group. Three or four blocks away youngsters may be experiencing formalized play under the direction of a playground supervisor. While a good supervisor may keep the atmosphere so relaxed that the group approaches the informal type, there is a tendency to *organize* the children on the playground into units with their own symbols and names, because in any administrative program it is easier to deal with social units (consisting of several individuals) than to deal with each individual separately. The formal group in such a case is a device to help the program along, leading in the long run to greater benefits for all of the individuals, as some orderliness is substituted for what might very easily turn into chaos.

Adults also have their informal groups. These arise in response to certain social needs without necessarily moving toward the creation of a formally organized social club. Such a social clique may eventually become the nucleus for setting up a fraternal order or a country club, but most social cliques never elect officers or worry about membership requirements. Their members may not even be aware that the clique is well defined to outsiders, since to the members it is a source of enjoyment and even a refuge from many of the highly organized aspects of life in which they participate.

Much if not most of the culture (social heritage) of a community, particularly the values and the norms, is passed on from one generation to the next through the informal groups: the family, the neighborhood, the play group. This is clearly demonstrated on a smaller scale in a college or university where the real traditions of the institution are passed to new students, not so effectively in the formalized orientation sessions, but in the informal, off-the-record remarks of the older students talking in the corridors between classes, having coffee at the Student Union, or in the small-talk of the fraternity, sorority, or dormitory. The same process, in a more complex way, holds true for the local community in which the educational institution is located.

Both the informal and formal groups are part of the communication network discussed in Chapter 4, but each type serves in a different way to diffuse information. Each type, as Chapter 10, on social control, will show, brings pressures to bear upon individuals to prepare them for community living and to keep them in line with the expectations of the people of the community. As indicated in the discussion of social layers, most of the informal cliques are tied in with a definite social layer, and shifts in membership in such cliques are tied in with mobility up or down the social scale (6).

FORMAL GROUPS WITHIN THE COMMUNITY

Studies both of a simple, agricultural community such as Pelpola, Ceylon, and of an industrialized urban area such as New Haven, Connecticut, show the widespread existence of informal, primary groups. In Detroit, Michigan, to cite a study made by Morris Axelrod, it was found that "informal group association was well-nigh universal with only a small segment entirely devoid of such association." Here, too, "relatives emerged as the most important type of informal group association."[3] Granted, then, that these informal groups exist, what about the formal associations? Mr. Ezra Smith, whose daily activities were previously detailed, participated not only in the informal but in the formal types. He went to the Lions Club, the P.-T.A., and the cub scout pack meeting; he attended church and a crippled children's home board of directors meeting; he was active in a veterans' organization. But an important question remains: Is Mr. Smith typical or is he the exception in holding so many organizational memberships (7, 13, 24)?

The Extent of Participation in Formal Groups. In the Detroit study made in 1952 and 1953 it was found that nearly two-thirds of the population are members of formal groups. One-half of all members belong to only one group and three-quarters to no more than two groups. So Mr. Smith is not typical of the Detroiter in general, since he belongs to several groups rather than to only one or two. He is also unusual in that he is a conscientious, active member of the

[3] Morris Axelrod, "Urban Structure and Social Participation," *American Sociological Review,* XXI (February, 1956), 18.

groups to which he does belong, whereas in Detroit about one-quarter of the members had not attended any meetings during the three months preceding the study, one-third had attended rarely, and one-quarter had attended frequently. The remainder—about one-fifth—could be considered very active. Reduced to percentages, this means that 19 per cent of the members but only 12 per cent of the population were very active in formal groups.

Further study of the data shows, however, that participation varies with income, and here Mr. Smith assumes a more typical position: higher income is associated with a greater probability of membership and higher activity. Less than one-half (42 per cent) of those whose family income is under $3000 have formal group membership, while twice this proportion (81 per cent) among those whose family earnings exceed $7000 are group members. (Compare the lower figures already cited for working-class family heads in New Haven, Connecticut.)

Education is important, too. More than three-quarters of all persons with some college experience have formal group membership, while only half of those with grade school education have formal group membership. Also, where the head is engaged in a white-collar occupation, the family members are somewhat more likely to belong to a formal group. As Axelrod points out, "The factory worker at the conclusion of his day's work may dismiss his work from his mind. The professional or the executive finds the dividing line between his work and his other activities a tenuous one."[4]

Since formal organizations do not have a greater *direct* influence upon the total population of a community, either in terms of numerous memberships or of intensive activity by those who are members, why is there so much emphasis upon clubs and associations by those engaged in community planning? This study of Detroit ends with the suggestion that the importance of formal groups lies in the fact that *these groups, through the active members, link together the underlying network of informal association in the community at large.* Perhaps several of Mr. Smith's neighbors and acquaintances are not active in formal groups, but when some matter of importance does come up he can act as their spokesman through the organizations of which he is a member.

Locality and Participation. In order to get a clearer picture of the importance of formal groups sociologists in particular have been making use of F. Stuart Chapin's social participation scale (8). One such study by Selz C. Mayo and C. Paul Marsh of two rural locality

[4] *Ibid.*, p. 16.

groups in Wake County, North Carolina, raised the question of the degree to which participation in such groups was limited to the immediate locality in which the members lived (16). Their chief finding was that the participation of the residents of a locality group with high group consciousness is confined to the locality to a much greater degree than that of the residents of a locality group with a low degree of group consciousness. The same would probably hold true for the subcommunities of a city in a general sense: where some area is highly self-conscious, has much pride, and contains organizations with appealing programs, the people of that area would be less apt to belong to formal groups in other parts of the city. The chances are, however, that the leaders of these groups would have numerous contacts in other organizations outside the area (11).

Further information about neighborhood residence and formal group participation is given in a study of four different kinds of neighborhoods in San Francisco (5). Wendell Bell and Maryanne T. Force report that, with the exception of the labor union, power through the activity of formally organized groups seems to rest largely in the hands of those men living in high economic status neighborhoods. These investigators also conclude that the associational behavior of urbanites, regardless of the social type of neighborhood in which they live, is largely a manifestation of a special interest which they share with other persons of similar status. Also, men living in high economic status neighborhoods had relatively more memberships in the general interest type of associations (Chamber of Commerce, service clubs, church-connected groups, fraternal organizations, etc.), whereas the stratum interest (war veterans' groups, labor unions, parent-teacher groups, nationality, professional, political, and business associations, etc.) seems more important in the associational behavior of men of low economic status.

Since suburbia is one of the most rapidly changing parts of the American social scene, it is well to inquire into formal group participation there. One study by Alvin H. Scaff concerns the commuter and participation in Claremont, California (21). His findings are worth checking with the suburbs in other parts of the United States.

1. The suburban town is a community with an increasing commuter population. A significant proportion of the young adult male population commutes to outside jobs. . . .
2. Whatever community interest the commuter expresses is likely to be divided between his place of residence and his place of work. This often complicates the task of the Community Chest and other agencies dependent upon private, volunteer, local support.

3. Usually the commuter participates very little in community affairs. Thus, the organizations of the community are largely left in the hands of elderly retired people or women.

4. The presence of a large group of commuters does help to balance the age groups in the population, but with the additional child population the tax burden for providing adequate schooling and the pressure for park space are increased.

5. Without any conscious effort to be exclusive, the organizations in the community are highly selective of the educated and professional groups. Education and membership in a profession become a badge of acceptance. High participation scores are thus made by these groups; the lowest participation scores, by the poorer educated and the employees in industry. . . . The commuting process has in fact given Claremont a cosmopolitan population without developing at the same time a cosmopolitan pattern of community organization.[5]

Many other studies of participation for rural, small town, and urban communities could be cited to show that numerous aspects of group life are affected by the statuses their members hold in the community. This means that each group is apt to fit in somewhere with reference to other similar groups in the community, and the effectiveness of its operation is raised or lowered in terms of this position and social acceptance. In a sense the community, or certain aspects of it, constitutes the environment of the social group. As such it sets limits to the behavior of the group without necessarily predetermining specifically what this behavior will be. The community, in turn, is affected as a social system by what happens within certain strategically placed groups as well as by the type of interaction occurring among the groups of the community.

REFERENCES AND SUGGESTED READINGS

1. *The American Journal of Sociology*, XLIV (May, 1939). Complete issue on The Individual and the Group.

2. AXELROD, MORRIS. "Urban Structure and Social Participation," *American Sociological Review*, XXI (February, 1956), 13–18.

3. BALES, R. F. *Interaction Process Analysis: A method for the Study of Small Groups*. Reading, Mass.: Addison-Wesley Publishing Company, Inc., 1950.

4. BATES, ALAN P., and CLOYD, JERRY S. "Toward the Development of Operations for Defining Group Norms and Member Roles," *Sociometry*, XIX (March, 1956), 26–39.

5. BELL, WENDELL, and FORCE, MARYANNE T. "Social Structure and Participation in Different Types of Formal Associations," *Social Forces*, XXXIV (May, 1956), 345–50.

6. BLAU, PETER M. "Social Mobility and Interpersonal Relations," *American Sociological Review*, XXI (June, 1956), 290–95.

7. BUSHEE, FREDERICK A. "Social Organizations in a Small City," *American Journal of Sociology*, LI (November, 1945), 217–26.

8. CHAPIN, F. STUART. *Social Participation Scale, 1937*. Minneapolis: University of Minnesota, 1948.

[5] Alvin H. Scaff, "The Effect of Commuting on Participation in Community Organizations," *American Sociological Review*, XVII (April, 1952), 219–20.

9. CLINARD, MARSHALL B. "The Group Approach to Social Reintegration," *American Sociological Review*, XIV (April, 1949), 257–62.
10. DOTSON, FLOYD. "Patterns of Voluntary Associations Among Urban Working-Class Families," *American Sociological Review*, XVI (October, 1951), 687–93.
11. FOSKETT, JOHN M. "Social Structure and Social Participation," *American Sociological Review*, XX (August, 1955), 431–38.
12. HOMANS, GEORGE C. *The Human Group*. New York: Harcourt, Brace & Company, 1950.
13. KOMAROVSKY, MIRRA. "The Voluntary Associations of Urban Dwellers," *American Sociological Review*, XI (December, 1946), 686–98.
14. LEWIN, K. *Resolving Social Conflicts: Selected Papers on Group Dynamics*. New York: Harper & Brothers, 1948.
15. MANN, PETER H. "The Concept of Neighborliness," *American Journal of Sociology*, LX (September, 1954), 163–68.
16. MAYO, SELZ C., and MARSH, C. PAUL. "Social Participation in the Rural Community," *The American Journal of Sociology*, LVII (November, 1951), 243–47.
17. MERTON, ROBERT K. *Social Theory and Social Structure*. Chicago: Free Press, 1949. See Chapter 1.
18. MORENO, J. L. *Who Shall Survive?* Rev. ed.; Beacon, New York: Beacon House, Inc., 1953.
19. POWELL, REED M. "Sociometric Analysis of Informal Groups—Their Structure and Function in Two Contrasting Communities," *Sociometry*, XV (August–November, 1952), 367–99.
20. RYAN, BRYCE. "Primary and Secondary Contacts in a Ceylonese Peasant Community," *Rural Sociology*, XVII (December, 1952), 311–21.
21. SCAFF, ALVIN H. "The Effect of Commuting on Participation in Community Organizations," *American Sociological Review*, XVII (April, 1952), 215–20.
22. SMITH, JOEL; FORM, WILLIAM H.; and STONE, GREGORY P. "Local Intimacy in a Middle-Sized City," *The American Journal of Sociology*, LX (November, 1954).
23. STRODTBECK, FRED L., and HARE, A. PAUL. "Bibliography of Small Group Research (from 1900 through 1953)," *Sociometry*, XVII (May, 1954), 107–78.
24. WARNER, W. LLOYD, and LUNT, PAUL S. *The Social Life of a Modern Community*. New Haven: Yale University Press, 1941.

Chapter 8

THE COMMUNITY AS AN ARENA OF INTERACTION

The central theme of this book is that a community, like a group, is essentially a system of social interaction. But many facts of community life are related to this interaction. To name some of these is to review briefly the earlier chapters.

The community as a place is a setting for interaction; it is the locale. An analysis of ninety-four definitions of the community showed wide variation about many points; but, with the exception of the purely ecological definitions, there was unanimous agreement that the concept of community was to be found within the broader concept of interaction, which occurred in an *area* of common ties (6).

As defined here, a community—this system of interaction—cannot involve just men or just women, just children or just adults. It must consist of people representing all of the age groups, the younger being prepared to take over the work of the older people. It differs from population aggregates which are sometimes called communities (such as monasteries or army camps), by recruiting members through the biological process of birth. In other words, the *actors* in community interaction are of all ages, of both sexes, and frequently of different racial or ethnic backgrounds.

Much community interaction centers about jobs and services, since these are the important means of subsistence in our society. Unless the locality is able to satisfy most of the daily needs of most of its members, it fails to qualify as a community; that is, it must have more than just one or two services such as one finds in a general crossroads store: it must consist of a nucleus which can take care of health needs, educational requirements, and a wide array of economic services which become increasingly more highly specialized.

The communication network is itself a system of social relationships through which the mechanical media are operated and through which much information, news, and gossip are spread by means of informal contacts, many of which are regularly structured. For example, a man may stop to buy a paper at the same place every day and exchange a few words with the newsboy. "Have you heard," the newsboy asks, "that there is a big fire over on the other side of town?" And the buyer of the paper may reciprocate by reporting that the stock market fell some yesterday and is expected to dip even lower today.

The dominant traditions and value orientations have much to do with the kind of interaction that goes on in the community. Whether one likes it or not, the "dead hand of the past" is present in every community and is an important influence. This is seen in the fact that a certain value orientation will stress one kind of interaction, such as competition, while in another community the stress is upon cooperation.

The study of social layers, too, shows that certain accepted roles are connected with those who hold certain statuses. It is quite correct to speak of "social worlds" within a community, and these worlds are apt to be identified with the stratification which exists and with the occupational complexes within these strata.

Finally, as the previous chapter has shown, groups are the chief units of interaction within the community. One cannot understand such interaction without some knowledge of the units in existence and of how these are related to each other in terms of previous performance.

All of the discussion thus far has therefore paved the way for the view of the sociological community as an arena of interaction.

THE NATURE OF INTERACTION

The view of the community as an arena of interaction may seem at first an oblique approach to the daily activities one observes in a home town. "Everybody knows" that the county school board does not get along well with the city school board; that the Lions and Kiwanis clubs will always cooperate when there is some worthy community project under way; that there is apt to be trouble at the small steel mill every three years or so when the national labor union representing the workers negotiates a new contract with the management of the big steel companies; that the Country Club excludes certain ethnic elements of the population and consequently this minority group has organized a country club of its own; that certain businessmen are looked down upon by other businessmen for what the latter consider "shady practices" in selling cars or real estate. Also, the community has been disturbed over juvenile delinquency since a gang of boys from a good residential area was caught stealing crates of candy bars from a railroad car. Item after item could be listed to illustrate the kinds of interpersonal relationships found in a community. In order to deal analytically with these one can use the concept of interaction—the observable and meaningful behavior of groups and individuals with each other.

In the case of interaction a single definition does not really convey all that is involved (19). Therefore, it is helpful to tie in what has already been said with other concepts such as communication, process, function, and dynamics.

Interaction and Communication. These two words are really interchangeable if communication is given the second meaning used in Chapter 4: the contact of mind with mind, the interchange of meaningful symbols between two or more people. Anyone who watches the spy stories on television or at the movies realizes that the major problem in intelligence work is that of communicating, of interacting with some other agent, without being caught. The reason for this difficulty is the readiness with which a third party can observe the various levels of communication, whether a nod of the head, sign language, an exchange of messages, or clandestine or open conversations.

Anyone studying community behavior soon learns that many group and community differences arise because of the failure of those involved to communicate effectively. Proposals are often presented in such vague, ambiguous language that one person will make one interpretation while a second and third person will reach very different interpretations. Some people in the community may be considered "haughty" or "uncooperative" because this is the impression they communicate to others, whereas they may really not think of themselves in those terms and would do much to change the impression if they understood the nature of what they were communicating. If meaningful symbols lie at the bottom of true communication (and therefore smooth interaction), then it is necessary for any person or group to be sure that others understand the meanings they attach to these symbols. This means more than that others are able to repeat the words used by the first party; the others must know the connotation given to those words. For example, groups which come together in the interest of more efficient government may find eventually that they *mean* different things when they speak of "efficient government." The League of Women Voters may stress orderly election procedures, a system of civil service, and a full debate of campaign issues by rival candidates in a public meeting. A businessman's group may think of efficient government as the one which costs the least, whereas a group of social workers may point out that in order to save money (in terms of the costs of human problems) governmental agencies may have to spend money (in terms of preventive programs) and that the test of good government is how the money is used in the public interest once it is collected. Political scientists may think of good government in some of the terms mentioned above but may also be interested in the exercise of constitutional powers by the different agencies of government. Therefore, the term "efficient government," unless it is spelled out in greater detail, is not an effective symbol of communication. It is apparently meaningful to most people, but the meanings attached to it will vary (8, 24).

Interaction and Process. A deeper inquiry into the nature of interaction makes one interested in how people arrive at the meanings they attach to different symbols. Although this process of socialization will be discussed more fully in Chapter 10, it is important to stress here that people who interact bring to this association certain expectations, a certain conditioning which greatly influences what they do. This was borne out in the description of Mr. Smith and the status-role bundle in the last chapter. He had been taught that certain behavior patterns were proper when he was a father, and others proper when he was a shoe salesman. These behavior patterns were social roles which were governed by the specific norms of the group in which he was participating and by the more general norms of the community of which he was a part. The totality of all this role-playing in the community is the same as the totality of all the social interaction of the community. The social roles are thus the active aspect of the social relationship, with statuses being the static aspect.

Although the term "social process" is not used as much by sociologists today as formerly, it still conveys some helpful ideas in relation to social interaction. A process carries with it the idea of flow or continuity, a sequence of occurrences. A given community is understandable only if one is aware of these continuities of behavior (25). Process is therefore useful in that it helps a person to think beyond the identifiable, observable acts of hundreds or even thousands of people and gives a term to use in describing what seems to be the net sum of these individual acts when viewed in some specified framework. To use simple illustrations, suppose that Guy Shaver went to school and gave the teacher a black eye for chastising his fourteen-year-old son; suppose that Mrs. O'Leary threw some clothespins over the back fence at Mrs. Patrono as a result of an argument;

or suppose it is customary in that same community for a drinking party to end in a brawl, whether the party be held in a back street saloon or in one of the finer houses on Main Street. In comparing such a community, where hand-to-hand violence is fairly common, with another community, where such situations almost never occur, one is in need of a descriptive term. In the former community, conflict may prove to be a dominant process which characterizes much of the interaction. Thus the totality of the roles where violence seems called for and is expected—that is, conflict—may be relatively higher in one community than in another.

Park and Burgess pointed out in one of the first standard sociology textbooks that social processes, such as have just been described, must be seen in conjunction with historical, economic, and other processes at work within the area covered by any community (15). To conclude, then, social process is made up of social interaction, but it refers to selected types of interaction, a selected series of occurrences, which are characteristic of the community. But no matter how ambitious the analysis of processes may be, one should always be able to relate a process step by step back to the role-playing of actual human beings in real life situations.

Interaction and Function. At first glance, it might seem that interaction and function are much the same thing. It is common to say that a thing functions when it "works" and certainly interaction, as used here, would describe the "working together" of individuals and groups within a community. For purposes of clarity, however, function has been given a different meaning in scientific writing from that of simply working. It more and more has come to mean the contribution that a unit, such as a social group, makes to the total environment, such as a community, of which it is a part. This means that in describing the community function of a particular group such as the Chamber of Commerce one does not ask merely what are the purposes of the Chamber as drawn up in its charter and as believed in by its members; instead, one assumes that the Chamber has connections with many other groups and groupings of the community and that one can best describe the actual functioning of the Chamber, from the community viewpoint at least, by tracing these social relationships between it and other groups. If, for example, the City Council will not decide on a problem of physical planning and zoning until it knows how the members of the Chamber of Commerce feel, then the connection between the Council and the Chamber has functional significance; if local labor leaders consider the activities of the Chamber somewhat antagonistic to their interests and tend to oppose any course of action proposed by the Chamber, then again the Chamber has functional significance in that it serves as a focus of cooperation among labor leaders and as a target for them in supporting what they consider the self-interest of their union membership. To continue the description would mean to ask about the interaction between the Chamber of Commerce and the Community Chest, the Farm Bureau, the Woman's Garden Club, the Boards of Education, to mention but a few possibilities. When one has traced all of the significant ramifications of the Chamber of Commerce's interaction with all other possible groups, then one has described the function of that particular organization.

Thus function is more than interaction in a general sense; it is rather an analysis of interaction between some part of the community structure and other parts. This is why it is almost impossible to talk clearly of function without thinking of structure, or the social organization through which functions are traced. "Social structure," a term not used heretofore in this text, consists of all the social relationships in a community viewed from the status standpoint. Those occupying at a given time the statuses of husband and father, wife and mother, daughter and sister, son and brother, are bound together structurally in a family unit; this unit becomes associated with other family units, and quite unconsciously on the part of the various members of the different families, these family units become the family aspect of the total structure. Just as in the case of the Chamber of Commerce, one can trace the function of the family as an important subsystem by showing how the family units interact with economic, political, religious, educational, or recreational units.

Robert K. Merton has correctly pointed out that many functions are *manifest* or evident (13). People know that the exclusive Nineteenth Century Club for many years has promoted the baby milk fund and considers this one of its most important community contributions during the year. This would be a manifest function to which members and nonmembers would readily agree. But the same group may serve a *latent* or hidden function which a few perceptive individuals may discern but which they are not apt to talk about or, at any rate, get much agreement about. Membership in the Nineteenth Century Club may serve the latent function of showing a small upper class that a woman has "arrived" socially and can therefore be invited to exclusive functions by the "best families" and that her daughter can be included among the list of debutantes. The members of this group when pressed to name the function of their club would stress the baby milk fund and the importance to them personally of the informative club meetings. Very few, if any, would list as a chief function this social selectivity which is decidedly "functional" for those who are trying to climb from the upper middle class to the upper class.

Through this and the other illustrations given, it should be clear that function can only be interpreted by watching the social interaction, but it goes a step beyond merely listing what happened in terms of activity or communication of symbols. The functional description must include the relevancy of this activity and communication to the community (or social unit) as a whole, taking account of both the manifest and latent aspects.

Interaction and Dynamics. When one speaks of a dynamic person one usually thinks of someone who gets things done, who radiates vitality, and who is definitely action-oriented. "Social dynamics," like many terms in the social sciences, has a connection with this popular meaning but requires a more precise definition. Pitirim A. Sorokin, who has done the most exhaustive study of sociocultural dynamics, would view the dynamics of a community or a society as dealing with that which is moving, changing (18). He also seeks to show that throughout this flux there are certain uniformities of change which can be discerned and analyzed.

This means that the concept of dynamics adds the element of *change* to interaction, which itself usually has a neutral tone. It is obvious that no two people and no two groups which interact are ever the same after the interaction; they are either on friendlier or unfriendlier terms as a result. Furthermore, without interaction change could not occur. Thus social dynamics would look at the community as a changing system and try to work out the laws governing the change within it. The concept of dynamics needs to be added to that of structure-function to give a complete account of a social system. Underlying it all is the basic fact of continuing interaction among the units of the community.

By comparing and even equating interaction with communication and by contrasting it with process, function, and dynamics one gets a clearer picture of the nature of interaction. But another purpose has been served as well—that of preparing for later analyses where these terms will be put to much fuller use and emerge as indispensable concepts in the understanding of community life.

Types of Interaction

Sociologists have worked out six terms to describe some of the chief types of interaction: "conflict," "accommodation," "assimilation," "competition," "cooperation," and "amalgamation." These are useful when characterizing *a single situation,* such as the interaction between the Women's Christian Temperance Union and the local bartenders' union, which in this case would probably illustrate conflict. The same six terms can be employed to describe a *series of occurrences* or the flowing of interaction through time, in which case one would call them social processes. They would still be types of interaction but would designate many single situations in sequence. A social relationship between two groups may move from competition into conflict, then into accommodation, and perhaps finally into cooperation. The description of what happened from one point of time to another is a description of the social process.

These terms, to be explained presently, are also useful when drawing up the social characteristics of a community. These characteristics refer to the over-all summation of social interaction discussed in the section on interaction and process. A community will tend to highlight one process more than others, with the result that the traditions of conflict or cooperation have much to do with the way interacting individuals and groups define the situation and either belligerently or peaceably try to work their way out of a problem. The two communities of Rimrock and Homestead, whose value orientations were compared, are good illustrations of variations between communities.

Although discussion here is limited to these six types of interaction, it should be remembered that there are many other social processes which are useful in describing what occurs in community life. For instance, ecological processes were mentioned in the treatment of the community as a place; in the next chapter attention will be paid to industrialization and urbanization and their connection with social change, and later on socialization and social control will be viewed as important motivational processes. All of these processes consist of human interaction, and each views some particular aspect of this interaction sequentially. The six processes being discussed here view interaction from the standpoint of goals of the participating units and the degree to which these units either help or hinder the other in reaching these goals.

Many different sociologists have written on these six processes, and each tends to follow some individualistic treatment. The most complete analysis of the social processes in the community setting has been done by Jessie Bernard, who treats organization, conflict, and competition as the basic concepts (2). She then works out on a continuum the stages through which conflict passes from elimination to assimilation and through which competition passes from the cut-throat stage to monopoly. She pays little attention to cooperation as a process.

On the other hand, Kimball Young, in his introductory sociology text (26), thinks of opposition and cooperation as the two basic processes: Opposition "may be defined as a struggle *against* another or others for a good, goal, or value; cooperation is joint striving with another or others for a good, goal, or value." He then divides opposition into competition and conflict, defining competition as a less violent form of opposition "in which two or more persons or groups struggle for some end or goal but in the course of which attention is focused chiefly on reward rather than on the competitor."[1] In conflict the person or group thwarts, injures, or destroys the opponent in order to secure the wanted goal or reward. Young looks upon the three processes—accommodation, assimilation, and amalgamation—as being derived from the others previously mentioned. (In this discussion he also takes up differentiation and stratification which were treated earlier in this text in chapters on the people and on the social layers.)

Accommodation as a process, according to Young, has to do "with the conscious efforts of men to develop such working arrangements among themselves as will temporarily suspend conflict and to make their relations more tolerable and less wasteful of energy." Assimilation means "the common blending and sharing of folkways, mores, laws, and ways of life generally of two or more groups or societies or peoples that formerly had distinctive patterns."[2] He treats amalgamation, particularly the biological type, as the only way to complete assimilation. However, other writers frequently think of amalgamation in the nonbiological sense of a business merger, for instance, where each of the interacting firms loses its original identity and becomes a part of a new firm which carries on independently. Churches, college organizations, and welfare agencies, for example, can amalgamate if some new group comes into being to take the place of two or more which formerly existed as separate units.

With this introduction to the types of interaction, each type will now be illustrated with reference to a community setting.

CONFLICT IN THE COMMUNITY

Conflict in American communities today can take a variety of forms and can arise over a number of issues. Also, what will disturb

---

[1] Kimball Young, *Sociology: A Study of Society and Culture* (2d ed.: New York: American Book Company, 1949), 64.

[2] *Ibid.*, p. 75.

one community will have almost no repercussions in another community thirty miles away. Some of the broad conflict areas deserve consideration even though none of these may be a particular problem at a given time in one's home town. These include such areas as industrial conflict, religious tensions, race conflict, oldtimer-newcomer conflict, and conflict between "liberals" and "conservatives" over political ideologies and methods of controlling subversives.

Industrial Conflict. In an excellent summary statement on industrial conflict and its mediation Clark Kerr describes, among other points, the nature of industrial conflict, responses to conflict, and tactical and strategical mediation (10; see also 1, 23). A review of some of his main points should prove helpful to anyone who wishes to understand the labor disputes which occur in a rapidly industrializing society.

In treating the nature of industrial conflict Kerr points out that it is inevitable for four reasons:

1. The desires of the parties are more or less unlimited, while the means of satisfaction are limited. Wages can never be as high as workers desire or profits or salaries as high as owners or managers might wish. . . .
2. Someone manages and someone is managed, and this is an eternal opposition of interest, which may be made bearable but can never be eliminated in a complex, industrial society. . . .
3. Industrial societies are dynamic. Even if a certain distribution of income and power could be devised which, in a given situation, was not subject to controversy (though this seems unlikely), the situation itself would change—because of new regulations by the state, changed expenditure patterns of consumers. . . .
4. If management and labor are to retain their institutional identities, they must disagree and must act on the disagreement. Conflict is essential to survival. The union which is in constant and complete agreement with management has ceased to be a union. . . .[3]

Furthermore, some aggressive conflict is even acceptable; it is not wholly evil. According to Kerr, there are three positive gains which may outweigh the injuries inflicted:

1. Out of aggressive industrial conflict or its latent possibility comes the resolution of many disputes . . . the parties find the bases for continued association and acceptance of each other . . .
2. Conflict, and particularly open conflict, reduces tensions. In modern industrial society the sources of unrest and hostility are enormous. The strike provides an outlet for them when they are so severe as to require forceful expression. . . . The chance to rebel against the other party on occasion establishes the independence of the group and of the individual, makes acceptance of the surrounding social system easier, and, therefore, can make a net addition to satisfaction and production . . .

[3] Clark Kerr, "Industrial Conflict and Its Mediation," *American Journal of Sociology,* LX (November, 1954), 231. Copyright, 1954, by the University of Chicago.

3. Out of the conflict of management and union . . . the worker is better served. As the two parties compete for his loyalty, his interests are advanced.[4]

While not advocating violence for violence's sake, Kerr does argue that limited antagonism serves a social purpose. However, he points out that conflict can be destructive as well as constructive and thus needs to be guided if the social fabric is to be protected and serious injury to individuals and groups avoided.

Responses to conflict may be of three broad alternatives: a party "may withdraw; it may seek to destroy or dominate the other party; or it may accept the adversary more or less permanently, adjust itself to the fact of conflict, and adapt itself to live with it."[5] In labor-management conflict only the third alternative is the realistic response and will be discussed under accommodation, where mediation is to be treated.

Of particular interest is what Kerr calls strategical mediation, which concerns itself with the manipulation of social situations and thus with factors quite external to the parties themselves. He writes:

From one point of view, society is a huge mediation mechanism, a means of settling disagreements between rival claimants—tax-payers and recipients of benefits, buyers and sellers, proponents of opposing political ideologies—so that people may live together in some state of mutual tolerance. Some societies mediate their disagreements, through their markets, their courts, their political processes, more effectively than do others. Society in the large is the mediation machinery for industrial as well as other forms of conflict.[6]

Kerr then lists six conditions which are most favorable to the nonviolent industrial conflict. These have much importance for any community where industrial plants operate:

1. Integration of workers and employers into society. To the extent that workers and employers consider themselves primarily citizens with roughly equal status, privileges, and opportunities, the sting is taken out of their relationship. The greater the social mobility, the more mixed in membership the various social associations, the more heterogeneous the community's occupational composition, the more accepted the institutions of workers and the greater their participation in general community life, the more secure the worker in his job and the higher his skill—the less violent will be the industrial conflict in the long run.

2. Stability of the society. The incidence of strikes is directly related to major changes in the operation of the society—particularly to the business cycle and to wars. . . . The parties normally can adjust more peacefully to gradual than to precipitous change.

3. Ideological compatibility. . . . Where people believe in brotherly love or the equality of man, for example, their disagreements will be fewer, less sharp,

[4] Ibid., pp. 232–33.
[5] Ibid., p. 235.
[6] Ibid., p. 243.

and more amenable to easy compromise. Where, however, they believe in the inevitable opposition of classes, in the rapacity of other men, then violent industrial conflict is more likely. . . .

4. Secure and responsive relationship of leaders to members. For the minimization of violent industrial conflict, it is desirable that leaders be (a) relatively secure in their position and (b) responsive to their constituencies . . .

5. The dispersion of grievance. The mass grievance, one which is held by many people in the same place at the same time against the same antagonist, grows and feeds on itself. Society can more readily accommodate and adjust the small grievance. . . . If the grievance is directed against several individuals and groups—the merchant, the landlord, the state, for example—rather than against an employer who provides housing, retail facilities, and law enforcement—it can have additional outlets . . .

6. Structuring the game . . . Rules which reduce the risks of the parties and limit the means they may employ, without unduly stifling the conflict, can make a substantial contribution to non-violent resolution of controversy or can mitigate the destructive consequences of violent conflict. [The employer, for example, may forego the use of strikebreakers, the discharge of strikers, or the blacklist. The union may forego sabotage, the boycott of products, or violence against officials of the company.][7]

These considerations show that community traits have much to do with the degree of violence accompanying a conflict situation; where strikes are prolonged and destructive, the people of the community may have to accept part of the blame along with the management and the strikers.

Religious Conflict. It is often assumed that religious conflict is confined to those churches of widely divergent views such as the Roman Catholic and Protestant. Undoubtedly, the relationships between these two large bodies have been undergoing considerable change with increased tension as a result. An analysis by John J. Kane of the editorial material in the *Christian Century,* a vigorous Protestant journal, and *America,* a Roman Catholic publication of the Society of Jesus, shows heightened verbal attacks on each other within recent years (9).

The traditional religious conflict in America, however, has not been that between Catholics and Protestants as much as schismatic conflict within a particular denomination, resulting in divisions or splintering off by those wishing to establish a new religious organization of their own. The story of such a split in one South Carolina community has been told by Gus Turbeville (21). It involves a Methodist church whose members refused to endorse the unification agreement of 1939 in which the Methodist Episcopal Church, South, joined with the Methodist Episcopal Church and the Methodist Protestant Church to form the "Methodist Church." This case illus-

[7] *Ibid.,* pp. 243–45.

trates the fact that often what may seem to be religious conflict really has other than religious roots and that what is frequently called heresy is not the cause for a schism but an excuse for it.

The Turbeville community had in 1945 a population of 653, of whom 150 were Negroes. The inhabitants have, for the most part, been traditionally Methodists, and for a living depend largely upon crops of tobacco and cotton . . .[8]

Some families have been more prominent than others. The Summerville family had been instrumental in getting a church, school, and post office for the community. As other families, chiefly the Browns, Newberrys, and Bettors, began to come into the community, some of them began to resent the dominant role being played by the Summervilles. . . . Neither side showed much inclination to cooperate with the other and, as a result, on almost any debatable issue that would arise, the Summervilles and their followers could be found on one side, and the Browns, Newberrys, and Bettors on the other.[9]

When the question of unification was brought up in Turbeville at the Pine Grove Church, the Summervilles seemed to think that it was a forward step in the advancement of Methodism. The Browns and their coteries could do nothing else but come out vociferously against it and advanced every possible type of argument to support their stand. They gained a larger following than did the Summervilles. Then matters began to happen in dramatic fashion.

On November 8, 1938, when it was time to appoint a new pastor, the stewards wrote to the bishop asking that the Conference not send them a preacher, since they were not a part of the newly formed "Methodist Church." This letter was ignored and a Mr. Williams was sent about the first of December.

The "antis" (the Brown group) began holding their services at a different time from those of the regularly scheduled services. They had to take any kind of preacher they could find.

On April 13, 1939, the "antis" posted notices, signed by the church stewards, calling for a conference on April 23. This notice was posted after the "antis" had requested the minister to call such a conference but he had refused.

At the April 23 meeting the three dissident trustees, who formed a majority out of the five, deeded the Pine Grove Church property to three of its own members for the sum of $5.00 with the provision that the latter were to hold the property in trust for the benefit of the members of the Pine Grove Methodist Episcopal Church, South.

[8] Gus Turbeville, "Religious Schism in the Methodist Church: A Sociological Analysis of the Pine Grove Case," *Rural Sociology*, XIV (March, 1949), 32.

[9] *Ibid.*, p. 32.

The "antis" then wrote a letter to the preacher forbidding him to use or trespass on this church property.

By the next Sunday the bishop who had been consulted helped the district superintendent and the minister get in touch with a lawyer who was able to have an injunction drawn up forbidding the dissident group from interfering in any way with the regularly scheduled service of the Methodist Church. The injunction did not forbid them from using the church at the other hours.

This was the beginning of a long legal battle with the Methodist Church on one side and the self-styled Southern Methodists on the other. Since this was something of a test case of the unification arrangement, the former body had six lawyers and the Southern Methodists had two lawyers. The Methodist Church finally won on all points before the Circuit Court as well as before the State Supreme Court and the United States Circuit Court of Appeals.

This so-called religious conflict has been accompanied by considerable social upheaval in the community. Both parties to the controversy have spread malicious gossip about the other; family relationships have been strained due to differences within the family over supporting the Summervilles or the "antis"; no social progress has been possible in the community, and even such matters as school board elections have been affected. An indication of the seriousness of the cleavage is shown by the fact that the "antis" have constructed a $25,000 church as well as a brick parsonage. Thus this small community of about five hundred white people is well churched but not prone to practice some of the cardinal Christian principles enunciated in the pulpits on Sunday morning. The conflict remains unresolved.

These discussions of two types of conflict, industrial and religious, are sufficient to illustrate the positive aspects and the negative aspects. They show how rational behavior in a conflict situation is subordinated to the desire to get even with or perhaps destroy the antagonist; they also show that conflict between any two groups inevitably has repercussions in the community (3).

ACCOMMODATION IN THE COMMUNITY

Accommodation is the process used for easing conflict so that people who have been wasting their energies fighting each other can get busy doing something else. It is rational in that men consciously begin to seek a way out of an impasse; it usually means that each party to the conflict has to yield some ground in order to develop working arrangements again. When some conflict besets a community, the first step to be taken by those interested in ending that conflict is to move it into accommodative channels. What are these? How is accommodation brought about?

Accommodation in Industry. The best-known step toward accommodation in an industrial dispute is mediation. As Kerr points out, this is guidance by a third party (10). Mediation "thus stands midway between conciliation, that is, adjustment of a dispute by the parties themselves, and arbitration, that is, decision by a third party."[10] The mediator, unlike the arbitrator, does not make the decision but tries to get the rival parties to work out an agreement among themselves. The potential contributions of the mediator are the following:

1. Reduction of irrationality. The mediator can bring the parties toward a more rational mood by giving the individuals involved an opportunity to vent their feelings to him, by keeping personal recriminations out of joint discussions, and by drawing the attention of the parties to the objective issues in dispute and to the consequences of aggressive conflict.

2. Removal of non-rationality. The mediator can aid the parties in reaching a full appreciation of reality by clarifying the intentions of the parties toward each other, the issues in controversy, and the pertinent facts and by leading each party to accurate calculations of the cost of aggressive conflict. . . .

3. Exploration of solutions. Not only can a skilled mediator help the parties explore solutions which have occurred to them independently, but he can create new solutions around which positions have not yet become fixed. . . .

4. Assistance in the graceful retreat. All, or almost all, collective bargaining involves some retreat by both parties from their original positions.

5. Raising the cost of conflict. A mediator may also raise the cost of conflict to one or both parties as an inducement to settle by bringing or threatening to bring public wrath down on their heads, etc. . . . These tactics are not normally pursued and are usually reserved for only the most crucial cases of great public concern.[11]

But whether the mediator, the conciliator, or the arbitrator is instrumental in bringing an end to the conflict for the time being, the possibility of future conflict still remains. Accommodation has, however, eased the tension and made possible a *modus vivendi,* a live-and-let-live arrangement (5).

Accommodation in Race Relations. Harry Walker has drawn up three stages in the development of the structure of race relations in the biracial communities of America (22). He characterizes these stages as follows: (1) the stage following the Civil War, in which personal contacts between whites and Negroes constituted the mechanism of racial understanding and adjustment; (2) a second stage, in

[10] Kerr, *op. cit.,* p. 236.
[11] *Ibid.,* pp. 236–39.

which, as a result of the evolution of a Negro social world based upon the growth of segregated Negro communities, Negro-white relationships tended to become more formalized, and in which the Negro community was represented by a type of leadership which performed a liaison function with leaders of the white community; and (3) the third stage, in which integration, in the sense of a more or less equal participation of Negroes with whites in community activities, is taking place. He points out that each community with a Negro minority tends to approximate one of these three stages.

Many of the rural and some of the urban communities of the South are characterized by the first stage where the accommodation has been worked out on the basis of personal relationships existing between the members of the two groups. Negroes who have grown up in the traditional plantation setting expect the whites for whom they work to help them in time of distress, protect them, gain favors for them, and thereby provide them with a sense of security. This friendliness between the two races is governed by "the etiquette of race relations" (4), and both whites and Negroes are supposed to abide by this etiquette or suffer consequences. The Negroes in such communities have not felt the need for being represented as a group, since each Negro family had its own personal relationships with white people.

As the towns and cities of the South grew, the Negroes became more separated from the whites and developed their own Negro institutions and associations. They began to move in a Negro world to a much greater degree, and many had relatively few contacts with whites. Thus they could not find security in the personal relationships with white people that an earlier generation of Negroes had enjoyed; the basis for racial adjustment which existed in these relationships was destroyed. As urbanization increased, even the Negroes who worked as domestic servants in white homes did not form intimate bonds with their employers but rather acquired new values and new conceptions of themselves in the Negro world. A Negro class structure came into existence and had great significance for the Negro because he came to feel that he had a chance to improve his status.

Many Negroes grow restive in the subordinate position given their race. The chief means of accommodation, however, is through the Negro leaders who become the spokesmen for their people and who themselves maintain fairly close contact with white people. In many communities these Negro leaders have been handpicked by the white people, and in order to maintain their position, they caution their Negro followers against any radical steps. At the same time, the Negro leadership in other communities has risen from among the Negroes themselves and assumes a more militant tone. These leaders are the product of a Negro world which is increasingly isolated from the white world and characterized by growing race consciousness and an increasing racial solidarity. These leaders, too, have to learn to accommodate, though perhaps not so willingly as the more conservative, older type of Negro leader. In any event, the fate of the relationships between the whites and Negroes of the community in this second stage is in the hands of the leaders of both races, who, though conflict situations arise, try to work out a means of getting along together.

The third stage—that of integration of Negroes in community activities—is a continuation of the accommodation process, since the integration concerns certain activities which cut across racial lines (7). The southern community which Walker studied had accommodated to the point that Negroes participated with whites in the Community Chest and in the planning of a new city park and recreational center for the Negroes. There was some integration in business, in education, and in health but most of all in political life, since Negroes began to vote and seek informal conferences with white candidates, participate in the local party meetings held by whites, and, more recently, began to be represented on the local Democratic committee. In this third stage there has been a tendency for the militant Negro leaders to rely upon political power to advance the interests of their race.

In the discussion of caste in Chapter 6 the emphasis was upon structure, or the relative position of whites and Negroes and even classes within the Negro caste. The presentation by Walker emphasizes the dynamic aspect—that of interaction—and reminds the student of the community that the relationships between the two races are constantly undergoing change. The change may not always move smoothly from one stage to the next—it may even seem to reverse the trend—but the process of accommodation is usually at work to resolve what could be tragic conflict if people of both races were not willing to search together for a mutually satisfying adjustment to day-by-day situations as they arise.

Assimilation Within the Community

Newcomers to the Community. When the people of an Alabama community were asked what they did with newcomers whom they did not like, one of the men replied, "Oh, we simply freeze them out." Further study of that community showed that that was really what happened. Even some residents who had married into the old, established families still were reminded that they were newcomers —though acceptable newcomers—after twenty years of residence. This behavior is not typical of all Alabama communities but does express the situation one finds when the most influential people are self-satisfied and opposed to change.

The study of a Kentucky community showed that its people, quite unconsciously on their part, had arrived at a way of assisting in the assimilation process. When any new professional man or the manager of one of the local businesses moved to town, he would be asked to join one of the civic clubs within the first year and would be given an important committee assignment. Shortly thereafter he was made an officer if he measured up and was thus given a chance to demonstrate to the community what capabilities he had. When this demonstration was added to the other qualities he and his family displayed, the people of the community had a good idea of how that newcomer fitted in.

Many cities use "welcome wagons" and other devices to make the new residents feel at home, but these usually acquaint the new-comer with businesses more than with possible informal associates. In many communities church groups are among the most active agents of assimilation, since rival denominational groups go to call on Protestants in an effort to gain them as members. Similarly, Catholics find a ready welcome in their own church-related organizations, as do minorities with other religious orientations.

Assimilation into a community, however, is different in some ways from assimilation into a group. A group is usually able to exercise some choice in the selection of its new members; it has carefully defined rules of attendance, paying dues, and other duties; and it has a self-identity that distinguishes it from other associations in the community. A community, however, has little direct control over those who settle there and cannot bring direct means to bear in the name of the community to teach the new people the values and role expectations of the older residents. Pressure must be indirect. Through various groups where such pressure is recognized and heeded, assimilation occurs; where it is ignored, the new elements remain indigestible lumps in the body politic.

Assimilation of the Foreign-born. Assimilation varies, too, with the degree to which newcomers become accustomed to the American way of doing things and, in many communities, to the regional way of doing things. Neighboring may be expected and encouraged in a western community, but the same act of "trying to be friendly" might be considered nosiness or forwardness in a New England community where individualism is valued and where neighborliness is reserved for time of real need. One problem, however, which almost all American communities have had to face is that of welcoming or finding a place for the foreign-born who come to establish homes in the New World.

People who live abroad constantly wonder at the ease with which America can take people from all parts of the world and within a generation or so make them completely loyal Americans who have only a secondary loyalty to the nationality group of their origin. It is somewhat baffling and yet interesting to try to explain to Greek villagers, living in houses perched on a mountainside, how native sons of that community have been turned so quickly into Americans. To those left behind in Greece, one is born Greek and cannot think of being anything else but Greek. If he goes to settle in Egypt, he remains Greek and does not become Egyptian in culture or identification; if he goes to settle in France, he still remains Greek. "How," the Greek peasants ask, "do you make people into Americans so quickly?"

In such a discussion it would have been most helpful to have had at hand the explanation presented by Mary Bosworth Treudley, who studied the assimilation of the Greeks in Boston (20). She thinks American communities have been so successful in absorbing immigrants because

... the Americanization process has been characterized by a balance between authoritarian structures to which the newly arrived immigrant and his children must adjust and autonomous structures which he creates and can modify to suit his needs and taste. Due largely to the externally imposed norms and behavioral patterns of coercive organizations and those developed by the ethnic group through its own voluntary associations, the United States has been uniquely successful in bringing about the changes in personality desired by the larger society, at a maximum rate of speed, with an economy of effort on the part of the dominant group, and at a relatively low cost in suffering to those undergoing "conversion."[12]

Professor Treudley then analyzes for various community subsystems the way the new arrivals from the rural villages of Greece had to conform to American work habits and accounting practices for the payment of income taxes. Their children were compelled by law to attend school, which brought about a difference between the older and younger generation. At the same time, these new Americans could have their own Greek church, which was relatively inde-

[12] Mary B. Treudley, "Formal Organization and the Americanization Process, with Special Reference to the Greeks of Boston," *American Sociological Review*, XIV (February, 1949), 45.

pendent and managed by each local congregation (or "community," as the Greeks call the formal organization of lay members); they could organize a lodge, and as Treudley points out, "A Greek starts to become an American when he stops frequenting a coffee shop and is initiated into a lodge."[13] These autonomous organizations, which the members can control, cushion the shock of transition. They maintain interaction among Greek-Americans, they make explicit the climbing systems within the Greek community, they help solve the problems which arise in shifting from a European peasant to an urban American, they provide an opportunity for the newcomers to practice American behavior in a congenial ethnic setting, and they help them consider over and over again their relation to Greek and to American culture. ("Shall we dance Greek or American?" is one way the adolescents phrase the basic question of culture conflict.)

Such an analysis shows how a situation which could have turned into a conflict situation over cultural differences becomes eased through accommodation and eventually is resolved through assimilation.

Competition Within the Community

Perhaps the process most consciously stressed in American communities is that of competition. It runs through the warp and woof of American life, receiving encouragement in school with the competition for grades, for membership in honorary societies, and for places on athletic teams. "Grading on the curve" is an expression of competition in education. Not only is there rivalry within the school, but competition between schools is highly accentuated, chiefly in athletics. Such competition builds up an in-group loyalty, but when very intense can affect other educational practices such as scholastic performance, hiring and firing of school officials because of interest expressed or not expressed in successful competition, and even the use of school funds for areas of competition in place of strengthening libraries, laboratories, and other facilities not involved in interschool comparisons.

Competition, furthermore, is looked upon as the process which keeps the free enterprise system operating successfully, although with increasing frequency the government has had to step in as an umpire, to organize agencies to watch over the stock exchanges, the trends toward monopoly, and public utilities. Churches compete for members and even organize their Sunday schools so that pupils com-

[13] *Ibid.*, p. 46.

pete with each other and classes with other classes. Much use is made of competition in youth groups, civic clubs, and women's organizations, both locally and nationally. Many of the rewards held out to those involved in community development are couched in competitive terms, with one community competing against another.

Political competition, especially with a two-party system, is deeply ingrained in the American way of life. Once a man enters politics he must think about re-election and continuing in a position of influence. This means that he must learn "the political game" and understand the nature of political competition. Communities vary in their willingness to support candidates who conduct what are frequently called "vigorous" campaigns by some and "dirty" campaigns by others; they demand different standards of performance from those who have been elected to office. Some communities show great indifference or apathy to political matters until conditions get so bad that the "general public" feels its interests are not properly protected or its sense of fairness has been violated. Then the people of the community rise up "to throw the rascals out," after which they sink into another period of unconcern and indifference.

To write at greater length is simply to describe again what is common knowledge. What is of interest is the difference between the effects of conflict and competition upon the voluntary associations of a community. A study of the formal associations in Minneapolis and St. Paul, Minnesota, was made by Arnold M. Rose (16). He defines conflict (or opposition) in much the same way as it is used in this chapter, stating that group conflict exists if two groups whose primary functions are opposed to each other are recognized by the leaders of both groups. Competition means that there exists within the same community at least two independent groups whose primary functions are the same and that the leaders of at least one of these groups recognize that their goals are the same as those of the other group. In initiating the study Rose set up hypotheses which he wished to test and came out with definite conclusions. He found that groups faced with opposition are more active in pursuit of group goals than are groups faced only with competition; they are more likely to develop a complex structure; they meet more frequently, are more likely to be flexible in activities and techniques, and have a more cohesive relationship among their members. But those facing competition develop these same traits to a greater degree than those groups which lack opposition or competition.

From the community standpoint, one of the most striking evidences of competition is that between organizations for recognition and prestige. Social status is involved. This struggle for social acceptability runs through all types of organizations but can become particularly acute with women's groups. A study which was made to investigate cleavage rather than competition among such organizations nevertheless reveals the results of competition. Mhyra S. Minnis worked out a prestige hierarchy of women's organizations in New Haven, Connecticut (14). A simple listing of the examples she gives will indicate how the ranking is done in one city, although it need not follow that some national organization named will have the same rank in another city:

Rank I. Our Society, the North End Club, the Junior League of New Haven, and the Garden Club of New Haven.

Rank II. The Auxiliary to the Hospital of St. Raphael, the Soroptimist, the Daughters of Patriots, the Daughters of the American Revolution, the Catholic Charity League, the American Association of University Women, and auxiliaries to the Church of the Redeemer, the United Church on the Green, and Temple Mishkan Israel.

Rank III. New Haven Woman's Club, the Council of Catholic Women, the Council of Jewish Women, the League of Women Voters, the Swedish Junior League, and auxiliaries to the American Legion and to the Congregational and Methodist Churches.

Rank IV. The Polish Falcons, Society Regional Marchegiana, and auxiliaries to Disabled War Veterans, to St. Luke's Church, to Howard Avenue Methodist Church (Negro), and to fraternal orders.

Rank V. The Mother's Club of the YWCA, the Salvation Army Home League, the Jr. R. and Jolifee Union, and the Ladies' Aid of the African Zion Church.

Within communities there are frequently borderline cases between conflict and competition. Two rival unions may be trying to organize the same nonunionized plant, each claiming the right of representing the workers with the management. As was pointed out earlier, the types of interaction being described here relate to the goals of the interacting parties. If the struggle between the two unions is merely that of getting the support of the workers of this plant, if both are after the same reward, then the interaction can be termed competition. If, however, this is a case in which the main goal is to try to eliminate as an organization the rival union and the support of workers is merely secondary to that primary aim, then the situation can be defined as conflict. In such a case the National Labor Relations Board will most probably be invited in to conduct an election among the workers to determine their preferences in the matter. This is the method of accommodation.

Cooperation Within the Community

Conflict and acute competition are spectacular; they catch the headlines. Cooperation is much more common and certainly more basic to the operation of the community life (12). Yet, cooperation is difficult to treat concretely, since there are so many ways in which there can be "joint striving with another or others for a good, goal, or value."

For example, there can be an impersonal cooperation, or symbiosis, which has been described earlier. It grows out of the division of labor and specialization of tasks which increase as society grows more complex. Certainly the men who collect the garbage in the early morning before the householder is up are engaged in a cooperative activity, since they render a service for which the householder has paid. Also, the householder has cooperated to the extent of wrapping the garbage in paper, putting it in proper containers, and locating these containers at some spot acceptable to the collectors. To try to describe all such types of cooperation in a community would be almost an endless task; what does become quickly evident is the breakdown in some chain of cooperation because some partner to the interaction does not play the role expected of him.

Another type of cooperation occurs in what might be called mutual aid groups. In early frontier days in America and even today in some rural areas people would come together to help a neighbor rebuild a barn that has burned or to assist a bedridden farmer get his crop in. In many cultures these mutual aid groups are important features of community life (17). In Brazil the word *mutirao* is used to designate a group of workers called upon in an emergency by a neighbor to aid without remuneration in completing rapidly a particular piece of work (11):

> When a farmer needs to make a road, clear brush, plant, cultivate, or harvest speedily but lacks sufficient help to carry out his tasks, he calls on the *mutirao* to come to his assistance. He agrees to reciprocate and pay back this service by himself being ready to work for the others when they call upon him. The day almost always ends in a fiesta which strengthens a moral obligation between the one who sought the cooperation and those who participated.[14]

Usually the day chosen for the *mutirao* is a Saturday or the day before a holiday, which gives everyone a chance to rest on the following day.

[14] J. V. Freitas Marcondes, "Mutirao or Mutual Aid," *Rural Sociology,* XIII (December, 1948), 374.

Similar accounts of mutual aid groups could be cited for every community because they are widespread social phenomena. Each community has its own pattern for these groups to follow with respect to the manner in which the invitations are to be issued, at what time of day people are to gather to work, who is to give the directions, when the workers are to stop to eat and drink and even what types of food and drink are to be served, and how the work contributed is to be repaid by the one who benefits. Some groups are made up of men only, others of women only, and in some communities both men and women participate. Thus there are norms governing this interaction.

It is but a step to move from these traditional, almost spontaneous mutual aid groups to the purposive formation of what are called cooperatives, or associations to further the mutual interests of those joining together. In one sense, the cooperative is primarily an economic union, but in many ways it goes beyond that and becomes a social outlet, a way of class expression for those who have become convinced of the need to stick together. It is of interest to note that the Labor Party in England grew strong and eventually took charge of the government under Clement Attlee not simply through a political organization. The labor movement in Britain consists also of the trade unions as well as a far-flung system of cooperatives in which many of the working class participated. Joseph W. Eaton, who has made a study of cooperative movements in several countries, has this to say:

In the European countries the members participate not merely because it is a means of saving money; they share working-class aspirations and an ideological affinity with working-class movements. American cooperatives, on the other hand, have little ideological support of this kind.[15]

The study of cooperation as a process within the community would take into account the existence of cooperatives as such, but these are only a small part of the over-all cooperative framework which makes community life possible. There may not be a single economic cooperative (such as a Farm Bureau cooperative), and yet the community may be characterized by a high state of cooperation.

This type of cooperation relates to the willingness of representatives of different organizations to join together in common efforts to achieve some community goal which they all agree is important. Frequently, such interaction goes on without the setting up of a specialized organization and is accomplished through frequent meetings of organizational representatives, necessary committees, and

[15] Joseph W. Eaton, "A Conceptual Theory of Co-operation," *American Journal of Sociology*, LIV (September, 1948), 127.

even a community mass meeting. When the project has been achieved, then the organizations which have cooperated may go their separate ways again until some new project demanding joint action is broached by parties interested in getting it launched.

It is an enlightening experience and one which restores confidence in what is termed "human nature" to trace for just a single day all of the instances of cooperation which a single observer knows have occurred within a community. Anyone doing so will realize that cooperation is a process too often overlooked by those training the leaders of the future.

AMALGAMATION

Amalgamation, the sixth process listed early in this chapter, deserves but brief treatment, since it is less frequently found than those which have been described. Groups decide to merge, or amalgamate, and lose their former identity in becoming a part of a new group. This happens over and over again in business and is best illustrated in the union of two banks, with the merger preserving in its name parts of the titles of the original banks. The Citizen's Bank merges with the Union Trust Company and becomes the Citizen's Union Trust Company.

Minor political parties find competition with the two major parties difficult and may regroup their forces under a new name. The case of the coming together of three branches of Methodism in 1939 (described under the discussion of conflict at the Pine Grove Church) resulted in amalgamation known as The Methodist Church. Illustrations could be multiplied to show this sixth type of interaction viewed from the standpoint of shifting goals of groups involved in the interaction.

By now it should be clear that the community is an arena of social interaction and that to understand this interaction is a great aid in understanding the community; without viewing the community in this light one misses its very essence. Yet, tantalizing though it seems, one can never completely understand this arena of interaction, since each response by an individual or group to another individual or group results in some social change. Thus interaction must not only be studied with reference to the goals of the participants; it must be studied in terms of the changes which it introduces into the lives of those who participate in it.

REFERENCES AND SUGGESTED READINGS

1. *Applied Anthropology* (now *Human Organization*), V, (Fall, 1946), special issue on "From Conflict to Cooperation: A Study in Union-Management Relations."

2. BERNARD, JESSIE. *American Community Behavior.* New York: The Dryden Press, Inc., 1949.
3. ————. "Where Is the Modern Sociology of Conflict?" *American Journal of Sociology,* LVI (July, 1950), 11–16.
4. DOYLE, BERTRAM W. *The Etiquette of Race Relations in the South.* Chicago: University of Chicago Press, 1937.
5. GARFIELD, SIDNEY, and WHYTE, WILLIAM F. "The Collective Bargaining Process: A Human Relations Analysis," *Human Organization,* IX (Part I, Summer, 1950; Part II, Fall, 1950; Part III, Winter, 1950).
6. HILLERY, GEORGE A., JR. "Definitions of Community: Areas of Agreement," *Rural Sociology,* XX (June, 1955), 111–23.
7. HOPE, JOHN, II. "Industrial Integration of Negroes: The Upgrading Process," *Human Organization,* XI (Winter, 1952), 5–14.
8. ICHHEISER, GUSTAV. "Misunderstandings in Human Relations: A Study in False Social Perception," *American Journal of Sociology,* LV (Part 2, September, 1949).
9. KANE, JOHN J. "Protestant-Catholic Tensions," *American Sociological Review,* XVI (October, 1951), 663–72.
10. KERR, CLARK. "Industrial Conflict and Its Mediation," *American Journal of Sociology,* LX (November, 1954), 230–45.
11. MARCONDES, J. V. FRIETAS. "Mutirao or Mutual Aid," *Rural Sociology,* XIII (December, 1948), 374–84.
12. MEAD, MARGARET (ed.) *Cooperation and Competition Among Primitive Peoples.* New York: McGraw-Hill Book Co., 1937.
13. MERTON, ROBERT K. *Social Theory and Social Structure.* Chicago: The Free Press, 1949.
14. MINNIS, MHYRA S. "Cleavage in Women's Organizations: A Reflection of the Social Structure of a City," *American Sociological Review,* XVIII (February, 1953), 47–53.
15. PARK, R. E., and BURGESS, E. W. *Introduction to the Science of Sociology* (Chicago: University of Chicago Press, 1924).
16. ROSE, ARNOLD M. "Voluntary Associations Under Conditions of Competition and Conflict," *Social Forces,* XXXIV (December, 1955), 159–63.
17. SANDERS, IRWIN T. "Selection of Participants in a Mutual Aid Group in Rural Greece," *Sociometry,* XVIII (1956). Special volume entitled *Sociometry and the Science of Man,* ed. J. L. Moreno, 326–29.
18. SOROKIN, PITIRIM A. *Social and Cultural Dynamics.* 4 vols. New York: American Book Company, 1937–1941.
19. TIMASHEFF, N. S. "The Basic Concepts of Sociology," *American Journal of Sociology,* LVIII (September, 1952), 176–86.
20. TREUDLEY, MARY BOSWORTH. "Formal Organization and the Americanization Process with Special Reference to the Greeks of Boston," *American Sociological Review,* XIV (February, 1949), 44–53.
21. TURBEVILLE, GUS. "Religious Schism in the Methodist Church: A Sociological Analysis of the Pine Grove Case," *Rural Sociology,* XIV (March, 1949), 29–39.
22. WALKER, HARRY J. "Changes in the Structure of Race Relations in the South," *American Sociological Review,* XIV (June, 1949), 377–83.
23. WHYTE, WILLIAM FOOTE. "Patterns of Interaction in Union-Management Relations," *Human Organization* (Fall, 1949), 13–19.
24. ————. "Semantics and Industrial Relations," *Human Organization* (Spring, 1949), 4–10.
25. WIESE, LEOPOLD VON, and BECKER, HOWARD. *Systematic Sociology.* New York: John Wiley & Sons, Inc., 1932, p. 243.
26. YOUNG, KIMBALL. *Sociology: A Study of Society and Culture.* 2d ed.; New York: American Book Company, 1949.

Chapter 9

SOCIAL CHANGE WITHIN THE COMMUNITY

Where things happen, as they do in any community, change is bound to result. Often this change is not at first evident even to those who are close at hand; indeed, it may be more obvious to someone who has been away—say, to college or on a job outside the community. A hill has been leveled to make a new parking lot; a big building has gone up on a once vacant field where boys played baseball; the railroad tracks which led through the center of the town have been moved to the outskirts because of the decline in passenger rail traffic. There have been material changes of other types: the women now go to the supermarket wearing blue jeans; kitchens in many of the homes have been modernized; coin vending machines impersonally dispense newspapers, combs, and a wide variety of articles that formerly required the attention of a salesman; children expect to be driven by automobile to all of their appointments, whereas a few years back they willingly walked; television sets dominate many living rooms; power lawn mowers putt-putt through the better residential areas.

Many other instances of changes in the material bases of life—the artifacts—could be mentioned. They are important for they are usually associated with changes in social relationships, but they reveal only one side of change within the community. If change is to be considered *social* it must focus on the changes which occur in the bonds between people, in the social groups, and in the community viewed as an arena of interaction. A brief look at a few studies dealing with social change reveals some of the numerous ways a community can be viewed as a dynamic social system.

SOME STUDIES OF CHANGING COMMUNITIES

To sample even a small part of the studies of changing communities is to take a trip around the world. Even more important than the cultural contrasts which they provide are the topics which their authors have included under the general rubric of social change.

Central Pennsylvania. In a study of four Pennsylvania bituminous coal mining areas William Wance and Richard Butler sought to explore "some of the human and social changes in family and community brought about by technological changes in the past generation."[1] One of the topics covered was the extent to which the young people followed the occupation of their fathers. New technological procedures, notably strip mining, have raised the production per miner, have increased the proportion of coal mined by machinery, and decreased the number of men required. What do these changes mean for the communities concerned? For one thing, this study revealed that there were more than twice as many miners as nonminers in the first generation, about equal in number in the second generation, and about 15 per cent fewer miners than nonminers in the third or present younger generation. The authors concluded as follows:

When the third generation left mining as an occupation they tended to enter skilled occupations primarily or to become operatives in factories or mills. They showed less tendency than farmers' sons to become proprietors or managers. The sons of miners who left their communities remained for the most part within a fifty mile radius of their homes, but a sizable number went to Cleveland and Erie. The third generation still in school does not wish to become miners. If they had their choice they would enter the more prestige-bearing occupations, especially the professions.[2]

Thus technological innovation affects occupational distribution and influences family ties in cases where young people must leave the home community in order to find any work or at least the type of work which they consider attractive.

Rural Quebec. In 1936–37 Horace Miner made a study of a French-Canadian community called St. Denis, located on the south shore of the St. Lawrence River about ninety miles east of Quebec city (17). He revisited this community in 1949 (16). What changes did he find after only twelve years? There were striking changes

[1] William Wance and Richard Butler, "The Effect of Industrial Changes on Occupational 'Inheritance' in Four Pennsylvania Communities," *Social Forces,* XXVII (December, 1953), 158.

[2] *Ibid.,* p. 162.

in the material culture. A main highway carrying Canadian and American tourists has replaced the once rough and graveled road and makes it possible for the villagers to go outside the community. Tractors are more numerous; the oxcart has disappeared. Rural mailboxes, telephones, electricity in every home (with milking machines in the barns), threshing by machinery instead of by horses, ready-made clothes, street lights, a new electric organ in the church, and new beach cottages—all are evidences of significant changes.

The economy, too, has felt the effects of new technology which has brought about an increasing dependence upon the outside world. People of St. Denis now participate in the old-age pension plan and the Canadian Family Allowance Act of 1944 which provides benefits for lower-income families. Other economic changes include increased cash income and the organization and expansion of cooperatives. More medical services are available; women have the unsought privilege of political suffrage. The birth rate has increased, probably temporarily.

The local social structure based on the "thrifty, close-family economy" has not, however, changed fundamentally, for the cash profits produced beyond the requirements of the old system have been turned into labor-saving devices on the farm. One reason for this has been the unwillingness of the girls to take up the heavy load that a farm woman had to carry while bearing ten or more children. The farm wife will continue to want mechanical assistance in her housework. Meanwhile, the development of a population surplus seems destined to continue.

Japanese Village Life. The most pervasive influence brought to bear by the American military occupational authorities upon the Japanese village was the program of agrarian reform which distributed land to over half of the farmers of Japan. Those who had been tenants now became owners; they joined farmers' cooperatives which tried to follow democratic procedures, and they were introduced to better farming practices. More people now take part in village affairs; the village heads are now elected by popular vote rather than by the village assembly; women have been given the ballot; and the public educational system has been improved. To Americans these all sound like changes in the right direction because of our value orientation. Apparently, from the studies made by Arthur F. Raper and his assistants, the majority of the Japanese villagers also welcomed these changes. One illustration of the extent of the revolutionary social change was the village of Yokogoshi, as seen in the following description by Raper.

. . . a conference was held with village officials . . . The meeting convened in the village hall assembly room. Looking up at the life-sized portraits of former village headmen—six of them—the officials said that not one of the present officials could have held office under conditions prevailing when these earlier mayors were in office. All of these former mayors were landowners, most of them members of the village's largest landowning family. Practically all of the assemblymen, too, prior to the agrarian reforms, had been from the village's small landowning group, despite the fact that 46 percent of the farmers when the Occupation began tenanted 90 percent or more of the land they cultivated, and 72 percent tenanted half or more of the land. The present mayor owns no land, was a clerk in the village hall, and long identified with the Farmers Union, which had agitated for improvement of the land tenure situation. Practically all of the assemblymen were new owners, as were most of the officers in the other public and private organizations in the village.[3]

Thus in Yokogoshi one finds not merely planned change but an arrangement whereby control of local affairs has passed from one economic group into the hands of another.

Rural Sweden. Sweden, too, has experienced some major changes in its local communities. David E. Lindstrom discusses the possible effects of a parliamentary measure in 1948 which reduced the number of local governmental units from about twenty-five hundred to nine hundred by 1952. This was the first major change in local government in over two hundred years and was necessitated by the increase in new social services, each of which is organized to be locally administered through the commune. Some of the communes had become so small in population that they were poor administrative units for these programs. According to Lindstrom:

Sociologically, the change will mean a change from primary to secondary group controls, a change which has already made considerable progress in other forms of organization in the country. The small commune in Sweden was often a neighborhood unit; people in it knew each other first hand. In the larger commune, control can be once or twice removed from the people. Rather than electing an entire council for their small commune . . . these people will elect only one man, if that, to a large commune council; or they may have their votes pooled with a neighboring commune for the election of a representative.[4]

The government will provide a much higher quality of professional service, and it will, of course, require more money. Whether value is received for this extra money will depend upon political factors outside the control of many of the local people.

[3] Arthur F. Raper, "Some Recent Changes in Japanese Village Life," *Rural Sociology,* XVI (March, 1951), 15–16.
[4] David E. Lindstrom, "The Changing Rural Community in Sweden," *Rural Sociology,* XVI (March, 1951), 54–55.

A *Mexican Town*. Oaxaca is a town of thirty thousand people at an elevation of five thousand feet on the great central plateau of Mexico. The changes there since 1910 have been described by Norman S. Hayner, who stressed particularly the differential change between the various social classes—the aristocracy or old upper class, the middle class, and the lower class (10). Social mobility can explain some of these changes.

. . . as the power of the old upper class weakened under the influence of revolution, expropriation and earthquakes, many of its members moved to Mexico City. Their places were taken in part by movement of aristocrats from smaller centers in the state and in part by vertical mobility from lower social classes. . . . The new and greatly enlarged middle class has been formed primarily by vertical mobility from below . . . It exhibits the greatest freedom in marriage, education, and the work of its women. In contrast, the lower class . . . is marked by the smallest personal mobility—ordinarily limited to the weekly trip to market—and the persistence of old ways in religion, housing, food, clothing, and the status of women . . . Probably the greatest hope for the future of the plebeian class and of Mexico lies in the great expansion of educational opportunities.[5]

What do these studies and hundreds like them show about the meaning of the term "social change"? Apparently, the one common thread running through them all is some change involving human relationships, whether reflected in their economy, their government, their class system, their family life. Besides, mention is made of technology, material possessions, acceptance of democracy. In view of the wide variety of the topics treated it is well to inquire more specifically into the nature of social change.

THE NATURE OF SOCIAL CHANGE

Change as Adjustment. Social interaction, as described in the previous chapter, consists of the totality of the behavior patterns of any group or community. Where conditions are relatively *static* these patterns undergo minor modifications but remain essentially the same through time. However, where dramatically new forces come in to shift the accents in human motivation or create new value orientation, the behavior patterns, or roles, change too. Groups such as political parties or business enterprises that will not change their methods to meet new conditions lose out in the struggle for support of the public; however, the fact that such groups do usually change means that their competitors must also change, and the changes carried out by these rivals in turn stimulate other change.

[5] Norman S. Hayner, "Differential Social Change in a Mexican Town," *American Journal of Sociology*, XXVI (May, 1948).

Under such conditions of change and counterchange we have a *dynamic* society. Change becomes built into the social structure and is accepted as one of the normal expectations of social life (24).

One of the most helpful ways of viewing the change within any community or segment of the community is to think of it as an adjustment by people to what they may consider new circumstances. William H. Harlan, in studying what has happened in St. Petersburg, Florida, under the influx of many aged people, makes use of the term *community adaptation*. He says:

> The functional relationships among the individuals and institutions of a community may be altered as a result of changes in demographic, economic, or social processes. As one segment of a community undergoes change, adaptive or adjustive modifications are to be expected in others. Distinctly social changes are described by the term "social adjustment," which has been defined [by E. W. Burgess] as "the adaptation to social change by modifications of social institutions." The term "community adaptation" . . . is more inclusive, covering both ecological and social changes. . . .[6]

Since a locality in our age of rapid communication is tied in with the total society of which it is a part, many forces producing change are generated outside the community (18). If war breaks out in Europe or Asia and the United States becomes involved, the participation in that struggle by the members of a single community is not theirs to decide as a community; they invariably are caught up in the wartime measures adopted by a more highly centralized federal government. Thus, they experience *regimentation*, a process leading to decreased autonomy by local people over their own affairs.

Or, as in the case of the Pennsylvania community mentioned earlier, the development of strip mining—at first in some area quite removed from the community—led to increased production per miner. The mine owners in Pennsylvania, in order to compete favorably, had to introduce some of the same technological advances, which in turn affected the occupational structure of the community. Machines tended to replace men, a process usually termed *mechanization*. Many cotton-growing communities have felt the impact of the use of machines in the cotton fields—not only for picking but for planting and cultivating as well. This has almost revolutionized the traditional landlord-tenant relationship in such communities.

Many communities, too, feel the impact of numerous features of dominant metropolitan areas. The young people of a community become attracted to the city and move there in search of work,

[6] William H. Harlan, "Community Adaptation to the Presence of Aged Persons: St. Petersburg, Florida," *American Journal of Sociology*, LXI (January, 1954), 332.

thereby leaving the older people and children behind to carry on life in the home community; or the conveniences of city homes have such a fascination for those in smaller communities that they, often at considerable sacrifice, seek to install them too. With these conveniences come many other patterns of city life, so that one can correctly speak of the process of *urbanization* as one covering not only the movement of people to the cities but the movement of city ways to rural areas where they are taken over by the people still living there (9).

When factories come to a community they introduce the process of *industrialization* to that town which is making an adjustment in the interest of what its people hope will prove to be greater economic gain. This process involves mass employment, but also the possibility of mass unemployment; it increases the social heterogeneity as far as occupational strata are concerned; it is usually accompanied by unionization, or the mass organization of workers into labor unions, to deal with those guiding the mass production of our economy.

Still another process of change is *commercialization,* which means that more and more aspects of life are brought under the influence of the businessman. Recreation, which may at one time have been cost-free, since it took place in informal groups and involved participation by the people themselves, becomes a business, and people pay to enjoy activities which fill up their leisure.

A final process of change necessitating adjustment is *secularization,* or the tendency to substitute rationality for tradition, to apply the scientific inquiry to areas formerly considered sacred or taboo (e.g., the Kinsey studies in sex), to vote for the candidate one prefers rather than for the party to which one's father belonged, to accept some impersonality in social relationships without feeling that one needs to know all of the intimate details about one's associates.

These processes—regimentation (in times of emergency), mechanization, urbanization, industrialization, commercialization, and secularization—are part of the American and Western European way of life and few communities avoid their impact. These not only characterize areas of life in which change is occurring but they typify certain major adjustments which the people of a community make to dynamic forces about them.

Change and Equilibrium. To the idea of adjustment—or reacting to major pressures—must be added the concept of equilibrium. A social unit, whether a group, a subsystem, or a community, cannot adjust too far in any one direction without changing so radically that its individuality is threatened. What is needed is a counterforce to serve as a balance to too great an adjustment. This tends to restore the equilibrium of the social unit.

Conservatism is one of the most useful counterforces in any community. As used here, "conservatism" means the tendency on the part of many people in the community to question some of the changes under way and to insist that old ways be preserved or to ask if there are not better alternatives than the proposed changes. At times this conservatism may seem narrow-minded to an outsider, but if he were familiar with the standards, values, and operational principles of that community he would see that for a time at least this narrow-mindedness is an essential step in slowing the tempo of change so that "a moving equilibrium" can be maintained. In the case of a moving equilibrium a previous condition of the social unit is never restored just as it was, but a balance is struck so that most of the people can go through their daily routines making use of most of their learned roles. They are not faced at every turn with a completely new situation for which they are unprepared.

Social planning, to be discussed more fully in Chapter 19, is also a counterbalance to social change. When certain trends (such as increased school enrollments, a rise in the number of the aged) can be anticipated, then provisions can be made in advance to soften the effect. Too much planning leads to regimentation, since the plan rather than the people to be helped becomes the main object of attention; too little planning means that many opportunities to prepare for change can never be recaptured.

The part played by local institutions in maintaining an equilibrium has long been recognized. Albert J. Reiss, Jr., in one of the most incisive monographs evaluating research on the community (21), sets forth four tentative postulates on change within the community:

1. Certain institutions, e.g., sustenance and residential institutions, primarily exist on a communal basis and function with respect to local orientations and actions.
2. Change always requires overcoming institutionalized resistances.
3. Communities may have certain institutionalized modes of change, unique to communal systems.
4. The orientation of residents of a community to change is a function of the level of integration of the communal system.

To illustrate the fourth point he cites the writings of Kreitlow and Koyen, who have studied the way Wisconsin communities accepted reorganization of their elementary school districts, and have indicated those factors which led to acceptance of and resistance to change (11).

Components of Social Change. In order to study change within any community one must use more specific terms than adjustment and equilibrium. These are basic to an understanding of the nature of change but must be supplemented by concrete examples of those units involved in social change. In the discussion of the community as a place in Chapter 1, a distinction was drawn between *habitat* and *culture*. The former was viewed as the natural environment and the latter as specifying the man-made environment. Culture in this sense is the broad term which encompasses any product of man's interaction, be it a material thing, a social group, or a system of ideas. Many community studies try to trace changes in all of these facets of human life and demonstrate how all three are intricately related. Frequently, people's ideas may change before they are willing to accept a new artifact; or in some cases they may start using it before they have accepted it psychologically or worked out a rationalization for continuing its use. Some communities set up formal organizations to introduce and speed up certain kinds of change while at the same time having other organizations whose most apparent function seems to be to "turn back the clock," but whose latent function may be to maintain equilibrium.

On the assumption that one is trying to understand the community as a social system, to figure out how it operates as a totality of interacting persons, the study of social change can be limited in scope to cover the area of social relationships. If these are the focus, then such a study would concentrate upon changes in status and role, in values and norms. It would be concerned not just with persons as social actors but also with groups and subsystems as partners in interaction. Obviously, attention would have to be paid to ecological and demographic influences, to the importance of economic and psychological factors (5), and certainly to historical continuity. But the starting point of the inquiry would be: What is happening to the relationships (in both structural and dynamic terms) among the social units of this community? As will be pointed out in the later discussion of the community as a social system, this approach provides the basis for a rewarding analysis with very practical applications.

MEASUREMENT OF SOCIAL CHANGE

Change itself is neutral. To describe it is to state what has occurred without necessarily telling whether this seems good or bad to the investigator. This is why social scientists do not try to *measure progress* but attempt to *describe change*. What seems progress to one group in the community (such as banning the sale of liquor within the city limits) may seem a step backward to those who are engaged in the activity. Any individual should be able to read the description of change, and then, from the standpoint of his own values, judge whether progress or retrogression has occurred.

The Temporal Aspect. Furthermore, change has a time dimension, since it indicates differences in relationships between two points in time. One must know what the relations were between the Methodist and Baptist churches at a given time if one is to trace what has occurred since that time. Likewise, to trace the changes occurring in race relations would imply that one could find out the situation as of a given date and then make the necessary comparison at a later date. The original description of relationships from which change is traced is often spoken of as the "bench mark" for measuring social change.

There are many communities which have been studied over a period of time by social science research groups. Some of the best known, however, have been done by one or two investigators. For example, Robert and Helen Lynd pioneered in community study by a survey of Middletown, an Indiana city, in the 1920's. In the 1930's they returned to make a resurvey, which they published under the title *Middletown in Transition* (14). Another trail-blazing community study was done of Tepoztlan, Mexico, by Robert Redfield, an anthropologist (20). This was restudied in 1943–44 and during shorter periods in 1947 and 1948, by Oscar Lewis, twenty-five years later (12). The later study showed not only that the community had changed but that social science methods and perspectives had matured considerably. A New England town labeled "Indecisive Hamlet" by Carle Zimmerman in his work *The Changing Community* (26), was restudied during the war by David and Mary Hatch, and called "Hilltown" in their published account (8). Mention has already been made of Horace Miner's research on St. Denis, Quebec.

As those who study the community develop better-defined methodologies, the restudies, known as *replications*, will be increasingly more valuable, especially if care is taken to follow the same methods and to work within the same conceptual orientation. The general tendency, however, is for the author of the restudy to incorporate new approaches and supplementary methods in the hope of making a more significant interpretation than would otherwise result (22).

This approach to social dynamics may result in what Donald J. Bogue has called "a static emphasis," since by using comparable data from successive surveys the investigators estimate the net change occurring between surveys. He correctly points out that one should also make use of questions which show more about the behavior of different individuals during this interval of time. He thinks this can be done by gaining mobility data which would indicate change of status or of function. Table 6 is one used by Bogue, since it shows the differences in the type of questions asked in the "static" survey and in that including the added data on mobility. Furthermore, in the column entitled "area of research" he lists a number of areas about which statistics can be collected and interpreted in terms of the social relationships which characterize community life.

The Specialized Study. The problem of measurement is much simplified when the researcher studies only one aspect of community life. If he is interested in the recreational patterns he can choose the research methods, work out a careful sample of the population, and then determine activities and preferences of those interviewed. Some new program can be launched and a later study made to see the effect of this program, providing other variables can be held reasonably constant. The same can be done in other fields such as health, advertising, political behavior, and education.

Without question, these specialized studies are indispensable to intelligent community planning and add to social science knowledge about certain areas of life. However, it is practically impossible to get a clear picture of the community as an operating system by simply adding together these miscellaneous specialized studies unless all were originally part of the total research design. A distinction should be made accordingly in what might be called general studies of the community (the over-all view of the social relationships) and the specialized studies (which contribute an insight into some one aspect).

A number of indices have been worked out for the specialized studies. These aid greatly not only in quantification but in comparing one's own city with other cities in such matters as contributions to the community chest, arrests for car theft, educational attainment, or fire insurance ratings, to give only a few areas of comparisons. One of the most ambitious efforts made to use such indices is found in R. C. Angell's study of the moral integration of American cities (1). Although his purpose was not to measure social change, the indices which he prepared, when studied through time, furnish certain clues as to what has happened between the dates specified.

What is often lacking in many of the specialized studies, largely because of their purpose, is an application of the data gathered and analyzed to the interpretation of social relationships. One can hardly be said to be measuring or indicating social change if he simply gives statistics about the number of passenger cars owned, the number of telephone calls made, or the average church memberships between two points in time. What might be called a "follow-through" is called for. The investigator, since he has probably obtained the best insight then available, should try to state, in tentative terms if necessary, what social relationships are affected by the data he has presented, what adjustments will most likely be made, and what statuses, roles, values, or norms may be altered. Later on, such interpretations can themselves be studied quantitatively and much learned about why some predictions were borne out and why others did not materialize.

ATTITUDES TOWARD CHANGE WITHIN THE COMMUNITY

A social scientist may carefully trace numerous changes within one community, publicize his findings, and create a ripple of interest which soon subsides; in another community, his report is greeted with great consideration, becomes the topic of animated discussion, and eventually proves the focal point for some planned community action. Such experiences indicate marked differences in attitudes between communities toward the introduction of new ideas and ways of doing things.

A community may be characterized by the way its leaders, who are responsible for deciding about matters of joint concern, react to social change as they try to establish what to them seems an equilibrium.

In the first place, they may resist change in all its forms to the best of their ability. They may feel that what they have is so good that it ought to be preserved; they may fear any alteration in their own position or situation if new forces begin to work within the community. To such people, the coming in of additional factories may seem undesirable. They fight their coming, frequently in open meeting, so that industrialists who may have originally thought of locating there shift to some other place. Such leaders may also resist a school bond issue which would help the community meet its educational needs. The reasons they give for opposition are complex, involving more than the objection to additional taxes which would have to be levied; they may even reveal an attitude that "ordinary people" should not be educated too far out of line with

TABLE 6

Prototype Form of Questions Asked To Collect Static Data and Mobility Data for a Variety of Subjects*

Area of Research	Static Question	Additional Question to Provide Mobility Data for Dynamic Analysis†
Area of residence	In what area does this person live?	In what area did this person live a year ago?
Community of residence	In what type of community does this person live?	In what type of community did this person live a year ago?
Marital status	What is the marital status of this person?	What was the marital status of this person a year ago?
Family status	What is the family status of this person?	What was the family status of this person a year ago?
Fertility status	What is the fertility-parity status of this woman?	What was the birth order of any children born to this woman during the past year?
School attendance	Is this person attending school?	Was this person attending school a year ago?
Educational attainment	What is the highest grade of school completed by this person?	Did this person complete a grade of school during the past year?
Employment status and class of worker	What is the employment status and class of worker of this person?	What was the employment status and class of worker of this person a year ago?

Occupation status	What is the occupation of this person?	What occupation did this person have a year ago?
Industry of employment	In what industry is this person employed?	In what industry was this person employed a year ago?
Income	What was the income of this person during the calendar year 1951?	What was the income of this person during the calendar year 1950?
Institutionalization	Is this person residing in an institution? If so, specify type.	Was this person residing in an institution a year ago? If so specify type.
Health	Does this person have a disabling illness?	Has this person had a disabling illness during the past year?
Church or other affiliation	Of what church is this person a member?	Of what church was this person a year ago?
Homeownership	Does this person own his home?	Did this person own his home a year ago?
Housing—type of structure	In what type of structure does this person live?	In what type of structure did this person live a year ago?
Farm mechanization	Is a tractor being used on this farm this season?	Was a tractor used in farming during the preceding season?

* It is assumed that the questions listed, or an appropriate rewording of them, would appear on a schedule containing several additional questions concerning the social and economic characteristics of the individuals to be enumerated and that the responses to these other items would be coded and cross-tabulated with the categories specifying mobility.

† A one-year interval has arbitrarily been used in wording the additional question to provide mobility data. The actual interval of time specified should be determined by such factors as obtaining reliable bases for rates, reliability of informant's memory, the length of time required to complete a change in status, and the relative frequency with which a given change takes place among the population.

Source: Donald J. Bogue, "The Quantitative Study of Social Dynamics and Social Change," *The American Journal of Sociology,* LVII (May, 1952), 567. Copyright, 1952, by the University of Chicago.

their social expectations. Not all of the people of the community agree with these leaders; yet they have little voice since they are not involved in the major decisions unless some issue is put to public vote.

In the second place, and much more commonly, one finds that the leaders are selective in their approach to social change. They recognize that change is inevitable; they have a philosophy of progress and lean toward the idea that a certain degree of social planning will help the people of the community arrive at goals considered desirable. Such leaders may also fight the coming in of what they think undesirable; they may also try to retain for the community some plant or government establishment which is about to be transferred elsewhere; they may also contribute generously to the development of an over-all metropolitan plan for the area in which they live. These leaders differ from that type of innovator, a few of whom are found in almost every community, who seem to think that any change is good and thrive on the excitement of a crisis situation (15).

Many communities, to mention a third reaction to change, seem to be apathetic or indifferent to change. In such cases, the leaders are often found to be deeply immersed in their own personal affairs and turn to community problems only when some acute difficulty has arisen and demands immediate attention. They have no real understanding of the nature of social change nor of its operation in the community; they seldom try to see the community as a whole or to think of its potentialities five or ten years hence. The rest of the community accepts conditions as they are, is little concerned about changes under way, and gives only token support to those members of the community who try to take positive action about housing, health, unemployment, or youth activities.

The attitude of the leaders toward change need not be just a matter of conjecture. It, too, can be studied, as shown by Marvin Bressler and Charles F. Westoff in their analysis of the reactions of leaders to increased industrialization in a semirural area of Pennsylvania (Bucks County). They were able to make the following inferences:

> The attitude towards social change in Lower Bucks County did not appear necessarily to be either stable or unidimensional, but instead frequently fluctuated between extremities of enthusiasm and vigorous opposition in the course of a single interview in accordance with the respondent's assumptions of one of his multiple roles . . . Thus while as a businessman a leader might evince great enthusiasm for the impending changes, he might be less enthusiastic as a homeowner, somewhat apprehensive as a father, and positively distressed at the

thought of the disturbance which the anticipated influx of new residents might impose on his ordinarily tranquil Sundays.

However, the roles which seemed to assume the highest priority for the respondent and appeared characteristically to be most influential in determining the direction of this attitude were those roles which involved current responsibility for his impending changes and entailed redefinition of his function . . . (For example, a local official might realize that his duties would increase tremendously, so he would be gloomy about the prospect of industrialization.)

Both the advantages and disadvantages accruing to Lower Bucks County as a result of the industrialization and urbanization process were perceived in tangible and material terms, primarily as it affected the economic sphere and the condition of community facilities and only secondarily in terms of expected alterations of cultural-ideological patterns and anticipated changes in the community as a result of the personal characteristics in the incoming population. (People thought concretely in terms of money, taxes, sewage system, crowded hospitals.)

Certain words and phrases seemed to possess the quality of independent symbolic imperatives so that they seemed capable of requiring responses which sometimes appeared to be at variance with the respondent's "real" attitude. (Such words were progress, planning, bigness.) . . .

[Furthermore] . . . the more powerful group manifests a higher degree of favorability than the less powerful group . . . This suggests the possible existence of a general mechanism by which an institutional role subtly influences individual cognitive and perceptual processes; those whose position in the social structure is vulnerable perceive any sort of change as still another threat to their security, while the strong and the powerful having already inherited the earth confidently expect that altered conditions, except those directly and specifically threatening them, will simply extend the range of their blessings.[7]

One of the clearest examples of the ways in which communities differ in their approach to social change was provided by the comparison of Rimrock and Homestead already cited in Chapter 5. The Mormon village of Rimrock, which would be considered by some as conservative theologically and socially, was receptive to economic change and had a social organization geared in with the development of such change; Homestead, many of whose members would be considered much less conservative in social conventions, was indifferent to the available changes.

Leaders must act within this value orientation or else run the risk of losing their following. Where they possess certain economic or political controls, and are not immediately and directly dependent upon prompt approval by the rest of the community for everything they do, they may feel that occasionally they can run counter to the value orientation or, to put it more correctly, rise above it and set it aside.

[7] Marvin Bressler and Charles F. Westoff, "Leadership and Social Change: The Reactions of a Special Group to Industrialization and Population Influx," *Social Forces*, XXXII (March, 1954), 236–43.

The differential attitudes toward change within a community may prove a source of local conflict. A *pro* and a *con* group arise to fight for or against some proposed change. Such disagreements may become bitter and result in impaired social relationships which affect community life for years to come. Oftentimes the *con* or *anti* group is fighting a losing battle, since it may be trying to resist some impersonal change which is already well under way in the larger society and is beginning to make its impact upon the local community.

On the other hand, the need to meet some crisis or community problem may draw many of the people of a community together. They may feel that they have had something to do with guiding change for their locality. Whether this is a correct interpretation or not, the fact that the people believe it, affects their relationships with each other and the zeal with which they will deal with future problems.

Preparing for Change

Most American communities are caught up in the dynamic changes which are part of the American way of life and many communities abroad have much the same prospect in store. Since a community is but one small part of a larger society, its members frequently have little to say about the impersonal changes which engulf them. But they do have much to say about the way they adjust to these changes. In the case of some communities a drastic change from outside is catastrophic, while the same impact upon another community causes the people to come together to seek a way out of the situation. In the case of the second community the chances are that there are present some leaders who have made it a practice to think about the future. They are asking such questions as: What do we need to be teaching our students in high school now to fit them for the kind of life they will be facing twenty years hence? What are we going to do if a law is passed and upheld that extends civil liberties to racial or religious minorities now experiencing discrimination? What are we going to do when the new thruway diverts most of the tourist traffic from the Main Street of our town? These are but illustrations of the kind of questioning that is needed if a community is to adjust to change with less severe strain. Such questions cannot have exact answers far ahead of an anticipated event, but instead of simply ignoring the change until it is too late to work out a rational solution, or running from it, communities can set courses which lead in the general direction of the change.

REFERENCES AND SUGGESTED READINGS

1. ANGELL, ROBERT COOLEY. "The Moral Integration of American Cities," *American Journal of Sociology*, LVII (July, 1951), Part 2.
2. BOGUE, DONALD J. "The Quantitative Study of Social Dynamics and Social Change," *American Journal of Sociology*, LVII (May, 1952), 565–68.
3. BOSSARD, JAMES H. S. "Social Change in the United States," *The Annals* of the American Academy of Political and Social Science CCLXV (September, 1949), 69–79.
4. BRESSLER, MARVIN, and WESTOFF, CHARLES F. "Leadership and Social Change: The Reactions of a Special Group to Industrialization and Population Influx," *Social Forces*, XXXII (March, 1954), 235–43.
5. BURGESS, E. W. "The Concept of Personal Adjustment," in Ruth S. Cavan *et al*, *Personal Adjustment in Old Age*. Chicago: Science Research Associates, Inc., 1949.
6. GITTLER, JOSEPH B. *Social Dynamics*. New York: McGraw-Hill Book Co., Inc., 1952.
7. HARLAN, WILLIAM H. "Community Adaptation to the Presence of Aged Persons: St. Petersburg, Florida," *American Journal of Sociology*, LXI (January, 1954), 332–39.
8. HATCH, DAVID and MARY G. *Under the Elms: Yesterday and Today*. Syracuse, New York: Syracuse University Press, 1949.
9. HAUSER, PHILIP M. (ed.) "World Urbanism," *American Journal of Sociology*, LX (March, 1955) (entire issue).
10. HAYNER, NORMAN S. "Differential Social Change in a Mexican Town," *American Journal of Sociology*, XXVI (May, 1948).
11. KREITLOW, BURTON W., and KOYEN, ROLAND. "First Progress Report: Longitudinal Study of Newly Formed Centralized Rural School Districts in the State of Wisconsin." Unpublished MS, Department of Rural Education, University of Wisconsin.
12. LEWIS, OSCAR. *Life in a Mexican Village: Tepoztlan Restudied*. Urbana: University of Illinois Press, 1951.
13. LINDSTROM, DAVID E. "The Changing Rural Community in Sweden," *Rural Sociology*, XVI (March, 1951), 49–55.
14. LYND, ROBERT S. and HELEN M. *Middletown*. New York: Harcourt, Brace & Company, 1929; *Middletown in Transition*. New York: Harcourt, Brace & Company, 1937.
15. McCORMACK, THELMA HERMAN. "The Motivation of Radicals," *American Journal of Sociology*, LVI (July, 1950), 17–24.
16. MINER, HORACE. "A New Epoch in Rural Quebec," *American Journal of Sociology*, LVI (July, 1950), 1–10.
17. ———. *St. Denis: A French-Canadian Parish*. Chicago: University of Chicago Press, 1939.
18. OGBURN, WILLIAM F. *Social Change*. New York: The Viking Press, Inc., 1922 and 1950.
19. RAPER, ARTHUR F. "Some Recent Changes in Japanese Village Life," *Rural Sociology*, XVI (March, 1951), 3–16.
20. REDFIELD, ROBERT. *Tepoztlan—A Mexican Village*. Chicago: University of Chicago Press, 1930.
21. REISS, ALBERT J., JR. *A Review and Evaluation of Research on Community: A Working Memorandum Prepared for the Committee on Social Behavior of the Social Science Research Council*. Mimeographed. Nashville, Tennessee, April, 1954.
22. SEWELL, W. H. "Field Techniques in Social Psychological Study in a Rural Community," *American Sociological Review*, XIV (December, 1949), 718–26.

23. WANCE, WILLIAM and BUTLER, RICHARD. "The Effect of Industrial Changes on Occupational 'Inheritance' in Four Pennsylvania Communities," *Social Forces,* XXVII (December, 1948), 158–162.
24. WASHBURNE, NORMAN F. *Interpreting Social Change in America.* Garden City: Doubleday & Co., Inc., 1954.
25. WATSON, JAMES B. "Four Approaches to Cultural Change: A Systematic Assignment," *Social Forces,* XXXII (December, 1953), 137–45.
26. ZIMMERMAN, CARLE C. *The Changing Community.* New York: Harper & Brothers, 1938.

Chapter 10

SOCIAL CONTROL

Another facet of a community which deserves special attention is the system of control within which its members must conduct themselves. In actuality, members control each other, but they have at their disposal certain inherited institutionalized ways of doing this which are more properly identified as communal or social than as individual. As has also been pointed out, there is some pattern—some rhyme and reason—to the intense social interaction which occurs and which is kept usually within circumscribed limits. Nor does social change seem such an ominous threat when one realizes that a community has already set up a system of control to deal effectively with innovation from without and deviation from within. The phenomena connected with social control will be described in terms of (1) the need for regularity and order in a social system such as a community; (2) the process of socialization, which prepares individuals for communal living; (3) the processes of social control and the techniques of effective guidance of interaction within the community; and (4) those who control these processes of community controls.

NEED FOR REGULARITY AND ORDER IN A SOCIAL SYSTEM

Any group to survive for long must have regularity and order. George C. Homans, whose work on *The Human Group* was mentioned in Chapter 7, points out that control over persons who threaten to depart from the norms of the group is often exceedingly effective but is not imposed from without. Instead it is implicit in the system of relations in the group (7). This same finding applies to the community whether it is viewed as a group or not. Indeed, the mere fact of moving into a community implies a willingness to conform to its prevailing patterns or accept certain consequences even though these be no more than the obvious disapproval of one's immediate neighbors.

Regularity and order are necessary for security. And there are three types of security which are important in community life. First, there must be physical security not only for one's own person and one's family but also for one's material possessions. In certain parts of New York City which were once fashionable residential neighborhoods, and are still occupied by upper middle class families, husbands do not let their wives return after dark from social functions unaccompanied, even though their apartment is within a block or so of a subway station. The environs of these neighborhoods have been "invaded" by families not yet assimilated into American life. Taxicab drivers have also been known to lecture women passengers returning to their homes in this area about the danger of being out alone without male escort. In time, this area of transition will be brought under effective control, but at present there is physical insecurity. In addition to protection from bodily harm, members of a community who invest their money in a building need to feel reasonably sure that that building will not be wrecked by vandals or by some unscrupulous business rival.

The fact that the community takes over the job, through its law enforcement agents, of providing this security means that individuals do not have to serve as their own policemen or set up special watchmen over every piece of property. Security facilitates economic specialization, since one is free to develop some skill or organize some service for others in the community. Nor does one have to interrupt a task to provide protective custody to some relative or friend ready to circulate in the community at large. One need only study the social waste of the vendetta or feud to realize how much more productive a community can be when there is physical security.

In addition, there is a second type of security, namely, psychological. It is attained when the unexpected and the unpredictable are kept at a minimum. It, too, is tied in with regularity and order. The individual who constantly worries about unemployment, the threat of a flood, or the possible necessity of getting to a distant hospital is a person whose efficiency is impaired. One of the reasons for living in a community is to reduce through group action the threat and the consequences of these unpredictable events. Knowing that neighbors are near to help in a crisis is a comfort to many who would feel inadequate as individuals to cope with such difficulties. The development of social welfare schemes, although frequently described in economic terms, contributes to the psychological security so necessary to sound community life. On the other hand, the presence of many who are psychologically insecure reinforces the disorganizing processes, in contrast to those processes which maintain stability. This does not overlook the fact that every individual needs to be somewhat psychologically insecure to motivate him into acceptable behavior, but it does stress the antisocial effects of exaggerated psychological insecurity. Communal action of many sorts can reduce the exaggerated type.

The third form of security, though closely related to the others, can be described as *societal* to distinguish it from the federal program of social security. This means that an individual feels secure in most social situations. He knows what roles to expect of his fellows and what roles they expect of him. This is not to say that he can run the whole gamut of social experiences within the community and feel "at home" in every situation; indeed, part of his training is to know where he is welcome and where unwelcome. So often a woman's concern about her dress prior to a social engagement reveals a deeper concern about her ability to behave as expected; the same may hold true when a man gives a number of reasons why he has not joined a certain club. Even a heterogeneous community, composed of many different population segments, can be societally secure if the individuals within a segment know how to behave with those from other segments. Where the pattern is one of marked subordination-superordination, those in the subordinate position, particularly a second generation, will become restive and try to move upward in the social scale. Many communities have regular channels for doing this which even help the individual acquire the new roles necessary for his changed status. Where, however, the community affords inadequate provision for socialization of the young and the control of deviants, there is apt to be societal insecurity.

Another matter closely related to psychological and societal security is that of community consensus, or agreement about topics of general concern. For a community to exist as community and not merely as a collection of isolated family units, there must be agreement on certain matters. One of these is *identification* with the community. People must feel that they belong to the same community or metropolitan area and that their individual fate is tied in with what happens to the community. If they feel detached, if they lack this feeling of "being in the same boat" with others, then one of the first ingredients of consensus is lacking.

As Chapter 5, on Traditions and Values, has shown, there must also be agreement about what is most important in life. Any two members of the community may not rank all values in the same order of importance or may not necessarily agree that a particular value is or is not important; but they will agree on enough of them to enable them to work out ways of reaching community decisions. Consensus on values is an aid in agreeing on the hierarchy of statuses. People who do this or that or have this or that are recognized as being at the top and are treated accordingly. When some individual supposedly occupying these high statuses fails to behave as expected, then over a period of time community sentiment may mobilize to the point that he is asked to change his ways or yield his position to another.

There must also be local consensus, particularly in American communities and others within the democratic orientation, about general institutional services such as government and education. Obviously, in any one community there cannot be two rival governments each with its right to collect taxes from all of the people and each trying to provide governmental services. There can be rival political parties and factions but there can be only one effective government. This calls for consensus as to the type of government, the identity of the duly elected or appointed officials, and the responsibilities of the citizen toward this governmental body. Likewise, in the field of education there must be some agreement. Whether the community is to rely upon public education, private education, or a mixture of both must be worked out. The financing of these systems, the enforcement of school attendance laws, and the public support of those in charge of the schools are important matters for agreement.

Communities may differ about the amount of individualism their members may express, about how much conformity is demanded, but there must be a reasonable degree of local consensus on this matter. Some communities with a strong parochial religious orientation, such as the Amish settlements in Pennsylvania, allow relatively little room for individual variation in social behavior, whereas other communities, such as the boom town, tend to accentuate individualism. Both types are "going" communities, and each has its own consensus without which there could be little regularity and social order.

The consensus does not happen by some mysterious process but is the result of time-tested ways of transmitting the culture from one generation to the next. The result of this inculcation of the traditions, values, and norms is the desire on the part of the individual to do what "is right." It may not even occur to him to do otherwise in many areas of life. Consensus, therefore, is based on motivation accepted as proper by the members of the community. Such motivation can be looked at from the standpoint of society and of the pressures which it brings to bear to assure a reasonable degree of conformity. "Socialization" is the motivational process which describes the *internalization*, or the automatic acceptance, of the appropriate roles, values, and norms; social control deals with the pressures toward conformity brought against the deviant, or the person who does not behave as though he had been properly socialized.

SOCIALIZATION AS A REGULATIVE, NORMATIVE PROCESS

It should be clear from the beginning of this discussion of socialization that the term as used here has no connection with the economic sense frequently given to this word in discussing "socialized medicine" or "socialization in Britain." Instead, the emphasis is upon personality development as viewed from the standpoint of society rather than from the standpoint of the individual. In this meaning, personality is considered a social product and socialization the process by which it is achieved.

One of the most stimulating discussions of this topic has been provided by David Riesman in *The Lonely Crowd: A Study of the Changing American Character* (16). He compares three types of society which enforce conformity and mold social character in definably different ways. Although he is careful to point out that he is talking about "ideal types" and not about any specific societies, he nevertheless can find numerous actual illustrations for the features described. Riesman's description of the social character and the ways this is produced is pertinent to the study of socialization.

The first society described is called *tradition-directed* because conformity is insured by the tendency of its members to follow tradition. Riesman writes:

The conformity of the individual tends to be dictated to a very large degree by power relations among the various age and sex groups, the clans, castes, professions, and so forth—relations which have endured for centuries and are modified but slightly, if at all, by successive generations. The culture controls behavior minutely, and, while the rules are not so complicated that the young cannot learn them during the period of intensive socialization, careful and rigid etiquette governs the fundamentally influential sphere of kin relationships. Moreover, the culture, in addition to its economic tasks, or as a part of them, provides ritual, routine, and religion to occupy and to orient everyone. Little energy is directed toward finding new solutions of the age-old problems, let us say, of agricultural technique or "medicine," the problems to which people are acculturated.[1]

[1] Abridged edition (Garden City, N.Y.: Doubleday & Company, Inc., 1953), p. 26. Original edition published by Yale University Press, 1950.

Riesman also points out that in such societies "relative stability is preserved in part by the infrequent but highly important process of fitting into institutionalized roles such deviants as there are. In such societies a person who might have become at a later historical stage an innovator or rebel . . . is drawn instead into roles like those of the shaman or sorcerer. That is, he is drawn into roles that make a socially acceptable contribution, while at the same time they provide the individual with a more or less approved niche."[2] The tradition-directed societies would number not only precapitalist Europe but also a wide variety of societies including the Hindus, Hopi Indians, Zulus and Chinese, North African Arabs and the Balinese.

The second type is a society dependent on *inner-direction*. As Riesman describes it, "Such a society is characterized by increased personal mobility, by a rapid accumulation of capital (teamed with devastating technological shifts), and by an almost constant expansion." Problems are so new and choices so numerous that people must learn to live socially without strict and self-evident tradition-direction. "The source of direction for the individual is 'inner' in the sense that it is implanted early in life by the elders and directed toward generalized but nonetheless inescapably destined goals."[3]

According to Riesman, inner-directed society can be characterized as follows:

As the control of the primary group is loosened—the group that both socializes the young and controls the adult in the earlier era—a new psychological mechanism appropriate to the more open society is "invented": it is what I like to describe as a psychological gyroscope. This instrument, once it is set by the parents and other authorities, keeps the inner-directed person . . . "on course" even when tradition, as responded to by his character, no longer dictates his moves. The inner-directed person becomes capable of maintaining a delicate balance between the demands upon him in his life goal and the buffetings of his external environment.[4]

The third type of society is *other-directed*, best typified by the upper middle class of New York and Boston. As seen by Riesman:

What is common to all the other-directed people is that their contemporaries are the source of direction for the individual—either those known to him or those with whom he is indirectly acquainted, through friends and through mass media. This source is of course "internalized" in the sense that dependence on it for guidance in life is implanted early. The goals toward which the other-directed person strives shift with that guidance: it is only the process of striv-

[2] *Ibid.*, p. 27.
[3] *Ibid.*, pp. 29–30.
[4] *Ibid.*, pp. 31–32.

ing itself and the process of paying close attention to the signals of others that remain unaltered throughout life.[5]

This indicates a strong need for approval.

In a summary comparison of the three types, Riesman notes the emotional sanction or control in each type:

> The tradition-directed person feels the impact of his culture as a unit, but it is nevertheless mediated through the specific, small number of individuals with whom he is in daily contact. These expect of him not so much that he be a certain type of person but that he behave in the approved way. Consequently the sanction for behavior tends to be the fear of being *shamed*. . . .
>
> Since the direction to be taken in life has been learned in the privacy of the home from a small number of guides and since principles, rather than details of behavior, are internalized, the inner-directed person is capable of great stability. . . . Getting off course may lead to the feeling of *guilt*.
>
> Contrasted with such a type as this, the other-directed person learns to respond to signals from a far wider circle than is constituted by his parents. The family is no longer a closely knit unit to which he belongs but merely part of a wider social environment to which he early becomes attentive. . . . The other-directed person is cosmopolitan. For him the border between the familiar and the strange . . . has broken down. . . . The inner-directed person is, in a sense, at home everywhere and nowhere, capable of a rapid if sometimes superficial intimacy with and response to everyone. . . . The other-directed person must be able to receive signals from far and near; the sources are many, the changes rapid. What can be internalized then, is not a code of behavior but the elaborate equipment needed to attend to such messages and occasionally to participate in their circulation. . . . The one prime psychological lever of the other-directed person is a *diffuse anxiety*. This control equipment, instead of being like a gyroscope, is like a radar.[6]

This study, together with others concerned with socialization, provides an insight into the mechanisms by which the values of the community or society become a part of the personality. In both the tradition- and inner-directed types the family was the key group, being strongly reinforced by kinfolk, older people in the neighborhood, and religious activities. In the other-directed society, the role of *peer-group*, that is, one's contemporaries, assumes a prominence it did not have before. It becomes a *reference group* (19), or one in terms of which an individual sets his goals and gauges his action.

Lest the impression be created that all of middle-class America has moved into the other-directed type—a claim which Riesman does not make—it would be well to look at a study of a suburban town by Frederick Elkin and William Westley (3). They studied adolescent culture in an effort to see if the young people were violently rejecting adult standards of judgment and compulsively conforming

[5] *Ibid.*, p. 37.
[6] *Ibid.*, pp. 40–42.

to peer group patterns. Since their work is based on a relatively small number of cases, their findings are suggestive but not definitive:

One dominant pattern in Suburban Town is that of adult directed and approved activity. The activities of the adolescent take place almost completely within the suburban community and in view of adult figures. The adolescent, in effect, has little unstructured time. Typically, on school days, he spends his time out-of-school doing two hours of homework; helping in household activities; and participating in school organizations, directed sports, or church and "Y" activities. On weekends, with more free time, he participates in some family projects, has certain allotted household tasks, and often attends gatherings at which adults are present. In summers he either works, attends camp, or vacations with his family at a summer cottage.[7]

The authors found that family ties in this suburb are close and the degree of basic family consensus is high; there is frank discussion between parents and adolescents on all matters except sex; the adolescents acknowledge the right of their parents to guide them and the parents express relatively little concern about the socialization problems or peer-group activities of their children. The continuity of socialization is more striking for this sample of adolescents than the discontinuity. The young people have internalized "responsible" and "adult" perspectives. Elkin and Westley, basing their comments on other studies, describe the deferred gratification pattern among upper middle and mobile low class adolescents as follows:

The child learns to forego immediate indulgences for the sake of future gains and thus inhibits his aggressive and sexual impulses, strives for success in school, and selects his associates with care. This pattern is in direct contradiction to the implications of a strong and pervasive youth culture. The individual who internalizes a deferred gratification pattern does not act solely in terms of irresponsible pleasure seeking and conforming in terms of pressures and, much as he may apparently be absorbed in dances, gang activity, and sports, he does not lose sight of his long run aspirations.[8]

There is widespread disagreement over the extent to which young people today are more influenced by their parents or by their contemporaries. The problem cannot be settled here, but the controversy can effectively point up some of the main features of the socialization process.

But this process consists of more than gaining values: it calls for the development of certain social and economic skills. Many of these skills can be learned at home, but an increasing number are being taught outside the home—at school, at public playgrounds, in Boy

[7] Elkin, Frederick and Westley, William A., "The Myth of Adolescent Culture," *American Sociological Review*, XX (December, 1955), 682.
[8] *Ibid.*, p. 683.

or Girl Scout meetings, and in part-time jobs. Since learning to drive a car is part of the socialization process of the average American youngster, many communities through the schools are providing driving courses to insure that this skill is learned well and that safer drivers use our highways.

The ultimate aim of socialization, as previously pointed out, is to make socially-acceptable patterns seem second-nature to those growing up in a society. It is the surest way of getting consensus on which order and regularity depend. Yet, in our dynamic society, some young people stress some patterns more than others and grow up with characteristics not shared by those in other social layers or even in other parts of the country. This is the price paid for change and complexity; yet, within the community such differentiation can be kept within bounds so that basic life needs can be met.

The Processes of Social Control

Figure 14 shows the major processes of social control. Of course, these four processes occur in every community, but the more totalitarian the society the greater the emphasis upon the fourth process

SOCIALIZATION	SUGGESTION
To so control the social environment that the child while growing up incorporates into his own personality structure as attitudes the values set forth by the community; accepts as "natural" the hierarchy of community statuses; and learns as "proper" the officially prescribed norms, or rules, governing the behavior of those occupying the various statuses, together with the reinforcing explanations as to why the social world is as it is.	To set up as copies to be imitated those whose behavior best conforms to the values of the community, indicating the rewards which follow such emulation. To initiate thoughts which will cause community members to think that they have arrived at conclusions on their own.
PERSUASION	COERCION
To gain concurrence by appeal both to emotion and reason, using both formal media and informal, face-to-face discussion.	To gain acquiescence to community demands, using nonviolent psychological pressure to induce compliance (threat of punishment) and violent physical force to bring about submission.

Fig. 14. Types of control* (from the standpoint of those exercising control).

* Adapted from Earle Edward Eubank, *The Concepts of Sociology* (New York: D. C. Heath & Company, 1932), p. 234.

of coercion. Communities, like whole societies, differ in the emphasis which they place upon these four processes.

But why should any control be necessary? Cannot individuals do what they want to do and each man take care of himself? Obviously, they cannot, for the result, as social philosophers through the centuries have pointed out, would be anarchy or at best the rule of only the physically strong. Thus each individual has to sacrifice some of his own individual longings for the security provided when social stability is maintained by various methods of control.

Some individuals do "get out of line" in the views of many people living in a community. They do not conform. They may be eager to flaunt the social conventions and behave in ways considered by others around them as quite improper. They may violate the sex mores, proclaim political ideas that are considered treasonable, or assert religious views thought to be heretical. Many people in the community consider them troublemakers. By the time their behavior has become recognized as "irregular" it is obvious that the processes of socialization and suggestion no longer are effective controls. At this point persuasion is brought into play. Their relatives or others who supposedly have influence with them are asked "to talk some sense into their heads." This appeal, as the chart indicates, is both to emotion and to reason. They are reminded of the shame they are bringing upon their loved ones and of the ways in which their action is jeopardizing their own future. Appeals may also be made in the name of religion or in the name of justice and fair play. With many people, persuasion is effective. The weight of social pressure of this sort is sufficient to make the individuals agree to conform more fully than in the past. They may still think that what they were doing or saying was perfectly right and proper but consent to keep such "dangerous" matters to themselves.

In spite of all of these pressures, however, some individuals cannot be dissuaded from the course they have either set for themselves or into which they are drifting. Persuasion, whether by a juvenile court judge, a clergyman, or a grown daughter, seems to be of no avail. The community then brings into play the techniques associated with the process of coercion. At first, there may be social ostracism. People whom the deviant counted as friends pass him by; doors that were once open to him are now shut; pastimes he once enjoyed no longer are fun, because of the reaction of those about him. Whatever occupation or profession he is pursuing in the community becomes affected, so that he can measure the ostracism in dollars and cents. But added to the effect upon himself is the effect such community behavior has upon his wife and children, who are made just as much the targets of this nonviolent psychological pressure as he is. He may know that in the larger society there is general approval of what he is doing or of the ideas he is championing (race relations, religious tolerance, citizen responsibility) but the community, with its present structure and set of traditions, finds this deviant irritating and unwelcome. If the deviant is obviously breaking the laws (the criminal code), then violent physical force in the form of the police is brought into play, and the individual may even be restrained against his will behind bars until his case is heard in court and he is freed or given some other punishment, varying from probation to the death sentence—the supreme form of control in the hands of the state.

For the purpose of further illustrating the nature of social control and the techniques used in its enforcement it is sometimes useful to step completely out of a social setting with which we are familiar into one where many differences exist. This is done in Figure 15, which sets forth in diagrammatic form the deviant types and regime controls one would find in a community of a Communist-dominated country. Notice that, according to the chart, the government is chiefly concerned about three areas of deviance: the ideas and beliefs which people hold; their efficiency on the job at which they work; and their general social conformity. For each of these three areas one can distinguish selected types of deviants, or those who fail to conform to the expectations of the regime. Where there are such deviants, the local Communist leaders and their supporters can call upon a variety of techniques which relate to the control processes of suggestion, persuasion, or coercion. No one of these is to be identified solely with a single type of deviant but is part of a whole battery of means at the disposal of those able to exercise power in the pursuit of what is interpreted to be the "official" purposes of the regime. This is only a partial list, since many more ways of inducing social pressure might be mentioned, but this list is sufficiently detailed to show that much conformity can be induced without recourse to any terror tactics—the threat of them is often enough.

But these processes of social control do not operate mysteriously; they are incorporated in the interaction which one can observe on every hand. In other words, it is not necessary to try to keep a weather eye on the whole community all at one time in order to see these processes at work. The neighborhood gossip who relates some choice bit about the young widow down the street is setting herself up as a sort of "community conscience." Sunday morning sermons may be directed at her kind of bearing false witness and community

AREAS OF DEVIANCE (from regime standpoint)	SPECIFIC TYPES OF DEVIANTS (with possible examples)	REGIME CONTROLS (Techniques illustrating suggestions, persuasion, coercion)
Ideas and Beliefs	Those holding to traditional nonregime ideas and beliefs (e.g., middle-aged parents, parish priests, peasants) Those accepting new (nontraditional) ideas and beliefs competing with those of the regime (e.g., the bourgeoisie, Party deviationists, soldiers or diplomats serving abroad, students reading "Western publications")	Information monopoly Rewards and privileges for regime supporters Censorship Forced newspaper subscription Indoctrination courses (in clubs, in school, at work) Educational preferment for conforming Use of symbols (fatherland, heroes, etc.) Rewriting of history Glorification of selected authors Politicization of art Censure, purge
Productivity	The ill (including alcoholics, cardiacs, etc.) The inefficient (those who lack ability or who are feebleminded, crippled, etc.) The unmotivated (the discontented, etc.) The "saboteurs" (those who slow down or destroy property or interfere with a program)	Quota on medical excuses Wages Bonuses and premiums Differential norms Production promotion (Stakhanovism) Job promotion policies Economic privileges (housing, vacation, etc.) Production goals Wall newspapers, etc. Favorable and unfavorable publicity Workers' and other occupational clubs Job transfer Labor camps
Social Conformity	The unaffiliated (those who fail to join mass organizations, attend meetings, or participate in voluntary projects) The antiregime spokesmen Organizers of the opposition The nonpolitical criminal The overt physical aggressors against the regime	Pressure to join groups, contribute to drives, sign petitions Medals, awards Informal sanction (gossip, etc.) Political preferment (rise in official hierarchy) Organizational monopoly (only official groups allowed) Legal sanctions Threat of arrest (terror) Arrests Capital punishment

Note: Any one of the above techniques can apply to any area of deviance.

FIG. 15. Deviant types and community controls under a communist regime.*

* Used by permission of Associates for International Research, Inc., for whom the author prepared this chart.

meddling, but she continues blithely on her course of trying to structure public opinion to her way of thinking, often successfully when the object of her attention is particularly vulnerable and defenseless.

Within various groups one finds community controls working. "Why," a high school English teacher asks, "do all of you girls come to school wearing white bobby socks? Can't any of you ever wear yellow or pink socks? Are you all conformists?" In the corridor a few minutes later the girls agree that they will "show that teacher up" and that they will all appear in different colored knee-socks. "But," as one of the girls pointed out, "each of us only agreed to this when the rest of the group had agreed. No girl decided on her own that she would make the change."

As one observes life in the community, he is made aware of this sensitivity of many kinds of people to what others will think. Each segment of the community is apt to have particular *reference groups* whose approval is most desired and who therefore tend to represent the whole community in the sense that they pattern the behavior, within limits, of those sensitive to them. A businessman will ask another businessman he admires, "What kind of a new car are you going to buy?" and may be influenced accordingly; a woman will ask another woman whose approval she seeks, "Where do you buy your clothes?" and may be seen the next day in that store. The individuals to whom these questions are addressed are important not so much as individuals to the ones putting the questions but rather as symbols of the "type of people" upon whom the questioners want to make the greatest impression. And when these "symbols" speak disapprovingly of certain actions or of certain people, those seeking their approval are quick to note these points and remember them in future social situations.

These occurrences just described are what are called the *informal* mechanisms of control. Kimball Young characterizes them as largely symbolic means, since they occur chiefly through talk and writing. Some of these devices, as he lists them, include praise and flattery, indoctrination, advertising, propaganda, slogans, rewards, badges, medals, uniforms, insignia, gossip, satire, laughing at others, calling names, commands, and threats (21).

But in addition to being aware of these informal or chiefly symbolic means of control one must be aware of the formal means where force in one of its forms is actually applied. This resort to force often finds expression in the decisions of official bodies, such as a school board's dismissal of a school principal, a labor council's calling of a strike, the banning of a motion picture for the members of a particular religious group by its board of censorship, a jury's verdict of guilty, a reduction by the local fiscal court of the recreation budget because of some unfavorable publicity given to one of the amateur night programs staged two months before. Each of these might at first seem to be an isolated event involving only a few people, but upon closer examination one finds that any one of them has wide community implications in that these decisions will in the future influence others in positions of responsibility to act in such ways as to avoid the censure of such groups.

WHO CONTROLS THE PROCESSES OF COMMUNITY CONTROL?

Knowing about the processes of control is not enough. For a real knowledge of a community it is also necessary to know who guides or controls these processes. Three considerations are involved in answering this question. First, the past still plays an active part in the present; second, each individual exercises some control, particularly in face-to-face contact; and third, most communities have what is usually termed a "power structure" whose upper echelons make many important decisions of community-wide scope.

The Controls from the Past. Every now and then one becomes acutely aware of the "dead hand of the past" in learning about some conditions set by a person long since dead. For example, a leading family of a Massachusetts town in a truly generous gesture donated an excellent beach to the town many years ago but stipulated that no man could use the beach unless he was wearing a two-piece bathing suit, a provision difficult to enforce in these days of bathing trunks. Other communities have to wrestle with problems growing out of large bequests set aside for the use of foundlings or to take care of horses too old to work any longer. These exceptional instances are often cited as illustrations of how the past, through specific legal documents, controls the present.

But the past, as the discussion of socialization has shown, makes its greatest contribution in that it has worked out such satisfactory solutions to many problems that these have been incorporated into the lifeways of the society and passed on from generation to generation. To the extent that these are accepted by each new generation—to that extent people are free to devote their attention to other problems. The problems solved in the past cover a vast variety of human behavior, ranging all the way from the development of techniques of medical care to the small details of etiquette, such as the custom of gentlemen standing when a lady enters a room. Thus in the development of American society, to which all American communities are inevitably bound, there is a unique approach to the meeting of economic needs, a system of public education worked out long ago and continuously implemented through the years, a pattern of the separation of church and state, as well as the formulation of a distinctive American political credo which, though not always obeyed, still remains an important social force in our lives.

Whenever some part of the social heritage is considered sacred by most of the members of the community (such as the practice of monogamy) or even highly desirable (such as the owning of one's home), the traditions and socially inherited values may be said to be generally in charge of the processes of control. This would be particularly marked in the tradition-directed society, as described by Riesman, but would hold true for any surviving society, since no generation is capable of starting anew to solve all of the problems that arise before it. In most matters it accepts the controls from the past, leaving its own imprint upon them as it transmits them to a succeeding age group.

It is in this sense that the dominant institutions of a community provide basic controls. Those seeking to strengthen or maintain an institution, whether they realize it or not, are actually promoting and perpetuating in their own lifetime the formulas for living, the accepted practices, and the systems of rewards and punishments which long ago were built into the institutional complex. Thus religious leaders and the men of science are each in turn attempting to stress solutions worked out by predecessors. In the case of religion, it may involve ways of establishing relationships with the supernatural and of living with one's fellowman; in the case of science, it may mean applying the scientific method, whose lineage is ancient, to wider and wider areas of life. As skillful adjustments are made to new situations, culture lag is avoided; on the other hand, when the past is in complete control, serious lags develop between the solutions provided by the past and the needs of the present. But the fact remains that in most matters the past provides ready-made solutions, and to the extent that these are followed, the past is exerting social control.

Control Exercised by the Individual. An individual, simply by being present in a social situation, exercises control over others. "Two's company, three's a crowd" is often quoted to show the impact that a third person can make. Or the woman who jokingly says that she had better go to a bridge party or a church supper "just so they won't talk about me" recognizes that her presence is apt to have at least an inhibitory effect upon those about her. If she belongs to some minority religion, out of politeness to her the others will not make that subject a topic of their discussion; if her husband is a politician, people will be reserved in their remarks about those in public office; if she brings an out-of-town visitor along, the other women will be even more restrained in what they say until they learn a little more about the visitor.

In addition to mere presence, however, an individual by his actions can encourage or discourage behavior on the part of others. Showing a readiness of response, an eagerness, can stimulate others to continue some course of action; expressing indifference or disapproval can cause others to shift to different behavior patterns. Furthermore, the registering of apathy by followers can lead to frustration by self-appointed or even elected leaders with the result that group activity weakens.

Nevertheless, those individuals who go into some social situation with a conscious purpose to fulfill are truly agents of social control. Whether they have tickets to a hospital bazaar or a firemen's ball, their persuading of others to buy and attend is a simple case of control. Or, the pressures may be more far-reaching in that they seek to influence some community decision (the location of the new waterworks, the advisability of keeping out any additional industry, the curtailing of advertising support for a newspaper whose editorials are considered "meddlesome" or "troublesome" by those whose activities are affected).

Thus every individual in his own social space, in his network of acquaintances and associates, is in position to exercise some kind of social control. The more intimate the relationship, such as in the family, the greater the likelihood of control; the more active and respected a person is in a social group to which he belongs, the greater his influence there; the greater a person's access to the chief means of communication, the more likely he is to influence others. The business man through advertising, the judge through interpreting the law, the worker by influencing other workers to better standards of performance exercise control within their individual spheres.

Most people of the community, however, live and move in a relatively restricted social space. They are concerned chiefly with making a living, having a good family life, enjoying their leisure; they feel no great urge to control the whole community. In many ways they do control more than they realize: it is they who are the ultimate consumers to whom the businessman appeals; it is their actions that raise or lower the standards of morality for the community as a whole; and it is their vote which settles many matters of wide importance. But this control is more a by-product of their reaction to the world about them and represents little in the way of a drive toward control.

The Role of Community Power Structure. Power, or the ability of an individual to control others, is distributed in unequal degree throughout the community. Parents have more authority than their children, an employer more power than his employees, and the police more power than a rowdy individual disturbing the peace. Each of these, however, is exercising a type of power derived from a different source, such as the family, the economic sphere, and government. These are institutional networks, or major community systems (to be described in Part Two), which serve as a means of distributing power throughout the community. But what has come to be called the *community power structure* refers more to the informal decisions made by a relatively few people at the top of their respective social and occupational hierarchies about matters of community-wide concern. These are the people "who run the town," or they are considered the "most important people." They are "the people to see" if a person is interested in promoting some big program in the community, for without their help no large-scale undertaking is likely to succeed. Who are these people who have such control? How did they gain it? How do they use it? For answers to these questions it is best to turn to studies of actual communities.

One of the earliest full-fledged sociological studies of a community was *Middletown,* by Robert and Helen Lynd (discussed in Chapter 9). The authors restudied this Indiana city in the middle 1930's (9). Here the power structure centered around a leading family of three brothers and their immediate kin who through the years had accumulated considerable wealth. This in turn meant that they became directors and officials of a major bank and could decide who should and should not have credit. The glass plant which they owned was a leading source of employment and became the biggest factory of its type in the world. Other business interests included the ownership of the largest department store in the city, much real estate, and stock in a daily newspaper. Members of the family were directors in other businesses which they did not own. Furthermore, they were active politically, and they held positions on the local school board and other civic bodies as well as being prominently represented in philanthropic and charitable organizations. Part of their power lay in the generous contributions they made to various causes, since because they were large donors, whatever suggestions they might make with respect to personnel would be taken much more seriously than the suggestions of others with less financial power.

In reading this study one does not gain the impression that this family was hungry for power or intent on exploiting the community. Its members as a rule seemed interested in community service, a fact which definitely enhanced their community standing even more. As they prospered financially the members of the family sought more and more outlets for their accumulated wealth, thereby gaining greater economic control. Thus the power held was a result of success in several lines and the tendency to take an active interest in what was going on in the community.

There are still communities where a single family group exercises the type of control described here, but today this is a much less common type of power structure than it was thirty to forty years ago in American towns and cities.

Lorain, Ohio, with a population of 50,000, is about the same size as *Middletown* was when it was studied by the Lynds. Although a steel mill provides more than half of the local jobs, there is no concentration of power similar to that of Middletown. There are three major strata, with the upper stratum consisting of the managers who operate the industrial, banking, and utility firms, the owners and operators of the larger local business enterprises, and a small group of upper professionals. The middle stratum consists of the small retail merchants, the white-collar and supervisory employees, and the lower professionals. The third stratum, numerically the largest, is the working class, most of whom are steelworkers (11). In addition, "race, ethnicity, and religion" are important dimensions of status. For example, managerial status not only means a high functional position but also contains ethnic and religious definitions.

According to some theories of community structure one would expect the power to reside in the upper stratum, since its members have not only prestige but the means to enforce many decisions through the industrial bureaucracy. In Lorain, however, a competing power bloc—the industrial union—has forged into prominence and has begun to play an active part in politics and civic affairs. It has proved to be the mechanism through which lower-status groups might be effectively united to wield political power in the community. Where numbers of votes can be made to count, as in municipal affairs and in control of the school system, the union has become the decisive force. It has also been accepted as a participant in the Community Chest and mobilizes working-class support, making possible the tripling of the budget over the last decade. Nevertheless, labor does not dominate decision-making in civic welfare.

James B. McKee, who made this study of Lorain, has listed three effects of the emergence of organized labor which has broken down the monopoly of decision-making once held by the upper stratum and created channels of influence for the low-status groups.

1. The alteration of power relations has disturbed the community's status system, since members of low-status ethnic groups, through achieving leadership in politics, local government, and the union, constitute a new elite in the community.
2. The union has taken over some decision-making once the prerogative of the upper stratum-managerial group, with the result that one group can no longer be considered the ruling group.
3. The organization of political power in the community contrasts with and contradicts the system of power and authority in the corporation. In the community, decision-making is more democratically structured than in the industrial bureaucracy where authority is located at the top, for those of low status can now have some share in community decision-making.

McKee feels that in an industrial society it is incorrect to think of the social order as a pyramid, with power and authority located at the apex. Instead, there are several pyramids of power, each concerned with a different type of decision-making. And this suggestion is borne out by a study made by Floyd Hunter of a southern metropolis of half a million people (8). Hunter has identified and described forty top leaders, pointing out that this power elite is divided into various cliques whose members interact informally, without publicity, and with no need of any formal structure for arriving at decisions. Once decisions are reached by these few (twenty-three executives of large manufacturing, financial, or commercial companies; five wealthy leaders of social or civic organizations; five corporation lawyers; four government officials; two labor leaders; one dentist), several hundred lesser leaders are called into action. These serve on numerous committees and boards and are called by Hunter the "executors" of policy. The Negro grouping is considered a subcommunity and has thirty-four top leaders of its own. Another point made by Hunter is the interlocking of some of the top leaders of this southern metropolis with the state and national power structures, which means that they have much to say not only about what goes on in the local government but in the state capital as well, with some influence also being wielded in Washington.

A fourth study, this one also of a southern city of two hundred thousand called "Bigtown," shows the prominent role played by the absentee management of a large corporation which has a factory there (15). In this case, members of the power structure, or at least an important segment involved in decisions affecting the community, live outside of the community. Their silent influence is pervasive in the sphere of community action and is certainly one factor to be taken into account in trying to determine who controls the processes of control.

These brief illustrations of the distribution of power within a community show the wide range of differences which one might find from one city to the next. In one place a leading family group, in another forty top leaders, in a third the labor union along with the upper stratum, and in a fourth the absentee management of a corporation are credited with having much to say about what goes on in the community. Such a summary, of course, puts the matter much too simply, but it does reveal striking variations in the pattern of control.

This whole treatment of social control takes on even more meaning when not considered as a general topic by itself but when tied in with the analysis of a community as a social system, the subject-matter of the next chapter.

REFERENCES AND SUGGESTED READINGS

1. BENDIX, REINHARD, and LIPSET, SEYMOUR MARTIN. *Class: Status and Power.* Chicago: Free Press, 1953.
2. BIERSTEDT, ROBERT. "An Analysis of Social Power," *American Sociological Review,* XV (December, 1950), 730–38.
3. ELKIN, FREDERICK, and WESTLEY, WILLIAM A. "The Myth of Adolescent Culture," *American Sociological Review,* XX (December, 1955), 680–84.
4. GIST, NOEL P., and HALBERT, L. A. *Urban Society.* New York: The Thomas Crowell Co., 1956, pp. 380–87 on "The Power Structure."
5. HERTZLER, JOYCE O. *Society in Action: A Study of Basic Social Processes.* New York: The Dryden Press, Inc., 1954, pp. 303–59.
6. HOLLINGSHEAD, A. B. "The Concept of Social Control," *American Sociological Review,* VI (April, 1941), 217–24.
7. HOMANS, GEORGE. *The Human Group.* New York: Harcourt, Brace & Company, 1950, ch. 11.
8. HUNTER, FLOYD. *Community Power Structure.* Chapel Hill: University of North Carolina Press, 1952, entire book.
9. LYND, ROBERT S. and HELEN M. *Middletown in Transition.* New York: Harcourt, Brace & Company, 1937, ch. 3.
10. MAYER, KURT B. *Class and Society.* Garden City: Doubleday and Company, Inc., ch. 6.
11. McKEE, JAMES. "Status and Power in the Industrial Community," *American Journal of Sociology,* LVIII (January, 1953), 367–71.
12. MERTON, ROBERT. "Patterns of Influence: A Study of Interpersonal Influence and of Communications Behavior in a Local Community," *Communications Research*

1948–1949, ed. by P. F. Lazarsfeld and F. Stanton (New York: Harper and Brothers, 1949).

13. MILLS, C. WRIGHT. *White Collar*. New York: Oxford University Press, 1951.
14. PARSONS, T. *The Social System*. Chicago: Free Press, 1951, pp. 249–325.
15. PELLEGRIN, ROLAND J., and COATES, CHARLES H. "Absentee-Owned Corporations and Community Power Structure," *American Journal of Sociology*, LXI (March, 1956), 413–19.
16. RIESMAN, DAVID, GLAZER, NATHAN, and DENNEY, REUEL. *The Lonely Crowd: A Study of the Changing American Character*. Abridged edition. Garden City: Doubleday & Company, Inc., 1953.
17. Ross, E. A. *Social Control*. New York: The Macmillan Co., 1920. A classic, originally appearing in 1901.
18. ROUCEK, J. S. (ed.) *Social Control*. Princeton: D. Van Nostrand Co., Inc., 1947.
19. SHIBUTANI, TAMOTSU. "Reference Groups as Perspectives," *American Journal of Sociology*, LX (May, 1955), 562–69.
20. WARREN, ROLAND L. "Toward a Typology of Extra-Community Controls Limiting Local Community Autonomy," *Social Forces*, XXXIV (May, 1956), 338–41.
21. YOUNG, KIMBALL. *Sociology: A Study of Society and Culture*. 2d ed.; New York: American Book Company, 1949, pp. 544–46.

Chapter 11

THE COMMUNITY AS A SOCIAL SYSTEM: SETTING AND COMPONENTS

The task of this chapter, as well as that of Chapter 18, is to describe the community as a social system (10). As a system it must possess certain properties capable of being singled out and analyzed (4, 13). For example, it must have an identity and be distinct from other communities and from other types of systems such as the personality system or the total society. It must also consist of parts or components which have definite functional relationships to each other. That is, if one part behaves in a certain way, then other parts will be affected in a specified, predictable manner. Furthermore, this social system can be viewed in terms of the operations which keep it going as a system and which help it adapt to changing situations. It must also be able to take corporate action when this is necessary in order to stave off some threat or meet an emergency.

THE SETTING OF THE COMMUNITY SOCIAL SYSTEM

In the description of the community as a social system it should be made clear from the beginning of the discussion that reference is made to the sphere of social relationships. Many other aspects of a community are important and interesting to analyze but do not constitute the main focus. Figure 16 shows that the social system is central to the interpretation undertaken here. Surrounding it are five factors of the setting, each of which helps define the community system and has considerable influence upon the way the system behaves (15).

Ecology. The first factor in the setting of a community is ecology, which traces some of the adjustments man has made to the natural environment and was described at some length in Chapter 1. Any system of social relationships, whether viewed as a group, a commu-

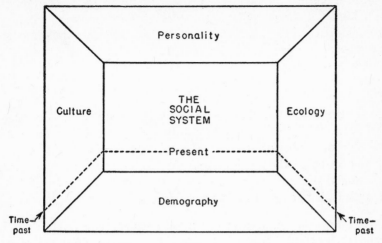

Fig. 16. The setting of the community system.*

nity, or a whole society, must bear some connection to the *place* in which its members must carry on their activities. Community life in the Sahara Desert is much different from that in the lush tropical growths farther south in the African continent, and a New Hampshire village has a different flavor from a settlement in Southern California. For any community one wishes to study it is necessary to learn about the adjustment of the people to their natural resources, climate, and the surface features.

Demography. A second background factor is that of demography, or the consideration of the people as a population rather than as interacting personalities. Chapter 2 has pointed out many of the demographic considerations which have a direct bearing upon the behavior of a community as a social system. These influence not only the quantity but frequently the quality of social relationships. A community made up of many diverse ethnic groups has different problems of assimilation and integration from one in which the population is homogeneous. Increasing or declining numbers, changing sex ratios or age composition, have subtle but no less real impact upon the social behavior within the community. City planners, for instance, must pay close attention to population growth and mobility if they are to anticipate community needs well in advance.

* This and the other figures in this chapter are adapted from charts prepared originally for Associates for International Research, Inc., Cambridge, Massachusetts. Used by permission.

Culture. A third factor of the setting is culture, or the social heritage, which was dealt with in Chapter 5. The cultural aspects are so much a part of our every act that one can separate them out only for purposes of analysis. If we were to place culture in the central position of Figure 16, shifting the social system to the side as one of the background factors, then instead of stressing social relationships we would be paying close attention to values, traditions, norms, belief systems, and the general themes which run like golden threads through the life of a given community with all their variations and contradictions. The knowledge of such matters is essential if one is to interpret correctly the interaction between the component parts of the social system; but in this present analysis, the cultural factor, rich as it is, is background and not central.

Personality. Few community studies, because they try to describe a different level of the social universe, get into the problem of personality development and personality types within a given community. When such topics can be incorporated the picture of community life assumes a new dimension. In our analysis this fourth factor of the setting indicates whether or not there are any special personality types developing within or attracted to a given community. It throws light on the prevalent attitudes and their formation (relating these to the belief systems), and it gets at the problem of motivation of the community members to conform to or deviate from the established patterns of conduct. In view of the complexity of these psychological problems and of the different methodological procedures involved in their study, most sociologists accept as granted the fact that the community is made up of persons who have been "socialized" into the ways of that community and who are sufficiently motivated to act as reasonable, relatively predictable participants in group and community life. Although personality is here placed as a setting factor, this does not mean that it is irrelevant or unimportant but rather that it is being studied in this connection in terms of how it influences the social system, which is the main focus at this time. More will be said about personality in this connection in the section which follows on components of the community as a social system (page 190).

Time. The past definitely lives on in the present; without a knowledge of this past, contemporary events cannot be fully understood. The temporal factor should involve more than just tracing a sequence of events; it should also include some effort to reconstruct the interrelationships which existed at a given time in the past among important social units of the community and the relevance of such interrelationships to present behavior in the community. The study of the past also helps one find out why communities which are reasonably close together and quite similar from the standpoint of the physical environment and population characteristics differ so much in their approach to many problems of the day, the reason being that the social heritage is of a different order, as the illustrations of the communities of Rimrock and Homestead have clearly pointed out.

The Setting Factors and a Definition of the Community. The setting also serves another useful purpose in helping to work out a definition of the community, a problem which has purposely been avoided until this point. Each factor of the setting has a significant contribution to make in this respect:

Ecology: A community is a territorially-organized system co-extensive with a settlement pattern in which (1) an effective communication network operates, (2) people share common facilities and services distributed within this settlement pattern, and (3) develop a psychological identification with the "locality symbol" (the name).

Demography: A community consists of a population in all stages of the life cycle, so that new members are recruited through the biological process of birth. Furthermore, the population must possess sufficient technical skills and knowledge to sustain life, whether on a self-subsistent level as in some peasant communities or through specialized production which depends upon exchange at a central market.

Culture: Community welfare is a value in itself and "community ends are standards by which competing groups judge and adjudicate their claims." Also, the community achieves a normative integration of its own "since the ends of a community are more inclusive than any specific group or groups within the community."[1]

Personality: A community has its own mechanisms for the socialization of new members and the development of the psychological identification with the "locality symbol" (referred to above).

Time: A community persists through time. It takes time to acquire a distinctive culture.

Community Research and the Setting Factors. One of the dilemmas faced by anyone doing sociological research is that of either

---

[1] Albert J. Reiss, Jr., *A Review and Evaluation of Research on Community* (Nashville: 1954. Privately mimeographed), p. 83.

giving too much or too little time to the study of the factors of the setting. In actual research experience, however, the dilemma is usually resolved by the "mind-set" of the researcher himself, who is so sensitized to all the setting factors that they become helpful clues in his interpretation of some aspect of community life. In other words, in one phase of the operation of the community as a social system, the persistence of some cultural trait may be a major influence; in some other phase, the personality of a dominant leader may be the clue; while in a third phase the changing population composition may offer a valuable insight.

Fortunately for students of the community an increasing number of research projects are exploring in detail the methods of social systems analysis (1, 2, 8, 9) as well as the connections between each of these setting factors and the social system. Future students of the community will, therefore, have an even firmer base upon which to build.

THE COMPONENTS OF THE COMMUNITY AS A SOCIAL SYSTEM[2]

Any system, even one that is moving very fast, has parts. In the case of a social system these parts may really be patterns of interaction (for that is what a group is). In other words, the dynamic aspect may be frozen at one point in time so that an analysis can be made of its structure, or of the relationship of the parts to each other. The comparison is often made with a motion picture film which tells the story only as it moves from one frame to the next. But it is possible to halt the camera and project one particular frame on the screen as long as desired so that some special detail can be studied. Social scientists have to catch "society on the run," since people never stop interacting, but they can trace the patterns of behavior and separate out a particular cluster of these behavior patterns for further study. It is in this sense that one can talk of components of a social system.

Since these components are analytical concepts, or a part of the social world set aside for study, it is possible to select those which deal with a relatively few people or those which deal with many, depending upon the kind of problems one wishes to study. The accompanying Figure 17 shows their range in size, moving from the single person through successively larger units to the total community. One could, of course, relate the community to a region and a whole society by continuing this figure into more comprehensive components. The figure should be carefully studied before moving

[2] Extensive use is made of charts in this chapter, since they provide one of the quickest and easiest means of outlining and summarization.

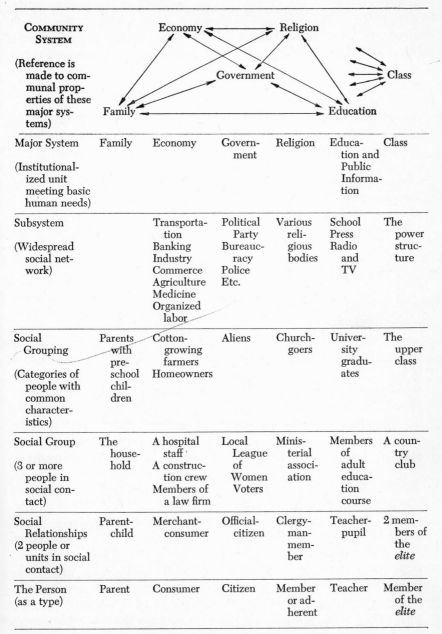

COMMUNITY SYSTEM

(Reference is made to communal properties of these major systems)

	Family	Economy	Government	Religion	Education and Public Information	Class
Major System (Institutionalized unit meeting basic human needs)	Family	Economy	Government	Religion	Education and Public Information	Class
Subsystem (Widespread social network)		Transportation, Banking, Industry, Commerce, Agriculture, Medicine, Organized labor	Political Party, Bureaucracy, Police, Etc.	Various religious bodies	School Press, Radio and TV	The power structure
Social Grouping (Categories of people with common characteristics)	Parents with preschool children	Cotton-growing farmers, Homeowners	Aliens	Church-goers	University graduates	The upper class
Social Group (3 or more people in social contact)	The household	A hospital staff, A construction crew, Members of a law firm	Local League of Women Voters	Ministerial association	Members of adult education course	A country club
Social Relationships (2 people or units in social contact)	Parent-child	Merchant-consumer	Official-citizen	Clergyman-member	Teacher-pupil	2 members of the *elite*
The Person (as a type)	Parent	Consumer	Citizen	Member or adherent	Teacher	Member of the *elite*

FIG. 17. Components of a community system, with examples.

on to the discussion of each of the components. Note that the basic unit of analysis for the study of a community is the subsystem (combined into major systems) and that the behavior of a community as a total system is greatly dependent upon the interaction among these subsystems. These subsystems are in turn made up of widespread networks of groups, which give expression to the kinds of activities associated with each subsystem; the groups are for their part made up of social relationships. The component called a "grouping" is introduced because it refers to certain categories of people, or publics, found in any community. Although these are not related to each other by bonds of interaction, they nevertheless constitute a component of importance for the community as a whole, as later discussion will show.

The Person. Again we meet the person, or the socialized individual, so frequently alluded to in previous pages and given the name of Ezra Smith in Chapter 7. Although he is a social product in one sense, he also becomes a partner in teaching what he has learned to those about him, particularly the younger people whom he may be trying to influence in definite directions that he considers proper. Whether his psychological mechanism is more similar to a gyroscope (as in the case of Riesman's inner-directed person) or a radar (as with the other-directed person), he is nevertheless able and ready to interact with other people in ways he considers expected and appropriate. Since the focus of this volume is upon the community rather than upon the individual as such, it is sufficient merely to indicate the connection between personality development and the social milieu in which one grows up and to stress the importance of viewing people as persons and not merely as biological organisms, each a separate entity unto itself.

It is through the acquisition of personality that one becomes social and moves from the animal plane to what might be called the human plane. (This is a useful generalization even though one might argue that certain animals have "personalities.") The social isolate cannot function as a person indefinitely, since his personality derives from and sustains itself through interaction with others. As Figure 17 shows, the person occupies many different statuses (parent, consumer, citizen, church member, teacher, etc.) within a community, filling some more adequately than others but nevertheless revealing different facets as social situations vary.

The Social Relationship. Since the nature of a social relationship was discussed in considerable detail in Chapter 7, mention need be made here only of the usefulness of this concept for community analysis. The generalized social relationship, such as that between any parent and child, merchant and consumer, official and citizen, clergyman and church member, or teacher and pupil frequently provides a convenient way of looking at some of the crucial characteristics of groups or even subsystems. It is a fair question to ask, "In this community, what is the relationship between the worker and management?" The person will understand the meaning of the question and may try to generalize in one of several ways. If labor is unorganized in the community and each worker seeks to establish a personal connection between himself and his employer, then this worker-manager relationship will be described in such terms; if labor is highly organized, militant, and powerful, then this particular relationship will be described in different terms. Or, if the picture is spotty, with some firms unionized and others not, then a third variation appears. This illustrates in quite simple terms how the analysis of any one relationship might give considerable insight into some of the important areas of social life.

The class (or caste) relationships between race or ethnic groups, the generalized relationships between husbands and wives, between Catholics and Protestants, between college people and townspeople —all reveal much about a community even though the analysis of each of these is in terms of those occupying two particular statuses. At times the situation varies so much from person to person that generalization about some relationships should be avoided; but even this fact itself has social significance, for it shows the existence of at least deviant behavior patterns and the possibility of variant values.

Although the examples in Figure 17 do not indicate this, social relationships can exist between groups or subsystems in as real a sense as they exist between persons. This should be borne in mind as these more inclusive units are fitted into the general scheme of the community system.

The Social Group. A quick review of Chapter 7 should show the part that social groups play as components. Their types are many and their number, even in a medium-sized city, difficult to calculate, particularly as one thinks of the informal cliques as well as the recognizable formal organizations. Through them things get done or proposals get blocked; in groups people spend their leisure, carry on their jobs, worship, acquire schooling, and become acquainted with those who later are to become their mates.

Beyond any question someone who could trace the behavior of all the groups of a community would have an omniscient view of that community, but such a comprehensive view is impossible even with the most ambitious research designs. What is possible, however, is the study of the behavior of various types of groups, with enough samples of each type to enable one to generalize about that type. For instance, men's service or luncheon clubs fall into a general pattern about which a great deal can be said without knowing the specific details of every such club in the community. Another approach sometimes used is to determine through a preliminary survey what specific groups in the community have a bearing upon the special research problems under investigation and then study these groups in great detail.

Whatever the approach, if one is intent upon a community study, the groups which are studied must be seen not as entities within themselves but as components of a larger social system. This means that one will stop and ask such questions as, "What would this community lack or what changes would be effected if this particular group (or others like it) were to disappear?" If definite answers can be made to that question then one is describing "the function" of that group in the community. If family groups were to be abolished, certain consequences would follow; the same would hold true for particular kinds of economic, governmental, religious, and recreational groups upon whom the community members seem to have developed a dependence even though not all of them are participants in this group. Relatively few people serve on the City Council, but without the proper functioning of this Council many community services would suffer and almost everyone in the community would be affected. It thus follows as a matter of definition as well as of fact that if a community is a system (with interrelated parts), the failure of any one significant part to perform as expected impairs the functioning of other parts closely tied in with it and eventually cripples the whole system.

The problem of analysis then turns to the meaning of the term *significant part*, for in a community as in the bodily organism there are parts such as the appendix which have little to do with the operation of the system. They may be fleeting and evanescent or may be so old that they have outlived their usefulness. Albert J. Reiss, Jr., would consider as *communal* only those forms of interaction which arise within the values which have been locally defined and implemented (put into practice). Therefore, he uses criteria internal to the system (14), since something is communal only if local people consider it so. This will be referred to again in the consideration of the subsystems and the widespread social networks connected with them. But before taking up this next component, which follows logically as a step beyond the group in inclusiveness, it would be well to consider a different kind of component—the social grouping.

The Social Grouping. For anyone interested in the study of public opinion in the community or in the planning of political appeals the *grouping* provides an important component. If the word *group* is reserved for those who are in direct social contact, then some other word such as *grouping* must be found for those who, because they possess certain characteristics in common, fall into the same categories, but who do not interact with each other on a face-to-face basis. Figure 18 provides one way of classifying these social groupings, each of which constitutes a special public to which action programs can be oriented.

BIOLOGICAL CRITERIA

AGE: children, youths, adults, aged
SEX: males, females
RACE: Negroes, Semites, Eurasians, etc.
NATIONALITIES: Serbs, Americans, Mexicans
OTHER PHYSICAL TRAITS: paraplegics, blondes, etc.

ECONOMIC CRITERIA

POSSESSIONS: home-owners, radio owners, stockholders, etc.
OCCUPATION: farmers, unskilled workers, skilled workers, managers, professional people
RESIDENCE: city-dwellers, villagers, townspeople, suburbanites

SOCIAL CRITERIA

POLITICAL ORIENTATION: Republicans, Democrats, New Dealers, Isolationists
RELIGIOUS ORIENTATION: Christians (Catholics, Protestants, Orthodox), Moslems (Shiites, Sunnites), Jews, Buddhists, etc.
FAMILIAL STATUS: single, married, divorced, widowed, parents, childless
SOCIAL VIEWS: liberals, conservatives, etc.

PERSONAL ACHIEVEMENT CRITERIA

EDUCATIONAL ATTAINMENT: illiterates, university graduates, etc.
FORMAL HONORS RECEIVED: Phi Beta Kappa, Nobel Prize Winner, etc.
RANK: presidents of civic organizations

CRITERIA OF COMMON INTERESTS

SPORTS: football enthusiasts, hunters, chess players, etc.
ARTS (AS AVOCATION): music lovers, museum-goers, etc.
RADIO AND TELEVISION: listeners to baseball broadcasts, devotees of Red Skelton program, etc.
HOBBIES: stamp collectors, amateur carpenters, tourists, etc.
"CAUSES": antivivisectionists, "Women's Righters," Advocates of Planned Parenthood, Esperanto enthusiasts, etc.

FIG. 18. Types of groupings in a complex community, with examples.

These groupings, many of which are included in the decennial U. S. Census, can be studied through statistical methods. Demographers concern themselves mainly with the groupings based on biological, economic, and some of the social criteria; the economists study some of these as well. Other social scientists, such as sociologists and social psychologists, have an interest not only in these but also in those involving personal achievement and common interests. Where the categories can be studied statistically it is possible to show the association between two or more of these groupings. For example, when the proportion of youth in the population rises, certain statistical correlations appear among such variables as family status, educational attainment, social views, and interests in sports. In other words, these relationships can be "quantified." Such findings have a bearing upon the study of the community as a social system when it can be shown that the behavior of the subsystems and their constituent groups are affected, a matter not too difficult to do when the statistical analysis has been carefully done and the theoretical model used is empirically sound.

The Subsystem. Groups, as has been pointed out, for the most part do not exist in isolation any more than does an individual. Most of them come into existence and survive in response to deep-seated human needs to which society has worked out numerous adjustments in the past. New groups arise as the life of the community becomes more specialized, and additional groups develop for the purpose of tying together into some sort of coordinated fashion the new groups of a highly specialized sort. For example, where occupation becomes so specialized that people learn only one narrow pursuit, classes in "do-it-yourself" spring up to impart to shopkeepers, busdrivers, insurance salesmen, and lawyers the ordinary technical skills which most men had in an earlier era. Coordinating councils of many kinds also become a necessity. These illustrate the fact that groups do become tied together in widespread interrelated social networks which in turn are a part of the age-old institutions which have been satisfying in various ways the familial, economic, religious, educational, and political needs of man. It does not matter that many of these felt needs are acquired (and therefore social) rather than biological; the fact that they exist is sufficient explanation for the presence of these institutionalized networks which we can call a subsystem.

But what are these networks and how does one know what groups are interconnected? As already indicated, the answer must be sought in the needs of the community system, for it is in response to these needs, felt and mediated by community members, of course, that the networks come into existence. Although the accompanying figure shows the types of subsystems in a total society, most of these are represented in a community as well. Whether a given subsystem suggested on this figure has much community significance will depend upon the value orientation of the community, but it is apt to be important where it is prompted by needs which can be said to be universal (such as biological maintenance).

Some Total System Needs	Particular Aspect	Subsystem—in Nation-wide Terms (A few examples of social networks)
Biological maintenance	Reproduction	Family (as a nation-wide subsystem of legitimized statuses and roles involving procreation and child rearing)
	Physical fitness	Medicine and public health
	Food and shelter	Agriculture; housing administration (see also material resources and service below)
Exercise of power	Decision-making	Informal power structure, governmental legislatures
	Bureaucratic enforcement of decisions	Each governmental department, dominant party
	Social control over individual behavior	Labor unions, political, women's, youth, nation-wide associations, religious bodies
	Use of physical force when other controls fail	Police, judiciary, military
Dissemination of knowledge, information, and "know-how"	Formal learning Information	Regular school at all levels, library Press, radio, television subsystems (involving control by appropriate bureaucratic agency)
	Teaching skills	Arrangements for apprenticeship and special courses outside regular school
Material resources and services	Production Distribution Professional services	Agriculture, mining, forestry, industry Transportation, commerce, finance Medicine, law, architecture, entertainment
Strengthening psychological security	Facing life crises	Some particular religious subsystem to which individual belongs
	Intimate response	Kinship (although intimate response comes chiefly from groups rather than subsystems)
	Welfare needs	Retirement, maternity, unemployment programs

FIG. 19. Types of subsystems in a total society.

The size of a community has much to do with the number of such networks. For example, in a large city there be many Methodist churches which for that community constitute a subsystem, or a network of interacting groups. But in a small town there will probably only be one Mehodist church and no "Methodist subsystem," although this single church is representative of the subsystem existing in the larger society. But in the small town there will be a family subsystem (as defined in Figure 19), a commercial subsystem, an agricultural subsystem, as well as others representing a joining of forces to meet community needs as highlighted by the value orientation of the community members. It is useful, however, to identify these subsystems as they exist in the larger society and then ask if their local counterparts are found within the community, remembering all the while that this analysis of the community as a social system is in terms of a theoretical scheme which may or may not apply one hundred per cent to any given community. But having such a scheme helps one know what components to seek and how to interrelate those that are found.

Major Systems. Some comment about the major systems listed on Figure 17, which arrays all of the components on a single chart, is necessary. These more inclusive units (family, government, etc.) are convenient analytical constructs for grouping together the subsystems into functional contexts. For example, it is only common sense to tie together the subsystems of agriculture, the professions, commerce, industry, transportation, banking, etc., into one major system called "the economy." When a person is describing the economy he is talking about the behavior of these subsystems toward each other and toward subsystems outside of the economy. The totality of the interaction of these subsystems, within limits at least, characterizes what might be termed the "economic segment" of the community. But the economy interacts with government, which in turn is made up of its constituent subsystems, and out of such interaction community welfare is influenced. A pointed illustration is the continuing debate as to whether there should be more taxes to provide more public services or lower taxes and decreased services to the citizenry. The tendency of government is to expand its activities, and the tendency of those in charge of economic matters is to resist its expansion and control.

Not all activities which occur within any one of these major systems is communal. Much that goes on within the home, the business office, or on the playing field is serving the private interests of those engaged in the activities there. The community, however, becomes directly involved when, for example, parents neglect their children or when a husband and a wife seek a divorce. This is another way of saying that the term *communal* must be understood with reference to the value orientation of a given community, since in one place what is considered a public matter is elsewhere considered a private matter. In one community a man may feel, and others will support him in his belief, that he has the right to beat his wife whenever she does not do what he tells her to do; in another community a wife thus treated could very quickly make it a community matter and gain considerable sympathy, even to the point of having her husband put into jail.

Social class, taken up in an earlier chapter cuts across the other major systems and can hardly be represented in the same social field unless a three-dimensional figure is used. Nevertheless, it is necessary to see that it is in itself a major system, frequently tied in with the power structure of the community (see Chapter 10) and has a reciprocal connection with the other systems. A later discussion of social mobility as an operation of the system will further elaborate this point.

This brief catalogue of the components of a community system should provide the basis for classifying and describing most of the social units in the community. Such an approach does indicate that in the study of a particular type of unit (such as an industrial plant) it is helpful to see that it too consists of components and is at the same time a part of a larger unit. It is important to remember that some of the components described are *concrete* and can actually be seen: a person, two people in a social relationship, a social group. The rest of these components are *inferred* from the behavior of people and their groups. One cannot at any one place or point of time see an economy, a family system, a religion, but one can see human behavior which demonstrates what we have come to associate with these major systems. This dealing with *analytic* as opposed to *concrete structures* (terms given special meaning by Marion J. Levy) (3) is common in any scientific research. We cannot see weight but we can see evidences of what weight does and so use it as a concept in everyday life as well as in the most intricate laboratory experiments. Therefore these complex patterns of relationships (subsystems and systems), so intertwined with other patterns that they cannot be separated even theoretically, assist one in finding out what is behind the observable group behavior and make possible not only the analysis of a community but the description of a total society as well (17).

REFERENCES AND SUGGESTED READINGS

1. BARBER, BERNARD. "Structural-Functional Analysis: Some Problems and Misunderstandings," *American Sociological Review*, XXI (April, 1956), 129–34.
2. BESHERS, JAMES M. "Models and Theory Construction," *American Sociological Review*, XXII (February, 1957), 32–37.
3. LEVY, MARION J. *The Structure of Society*. Princeton: Princeton University Press, 1952.
4. LOOMIS, CHARLES P. "The Nature of Rural Social Systems—A Typological Analysis," *Rural Sociology*, XV (June, 1950), 155–74.
5. LOOMIS, CHARLES P., and BEEGLE, J. ALLAN. *Rural Social Systems*. Englewood Cliffs, N.J.: Prentice-Hall, Inc., 1950.
6. ———. "A Typological Analysis of Social Systems," *Sociometry*, XI (August, 1948), 147–91.
7. LOOMIS, CHARLES P., and McKINNEY, JOHN C. "Systemic Differences Between Latin-American Communities of Family Farms and Large Estates," *The American Journal of Sociology*, LXI (March, 1956), 404–12.
8. McKINNEY, JOHN C. "The Role of Constructive Typology in Scientific Sociological Analysis," *Social Forces*, XXVIII (March, 1950), 235–39.
9. MEADOWS, PAUL. "Models, Systems and Science," *American Sociological Review*, XXII (February, 1957), 3–8.
10. MERCER, BLAINE E. *The American Community*. New York: Random House, Inc., 1956.
11. MERTON, ROBERT K. *Social Theory and Structure*. Chicago: Free Press, 1949.
12. NETT, ROGER. "System Building in Sociology—A Methodological Analysis," *Social Forces*, XXXI (October, 1952), 25–29.
13. PARSONS, TALCOTT. *The Social System*. Chicago: Free Press, 1951.
14. REISS, ALBERT J., JR. *A Review and Evaluation of Research on Community: A Working Memorandum Prepared for the Committee on Social Behavior of the Social Science Research Council*. Mimeographed. Nashville, Tennessee, April, 1954.
15. SOROKIN, PITIRIM. *Society, Culture and Personality*. New York: Harper & Brothers, 1947.
16. WIESE, LEOPOLD VON, and BECKER, HOWARD. *Systematic Sociology*. New York: John Wiley & Sons, Inc., 1932.
17. WILLIAMS, ROBIN M. *American Society: A Sociological Interpretation*. New York: Alfred A. Knopf, Inc., 1951.

PART II

The Major Systems at Work

INTRODUCTION TO PART TWO

"My Home Town" is a theme topic frequently assigned by instructors of Freshman English Composition in the early days of the semester when the new students' nostalgia for home and friends is very strong. The treatment of this theme runs from the highly emotional extolling of local virtues to the coldly analytical description of places and persons. As is to be expected, few if any freshmen use the concepts treated in the previous chapter, for they have not developed sufficient detachment to view their community as a social system. Nor do they have the specialized vocabulary which such a description requires. Perhaps much of the charm which such compositions frequently contain would be lost if they were fitted arbitrarily into a sociological mold.

Nevertheless, for purposes of the major community system descriptions which follow it is necessary to have in mind a general guide which calls attention to the points to be considered in a full-scale analysis.

First, the *structure* of the major community system must be delineated. This can be done by analyzing the subsystems of which it is composed, breaking these down into their constituent groups. Interrelationships among the subsystems must also be traced if one is to get a full structural picture. For some kinds of analysis the structure can be sufficiently indicated by a listing of the hierarchies of statuses of which it is composed or by describing significant social relationships contained in the system. Whatever the approach used, it is well to know what social units are being treated and how they are connected with each other.

Second, the *functions* of each major community system must be examined. This can be done with reference to the general operations of the system (see Figure 24), or it may be done simply in terms of specific activities which the system uniquely performs and without which the community would be seriously handicapped. At some point, the tie-in between the behavior of each system and other systems must be pointed up, since this reveals much about the specific functions of these systems in the community as a whole. This treatment of the functions will pave the way for a summary chapter on the operations of the community as a system to supplement the preceding chapter on the setting and components of the system. Only as the dynamic aspect is added to the structural aspect is a full picture of the total community system possible.

No attempt is made in the chapters which follow to use a single outline for each chapter. Instead, each major system will receive the kind of treatment which reflects not only the kind of research done in connection with it but which also brings out some of the uniqueness of that major system. From time to time, attention will be called to the connection between the system under discussion and other major systems in the community, although no attempt will be made to exhaust all—or even most—of the possible interrelationships that might be described. The chief purposes of these succeeding chapters, therefore, is to indicate important points to bear in mind when looking sociologically at major areas of community life and to suggest that such areas can be viewed in terms of the structure and the operations of the subsystems of which they are composed as well as in terms of the total community of which they are a part.

Chapter 12

LOCAL GOVERNMENT

A visitor to a Greek village, whether he arrives by donkey, bus, or private car, finds himself under the curious but friendly gaze of those who happen to be in or passing through the central village square. If he goes over to the coffee-house to sit in the shade and order a cool drink, he does not need to wait long before the village officially welcomes him in the person of the President of the Community Board. Here he sees local government in operation in a lively, hospitable way. A stay of even a short duration will show other examples of local government (11):

The policeman who assists a peasant who has imbibed too heavily home from the coffee house-tavern.

The "water caller" who regulates the flow of water into a man's irrigation ditches for a specified length of time and then calls the name of the next in line so that he can be on hand to control the water diverted into his ditches.

The meeting of the Community Board, whose members, officially elected, assemble to decide what public funds if any are to be turned over to the School Board or the Church Board.

The tax collector, from outside the village, who nevertheless makes the office of the Community Board his headquarters while he tries to get payment from recalcitrant farmers.

The request by the Community President to the Prefect that some representative of the national government (agricultural extension worker, health official, veterinarian, school supervisor, etc.) come to help out with some urgent problem.

These simple cases illustrate that where the village, easily demarcated geographically, is the unit of government, there is a close correspondence between the governmental unit and the sociological community. But in most countries where the village settlement pattern dominates, local government is chiefly a representation of the central government, which allows few local decisions to be made.

In the United States, on the other hand, school boards may be autonomous in many matters; counties and incorporated towns may have a larger voice in fixing the exact tax rates for the year; or the police officials may be employees of the local unit of government rather than state or federal employees. Nevertheless, local government in the United States depends entirely upon the legislative statutes of the state in which the unit is located, with different states allowing varying degrees of choice to units of different size. Furthermore, the political boundaries in the United States only occasionally correspond to the boundaries of the community as defined in this book. What then, is local governmental structure like and how as a major community system does it affect community life?

POLITICAL STRUCTURE IN THE COMMUNITY

Variety of Local Administrative Units. Students of local government in the United States have clearly shown the "crazy-quilt" pattern of local administrative units. They cite the special study made by the United States Census Bureau for 1942, which reveals that at that time there were 155,116 units of government in the nation. Of these 3050 were counties, 18,919 towns and townships, 16,220 municipalities, 108,579 school districts, and 8299 special districts. As is apparent, 70 per cent of the total were school districts, whose number has declined by several thousand because of consolidation since the study was made. Just the same, the variety of local units still is bewildering to anyone trying to bring about some approximation between the sociological community and these local administrative units.

This is in striking contrast to the situation in a country like Brazil, where there is one local administrative unit, the *município*, through which all political activities flow. These number 1575 and correspond roughly to the county governmental unit in the United States, but, as T. Lynn Smith (14) has pointed out, the city which serves as the seat of the *município* never has a corporate existence. Indeed, there is no such thing as the separate incorporation of a Brazilian village, town, or city, but the inhabitants of a *município*, whether they live in the center itself or the rural areas, must depend upon it for their governmental services, many of which are state-supported. One disadvantage of the *município* is the fact that people do not think of it as a unit of government close to them and serving them. In the United States, where there are these more numerous subdivisions, people may feel closer to their local government but, on the other hand, find that the profusion of such units makes it

very difficult to deal with problems that extend beyond the boundaries of that small unit. For example, health problems, as well as
many other kinds, can only be dealt with intelligently when incorporated places as well as the county cooperate in a combined
program. But the difficulties of such cooperation are only too evident in communities where sharp feelings exist over a matter like
the use of daylight-saving time. For example, in the heart of the
town whose council has decided in favor of "fast time," stands the
court house with its clock set one hour behind on "God's time" in
deference to the rural people who control the county unit.

Regional Differences in Local Government. The study of American
community life is not only complicated by the number of administrative units in a given area but by the fact that there are such differences from region to region. Luke M. Smith has studied this regional distribution and has sought to discover which types follow
trade and social areas. He finds:

In New England the territory of the State is divided into townships, most of
the local governmental functions being performed by them, although they are
grouped into counties as State court, sheriff, and land-recording districts; the
boundaries of the townships coincide rather closely with the trade or other social areas; legal separation of the social-trade centers from their rural hinterlands is rare . . . the township hall is almost always in the largest, sometimes
the only, urban center of the township. The Middle Atlantic States are transitional between New England and the Middle West.[1]

In the Middle West, on the contrary, the townships are the basic
units as in New England, but the counties perform more local functions. The townships, having been laid out into areas six miles
square, have little correspondence with trade or other social areas.
Furthermore, the social-trade centers become incorporated, legally
separating themselves from the rural areas, to a greater extent than
elsewhere in the United States. In the Far West the county assumes
nearly all the functions of local government, the townships having
been almost entirely abolished.

In the South, especially in the Southeast, the townships are reduced to
justice-of-the-peace districts and the counties are made virtually the sole units
of local government; the counties are smaller than they are elsewhere in the
United States and coincide more nearly with the trade or other social areas,
although not so closely as in the case of the New England townships; the social-
trade centers legally separate themselves from their rural hinterlands more frequently than in the Middle West; the county seats are often in the social-trade
centers of their counties, although they are more likely to be toward the easily

[1] Luke M. Smith, "Territorial Variables in American Local Government," *Social
Forces,* XXVII (May, 1949), 351.

accessible geographical centers . . . than they are likely to be in the largest social-trade centers.[2]

Principal Organs of Local Government (the "Official" Subsystem). In view of this variety and regional distribution, what, then, are the kinds of groups through which the governmental machinery conducts its business? Some kind of body must exist with powers to act. In every state except Rhode Island there is an elective county board (in Louisiana the parish is equivalent to the county). Most counties have boards consisting of three to five members, often called commissioners, whose duties and powers relate to finance, maintenance of highways, bridges, and other public works, charities and corrections, appointment and supervision of county officers, control of elections, and a large variety of other matters.

Cities, on the other hand, have one of three possible types: the mayor-council type, which still is the most prevalent form; the commission type, and the council-manager type.

In the mayor-council system, the councilors and mayor are elected, with the councilors representing the legislative side and the mayor the executive side of government. The work of the local government is carried out not by the council but by administrative departments, which vary largely in number but will include at least the following six:

. . . (1) a law department headed by the corporation counsel or city attorney, and charged with giving legal advice to the mayor, council, and all city departments, prosecuting and defending suits brought by or against the city, drawing up or approving city contracts, and drafting municipal ordinances; (2) a department of finance, commonly including the offices of city treasurer, city comptroller, auditor, and tax assessors or collectors; (3) a department of public safety, including the machinery of fire, police, health, and building administration; (4) a department of public works—usually the largest of all—with subdivisions or bureaus attending to streets, public buildings, parks and playgrounds, sewerage and water systems, and practically all the engineering work of the city; (5) a health department, charged with enforcement of the sanitary code; and (6) a department of education—although in numerous cities the administration of school and library affairs is handled by more or less independent school or library boards, chosen by popular vote or appointed by the mayor.[3]

In some cities the mayor may appoint the department heads, while in others they are popularly elected.

Under the commission plan, instead of a mayor and a council, one finds a small commission, usually of five members, elected on a general ticket. All of the legislative and most of the administrative

[2] *Ibid.*
[3] Frederic A. Ogg and P. Orman Ray, *Essentials of American Government* (6th ed.; New York: Appleton-Century-Crofts, Inc.), pp. 669–70.

authority is concentrated in their hands. Each member of the commission usually serves as the head of one of the five departments into which the administrative work is usually divided.

The third plan, the council-manager system, works through an elected city council or commission whose members have no administrative duties as they would under the commission plan but who turn such work over to a professionally trained city manager (1). He is supposedly a nonpolitical, highly competent, well-paid individual who follows the policies set by the council. He has general administrative charge over the work of the departments.

In the case of the New England town the authority for decision rests with an assembly composed of the town's qualified voters, although in areas of heavy population concentration this assembly is made up of duly elected representatives. It has an elected board of selectmen who serve as an executive committee between the annual town meetings. There is no mayor or chief executive. The townships of the midwest have either a committee or board of supervisors or trustees, and in some states the township has a well-defined head called the supervisor. But as was noted earlier, in these areas the role of the township is much less important than in New England.

In addition to these formal organs of local government (county board, city council, board of selectmen, supervisors, or trustees) one finds in many communities other governmental agencies or groups with considerable power.[4] These are such state agencies as the county court, a part of the state judicial machinery; there are state welfare agencies and numerous units of the federal government administering agricultural and other programs. Thus, not all government in a local community is local government, but it is all part of the resident's experience of government.

By now the official structure of local government in the community should be somewhat more clarified. If the community extends beyond the corporate boundaries of a town or city, as it usually does, one must include the county as well as the town or city government, identifying each agency connected with either body. To these must be added the district school boards, the state and federal agencies represented locally, and the connections, if any, between the county or city governments. Since some serve only a part of the community and others the rest of the community, these governmental units may tend to divide rather than unite the people in joint undertakings of mutual benefit.

[4] One of these is the agency devoted to physical planning and zoning. It will not be discussed here, since it is the central topic of Chapter 19.

The "official subsystem" consists, then, of the chief organ (council, etc.) and the departments and agencies connected with it, as well as its connections with other "official" agencies (county, state, federal, etc.). The interaction within this "official" subsystem can be studied in great detail, including the behavior of the police department toward the fire department, the public works staff, or vice versa (16, 17). It is important to know how the members for the subsystem are recruited: by merit examination, by the spoils system, or otherwise. Such a study would also trace the flow of power as originally outlined in the charter provided by the state legislature and try to determine to what extent the locus of power resided in spots other than that legally intended. The study of this subsystem would show whether the city and the county welfare workers shunted clients back and forth between them, how taxes were assessed differently in the county, township, and the city, and a number of other features involving two rival jurisdictions in the same community. Since the school board as well as other elected boards also appertain to this "official subsystem," their part in it must be fully understood. Here, then, is a network of social relationships, consisting of many, many groups and one marked by hierarchies of status throughout which power is supposed to reside.

The "Party" Subsystem. But setting down the formal structure of government, with its official organs and numerous departments and agencies, is only the beginning of the story of government. There is also a "party" subsystem consisting of local organizations of national political parties through which candidates for office are chosen, campaigns conducted, and rewards redistributed to those who supported the winning ticket. Such rewards may include appointment to official position or the grant of lucrative contracts (12).

Noel P. Gist and L. A. Halbert have this to say about such organizations in the city:

Supplementing the bureaucratic structure of formal government is the party organization, which in a large city, and even in smaller ones, may be complex. At the base of the organizational pyramid is the precinct worker whose responsibility is to get out the vote in his political division. A little higher up the political pyramid is the ward committeeman, usually a precinct executive who has been promoted because of his diligence and success. His duty is to supervise the precinct workers who operate within his political domain. At the apex of the political pyramid is the boss, the generalissimo of the party. . . . The local party organization is, of course, an integral part of a bureaucracy that is national in scope.[5]

[5] Noel P. Gist and L. A. Halbert, *Urban Society* (New York: The Thomas Crowell Co., 1956), p. 374.

More and more, elections to local government are being conducted on a nonpartisan basis, but even then mechanisms must be found for drawing up nonpartisan slates and publicizing these candidates so that the voters can make an intelligent decision.

Many studies are conducted each election year on voting behavior; consequently we are learning more about the way this "party" subsystem works (3, 6, 10). For example, Philip K. Hastings finds in his study of the nonvoter in Pittsfield, Massachusetts, that the following correlates of nonvoting exist: "(1) comparatively rare membership in voluntary associations; (2) minimum exposure to political communication; (3) meager information; (4) little identification with political organizations; (5) low frequency of substantive assumptions regarding the voting behavior of various political organizations; and (6) indefinite attitudes toward current politico-economic issues."[6] He also suggests, though he does not claim to have proved this point, that the politically apathetic individual probably depends politically "upon the local authority or leader symbols," thereby betraying a personal sense of inadequacy and insecurity. Studies such as these would indicate that a relatively few groups, closely identified with party affairs, really constitute the subsystem, with a large grouping of community members bearing the labels Democrat, Republican, Independent, who may or may not be excited enough to participate at election time. Between elections even the most enthusiastic campaigner is apt to subside and let the "party politicians" keep the subsystem operating.

Even though two or three local committees representing different parties compete with each other for the support of the voters they usually cooperate to keep the subsystem in operation and would prove mutually resistant to efforts made to infringe upon the power of the political parties as one of the elements of our governmental system. No matter what their political complexion they feel not only a loyalty to their own party but to the "party" subsystem—the arena of interaction in which their unit plays a significant part.

The "Citizen" Subsystem. In many communities one finds a third governmental subsystem in operation, and it might be termed the "citizen" subsystem. This includes voluntary joint efforts by citizens' groups to improve the quality of governmental services, to increase the honesty of elections, and to call forth a greater sense of civic responsibility on the part of the members of the community. In one way this might be thought of as a pressure subsystem

[6] Philip K. Hastings, "The Voter and the Non-Voter," *American Journal of Sociology,* LXII (November, 1956), 302.

which arises in response to other pressures brought to bear upon officials to show favoritism, split fees, and divert public funds for the private gain of themselves or others.

A copy of a single issue of the news letter of the Citizens' Civic Association, Inc., of Fort Wayne, Indiana, indicates the drive and approach of a particularly active and effective group of this sort (see Figure 20). The network of persons and organizations of which

Citizens' news letter CIVIC ASSOCIATION, INC.

608 FORT WAYNE BANK BUILDING • FORT WAYNE, INDIANA • TELEPHONE ANTHONY 4438
SUBSCRIPTION PRICE $2.00   THOMAS P. RIDDLE, Editor

NO. 74   APRIL 30, 1957
                    "TODAY'S FORESIGHT-TOMORROW'S COMMUNITY"

    There are many indications that we have entered a new and exciting era of community improvement and development in Fort Wayne and in Allen County. The following signs of impending progress reflect the imagination and leadership of heads of local government and of various civic organizations:

        MERGER OF CITY'S VARIOUS ENGINEERING DEPARTMENTS COMPLETED;
        MERGER OF SOME TOWNSHIP AND SCHOOL-CITY DISTRICTS PROPOSED;
        MERGER OF CITY AND COUNTY HEALTH DEPARTMENTS ADVOCATED;
        PLANNING OF METROPOLITAN AREA SEWERAGE WORKS BEGUN;
        COUNTY-WIDE SYSTEM FOR DESIGNATING HOUSES AND ROADS LAUNCHED;
        CITY-COUNTY LAND USE & IMPROVEMENT PLANNING TO BE INTEGRATED;
        SUBURBAN SEWAGE TREATMENT PLANTS TO BE CONSTRUCTED;
        RENEWAL OF DOWNTOWN FORT WAYNE CONTEMPLATED;
        CONSTRUCTION OF FORT WAYNE'S "FINE ARTS CENTER" PLANNED;
        SUCCESSFUL ANNEXATIONS TO CITY ATTRIBUTED TO CRITERIA USED.

    The building of a better community depends, in no small measure, upon the resourcefulness of public officials in adapting improved mechanisms of government to the solution of problems of over-all concern to city and county residents. IT ALSO DEPENDS UPON TODAY'S FORESIGHT.

    ****
    * CITIZENS' COUNCIL MEETING - WEDNESDAY, MAY 1,1957, 7:30 P.M. *
    *   KROGER STORE, "TRAINING ROOM" - 2201 SHERMAN BLVD.   *
    *   *
    *   THEME: "ACTS OF INDIANA GENERAL ASSEMBLY HIGHLIGHTED"   *
    *   *
    *   GUEST SPEAKER: DONNELLY P. McDONALD, JR.,   *
    *   REPRESENTATIVE TO THE STATE LEGISLATURE   *
    *   *
    *   "OUR EXPLODING SUBURBS" - AN INTERESTING COLORED FILM   *
    *   WILL BE SHOWN UNDER THE AUSPICES OF   *
    *   THE HOME BUILDERS' ASSOCIATION OF FORT WAYNE   *
    *   *
    *   ALL DELEGATES AND OFFICERS OF MEMBER ORGANIZATIONS ARE   *
    *   URGED TO ATTEND   *
    ****

    A CRYING NEED: Fort Wayne's three rivers offer opportunities for improvement, development and utilization of a natural resource of great potential public use and enjoyment. A NEGLECTED RESOURCE OF SUCH IMPORTANCE PROVIDES A CHALLENGING OPPORTUNITY FOR PUBLIC SERVICE.

                            NOTEWORTHY:

        "BEAUTY BREEDS BEAUTY" - IT'S TIME FOR NEIGHBORHOOD

        CLEAN-UP, PAINT-UP, FIX-UP, WAKE-UP CAMPAIGNS

FIG. 20. A civic association news letter.

it is an important part comprises in Fort Wayne the "citizen" sub-system, which pays considerable attention to those projects that can be accomplished through better local government.

The League of Women Voters, a national group with local branches scattered in most major American cities, is a good example of associations singularly dedicated to good government and more intelligent citizen participation.

The "citizens" subsystem is not as closely knit as the other two subsystems, but when local leaders do mobilize opinion and unite local groups into a network for "good government," the "official" sub-system begins to respond. Should it get to the point of actually selecting and campaigning for candidates the "citizens" subsystem turns into a unit of the "party subsystem." This does not inevitably occur, because many of the citizens' groups realize that their chief contribution comes when they maintain strict political neutrality as far as candidates are concerned and speak out only on the issues involving better government.

Within this network, when it does come into existence, there is likely to be stress and strain, since many groups who support such a move do so for a variety of different reasons. They find that they can unite on this one issue at this particular juncture of time, although they may otherwise constitute rather strange bedfellows (e.g., the Tax Reduction League, local branch of American Association of Social Workers, Ministerial Association, Freethinkers' Society). This explains to a large degree the nature of the instability of such a subsystem and shows why a new beginning has to be made periodically to correct recurring governmental abuses.

DIAGRAMMING THE GOVERNMENT AS A MAJOR COMMUNITY SYSTEM

Anyone who would understand not only the structure but also the dynamics of government in his community must first take the time to analyze the components of each of three subsystems just described. Most groups that have any important connection with government can be included under one of these subsystems. Furthermore, each subsystem must be viewed as a network. In many communities it is quite possible to have several groups interested in better government, each going its separate way without reference to the other and not constituting a network at all. If, however, several of these groups are aware of the others' presence, begin to respond to the action taken by the other groups, either by lending support or avoiding duplication or by sending a single member to talk over local problems with representatives of other organizations—then the subsystem is beginning to materialize. Likewise, in a community that has only one political party and where no rival slates are even entered one does not have a "party" subsystem in the sense used here. Instead, a single group is carrying on the work that the larger subsystem would conduct in a two-party community.

The second step, after each subsystem has been diagrammed separately, is to try to show the connections among the three subsystems: the "official," the "party," and the "citizen." How does the outcome of an election (engineered within the "party" subsystem) affect the "official" subsystem? Are all officeholders thrown out, are the department heads changed, or is there simply a turnover of the elected officials? To what extent is there such a close tie-in between the "official" subsystem and some division of the "party" subsystem that those with positions in the local government are forced to give "voluntary" contributions to the campaign chests of incumbents seeking re-election? To what extent do local governmental services grow more efficient as an election approaches? How well do the county officials enforce the election laws?

The "citizen" subsystem also interacts with each of the other two. What cooperation does a citizen group get from the major political parties when it asks for permission to have poll watchers in precincts where voting irregularities have been known to occur? To what extent are rival candidates for office willing to answer in specific detail a series of questions, put to them during the campaign, about their intentions if elected to office? How responsive are the officials at city hall to complaints about inefficient government services? Are they willing to have "beef sessions," as was Mayor Charles Farnsley of Louisville, Kentucky, who made himself available to listen to complaints of every sort and tried through the appropriate department head to take care of legitimate complaints? Since the possible courses of interaction between these subsystems are so numerous and since they will vary from community to community, it is sufficient here to indicate that this is a part of the analysis of local government that should not be overlooked.

The third step in diagramming local government, once the connections between the three subsystems have been charted, is to relate government to the other major institutions of the community. This quickly leads into the question of the functions of government, the topic to be considered next.

GOVERNMENT FUNCTIONS IN THE COMMUNITY

In listing the structural aspects of government one invariably chronicles many of the services government performs simply because the names of many of the groups to be identified tell what they do: the fire department, the health department, and the like. Their activities may be looked upon as functions, since whatever the government does for the people, according to this view, constitutes the functions of government (8).

Another way of describing the functions of government is to relate it as a subsystem to the workings of the total community, combining several activities into what might be called a "function." Directing traffic, arresting a criminal, or taking an expectant mother to the hospital are different activities in which a policeman could be involved any day of the week. But when we think of the police power we think of something more than these services: the authority inherent in the governmental body, through its official representatives such as sheriffs and policemen, to use force in maintaining order or in apprehending individuals who break the laws.

Social Control. One of the operations necessary in any social system is the control of deviant behavior, as Chapter 10 has shown, and the government is the ultimate agent of control in our society. The existence of actual or incipient conflict within a community is the reason for the designation of a major system as the means for resolving the conflict through a lawsuit, if it goes that far, or as an agent to see that a wronged individual does not resort to physical violence in an effort to settle the score. To be sure, the state rather than the local government tries those suspected of felonies or serious crimes; it also convicts and carries out extreme penalties. But the local law enforcement officers make the arrests and keep the prisoners in custody until the state takes charge.

This social control carries with it the idea of the allocation of power within the community, particularly of political power (7). Federal and state constitutions or city charters set forth the basis of much allocation of power, often putting restrictions upon those who may hold office and also setting limits to the length of terms. But all power is not allocated to the police and elected officials. Through the election process much of it is distributed to the community members in general, although far too often they fail to exercise this power placed at their disposal. The right to criticize those in public office and to suggest better ways in which they might do their job is a form of power which the citizen possesses, although he must avoid making libelous statements about another member of the community when exercising criticism.

It frequently happens that the "informal" power relationships differ markedly from the formal government structure. Some official, such as a county judge in the South, becomes more powerful than the rest. Or some community leader or leaders not in political life may provide guidance to the officials in many matters of their office; indeed they may be half-humorously referred to by some members of the community as the "powers behind the throne" (15).

Allocation of Goods and Services. In a socialist state the government plays the major role in the distribution of many of the goods and services available to the people; in a free enterprise system such as ours this function is left largely to the units of business comprising the economic system. Nevertheless, even in the American setting government plays a bigger role in this regard than is commonly supposed. Many public utilities are provided by privately owned business companies, but where these fail to offer services the local government frequently steps in to do so. The case of Los Angeles offers an interesting illustration of combined private and public ownership of utilities, even though the city uses only municipal governmental units for sewage, garbage, and rubbish disposal. Even though the following account is quoted rather fully, it affords one of the quickest ways of getting a picture of how local governments allocate certain types of goods and services:[7]

Water

. . . Now a city with a population of approximately 2,000,000, Los Angeles uses to capacity the sources of the Los Angeles River and the supply from the Owens-Mono Aqueduct. In 1948 a little more than 3 per cent of all water sold by the Los Angeles Department of Water and Power was supplied by the Metropolitan Water District. Future growth of the city is entirely dependent upon this source of supply.
. . . Today there is no restriction upon the amount of water a family in the metropolitan area may use. In the City of Los Angeles the average daily consumption per person is approximately 150 gallons, whereas in 1940 it was approximately 120 gallons. In Beverly Hills, a city with many fine gardens and swimming pools, per capita consumption is approximately 270 gallons per day. In some of the low-income areas of the metropolitan area it is only 100 gallons per day. If the community ever becomes so populous that it is necessary to limit use of water, certain luxury uses could be curtailed.

Energy

Without energy from distant sources the Los Angeles area would have reached stagnation in its development some years ago. . . . And if it were not now making plans to obtain still more energy from sources in other counties and other states its future would be in doubt.
The Los Angeles area today imports more natural gas and petroleum than it

[7] Mel Scott, *Metropolitan Los Angeles: One Community* (The Haynes Foundation: Los Angeles, California, 1949), pp. 69–79.

produces. Likewise it imports more hydroelectric power than it generates locally in steam plants utilizing heavy fuel oil or natural gas.

. . . Public and private power systems in the Los Angeles area are interconnected, so that in emergencies a city or town may borrow from sources other than those upon which it usually depends. This is a form of coordination achieved during the war, when the major suppliers of electricity established the Southwest Power Pool, in order to meet the threat of sudden dislocation of any part of the power facilities in this area and to be able to supply war industries with large amounts of energy as required.

Since 1940 the electrical energy sales of the Southern California Edison Company in the Los Angeles area have doubled, while those of the Los Angeles Department of Water and Power have more than doubled. New manufacturing plants, commercial establishments, and new homes have all created the demand for more energy. Aside from the increased demands of industry, proportionately more electrical appliances are in use today than before the war.

The Los Angeles area is now plentifully supplied with natural gas by wells in Santa Barbara, Ventura, and Los Angeles Counties, the San Joaquin Valley, the Permian basin of west Texas and southeast New Mexico, and the Hugoton Panhandle area of northwest Texas.

A 1204-mile pipe line that began operating in 1948 brings natural gas from the Texas and New Mexico fields. This supply previously was vented into the air for lack of a market. Geologists estimate that the Texas fields contain 400 trillion cubic feet of natural gas—the greatest known reserves in the world.

. . . The Los Angeles area consumes seven times as much natural gas in winter as it does in summer, since gas is the chief fuel used for heating homes. Because of the heavy domestic consumption in winter, gas companies cut off most industrial consumers during winter. These large industrial users immediately switch to other fuels, such as fuel oil, diesel oil, propane, or butane.

Waste Disposal

Sewers are among the "essentials" without which a modern community cannot function. Hidden from view, these underground disposal facilities make possible the very existence of large concentrations of population. If there were no quick and efficient means of removing body wastes, cities would become noxious, plague-ridden, and deadly.

Garbage Disposal

The Los Angeles area has no uniform system for disposing of kitchen and table wastes, or garbage. A few cities operate their own collection trucks and sell garbage to hog ranches, but most of the cities in Los Angeles County allow private contractors to collect garbage without paying any revenue to the municipality for the privilege. A few cities receive some revenue from the private contractors who operate their own trucks and dispose of the wastes collected. Beverly Hills has its own trucks and burns its garbage in a municipal incinerator.

The City of Los Angeles operates municipally owned collection trucks and sells wet garbage to ranchers for hog food. Through four sales contracts the city is able to dispose of all collections in the city.

Rubbish Disposal

No two cities in the Los Angeles area dispose of combustible and noncombustible rubbish in the same manner. Some have special services for the collection of refuse; others license private collectors to gather material and bring it to city-owned incinerators. Many cities now bury both combustible and noncombustible rubbish by the cut-and-fill method; others burn combustible rubbish and sell noncombustible rubbish to private companies that carry on salvage operations. Some cities collect tree and lawn trimmings; most do not. Few if any cities share joint facilities for disposal of street sweepings, house refuse, and garden trimmings. The City of Los Angeles, which licenses private collectors to gather rubbish, owns and operates an incinerator near the central area of Los Angeles and is planning to build four others.

Another illustration of the allocation of goods and services is found in the taxing ability of local government. Certain welfare legislation calls for the expenditure of large sums for the needs of those who are too poor to pay. This also holds true in education, in public health programs, and in highway construction. Most Americans seem to agree that there are certain minimum essentials which all persons should enjoy. Debates may rage about particular items, but there is general agreement that most of these essentials should be met. The only way such a function can be discharged by government is to collect taxes from those who are in a position to pay and use these funds to provide services for all the people. Local government, through property and other taxes, plays its part in just as real a sense as do the state and federal governments through the income and other taxes. This redistribution of wealth through taxation makes few people happy but continues to be exercised year in and year out in American communities as a necessary feature of our government at all levels.

Functional Interdependence of Government and the Economy. Although the economy has not yet been discussed as a major community system, it nevertheless seems appropriate at this point to indicate the close interdependence between the economy and government in the modern American community. In its original form local government existed to maintain law and order, protect property, and perform a limited number of services, such as repairing bridges. But as society has grown more complex and individuals have been less and less able to control many influences affecting their lives, government has been called upon to assume functions it did not formerly have. Much of this is done under the general welfare clause in the first paragraph of the Constitution of the United States, for there the purposes for establishing the constitution are listed as being "to form a more perfect union, establish justice, insure domestic tranquillity, provide for the common defense, *promote the general welfare* [italics added], and secure the blessings of liberty to ourselves and our posterity." This meant that government was no longer primarily interpreted as a protector of "property" but was rather the supporter of what was good for the general public. This latter shift was strengthened by the broadening of the franchise, under which the poor man's vote counted as much as that of the rich man. The shift was certainly accelerated by the breakdown of most of the economy in the depression of the Thirties and the need for government, particularly the national government, to step into the breach.

The connection between local government and the economic life of the community must be seen in historical perspective. Many businessmen hold firmly to the belief that the least government is the best government and believe that the fewer and lower the taxes the more efficient the government. Officials in the governmental hierarchy, on the other hand, often hold that they are "the servants of the people" and that the more they can do "for the people" the better they are carrying out their jobs. In the case of such contrasting points of view some accommodation is usually worked out: the businessman increasingly recognizes a responsibility for those in his community who need some form of help and the government officials admit that businessmen also are part of "the people." But while many businessmen argue that relief should be given through voluntary, private organizations and not through the government, others argue that only the government is capable of handling the needs of our highly mobile population.

In spite of wide divergencies in point of view, it is well to remember that many of the government officials themselves, such as councilmen and school board members, are apt to be active in the economic affairs of the community and that many businessmen have often held contracts with some branch of government. But to indicate the nature of the interaction of these two systems and their dependence upon each other, a few examples might be listed.

To attract new industry to the community, the Chamber of Commerce may persuade the local governmental council or commission to give such new industry a tax-free status for a specified number of years.

To erect a new school building, the local government may need to borrow money by selling bonds, which the business community is asked to buy in large amounts.

To avoid unfair competition through the "cutting of too many corners" in some businesses, such as the food industry, local government is asked to make periodic inspection to be sure that all competitors are measuring up to the sanitary code.

To gain an upper hand in a labor dispute, both labor and management seek to use court decisions as a weapon for their cause.

To increase local revenues, businessmen may have to cooperate in the added red tape involved in a sales tax, a payroll deduction for an "occupational tax," or even in the so-called "nuisance taxes" connected with tickets for entertainment features.

Such illustrations only begin to scratch the surface of the great number of ways in which the government and the economy are mutually self-supportive. These do not preclude the periodic "economy drives in government" by tax leagues nor an effort now and then to elect to the local council a slate of officials who will understand the businessman's problems. Nor should one forget that in many cities, as in the case of Lorain, Ohio, discussed in Chapter 10 in connection with the community power structure, organized labor is a growing political force which speaks for a more vocal segment of the economy. Were one to include what the state government does in the way of public utility commissions or the granting of alcoholic beverage licenses, or what the federal government does in its program of social security, one would find the ties between the economy and government numerous indeed.

Further insight into the workings of the two major systems (government and the economy) is contained in a report by Robert E. Lane, who studied the responses of Connecticut businessmen to the New Deal and the Fair Deal. His findings apply to local government as well as to the national scene and would relate particularly to efforts at planning and zoning or other community improvements that call for increased governmental regulation of business. In the first place, what are the real grounds for the dissatisfaction which businessmen express in connection with such regulation? In general, according to Lane, they may be said to include the following, listed in the order of emotional attachment:

1. Deprivation of power with respect to an organized opposing economic force (i.e., the government).
2. Deprivation of freedom to manage one's own economic affairs.
3. Deprivation of equity with respect to other social groups (such as labor).
4. Deprivation of money or the opportunity to make money.
5. Deprivation of certainty and security in an uncontrollable environment.[8]

A second result of his study, according to Lane, is the help it gives the administrator in anticipating themes of criticism, even though these are not related to the real deprivations just listed. As a possible guide to several of these themes a few of the covert causes are described in the following.

[8] Robert E. Lane, "Government Regulation and the Business Mind," *American Sociological Review*, XVI (April, 1951), 172.

1. "The regulation is confused or fails of its purpose." This theme is most likely to appear where there is weight of cultural or business approval for the measure which makes a frontal attack difficult or inadvisable. The prevalence of this theme indicates a broad area of consensus where ultimate objectives are immune from attack.

2. "The regulation is political or biased." This theme is likely to appear where there is a strong organized group who have demanded the measure and are rivals of the industry or segment regulated. It does not appear, for example, where the beneficiary is considered to be the consuming public.

3. "The regulation is coercive and arbitrary." This theme is likely to appear whenever there is considerable cultural distance between the requirements of the law and the normal mores of the business group. It is more likely to appear in relation to labor than in trade-practices regulation for this reason.

4. "The administration of the law and its personnel are inferior." This is integral to attitudes on the substance of the law and varies with relative disfavor. It is, in general, a declining theme and may not appear as important in future regulatory situations.[9]

These suggestions about possible connections between the government and the economy do not begin to exhaust the list of those which might be discovered; they simply indicate some of the types which have community-wide significance.

The Legal Profession

Although considerable mention has been made of public officials and the politicians perennially running for office, the system of government keeps going in America largely because of the legal profession.[10] Its members not only become the politicians, but many lawyers find that running even a losing campaign gets their names before the public long enough to help out their law business. More importantly though, the lawyer is able to guide the puzzled citizen through one legal maze after another, whether it be in bringing suit against a defaulting debtor or in working out legal ways of reducing one's income tax.

Walter I. Wardwell and Arthur L. Wood describe the lawyer's professional role as follows:

Whether the lawyer be functioning as *advocate* (pleader in court), *attorney* (agent or representative in negotiations), or legal *counselor* (adviser), he is subject to three general sets of obligations laid down in the canons of legal ethics—obligations to clients, to colleagues, and to society at large, the latter most specifically as an officer of the court. Although there are potential conflicts between

9 *Ibid.*, p. 172.

10 For an interesting insight into the lawyer's role see David Riesman, "Toward an Anthropological Science of Law and the Legal Profession," *American Journal of Sociology*, VII (September, 1951), 121–35.

these different role-obligations, as Carl Taeusch has adequately shown,[11] the obligations themselves are usually clearly stated, generally known to lawyers, and to a substantial degree observed by them.[12]

But in addition to the expected professional roles, there is the extra-professional or the citizenship role. What does the community expect from a lawyer outside the courtroom or his office?

The lawyer's citizenship role, according to Wardwell and Wood, excludes any behavior expected of any citizen as a citizen and includes only those special community role-expectations relating to the lawyer as a lawyer. This citizenship role relates only tangentially to the lawyer's relationships with other lawyers, who are supposed to associate with each other on a first-name basis outside the courtroom; it does not include his relationships with his clients whom he, as a professional person, should view as *cases* and not as *persons*. (For example, if he lets himself become involved in his client's emotional problems, he might not be able to provide him with efficient legal service.) Finally, his citizenship role is only partially tied in with the court and law-enforcement personnel with whom he develops some personal friendships.

The real content of the lawyer's citizenship role is threefold: first, it is generally accepted that the lawyer will be available as a public servant. Particularly in smaller communities, practically all lawyers are at some time officeholders or are otherwise active in politics; even in large cities the pressure toward such activities is present, although not as large a proportion of city lawyers become involved. Second, lawyers are supposed to be available for various kinds of nonpolitical leadership, particularly where a community service or philanthropic purpose is involved. Many such organizations think it necessary to have a lawyer on their board or on their important committees, since he is expected to give free legal advice in his capacity as a board or committee member. Third, the legal profession as a whole feels a collective responsibility for some law-related activities, such as legal-aid societies and lawyer-reference plans. These considerations show that the lawyer has "extra-curricular" obligations of a special kind simply because he is a lawyer.

There results a sense of urgency about the lawyer's citizenship role which does not exist in the case of other occupational groups. This is revealed both in the internalized feelings of lawyers and in the expectations and demands by

[11] See Carl Taeusch, *Professional and Business Ethics* (New York: Henry Holt & Co., 1926), chs. ii and iii.

[12] Walter I. Wardwell and Arthur L. Wood, "The Extra-Professional Role of the Lawyer," *American Journal of Sociology*, LXI (January, 1956), 304. Copyright, 1956, by the University of Chicago.

others that lawyers should be active in community affairs. From this point of view it makes little difference whether lawyers perceive community activity principally as a *means* of getting a reputation as a lawyer and building a practice or as *an end in itself*. There is no doubt that at least some segments of the public view the man who is active in community affairs as behaving as a lawyer should. Other things being equal, this man will be recognized professionally as a lawyer more quickly than one who is not active . . .[13]

As a person watches the lawyers of the community playing both their professional and extra-professional roles, he realizes that government is a human institution which rises to heights of nobility as those responsible for it render dedicated service; it also can stumble along ineffectively when community expectations and those responsible for it view it as a means through which the "ins" can enrich themselves at the expense of the public or the administration of justice fails to be impartial. The responsibilities of the official and the lawyer are great, but what they do or do not do is closely tied in with the expectations of the rest of the community. Where citizens demand much, they get more in the way of service.

Limitations of Government as a Major Community System

Arthur E. Morgan in his stimulating book *The Community of the Future* stresses the need for strong local government responsive to the needs of its citizens. At the same time he points out the necessity for a balance between this responsiveness and the inadequacy of local government to meet many of the major needs of our time. He writes:

There are various elements of local government in which efficient administration is possible only on a large scale, entirely beyond the range of local government. The administration of the post office is such a case. . . .

Other areas where it is not feasible for the locality to administer its own affairs are: rules for operating railway traffic through the town, automobile speed through the community, precautions against contagious diseases, the administration of social security (since people are constantly moving about), the right of childhood to be free from economic exploitation, the disposal of sewage and the control of stream pollution where it would affect other communities. . . .[14]

The fact that larger units are needed for certain tasks indicates to some the outmoded nature of certain forms of local government; yet other tasks are of such a nature that should the county unit disappear, something similar might have to be created to take its place. Although the services of local government are important Dr. Morgan

---

[13] *Ibid.*, p. 307.

[14] Arthur E. Morgan, *The Community of the Future and the Future of the Community* (Yellow Springs, Ohio: Community Service, Inc., 1957), p. 92.

would stress the spirit with which the officials go about their tasks in the performance of these services. He sees as one value of local community government its possibility as a training ground for the growth of good will. Thus it would become not so much a means of resolving conflict as a means of developing consensus.

Until the day comes when government is more truly communal in spirit, it will continue to have limitations in the accomplishment of community goals. The first such limitation is statutory. The government uses public money which is collected under well-defined statutes, and its officials can only spend that money in certain legally-specified ways. Many community problems arise which have not been anticipated by legislators or which are considered nongovernmental in character. For these, private funds must be found.

A second limitation stems from the nature of officialdom, which must retain a certain degree of official neutrality on crucial issues if it wants to be re-elected. The political appointee or the elected official shuns controversy unless it is apt to catapult him into favorable prominence. The same general caution motivates members of other bureaucracies in the community, whether industrial, educational, or religious. But many community issues, in the minds of many people, involve a "right" and a "wrong," and one who fails to take sides is definitely considered an ineffective ally in the struggle.

A final limitation, already mentioned, is the failure of the local governmental unit or units to correspond to the area of the sociological community. Where cooperation between all units can be gained, then the government can play a significant role in community development; where, however, one unit will support and another will not support some local undertaking, factionalism is apt to spring up and have a deleterious effect upon other community-wide efforts. In other words, there are limitations to what local government can and cannot do in solving community problems. One must be aware of the exact nature of these limitations before criticizing those in responsible government positions, because it may be that, as they correctly interpret their role, they must stay within those limitations or become subject to the charge of misuse of their office, no matter how noble their intentions.

References and Suggested Readings

1. Floro, George K. "Continuity in City-Manager Careers," *American Journal of Sociology,* LXI (November, 1955), 240–46.
2. Gist, Noel P., and Halbert, L. C. *Urban Society.* 4th ed.; New York: The Thomas Crowell Co., 1956.
3. Hastings, Philip K. "The Voter and the Non-Voter," *American Journal of Sociology,* LXII (November, 1956), 302–7.

4. HOIBERG, OTTO G. *Exploring the Small Community.* Lincoln: University of Nebraska Press, 1955, ch. 11.
5. LANE, ROBERT E. "Government Regulation and the Business Mind," *American Sociological Review,* XVI (April, 1951), 163–73.
6. LAZARSFELD, P.; BERELSON, B.; and GAUDET, H. *The People's Choice.* New York: Columbia University Press, 1948.
7. LEVY, MARION J., JR. *The Structure of Society.* Princeton: Princeton University Press, 1952, ch. X: "The Structure of Political Allocation."
8. MERCER, BLAINE E. *The American Community.* New York: Random House, Inc., 1956, ch. 12.
9. MORGAN, ARTHUR E. *The Community of the Future and the Future of the Community.* Yellow Springs, Ohio: Community Service, Inc., 1957.
10. ROBINSON, W. S. "The Motivational Structure of Political Participation," *American Sociological Review,* XVII (April, 1952), 151–56.
11. SANDERS, IRWIN T. "Village Social Organization in Greece," *Rural Sociology,* XVIII (December, 1953), 366–75.
12. SCHATTISCHNEIDER, E. E. "Political Parties and the Public Interest," *The Annals,* 280 (March, 1952), 18–26.
13. SMITH, LUKE M. "Territorial Variables in American Local Government," *Social Forces,* XXVII (May, 1949), 350–58.
14. SMITH, T. LYNN. *Brazil: People and Institutions.* Baton Rouge: Louisiana State University Press, 1947, ch. XXII.
15. WEIDNER, E. C., and PREISS, JACK J. "Rural Local Government and Politics and Adult Education," in C. P. Loomis *et al., Rural Social Systems and Adult Education.* East Lansing: Michigan State College Press, 1953.
16. WESTLEY, WILLIAM A. "Violence and the Police," *American Journal of Sociology,* LIX (July, 1953), 34–41.
17. YOUNG, WILLIAM H. "Governors, Mayors, and Community Ethics," *The Annals,* 280 (March, 1952), 46–50.

Chapter 13

THE ECONOMY

There are at least three ways to approach the study of the economy of an American community. One is the anthropological treatment, which picks out basic characteristics and cultural themes as an anthropologist would do were he to describe a primitive tribe. One such study summarizes in capsule form the economic system of the United States, and indirectly that of most American communities, in these terms:

> Economic [System]: finance capitalism, with a movement toward state capitalism; a machine economy closely related to scientific technology, which has resulted in worldwide exploitation of markets and materials and produced a tremendous quantity of durable and consumers' goods; corporate structure of business; a variety of finance and credit agencies; electric, coal, oil, and other fuels and energies, with atomic energy imminent; a laboring force dependent upon the vicissitudes of the economy and increasingly organized into trade unions for purposes of collective bargaining.[1]

Carrying the analysis a step further, Professor Sirjamaki discusses the economic conditioning of the culture—how business and industry primarily determine the physical layout of American cities and villages and the dispersion of population—as well as the cultural values of capitalism into which the individual is inevitably socialized. Such values are stated as "private property, individual initiative, free competition, and private profit." As a result, "the job determines not only the conditions of daily labor, but friends, personal and family life, interests and hobbies, and to an important extent social class position."[2]

In this anthropological approach many more effects of the central economic themes in American life could be traced: the emphasis upon progress, its utilitarian character, the tendency of Americans

[1] John Sirjamaki, "A Footnote to the Anthropological Approach to the Study of American Culture," *Social Forces*, XXV (March, 1947), 255.

[2] *Ibid.*, p. 258.

to be producer-minded and to esteem technical skills and efficiency.

A second approach, somewhat related but different in emphasis, is that in Chapter 3 in the discussion of the occupational structure (12). Quite a few sociologists have thought that one of the best ways of understanding community life was to begin with the analysis of the division of labor and the occupational distribution which resulted. They rightly claim that when they acquire this information they can state many important sociological characteristics of the society. Indeed, one of the essentials for any social system is the differentiation of its parts, since they supposedly have different tasks to perform. Thus in the study of the community it is important to look at the fact of differentiation as one of the basic operations (see Figure 24). Accompanying this operation is a mechanism by which individuals are persuaded to fill the necessary occupational statuses, whether the persuasion is based largely on prestige gained, salary earned, or the automatic assumption of the father's occupation as is done in the more traditionalistic societies.

A third approach, the one being followed in this volume, is to view the economy as a major system in the community and to analyze the subsystems of which it is composed. These subsystems, as in the case of government, are networks of groups. One could do as economists frequently do and view the subsystems on what might be termed a "product" or "industry" basis, for example, taking the "clothing industry" from the beginning of the acquisition of materials for the manufacture of clothes, through their manufacture, their distribution through several channels, and their selection and use by the ultimate consumer. To follow this approach, rewarding though it would be, would be too space-consuming here, inasmuch as each type of product, such as automobiles, paint, and electrical appliances, would have to be surveyed in turn. True enough, each of these, so viewed, would represent social subsystems in the sense used here.

However, a more practical way of viewing the subsystems, sociologically, at least, is to cut across the economy in terms of major segments and note what interconnections exist. Such a division would include the subsystems of commerce, industry, organized labor, transportation and utilities, finance, and agriculture. Each of these has social characteristics distinguishing it from the others, as will be shown in the treatment of their structure and their functions. As the discussion of the role of the lawyer in the previous chapter shows, the professions can be treated separately in terms of the major system with which they are most intimately connected, although it is recognized that they comprise an important part of the economy (14).

STRUCTURE OF THE ECONOMY AS A MAJOR SYSTEM

Variety of Economic Groups. The fact that the economy is a set of social relationships just as much as it is a collection of stores, factories, and railroad tracks is vividly revealed by the study of economic groups. Once a few of these have been seen it is easier to move to the larger units—the subsystems—and note how these in turn make up the total economy. Four groups or combinations of groups will be dealt with briefly: a restaurant, a district labor union made up of nine locals, a milk cooperative, and a public employment agency.

A restaurant. William Foote Whyte draws the following contrasts between the restaurant, the factory, and the retail store.[3]

The restaurant is a combination production and service unit. It differs from the factory, which is solely a production unit, and also from the retail store, which is solely a service unit. . . .

The contrast between factory and restaurant can be illustrated by this simple diagram, representing the direction of orders in the two structures:

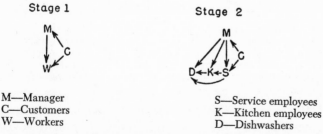

The problems of co-ordination and customer relations are relative simple in the small restaurant, but they become much more difficult as the organization grows. This may be illustrated structurally in terms of five stages of growth.

M—Manager
C—Customers
W—Workers

S—Service employees
K—Kitchen employees
D—Dishwashers

In Stage 1 there is little division of labor, but in Stage 2 the business has grown to the point that it is necessary to divide the work.

[3] William Foote Whyte, "The Social Structure of the Restaurant," *American Journal of Sociology,* LIV (January, 1949), 302–3.

Although the boss knows most customers and his employees on a personal basis, he nevertheless is faced with the problem of co-ordination. In Stage 3, however, larger quarters plus a more complex organization with supervisors and checkers are found:[4]

Stage 3

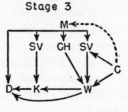

M—Manager   W—Waitress
SV—Supervisor   K—Kitchen worker
CH—Checker   D—Dishwasher
C—Customer

In time, the owner-manager finds that he can accommodate a larger number of customers if he takes one more step in the division of labor. Up to now the cooks have been serving the food to the waitresses. When these functions are divided, both cooking and serving can proceed more efficiently. Therefore, he sets up a service pantry apart from the kitchen. The cooks now concentrate on cooking, the runners carry food from pantry to kitchen, and the pantry girls serve the waitresses over the counter. This adds two more groups (pantry girls and runners) to be supervised, and, to cope with this and the larger scale of operation, the owner adds another level of supervision, so that there are two supervisors between himself and the workers.

Stage 4

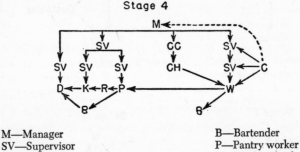

M—Manager   B—Bartender
SV—Supervisor   P—Pantry worker
CH—Checker   K—Kitchen worker
CC—Cost Control Supervisor   R—Runner
C—Customer   D—Dishwasher
W—Waitress

The fifth stage, which need not be diagramed, consists of tying together several units into a chain, "and one or more levels of authority are set up in a main office above the individual unit structures." In this study of twelve Chicago restaurants, with one to four months spent upon each restaurant, Whyte and his associates re-

[4] *Ibid.*

vealed how interaction flowed within this structure which is dia-gramed and indicated the trouble points that developed as "emo-tional tension experienced by the waitresses was transmitted, link by link, all the way to the kitchen."[5]

A labor union. The Toronto District of Amalgamated Clothing Workers of America has a structure of three chief elements, accord-ing to Herbert A. Shepard:

1. The local: The nine Toronto locals are based roughly on ethnic, linguistic, and craft distinctions. Each has an elected executive board "which handles routine business, deals with disputes among members, administers discipline, and prepares agenda for the local meeting."[6] The local passes resolutions and by-laws in addition to sending delegates to conventions and electing three members to the Joint Board.

2. The Joint Board: Of the three members which each local sends to the Joint Board, one is elected to the Board of Directors, the ex-ecutive committee for the Joint Board. Six of the representatives are paid officers, all of whom hold elective office except the district manager, who is appointed by the General Executive Board (higher than the district) but subject to district approval. Each of these paid officers, or business agents, is elected by a different group, such as the journeyman tailors, cutters, and trimmers (Italian-speaking and English-speaking locals) or the Jewish-speaking locals. The business agent does the more difficult bargaining with management and holds his office only so long as he pleases the fellow-workers who elect him. Therefore, he must be responsive to their opinion.

3. The shop organization: In addition to belonging to a local, each worker is a part of a shop organization consisting of the employees of the firm or department where he is employed. Within any one shop may be found members of several of the locals. Each shop has its own elected committee consisting of the shop chairman and several assistants. The shop chairman's office is particularly burden-some, for

. . . in some firms he must rearrange workers and modify the production line daily to guarantee a smooth flow of work. He plays a large part in the determi-nation of piece rates, wages, layoffs, transfers, promotions and training . . . Furthermore, his activities are carried on under the close surveillance of his electors, who are quick to criticize his inadequacies.[7]

[5] *Ibid.,* p. 305.
[6] Herbert A. Shepard, "Democratic Control in a Labor Union," *The American Journal of Sociology,* LIV (January, 1949), 311.
[7] *Ibid.,* p. 312.

This shop chairman tries to settle as many complaints as he can with the foreman, and failing this turns the matter over to the business agent (from the District Joint Board) to take up with higher management. Thus it can be seen that the district consists of a system of checks and balances; the shop committee in some ways checks on the activities of the locals and both check on the activities of the Joint Board. The labor network in this particular industry moves from the district to the General Executive Board of the international union, which has actually followed a policy of decentralization and nonintervention. The structure is present for exerting pressure upon management even though there have been no general strikes in the district for twenty-five years, a fact which makes it difficult at times for the labor leaders to maintain high membership interest in the organization.

A milk marketing cooperative. Agriculture has its groups as well. A fairly common type in dairy areas is the milk marketing cooperative. For a cooperative to procure a satisfactory volume to make its operations successful a large number of milk producers must be enrolled who guarantee that they will sell all of their milk through the cooperative. The particular Ohio cooperative studied by Chester M. Stephenson began its organization in 1922 and by January 1, 1924, had enrolled two-thirds of the ninety milk producers in the township, although its total membership came from an area of four thousand square miles. Thirty producers in the township did not join.

By 1949 the situation had radically changed, for the cooperative in twenty-five years lost forty-two of its original sixty members and added only three, a net decline of 65 per cent. On the other hand, the nonmembers (numbering thirty) lost nineteen of their original group, but added thirty-four producers, registering a net gain of 50 per cent. "Why," asks Professor Stephenson, "did the cooperative decline from an organization that controlled the milk marketing of two-thirds of the producers to one that controlled only a third?" He eliminates tenancy and inability to cooperate as causative factors in this situation, but shows that where there was cooperation the organizations involved were local affairs with their headquarters in the village township center. The headquarters of the milk marketing cooperative, by contrast, seemed far removed, since it was not organized on a local or township basis and the members did not feel a close tie of any sort:

At first, the cooperative was centered mainly around the milk routes of two men. These men knew everyone in the township, and were active in the development of the new farmer-owned enterprise. Later, all the country routes were reorganized and let out on bids. Thus, the cooperative producer had to ship his milk with whatever hauler had bid in at the lowest price, while the independent producer [who did not join the cooperative] could choose his own hauler [whom he usually knew personally]. The milk hauler is often the dairy farmer's chief contact with his distributor.[8]

Another matter of discontent on the part of the members was the fact that they received smaller pay checks than the nonmembers for the same amount of milk. This was due to the deductions made by the cooperative to pay for milk plants built, although in return for these deductions members were given stock which could be cashed in after twenty years. However, this seemed to many members a long time to wait. Another source of dissatisfaction was the restriction on the producer's freedom to market his milk when and where he pleased. Not only did he have to market all of his milk through the cooperative but he could resign only in the fall and could not be released until the following spring. Nonmembers were of course free to shop around among independent distributors for better deals. Those supporting the cooperative argue that they have served an important economic purpose since 1924 by furnishing competition to the independent distributors. They assert that the nonmembers are "riding on the cooperative's ticket." Nevertheless, at the time of the study, most of the producers in the township preferred to market their milk independently.

A public employment agency. This is a government-financed group set up to serve both employer and prospective employees. The interviewers in this agency receive requests for workers over the phone, fill out and file the order forms, interview the applicants for jobs, and then try to match the applicants' qualifications with the job requirements. If such a job is found, the client is sent to see the employer, and the interviewer later phones the employer to find out if the client has been hired. In one of these agencies studied by Peter M. Blau there were two sections of six interviewers each, and there was considerable competitiveness shown within the sections. This was heightened by the practice of passing around the statistics of how many placements each interviewer had made. As a consequence, the interviewers would resort to surreptitious methods in order to show up well in the statistics. One interviewer reported:

When you take an order, instead of putting it in the box, you leave it on your desk. There was so much hiding of orders under the blotter that we used to ask, "Do you have anything under your rug?" when we looked for an order. You

[8] Chester M. Stephenson, "A Case Study of a Milk Marketing Cooperative," *Rural Sociology,* XVIII (June, 1953), 170.

might leave an order you took on the desk, or you might leave it on the desk after you made no referral. . . . Or, you might take an order only partially; you write the firm's name, and few things; the other you remember. And you leave it on the pad (of order blanks). You keep on doing this, and all these orders are not in the box.[9]

In addition, the interviewers would often incorrectly fill out or file the form.

By studying the extent to which an interviewer filled the vacancies he had received over the phone with his own clients in excess of chance expectations, Blau was able to determine the competitiveness of each individual and of each section. The most important finding of the study was that the more competitive section was less productive than the less competitive one. It lacked as much social cohesion; individual members had to spend time trying to conciliate colleagues whom their competitive practices had alienated.

At first, these four vignettes of economic groups may seem to have little bearing upon the community as a whole. What goes on in a restaurant, a labor union, an agricultural cooperative, or a public employment agency is not necessarily communal. But restaurants by their attractiveness and quality of service do play a part in the impression created upon visitors and local people alike; and in fact, the local people often derive their view of whether or not they have a good community from the comments made by the visitors. Labor union policies do at times assume communal significance as do the practices of cooperatives. Furthermore, the productivity of the employment agency adds to the efficiency of the economic system. These illustrations are useful reminders that the economy must be seen in terms of such groups as these, for out of them the subsystems come into existence and find expression.

Selected Economic Subsystems

No effort will be made here to take up all possible economic subsystems; rather attention will be centered on some of the more important ones. Careful observations of the interconnections between these subsystems will help furnish a skeletal picture at least of the social structure of the economy.

The Industrial Subsystem. The center of the industrial subsystem is the plant or factory. To raise money for the construction of the building and the purchase of necessary equipment and raw materials, those undertaking the venture must issue stock to those who

---

[9] Peter M. Blau, "Co-operation and Competition in a Bureaucracy," *American Journal of Sociology*, LIX (May, 1954), 530.

want to become part owners in the hope of receiving periodic dividends or sell bonds to those who wish to invest their capital for the sake of the interest they expect to derive. Thus an important grouping in the industrial subsystem consists of owners and investors whose funds made the plant possible. If a few people own the major factory in a town, as was true in the case of Middletown (see Chapter 10), that fact produces different community effects than if the ownership is widely scattered; or if the plant is owned almost entirely by outside people—as in the case of Bigtown—that too has community implications.

In today's industrial subsystem the owners are not usually the managers, which means that there is a separate group which "runs" the factory in an effort to make the maximum profit for the owners (11). The members of this group range from the top executives through various ranks of junior executives down to the foreman in charge of the work within a particular shop or department of the plant. Many studies have been made and continue to be made about the conflicts which occur between staff and line managerial officers (7) and the steps by which executives rise up the managerial ladder (8). Also, more is being learned about the informal organization, quite apart from that shown in the organizational blueprint of the company, and the way these informal cliques support or interfere with the carrying out of policies determined by top management.

A key figure in the industrial subsystem is the foreman. According to Donald E. Wray, there are two prevailing conceptions of his role, neither of which is altogether accurate. One view holds that the supervisor is definitely a part of management, being the first point in a clear-cut "line of authority." A second view, held by the Foreman's Association of America, states that the first-line supervisor is the man in the middle who as a mere representative of management has no power to make decisions. Wray points out that part of the foreman's problem is the disparity between the norm (that he does make and enforce decisions) and actuality where he finds himself with no authority to do this. He concludes:

The foreman, . . . is less than a full member of the management line; he shares with those higher up the responsibility for carrying out policies but does not share in the making of them. Furthermore, his position differs from theirs in that those higher up give orders to people who are identified with management, while the essence of the foreman's job is that he must transmit them to people who are clearly not of management. In short, the position of foreman has some of the characteristics of management positions but lacks other crucial ones. Such marginal positions are common in society, and there is reason to believe that they are especially difficult to occupy effectively and with peace of mind.

With respect to management, the foremen's position is peripheral rather than in the middle.[10]

A number of other statuses which are related to the management of the industrial subsystem would have to be described in full if one were to do justice to this very important aspect (7). The more one knows about the different occupational positions and accompanying role expectations, the better one is able to interpret the kinds of interaction which frequently assume community-wide significance.

The third important human element is the worker (21), who is paid wages instead of a salary and usually, if unionized, thinks of himself as a distinct group from management, with whom he must use collective bargaining to secure the goals he has in mind (10). Workers vary greatly among themselves as to skills, ethnic background, religious orientation, and attitudes toward labor unions, but they all share *the job* as a common concern. They even accept and develop myths about their work which though untrue affect them as though they were true. For example, some machines are believed to be "faster" than others, even though scientific tests showed the myth to be false, and workers react to these machines accordingly (23).

Robert H. Guest found in a study of workers on an automobile assembly line that they were not looking for and did not expect jobs which would give them a higher economic and social status within the existing organization.

Instead, they hope for the break which will relieve them of the anonymity and impersonality of the line. They want jobs which they can handle as they grow older and which will give them more individual control over work pace. Their inability to achieve even these short-run immediate gains was found to be a source of frustration.

In the long range picture, assembly line workers entertain hopes, on the verbal level at least, which are in keeping with the deeply rooted American tradition of opportunity. They want to quit the present job altogether and strike out on their own. Yet to leave means facing the unknown. The present imperatives of security and a reasonably steady income outweigh the attractions of the job world outside. . . .[11]

This one study is simply indicative of the type of work being done in industrial sociology, which includes as part of the total picture the relationship between the worker and his job (5, 26) as well as that between him and his supervisors and fellow workers.

[10] Donald E. Wray, "Marginal Men of Industry: The Foreman," *American Journal of Sociology*, LIV (January, 1949), 301.

[11] Robert H. Guest, "Work Careers and Aspirations of Automobile Workers," *American Sociological Review*, XIX (April, 1954), 163.

As already intimated, industrial sociologists and social psychologists are making many studies of the kinds of social relationships found within a given plant and are studying those variables which affect these relationships (18). But one begins to get a picture of the industrial system of a community only as he sees how one plant is connected with all of the rest. For example, the feeder plant, a rapidly growing type, is much more intimately connected with the rest of the industrial system than was the small plant of a generation or two ago. William J. Goode and Irving Fowler describe it as follows:

A small plant, organized independently or with the aid of a parent company, is a contractor or feeder plant for the parent company. All its production goes to the parent company, and is tailored specifically to the needs of the latter. It has no choice over the products, and naturally has little opportunity to gear its production to a broader market. It is, thus, dependent on a larger organization which fosters competition and consequent price cutting and which does not concern itself with the labor relations of the small plant or its wage policies.[12]

In addition to this "linkage" or the interdependence of one plant upon others one finds that within any community there is a general tendency for those who manage industrial plants to view many problems in the same way. These include employment practices, labor policies, contributions to various financial drives for many causes, reactions to planning and zoning and to proposals for improvement of transportation and public utilities. Each company may differ as to the specific way it works out the problem, but there is apt to be a "common definition of the situation" by most of the managers. This tends to give a consistency to the subsystem, which is reinforced if the managers all participate in and are influenced by outside trade associations or such groups as the National Association of Manufacturers.

Transportation and Public Utilities. Mention need be made only in passing of the subsystem of transportation and public utilities whose rates are regulated by semiofficial bodies set up at the state level. Although there is competition among many carriers such as railways, buses, trucking firms, and airways, they also operate under a franchise which gives them the right to conduct business between certain specified points, in return for which they have to provide certain kinds of service. Where it seems justified they may be given a monopoly—such as a city bus system—since it appears obvious that two competing bus companies in a small town, for example, could hardly expect sufficient income.

[12] William J. Goode and Irving Fowler, "Incentive Factors in a Low Morale Plant," *American Sociological Review*, XIV (October, 1949), 619.

The same holds true of private utilities such as gas, electric, water, and telephone companies, which are regulated as to the rates they can charge but at the same time are protected from any competition within the area covered by their franchise. The firms which comprise this subsystem are faced with some different problems from those in other types of business. Although an electric company may seem to have a monopoly, it is faced with competition from natural gas or oil companies which try to prove that their particular fuel is more economical. At the same time, since they operate under what is tantamount to a public trust, they must devote much advertising to winning and maintaining public support so that their position will not be infringed upon or restricted by local ordinances or state legislation which an irate public might demand.

A detailed knowledge of this subsystem would call for an analysis of the way financing is conducted, the composition of boards of directors of the utilities, the relations maintained with the state agencies which regulate them, and the attitude of the members of the community toward the kind of service being offered. It often happens that one unit of the subsystem, such as bus service in Washington, D. C., is the subject of a great deal of public scorn while other private utilities in the same community are recognized as rendering outstanding service. It also happens that in many communities some of the utilities are privately owned and some publicly owned, and there are usually those in the community who argue in favor of getting the publicly owned ones back into private hands or else take the contrary view that local government should acquire some of the private utilities. Such arguments go back to one's philosophy of government mentioned in the previous chapter but illustrate a possible source of strain within this particular subsystem to which most of the other economic subsystems are not subject.

Organized Labor as a Subsystem. Since unions cut across many of the subsystems, including in some communities many workers in retail establishments, laundries, transportation, and the professions as well as in industry, it seems appropriate to look upon them as part of a separate subsystem. Of course, this subsystem does not exist in those communities where there are no local unions. But where unionization has been carried out on a large scale, definite subsystems come into being. This is often best symbolized by a community-wide labor union council, given various names in different communities. Through this council the constituent unions decide what kind of participation they will have in the Community Chest or whether a group of workers not directly affected by an issue involved in a strike will decide to call a sympathy strike; and in some cases they employ it to reach decisions as to which political candidates have records most friendly to labor.

The union hall of this council may serve as a social center for some of the officers of local unions, although each district union may have its own headquarters to serve the rank and file of its membership. But in the United States the union has not emerged as the social and educational center which it has frequently become in England. Instead, it serves primarily an economic function with occasional social overtones represented in varying degrees of social solidarity and unity of action.

A question of considerable community interest has to do with the type of people who became union leaders. Who are they? Where do they rank in the workers' status system? A study of twenty local unions by George Strauss and Leonard R. Sayles (30) indicates that the elected local union officials are generally higher paid and more skilled than the rank-and-file workers they represent. Those with higher seniority and in a position to communicate with other workers are more likely to be elected, but exceptions occur when the union is new or when there is a state of disequilibrium or crisis in which the lower status workers lose confidence in their leaders.

Such leaders of local unions, totaling somewhere between sixty-five and seventy-five thousand in the United States, are considered the backbone of the labor movement because they influence the attitudes of the members and employers toward it. Frequently they identify themselves closely with the union and believe it has brought about substantial gains. Indeed, some studies show that to these leaders "the union has become a way of life, serving the needs of its members apart from, and in addition to, the reasons that initially brought it into existence."[13]

An integral part of the system is the union organizer, who is considered by many members of a nonunionized community as a social irritant. This is because he "probes for dissatisfaction and seeks to transform individual unrest into a collective phenomenon. He has no set rules by which to operate but must emphasize that aspect of unionism that will be attractive to the workers he is trying to convince. To workers with little or no prior union experience the union is an abstraction, and their judgment may turn on their esti-

---

[13] Joel Seidman, Jack London, and Bernard Karsh, "Leadership in a Local Union," *American Journal of Sociology*, LVI (November, 1950), 229–37.

mate of the personality of the organizer."[14] But the community
reported here would probably not have become unionized simply
because an organizer visited it; previous organizers had failed.
There needed to be present a spirit of dissatisfaction upon which
the organizer could capitalize.

But when the whole subsystem of organized labor is viewed on
a national rather than a community scale, the role of unions appears
somewhat different. According to George H. Hildebrand:

> . . . despite their rapid growth since 1933 and contrary to expectation and
> professed programs, unions appear to have had little influence on the economic
> position of the organized third of employees through altering the distribution
> of incomes. Their major effect upon stratification has been the limiting of author-
> ity of management at the place of work. As a loose grouping within a middle-
> class-oriented political coalition, they have had an appreciable effect upon social
> and economic structure through government action—a condition which may be
> expected to continue, though it is contrary to their ideology.[15]

This subsystem has considerable power, however, where it is
militantly organized. Hildebrand concludes:

> It seems reasonable, then, to describe the American unions as what De
> Tocqueville called "secondary powers" in society, that is, the unions are private
> associations that perform functions of rulemaking and control independently of
> the state. As such, they are essentially conservative institutions in and of the
> existing order. In this way, the unions aid in the solution of problems that are
> common wherever work groups are found, without recourse to the central gov-
> ernment. To an important degree, therefore, industrial society is being remade
> on the job and in the here and now by a slow process of pragmatic accretionary
> change. . . .[16]

If one accepts this thesis then what is going on in the individual
plants in individual American communities determines the influence
of the organized labor subsystem just as much or even more than
decisions that are made in state capitals or in the national capital.

Finance. The banking institutions, loan companies, and firms
trading in securities comprise a subsystem which for purposes of
analysis can be separated from the rest of the economy. Money is
the chief article with which these groups deal, although a stock or
a bond may replace actual cash. Along with such functions goes
the administration of estates, often in the hands of the trust departments of banks. Within a particular community the banks usually

[14] Bernard Karsh, Joel Seidman, and Daisy M. Lilienthal, "The Union Organizer
and his Tactics: A Case Study," *American Journal of Sociology,* LIX (September,
1953), 113.

[15] George H. Hildebrand, "American Unionism, Social Stratification, and Power,"
American Journal of Sociology, LVIII (January, 1953), 381.

[16] *Ibid.,* p. 390.

have a clearing house through which checks pass and in which records are kept of the claim of one bank against the others. This serves as a coordinating agency, although the banks of the region are also members of their district branch of the Federal Reserve System, which was created to assist member banks with many of their activities.

One of the perennial problems found in most communities is the difficulty faced by the poorer people when they have to borrow money for some emergency. Rates for loans of $300 or less are customarily high, whether the lender be a commercial bank, industrial or Morris Plan bank, industrial loan company, credit union, or consumer finance company (25). Such conditions lead to the activities of the "loan sharks" (unlicensed lenders), who thrive where a fixed legal rate of interest is so low that licensed firms are driven out of business or where the people, because of their inexperience and ignorance, are not aware that they could obtain loans at fairer rates of interest from legitimate sources.

The financial subsystem is usually regulated by state and federal laws and agencies rather than by local ordinances. But how it operates in a given community will depend considerably upon a number of factors: the values toward thrift and debt; the complexity of the economic structure and the requirements for many kinds of financial services; the distribution of wealth and income in the community and the number of those who invest in securities.

Since ours is a money economy, the part of the banker is strategic. He determines who may and who may not obtain credit at reasonable rates in the community; he knows what business moves are intended and where profitable investments can be made; he knows about the financial condition of many individuals and firms within the community and is often called upon for advice about matters outside the field of finance. Any community study claiming comprehensive coverage needs to list and briefly characterize the components of this financial network and describe how they fit into the general economic structure and cultural orientation of the community.

Commerce. Community members as consumers are most intimately involved with the commercial subsystem through which they obtain the goods and services which they require. As was seen in the case study of the restaurant, each such unit varies in what it has to offer the public and in size and complexity of operations. A study sponsored by a large merchandising chain of thousands of employees in many units of the chain shows that both increasing size and increasing complexity of organizational structure make effective integration difficult and contribute to the progressive deterioration of management-employee relations (34). This illustrates the fact that each commercial establishment, like each industrial plant, is a set of human relationships which can be studied with respect to those variables which influence them.

Chapter 3 has provided sufficient background to indicate the interrelatedness of these business groups, whether as wholesale companies serving retail stores, or as laundries serving hotels. There is such a continuing interchange within the subsystem that it would be difficult to trace even in minimum detail. But the orientation of the businessman, be his company small or large, is to make a profit. This means cutting down his costs, charging whatever prices the general public seems willing to pay, and rendering the type of service that will result in consumer satisfaction. It also means, in theory at least, getting a full day's work from each employee. In other words, Main Street tends to develop a subculture of its own which not only pervades the commercial subsystem but strongly influences the other systems of the community.

Although the commercial subsystem is held together primarily through the impersonal processes of supply and demand, of competition and the other basic characteristics of the free enterprise system, it nevertheless has some formal organizations which exist to serve its interests. One of these is the local Chamber of Commerce, whose executive is supposed to see that business interests are protected in the community at large. Many other local businessmen's groups spring up in the larger cities. These are based on the type of establishment or special occupational status and hold periodic meetings with appropriate programs. In some communities the Salesman's Club is active, in others all dealers in real estate may have an over-all Realtor's group. These coordinating groups in turn interlock to give a consistency to the subsystem.

As businesses prosper and grow, as their management becomes more complicated, they more and more demand the services of the business executive, a specialized status in urban areas. Many studies have been made of persons occupying this status, for in understanding them one gains an insight into many important features of local business life. One study by William E. Henry, which involved data gathered from over one hundred executives in various types of business houses, contains some very positive findings. The following quotation is the beginning of the Henry report.

The business executive is a central figure in the economic and social life of the United States. His direction of business enterprise and his participation in informal social groupings give him a significant place in community life. In both its economic and its social aspects the role of the business executive is sociologically a highly visible one. It has clearly definable limits and characteristics known to the general public. These characteristics indicate the function of the business executive in the social structure, define the behavior expected of the individual executive, and serve as a guide to the selection of the novice.

Social pressure plus the constant demands of the business organization of which he is a part direct the behavior of the executive into the mold appropriate to the defined role. "Success" is the name applied to the whole-hearted adoption of the role. The individual behaves in the manner dictated by the society, and society rewards the individual with "success" if his behavior conforms to the role. It would punish him with "failure" should he deviate from it.[17]

After pointing out that participation in this role is related to personality structure, Henry goes on to list some of the personality characteristics which business executives have in common. These may be summarized as follows:

Successful executives show high drive and achievement desires.

They have strong mobility drives.

They look to their superiors as persons of more advanced training and experience, to be consulted on special problems, and from whom they receive certain guiding directives.

They have a high degree of ability to organize unstructured situations and to see the implications of their organization. That is, they see relationships between several isolated events.

They can be decisive in the sense of choosing a course among several alternatives, whether this be done on the spot or after detailed consideration.

They know what they are and what they want and have well-developed techniques for getting what they want.

They are active, striving, aggressive persons, with this activity and aggressiveness channeled into work or struggles for status and prestige.

The successful executives are "self-propelled" and need to keep moving always and to see another goal ever ahead, which also suggests that cessation of mobility and of struggling for new achievements will result in inversion of this constant energy. They will worry about their health, be dissatisfied in their social relationships. There is always present the fear that they may not succeed.

Strong executives are thoroughly oriented to immediate realities and their implications.

The successful executives in general look to their superiors with a feeling of personal attachment and tend to identify with them. On

[17] William E. Henry, "The Business Executive: The Psycho-Dynamics of a Social Role," *American Journal of Sociology*, LIV (January, 1949), 286.

the other hand, they look to their subordinates in a detached and impersonal way, seeing them as "doers of work" rather than as people. They are "men who have left home." They feel and act as though they were on their own, as though their emotional ties and obligations to parents had been severed. The tie to the mother has been mostly clearly broken but the tie to the father remains positive as the emotional counterpart of the admired and more successful male figure. Without this image, struggle for success seems difficult.[18]

No business executive of one's acquaintance will fill each one of this bill of particulars, but the successful ones will tend to approximate the general picture described. Since individuals of this sort are at the helm of the commercial (and some of the other economic) subsystem, one readily understands the dynamic effect of such a subsystem upon community life.

Agriculture. Since most communities, sociologically defined, spill out over the settled urban area they include rural people who farm full-time, part-time, or not at all. Within the center of the community one finds business groups which buy, store, process, and ship agricultural products and cater to the needs of the farmer, who is in a very real sense a businessman himself. Although each farm is an independent firm, the farmer, particularly if he is successful, joins various agricultural groups that carry on activities in his interest. If he has many cattle he may participate in a livestock breeding association, or if he grows oranges he may belong to a cooperative specializing in the distribution of citrus fruits. He is apt to be a member of a Farm Bureau, the official organization representing farmers in his community, and his wife will belong to the Homemakers' Clubs. His children will participate in 4-H or Future Farmers of America activities.

Furthermore, he will probably make use of the materials and services provided by the Cooperative Extension Work in Agriculture and Home Economics, the federal-state-local program that has been in operation for over forty years. The County Agent will often work through the Farm Bureau, and the Home Demonstration Agent through the Homemakers' Clubs. Both of these are known as "extension workers" in that they are supposed to carry on adult education among the rural people of the county. Many studies of extension work indicate that the farmers with highest socioeconomic status are most often reached by the extension program (6).

Many recent changes, such as industrialization and mechanization, have altered the character of the agricultural subsystem in many

[18] *Ibid.,* adapted and abridged from pages 287–91.

areas. Cotton-producing regions which relied traditionally upon a landlord-tenant relationship are now shifting to the use of laborers paid daily or weekly wages. Commercial farming is thus spreading to the point that most of the farm products an urban family consumes come from a commercial rather than a family farm.

But the agricultural subsystem is also held together by a number of government programs in addition to the extension service. Soil conservation, rural electrification, farm credit associations, bring an influence to farming that it lacked only two or three generations ago. Rural development programs cater to the poorer farmer with a small holding or one consisting of unprofitable land. There is thus a self-consciousness, a feeling of identity within the agricultural subsystem of a community.

These brief descriptions of selected economic subsystems are designed to call attention to the kinds of socioeconomic networks which exist in most communities. For some research purposes, the economic system may be viewed in different ways, with the result that other subsystems will prove better analytical tools; yet, the average members of the community identify and understand the subsystems delineated here, which is a sufficient reason for their use in a volume such as this.

Once individual subsystems have been singled out and portrayed, the task remains of putting them back together into the major economic system. This calls for the spelling out in detail of the ways in which each is tied in with all the rest, a task which has already been partly done in the earlier discussion. For example, the connection between organized labor and the industrial subsystem is readily apparent, although some of the unofficial relations are not frequently recognized (29). The connection between the financial institutions and the other segments also are obvious, but the nature and extent of the control exercised will vary from community to community. The coming in of industry and the development of that subsystem have a profound effect upon the rest. For example, it may cause marked shifts in agriculture as people shift from full-time to part-time farming, supplementing their income by work in the factory.

This subsystem approach should emphasize also that there is no single person or small group of persons who can speak in behalf of the whole economic segment of the community. Various subsystems have their spokesmen, and even within subsystems there are conflicting voices.

The Economy and the Operations of the Community as a Social System

Even if one gains some idea, through the subsystem analysis, of the structure and workings of the economy as a major system, there still remains the problem of relating the economy to the community as a total system. As Figure 24 (Chapter 18) shows, there are several operations which must be carried out if the community is to survive as a social system. Some of these are obviously carried out through the economy.

Differentiation and Allocation of Occupational Status. In the introduction to this chapter reference was made to the division of labor in the community and the need for specialists to develop as new needs required them. This operation is termed "differentiation" and accompanies advancing technology and increased social complexity. The contrast between the occupations found in a small Guatemalan agricultural community (Chapter 3) and in the modern city demonstrates clearly this operation at work. Differentiation need not be confined solely to occupations but can include distinctions based on race, nationality, religion, class, and caste; but certainly where it is occupational it has developed in response to economic needs.

Therefore, the economy serves the functions of rewarding those who learn new specialties considered useful to the members of the community. If many members of a suburban community should decide to commute to work daily by helicopter, then specialized helicopter mechanics would probably spring up around the places where the "copters" were parked. If many of the members of a community manifest a lively interest in golf, then driving ranges may develop in response. Somehow or other, in a free enterprise system there is a tendency for specialties to develop in direct answer to felt needs. Where the specialty is economic, of course, the new specialist has hopes of gaining sufficient monetary return to make his efforts worthwhile.

Adding to the specialties of a community takes care of only part of the problem; people must be persuaded to fill these occupational statuses as new replacements are needed. Here again the economy is one of the major systems involved along with education. There is always talk of some occupational shortages. For example, with the changes in our way of life there is increased demand for trained nurses, but their supply is insufficient. The same holds true for certain types of scientists. Increased monetary remuneration may in part provide sufficient attraction, but the chances are that in the case of both nurses and scientists some noneconomic incentives need to be worked out. These would include greater glamor in the case of nursing and more equation in the prestige of the scientist and that of the business executive. But economies are often able through impersonal processes to arrange such shifts in emphasis over a period of time, with the result that the essential occupational statuses become staffed and community needs are met.

Allocation of Goods and Services. This operation, already touched upon in the discussion of government, applies with even greater force to the economy. An economic system, through the filling of necessary occupational positions, supposedly takes care of the production of all the material goods needed, as well as its distribution. But this distribution should not be thought of as simply a geographical parcelling out of what is available. Instead, it takes place in a free enterprise system through the distribution of income, which varies with the different kinds of jobs. Some jobs pay much, others pay little. Those people who receive the most pay can buy the most goods and services in contrast to those with little income. Thus Cadillacs and second-hand Chevrolets get distributed throughout the community, as do women's permanents in the high-class beauty salons and in the less expensive do-it-yourself kits. The economy, then, is the system that determines to a great extent who gets what and how much of the material goods and services as well as many of the more intangible benefits of community life.

Social Mobility. Related to both of the preceding operations is a third requirement of a dynamic community system, namely, the rise of people of ability and ambition to the higher positions in the society, with a consequent possible downgrading of others. Through the occupational structure (29) individuals are able to "better" their social station, and this mobility has a stimulating effect upon the members of the system. Supposedly, in a closed society, where people have little opportunity to change their station, incentives for progress would be lacking, and individuals would expect to end their lives in about the same relative position as they began it. In American society, according to some of the points of view cited in Chapter 6, the attitude toward progress is tied in with the expectation of advancement on the basis of merit and hard work. Just how real is this American dream is still subject to debate, but in most communities there is sufficient social circulation to guarantee that capable people, even though not always the most capable, fill positions

of responsibility. Economic considerations enter largely into the
question of who rises and how far.

The Economy and Community Change

The very listing of these three illustrative operations should indicate that the economic system is dedicated to change largely because it is based on technology and the satisfaction of an increasing
appetite for consumers goods. This year's automobile is dated after
it has been out two months, for the automobile trade begins to talk
about next year's model. The current radio or television idol will be
replaced in time by someone else with a higher audience rating. The
shift from one chief source of fuel, such as that from coal to oil or
gas, and from oil or gas to atomic power, carries with it changes of
many kinds.

Furthermore, the economy, like the government, is closely geared
in with the economic system outside of the community. National advertising (3) and mass merchandising penetrate the small town and
medium-sized city to the point that they determine what the customers demand from the merchants, although department store
buyers well-versed in local tastes can still play a role in setting the
limits of new fashions. The increasing use of brand names, as the
result of a consistent effort on the part of those promoting various
products, tends to standardize consumer tastes.

Accompanying these changes, as Chapter 9 has shown, are modifications in values and in behavior patterns. When the automobile
became popular, men stopped wearing top hats and carrying canes
which could be managed quite conveniently in a roomy horse-drawn
carriage but not in the motor car. Thus, in ways too numerous to
mention, the economic system brings in material changes. Shifts in
occupational structure and in distribution of income affect social
relationships; redistribution of power through organized groups
serving economic ends influences the behavior of subsystems toward
each other; and the quality of community life changes as one major
system, such as the government or the economy, gains ascendancy
over the rest. Such competition among systems is reflected in the
shifting positions of those most closely identified with those systems
and can be gauged by rising or declining influence in the community as a whole. Change is occurring, therefore, when the new industrial managers replace the landed aristocracy in the community
councils, when politicians listen to the labor leaders as much as they
do to the bankers, and when professional people as well as businessmen are asked their opinions about local affairs.

REFERENCES AND SUGGESTED READINGS

1. *Annals* of the American Academy of Political and Social Science 274 (March, 1951). Entire issue devoted to "Labor in the American Economy."
2. ARENSBERG, C. M. "Industry and the Community," *American Journal of Sociology*, XLVIII (July, 1942), 1–12.
3. BAUR, E. JACKSON. "The Functions of Ceremony in the Advertising Business," *Social Forces*, XXVII (May, 1949), 358–65.
4. BLAU, PETER M. "Co-operation and Competition in a Bureaucracy," *American Journal of Sociology*, LIX (May, 1954), 530–35.
5. CHINOY, ELY. "The Tradition of Opportunity and the Aspirations of Automobile Workers," *American Journal of Sociology*, LVII (March, 1952), 453–59.
6. COLEMAN, LEE. "Differential Contact with Extension Work in a New York Community," *Rural Sociology*, XVI (September, 1951), 207–16.
7. DALTON, MELVILLE. "Informal Factors in Career Achievement," *American Journal of Sociology*, LVI (March, 1951), 407–15.
8. ————. "Conflicts between Staff and Line Managerial Officers," *American Sociological Review*, XV (June, 1950), 342–51.
9. ————. "Unofficial Union-Management Relations," *American Sociological Review*, XV (October, 1950), 611–19.
10. DRUCKER, PETER F. "The Employee Society," *American Journal of Sociology*, LVIII (January, 1953), 358–63.
11. DUBIN, ROBERT. "Decision-Making by Management in Industrial Relations," *American Journal of Sociology*, LIV (January, 1949), 292–97.
12. FORM, WILLIAM H., and MILLER, DELBERT C. "Occupational Career Patterns as a Sociological Instrument," *American Journal of Sociology*, LIV (January, 1949), 317–29.
13. GARDNER, BURLEIGH. *Human Relations in Industry.* Homewood, Ill.: Richard D. Irwin, Inc., 1945.
14. GOODE, WILLIAM J. "Community Within a Community: The Professions," *American Sociological Review*, XXII (April, 1957), 194–200.
15. GOODE, WILLIAM J., and FOWLER, IRVING. "Incentive Factors in a Low Morale Plant," *American Sociological Review*, XIV (October, 1949), 618–24.
16. HENRY, WILLIAM E. "The Business Executive: The Psycho-Dynamics of a Social Role," *American Journal of Sociology*, LIV (June, 1949), 286–91.
17. HILDEBRAND, GEORGE H. "American Unionism, Social Stratification, and Power," *American Journal of Sociology*, LVIII (January, 1953), 381–90.
18. HUGHES, EVERETT C. "The Sociological Study of Work: An Editorial Foreword," *American Journal of Sociology*, LVII (March, 1952), 423–26.
19. KARSH, BERNARD; SEIDMAN, JOEL; and LILIENTHAL, DAISY M. "The Union Organizer and his Tactics: A Case Study," *American Journal of Sociology*, LIX (September, 1953), 113–22.
20. KNOX, JOHN B. *The Sociology of Industrial Relations: An Introduction to Industrial Sociology.* New York: Random House, Inc., 1956.
21. MEADOWS, PAUL. "The Worker: Archetype of Industrial Man," *Social Forces*, XXV (May, 1947), 441–45.
22. MOORE, WILBERT E. *Industrial Relations and the Social Order.* New York: The Macmillan Co., 1946.
23. MYERS, RICHARD R. "Myth and Status Systems in Industry," *Social Forces*, XXVI (March, 1948), 331–37.
24. ODAKA, KUNIO. "An Iron Workers' Community in Japan: A Study in the Sociology of Industrial Groups," *American Sociological Review*, XV (April, 1950), 186–95.
25. PHELPS, CLYDE WILLIAM. "The Social Control of Consumer Credit Costs: A Case Study," *Social Forces*, XXIX (May, 1951), 433–42.
26. ROY, DONALD. "Quota Restriction and Goldbricking in a Machine Shop," *American Journal of Sociology*, LVII (March, 1952), 427–42.

27. SEIDMAN, JOEL; LONDON, JACK; and KARSH, BERNARD. "Leadership in a Local Union," *American Journal of Sociology*, LVI (November, 1950), 229–37.
28. STEPHENSON, CHESTER M. "A Case Study of a Milk Marketing Cooperative," *Rural Sociology*, XVIII (June, 1953), 169–70.
29. STEPHENSON, RICHARD. "Status Achievement and the Occupational Pyramid," *Social Forces*, XXXI (October, 1952), 75–77.
30. STRAUSS, GEORGE, and SAYLES, LEONARD R. "Occupation and the Selection of Local Union Officers," *American Journal of Sociology*, LVIII (May, 1953), 585–91.
31. WALKER, CHARLES R.; GUEST, ROBERT H.; and TURNER, ARTHUR N. *The Foreman on the Assembly Line.* Cambridge: Harvard University Press, 1956.
32. WARNER, W. LLOYD, and LOW, J. O. *The Social System of the Modern Factory.* New Haven: Yale University Press, 1947.
33. WHYTE, WILLIAM F. *Industry and Society.* New York: McGraw-Hill Book Co., Inc., 1946.
34. WORTHY, JAMES C. "Organizational Structure and Employe Morale," *American Sociological Review*, XV (April, 1950), 169–79.
35. WRAY, DONALD E. "Marginal Men of Industry: The Foreman," *American Journal of Sociology*, LIV (January, 1949), 298–301.

Chapter 14

FAMILY, RELIGION, AND MORALITY

One of the most popular fields within sociology is "the sociology of the family," and another which promises to assume increasing importance is "the sociology of religion."[1] Each of these subjects could be discussed as major systems in American society or any society at great length, and such discussion would be both interesting and profitable. However, since the community is the central theme of this volume, these two systems will be viewed chiefly in terms of their connection with the community, although some brief characterization of each will first be necessary.

THE FAMILY SYSTEM

Differences in Family Types. Professor Sirjamaki, whose summary of the economic system was quoted in the last chapter, characterizes the American family system as follows:

> *Family:* monogamous marriage; conjugal family with limited kin reckoning; considerable divorce and remarriage; family reduced in size and functions; increased individuation of family members, with approaching husband-wife equality and particular emphasis on children; marriage as a sacrament, but with considerable secularism.[2]

Although such a description accurately describes the over-all family system in the United States, marked regional variations still remain. The Spanish-American family in New Mexico differs from the middle-class suburban family of Lake Forest, Illinois, in the

---

[1] "The sociology of religion may be defined as the scientific study of religion as a social institution, including its interrelationships with other social institutions and other aspects of society and culture." See Earl D. C. Brewer, "Sect and Church in Methodism," *Social Forces*, XXX (May, 1952), 400.

[2] John Sirjamaki, "A Footnote to the Anthropological Approach to the Study of American Culture," *Social Forces*, XXV (March, 1947), 255.

authority accorded the father. The rural family of the Appalachian mountains has traits which seem most unusual to long-time residents of Flint, Michigan. In a few communities and among some social groupings the home is a place to eat and sleep but most activities are carried on elsewhere; in most communities though, even where the patriarchal tradition no longer prevails, the home is much more than a boardinghouse.

Furthermore, there seem to be differences between the social classes in many family behavior patterns. Two studies, one made in Boston and the other in Chicago, agreed that:

> The lower class is more severe in punishment in toilet training.
> The middle class has higher educational expectations of their children.
> Middle class children are allowed more freedom of movement away
> from home during the day.[3]

On the other hand, the studies showed that there was no class difference in amount of care given the children by the father and no class difference in display of aggression by children in the home, excluding aggression toward siblings. But there are sufficient indications of family differences within any community to make it extremely dangerous for one to assume that one's own family or that of a close friend can be used as a basis for generalization about the community as a whole. Racial, religious, and occupational factors all play their part, as do such traumatic experiences as divorce, desertion, or death, which lead to "broken homes."

Nevertheless, it is fair to say that a visitor to America from some peasant society such as India would be more impressed by the similarities he observed in all American families than by the differences, because he would be comparing what he saw with the family-centered, traditionalistic society in which he had been reared.

The Family and Other Major Systems. No family, particularly if it consists of lively, adventurous youngsters who venture into many parts of the community, can remain aloof from community influences. Even those parents supposedly "set in their ways" are not immune to the nonfamilial forces at play about them. As these new ways become accepted by the parents, they incorporate them into their child-rearing practices or into the system of beliefs which they transmit to their children, thereby producing within the community new members whose orientation is different from that of the previous generation (14).

[3] Robert J. Havighurst and Allison Davis, "A Comparison of the Chicago and Harvard Studies of Social Class Differences in Child Rearing," *American Sociological Review,* XX (August, 1955), 441.

What are some of these influences which have a bearing upon family life? One area of close interdependence is that between family and religion. Lee G. Burchinal has noted that earlier marital prediction studies indicated that success in marriage was associated with "pre-marital participation in church activities, a church-sanctioned marriage, being a church member before and during marriage, and attending church regularly."[4] He also observed contradictory findings in some of these studies and therefore set out to check on them. But at the end of his research he concluded that the association between church activities and marital satisfaction generally held true.

But some studies suggest that the contemporary family is declining as a religious force, and they consider this trend as an urban rather than a rural phenomenon, one which affects various religious bodies differently (5). Although John L. Thomas made a careful, extensive study of religious training in the Roman Catholic family to find out whether this decline was real or not in that religious body, he was unable to discern any trends which could be stated with confidence. Regional differences as well as rural-urban differences did assume a significance when the religious training of the pre-school Roman Catholic child was analyzed (25). Until more evidence to the contrary is available for other religious groupings as well, it is possible to assume that family life is becoming more secularized in the United States and that parents are increasingly leaving what might be called specific religious training to the Sunday Schools and other types of instruction, such as parochial schools provided by church authorities; but even such trends can experience reversal if parents should decide to play a more active part in these matters.

The effects of transition in national economies upon family life are too well known to need much elaboration (13). But these seem to differ in different cultures (24, 11, 26). In Japan, according to Irene B. Taeuber, where industrialization and urbanization occurred on a broad scale, the family system rather than the individual worker became the unit which responded to and guided the changes under way.

The process of economic readjustment . . . was achieved primarily through the reallocation of youth, and that reallocation occurred through the family system. The movements for employment and for marriage that created one of the most rapid urbanizations in the modern world were controlled through a household system whose ancient roots and modern formation were alike components of a feudal social structure. . . . Industry and commerce become added

[4] Lee G. Burchinal, "Marital Satisfaction and Religious Behavior," *American Sociological Review*, XXII (June, 1957), 306.

functions of a family whose cohesiveness in the metropolis became in some ways even greater than it had been in the village, and monetary values permeated a culture sizeable portions of whose people worked without wages.[5]

The pre-eminence of the family in the Japanese economy is shown by the fact that it also served as the function of a social security system. Anyone losing his job in the commercial economy could rejoin his original family, secure subsistence, and work in the family enterprise whether it was a farm, small shop, or piecework. Furthermore, women entered the labor market in ways consistent with their family role; that is, they worked within the home or in the family enterprise, not outside it, even though they were gainfully employed. Changes were being fashioned, however, by the migration of young people to industrial centers, and additional changes were introduced by the democratic reforms set up during the American occupation of Japan. These legally abolished the responsibilities and obligations of the household head. Women were given independence of action not known before. In short, individualism was to replace familism, equality to replace feudalism. Western-type social welfare services by the state were to replace those of the family. Whether these imported ideas will win out over the entrenched traditional family system is a contest which social observers are watching with keen interest. It is significant that the Japanese response to industrialization and urbanization was different from that of the Western nations. In Japan the family persisted as the important economic unit; in the West, where individualism developed, the family tended to lose some of its economic functions, especially those having to do with production.

The family and government as major systems interact at many points. Family dependents figure prominently in the fixing of individual income tax rates, since allowable deductions are permitted for each dependent. In the United States child welfare and old-age assistance programs, parts of the federal social security legislation administered through state agencies, reveal the effect of government upon family life. For example, does the existence of such provisions for elderly people mean that grown children feel less responsible for their aged parents? Are they more apt to think that the community, through the mediation of the government, should take care of their parents, comforting themselves with the thought that they need to spend what income they have on their own children? With increasing urbanization the trend toward a lessened sense of responsibility for parents was becoming pronounced even before the

[5] Irene B. Taeuber, "Family, Migration and Industrialization in Japan," *American Sociological Review*, XVI (April, 1951), 151.

old-age assistance provisions were passed as part of the Social Security Act of 1935. At any rate, government has an important influence on such family relationships today.

Government has long been involved in the registration of marriages and, more recently, in the premarital health tests required by some states, chiefly in the interests of preventing the spread of venereal desease. When divorce is contemplated or carried through, the government too is closely tied in with the fate of the members of the family unit being dissolved, since it determines whether or not the wife receives alimony and what provisions are to be made for the children. Even the services of marriage and family counselors are provided by some units of local government, chiefly the larger cities, where there are Courts of Domestic Relations.

The family, as one of the major community systems, is closely tied in therefore with the other systems, and its changing character must be seen against these interrelationships.

Functions of the Family. One writer, Blaine E. Mercer, takes strong issue with those who claim that the American family is *losing* many of its functions. He states:

> Affectionally, it (the family) is more significant than ever in an increasingly industrial society in which an individual can be "lost in a crowd." Economically, family, while not so important as formerly as a production unit, is the basic earning and spending unit. Protectively, it is in the family that concern for individual welfare is still most effectively expressed. Recreationally, we have recently experienced a revitalization of family activities. . . . Educationally, the family is expressing concern for child training through growing membership in P.T.A. and other home-school organizations, through emphasis on the study of child psychology, care in selection of books and recordings; even the recent outcries against unfunny comic books and horror films have come largely from parents and family life organizations.[6]

Mercer receives considerable support for his position from Charles E. Ramsey and Lowry Nelson who were also aware of the many statements being made about the loss of functions (21) believed to be associated with changes in values and attitudes toward the home and family (9). They decided in 1952 to repeat a 1939 study of the attitudes of high school juniors and seniors of Mora, Minnesota, toward family relations. To their surprise they found that for this one community at least there was no support for the hypothesis that changes had occurred in family adjustment or in values and attitudes toward specific family relations. The one exception was the finding that the girls in the 1952 sample had less sense of obligation to the

[6] Blaine E. Mercer, *The American Community* (New York: Random House, Inc., 1956), p. 198.

family than those in the 1939 sample. The authors made two suggestions which might account for their results. First, it may really be true that despite high divorce rates "the family is achieving a successful adaptation to what are often called urban influences; that is, whatever changes may take place in other family functions, the basic confidence and loyalties of members to each other are not measurably affected." Their second suggestion was that "the age group included in this sample is not influenced in attitudes by changes in the social 'climate'; their lives are sheltered from the changes in the social economic order—changes which may be more immediately reflected in changes in the attitudes of adults."[7]

The functions of the family, as discussed thus far, are stated chiefly in terms of the individual. That is, what does the family do for him? It is necessary also to see how the family participates in the operation of the community as a total social system. One of the most important contributions of the family in this regard is so obvious that it hardly needs to be stated: namely, the biological replacement of the population. But even this function is subject to various pressures. A case in point is Hamtramck, Michigan, an immigrant Polish Catholic community, which had four of the characteristics ordinarily associated with high fertility of its residents: rural origin, foreign birth, low socioeconomic status, and Roman Catholicism. In 1920 its birth rate was much above the average in the United States; by 1950 the two were very similar. What had happened, in spite of the characteristics mentioned, to make the rates there more like the rest of the country? Albert J. Mayer and Sue Marx, who tried to account for the change (20), suggest that the Poles had as their reference group Americans with a higher standard of living, particularly for the children. They desired to avoid group ridicule, to enjoy this higher standard of living. And they found it increasingly difficult to support a large family at even a subsistence level. Also, they had a decided prejudice against accepting welfare funds. These pressures and incentives were strong enough to make the people prefer small families and resort to birth control. Furthermore, Hamtramck was such a cohesive and close-knit community that once the values related to lower birth rates began to be accepted, the knowledge of birth-control methods could rapidly spread through the community.

Another very important contribution made by the family to the operation of the community as a system is the socialization of the

[7] Charles E. Ramsey and Lowry Nelson, "Change in Values and Attitudes toward the Family," *American Sociological Review*, XXI (October, 1956), 609.

young, which also aids in the socialization of parents, involving them much more in community affairs than would otherwise be the case. Certainly, participation in community affairs seems definitely linked with the presence of children in the home, and particularly younger children, according to evidence from a study of Prince Georges County, Maryland.[8] The parents themselves go through a socialization process, which gives them a more active community concern, although when the children grow up and move away, interest in organized community effort may hold much less attraction unless such participation is "good for business" or unless prestige-involvement provides sufficient motivation.

Thus a study of any community would have to take into account not only what the family system is like but those changes within the systems, such as lowering birth rates, which may affect the future of the community. The family as a major system lacks the several subsystems that the economy possesses, for it lacks the differentiation of statuses found in the economy. As far as family life is concerned, people are distributed into small disconnected but roughly similar units. Such units can be typed by size and composition, but those conforming to a given type, such as three-member families, do not comprise an extended network of social interactions. The only major intermediary network in America between the individual family groups and the total family system (as an institutionalized set of statuses, roles, values, and norms) is the kinship group, which again binds only a relatively few people together and does not cut across most communities in the way that subsystems previously described would do. In a familistic, peasant society the kinship group would step in to exercise social control when this was necessary, but in most American communities each individual family unit operates independently. When these family units fail to perform their functions effectively, the community becomes acutely aware of juvenile delinquency, truancy, desertion, and a breakdown in consensus about dominant values. It is only as these "problems" become evident that the average citizen realizes that the family system, though working in small units, is actually in its totality a major system in the community.

THE RELIGIOUS SYSTEM

In spite of all of the talk about the emphasis upon the secular aspects of our culture the proportion of the American population

---

[8] See W. C. Rohrer and J. F. Schmidt, *Family Type and Social Participation* (College Park: Agricultural Experiment Station, University of Maryland, Misc. Publication No. 196, June, 1954).

enrolled as church members has reached an all-time high (4). What accounts for this interest in religious matters? Is there a "return to religion," or is religious membership one of the important steps in acquiring and maintaining higher social status in the American community? Obviously, the motivation will vary with different people, but the interest in religion, as shown by the popularity of religious books on best-seller lists (22), is one of the sociological facts of our time.

The Church and the Sect. In order to speak with clarity and accuracy about religion and society, sociologists find it necessary to make distinctions between the different kinds of religious bodies. For example, there are such tremendous differences between Jehovah's Witnesses and the Eastern Orthodox Church that each will have a different relationship to its social environment, although as religious organizations they will have some points in common. Each writer in this field is apt to formulate his own system for distinguishing between religious bodies, but the most widely used classification centers around the use of the terms *church* and *sect.* Harold W. Pfautz has found it desirable in his discussion of the development of Christian Science to use a five-fold classification of religious bodies based on degree of secularization, as shown in Figure 21.

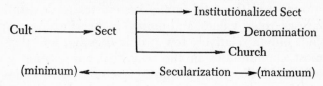

From Harold W. Pfautz, "The Sociology of Secularization: Religious Groups," *American Journal of Sociology,* LXI (September, 1955), 121.

Fig. 21. Development relationship among types of religious "groups."

According to Pfautz[9] five distinct frames of reference can be employed in the construction of types: the demographic, ecological, associational (oriented to group organization), structural (social differentiation within the group and type of leadership), and social-psychological. Once a sect has developed, it can become either an institutionalized sect, a church, or a denomination. Figure 22 summarizes Pfautz's main points. This figure should prove particularly useful in indicating the main points stressed by sociologists in their study of religion as a social system. Indeed, many of the terms used in the typology should have a familiar ring, since they were dis-

[9] See his article for reference to those (Troeltsch, Pope, Niebuhr, Yinger) who have been most responsible for the development of this terminology and on whose work he bases his classification.

cussed in other connections in earlier chapters. But in order to make
the discussion in this chapter briefer and less detailed, we will use
the three-fold division of cult, sect (including the sect and the institutionalized sect), and the church (including both the church and
the denomination). It also follows more closely the everyday use of
the word *church*. Whatever typology one accepts as most useful for
a particular study, it is important to remember that in spite of many
similar characteristics, various religious bodies do have strikingly
different appeals, with the result that the American has a wide
choice of religious orientations from which to choose, some of which
include world religions other than Christianity.

Many studies have shown that new sects are closely connected
with socioeconomic status, which has some bearing upon the choice
that an individual makes (3, 7). Benton Johnson sees the sect as a
powerful agent in socializing lower-class groups in the values and
usages of our predominantly middle-class society (15). In his study
of Columbus, Ohio, Russell R. Dynes verified the hypothesis that
Churchness (represented by Episcopalians and Presbyterians) is associated with high socioeconomic status and, conversely, that Sect-
ness (Holiness, Pentecostal, Church of God, Church of the Nazarene,
and Baptist) is associated with low socioeconomic status (6).

Religious Subsystems. Each denominational subsystem is replete
with its own professional leaders, or functionaries, who differ in
their ideas about the extent to which they or their parishioners
should become involved in community affairs. Their job as functionaries is not to represent the community but rather their own denomination and in many cases their own local congregation. The
long training that most of them have had in theological seminaries
plus the special roles, which in some ways set them apart, makes
most of them content to leave community problems to others.

But the subsystem, in addition to the functionaries, has its own
set of beliefs—perhaps formulated in creed and worked out as theology—which gives it a distinctiveness from many other though
not all religious bodies. Particularly in the case of the newer sects,
as well as periodically with the more established ones, a feeling of
being different heightens the *esprit de corps*. This difference may
be that of a minority group conscious that only as all members stick
together will any of them gain; or the sense of difference may be
one that grows out of the feeling of being "better" or "more pious"
than nonmembers. These beliefs, in addition to embracing creed,
also indicate conduct and practice, thereby giving guidance for
daily life. To be told that one should not consume pork products,

SOCIOLOGICAL PERSPECTIVE

Type of Religious Body	Demographic	Ecological	Associational	Structural	Social-Psychological
Cult (many "store-front churches")	So small that every member is acquainted with others personally Heterogeneous in racial and ethnic composition	Confined to local community and technically segregated because of smallness	Lacks internal differentiation Members interact with one another totally Typically isolated *outside* the mores Interaction chiefly nonsymbolic (Note 1) Recruitment voluntary	Little status differentiation present Leadership is personal, residing more in personal qualities of leader than in social response and definition Rules few but contain a total way of life	A fellowship; affectual motives are primary, solidarity based on psychic dividends
Sect (Dunkers and Amana Society)	Increases in size to point where secondary relationships are necessarily reached Remains heterogeneous	"On the move" Because of its conflict ideology, as well as smallness, it remains ecologically segregated; if it disperses, does not do so at random	Increasing internal associational differentiation Symbolic elements increase because goals (ideology) become clarified In conflict with larger society Recruitment primarily voluntary	Status differentiation has increased Functionaries identified Leadership has become charismatic (Note 2) Norms more specific but continue to cover entire range of social life Prestige low	A following in which affectual and value-rational motives are combined
Institutionalized Sect (Quakers, Mormons, Christian Scientists)	Too large for all members to know each other even impersonally Grows more homogeneous, since recruiting is more selective	National and even international in distribution Highly segregated	Much internal differentiation; numerous formal groups develop; balance between symbolic and nonsymbolic elements Conflict with larger society institution…	Formal status more common Leadership is official but not professionalized Directives for conduct highly specific	Approximates a "community" with a balanced motivational texture among the emotional, the self-interest, the traditional, and value-rational

258

				(top of cell cut off) … groups in larger society; "respectable"	An institutional locus of control in the larger society Membership conveys prestige
Church (Roman Catholics)	Large but heterogeneous Grows as larger society grows	Members scattered and not segregated	Traditional membership becomes significant Highly differentiated assimilated into larger society Recruitment traditional rather than voluntary	Social structure complex and formal Leadership official and professionalized Normative system explicit, specific, comprehensive	
Denomination (more important Protestant bodies)	Large but homogeneous Growth slow, may be static	Segregated	Highly differentiated symbolic elements outweigh nonsymbolic Relationship to larger society is accommodative Members belong because parents belonged	More power than institutionalized sect but less than the church, with such power employed for reform "Respectable" Behavior as institution relatively rational	Associations rather than communities

Source: Adapted from Harold W. Pfautz, "The Sociology of Secularization: Religious Groups," *American Journal of Sociology*, LXI (September, 1955).

Note 1: "Throughout religion *symbolism* plays an important part. Symbols are substitutes or representations of some object or situation. They may be verbal or tangible. A commonly recognized religious symbol assists the person to identify himself with his fellows. It promotes a sense of solidarity. . . . For the religious worshiper, the object and its symbol are combined ino an indivisible emotional experience that asserts itself whenever the situation calls for contact with the supernatural powers." Kimball Young, *Sociology: A Study of Society and Culture* (New York: American Book Co., 1949 2nd edition), p. 372.

Note 2:. Charismatic Authority: resting on devotion to the specific and exceptional sanctity, heroism or exemplary character of an individual person, and of the normative patterns or order revealed or ordained by him. A. M. Henderson and Talcott Parsons [Translators], *Max Weber: The Theory of Social and Economic Organization* [New York: Oxford University Press 1947], p. 328.

Fig. 22. Types of religious bodies within American Christianity.

as is the case of some of the small sects in the Protestant tradition, sets the members apart from those people who do eat pork. This is a part of the belief system one embraces in joining that particular group.

The religious subsystem, like other subsystems, is composed of social groups or organizations. In some churches[10] this phase receives such stress that much time is put into many activities which to the outside observer have little connection with traditional religious behavior. But those in charge of such programs visualize the church as a social as well as a spiritual center, pointing out oftentimes that there is little difference between the two. Other church groups try to set up a rigid distinction between the human and social on the one hand and the divine and spiritual on the other. All of these differences have a marked influence on participation in community affairs. Where a church satisfies most of their social needs, its members are much less interested in becoming involved in community matters; where a compartmentalization takes place between religion and everyday life, the individual brings to community activity a different orientation.

Along with creeds and ethics go important symbols, which signify to the fully initiated member much that words fail to convey. Symbols too can be divisive in the community sense, as in the case of Jewish minorities to whom the Star of David is as meaningful as the Cross is to Christians. At a certain level of communal activity, however, it is possible to work out an accommodation—at high school commencement exercises, for example—where a Catholic priest, a Protestant clergyman, and a Jewish rabbi can all participate without conflict of symbols or at least with a toleration of their use by the rest.

Usually, too, there is some kind of established hierarchy within a given religious subsystem. Great honor is paid to the hierarchy, which consists of those persons most closely associated with the more sacred aspects of the religious body. Quite often, in the case of laymen, the hierarchy does not correspond to social position in the community, since individuals who have been blocked in mobility drives in other ways find genuine satisfaction in devoting most of their energies to working in church groups. This is a common phenomenon in community life which applies to masonic orders, civic and woman's clubs, as well as to religious bodies.

[10] The typology in Figure 22 refers to national bodies, where it is possible to distinguish usefully between church and denomination. In the discussion of religion in the local community the word *church* will be used in the everyday sense and will refer to the local groups of all religious types.

However, these various religious subsystems from time to time find themselves in severe competition and occasionally in conflict. Religion, for example, may be the precipitating cause of some unfortunate incidents in the community when actually other causes may have been more basic. As a matter of fact, most church bodies may be characterized under one of three types. There is the *circumscribed* church whose leaders and most of whose members keep to themselves and have little to do with community problems or other churches. There is the *militant* church which is trying to grow in numbers, power, and prestige at the expense of all other church groups. Far from having a "live and let live" policy, its leaders are out on a mission to persuade the whole community to their way of thinking without calculating the social effects of their militancy. And there is the *cooperative* church which, though strongly believing in the correctness of its message and organization, still conceives of itself as being part of a larger system in which churches of different types have different purposes to perform. The minister of such a church usually joins the local ministerial union, participates in community events, and is willing to see the church building used by the Boy Scouts and other groups needing a regular place to meet. It is necessary to identify and classify the church bodies in this fashion if one is to see the part each plays in the total religious system of the community.

The Clergy. A familiarity with the official behavior patterns of the clergy in different church bodies reveals much not only about the interaction of these bodies with each other but also with the community. For example, if one compares the ministers in the congregational-type denomination with those in the episcopal-type denomination, interesting differences emerge. Luke M. Smith, who has studied this question, points out that clergymen in the congregational-type denomination are hired and fired by the parishioners; the denominational officials are little more than an employment agency without any authority to intervene. In an episcopal-type denomination the clergymen owe their jobs to denominational officials, who may or may not follow the wishes of the clergymen or the parishioners. There is also another important difference between the two types: the episcopal type leans toward *sacramentalism,* where denominational offices, structure, and rituals are ends in themselves. In contrast, *instrumentalism* is stressed in the congregational-type with the offices, structure, and rituals considered merely as instruments or means with no particular sacredness attached to them.

If a clergyman is to be considered successful, he must behave differently in the two types: in the episcopal-type he must fulfill formal ritual duties, conform to a traditional order, and be more willing to remain in the same parish; in the congregational-type his goal is to move from one parish to another, always trying to obtain a parish of higher prestige. Professor Smith views some of the relationships in economic terms:

> For purposes of comparative study, the episcopal-type can be generalized as *bureaucracy*, i.e., control is exercised by the managers; and the congregational-type as an *open market*, i.e., control is exercised by the clients or customers. There is also a tendency toward control by a third set of social positions, the workers, in this case the parish clergy. This type of authority will be called the professional. Thus a religious denomination is generalized as a set of social relationships between clients or customers, workers, and managers. About these social positions the authority structure may be institutionalized in a variety of ways, and there may be a certain amount of uninstitutionalized struggle between these positions for control.[11]

To test the generalizations which he has made, Smith has studied the migration of clergymen from one parish to another to determine whether moving patterns differ in the different types of denomination. Here are some of his findings based on interviews with twelve Episcopal and twelve Congregational clergymen in one metropolitan area:

> Clergymen of both denominations move more frequently during the early years than later, although Congregationalists continued to move during the later years whereas Episcopalians tended to settle down.
>
> Congregational clergymen moved a greater distance than Episcopalians.
>
> The Episcopalians, in telling about how they obtained their parishes, made much greater mention of denominational officials, whereas the Congregationalist mentioned church boards more frequently.
>
> Both sets of clergymen were equally concerned with pastoral counseling and calling. However, Episcopalians were bureaucratically oriented toward obtaining denominational offices and honors, whereas Congregationalists were professionally oriented toward interdenominational and interfaith activities.
>
> Episcopal clergymen were more concerned with improving economic conditions of the parish and with community welfare; Congregationalists more with obtaining loyalty of parishioners to the parish.
>
> In the Episcopal Church, where the clergyman is by canon law actually rector or ruler of his parish, there was little organized opposition to him and little evidence of factionalism in the parish. Such strains that arose were between the rector and individuals rather than factions. In the Congregational Church there were many evidences of strain arising between the minister and a faction or between factions. These latter strains arise because the minister has no official backing from the denomination, he is entirely on his own in his parish, and yet his authority is divided and must be shared with the church committee which

[11] Luke M. Smith, "The Clergy: Authority, Structure, Ideology, Migration," *American Sociological Review*, XVIII (June, 1953), 243.

is elected by the congregation. He does not even have authority to say who may and who may not hold services in his own church. His tenure often depends upon making particularistic relationships, yet in doing so he is in danger of alienating other factions.[12]

As a consequence of these and other factors, according to this report, clergymen under control of "clients" (Congregationalists) move more frequently than those under the control of "managers" (Episcopalians).

Another dimension to understanding the role of the clergyman in the community is given by Charles Y. Glock and Benjamin B. Ringer, who made a study of the attitudes of ministers and parishioners on social issues. They too made use of the Episcopal Church in an effort to see the climate of opinion of the general membership about official church policy on social, economic, and political issues. They also wanted to know the position of the clergy on those issues where there was a conflict between the official church policy and the sentiment of the parishioners. They find the danger of conflict greatest on issues bearing directly on the distribution of power in society (war, labor, government control, and political control of the church). On issues of an ideological or moral character the church can express itself through strong and clear-cut pronouncements.

But what about the minister who is the crucial link in communicating church policy to the church's membership? According to Glock and Ringer, a minister's attitudes clearly tend to reflect church policy, compromising with the views of his parishioners when the church has compromised on an issue. Where, however, the church has taken a partisan view, the minister identifies with this view even though a substantial segment of his parishioners object. "Where the church has made up its mind, so have the ministers; where the church is equivocal, so are the ministers."[13]

The complexity of the minister's status in a community is shown most fully, however, in a study conducted by Samuel W. Blizzard, who based his findings on a study of 690 Protestant ministers (2). Six practitioner roles were distinguished within the work of the parish minister, as follows: (1) *administrator*, or manager of the parish, involving him in official board and staff meetings, publicity, clerical and stenographic work, financial administration and promotion, physical plant supervision and general church planning; (2) *organizer*, or leader, participant and planner in local church associations

[12] *Ibid.*, pp. 243–47.
[13] Charles Y. Glock and Benjamin B. Ringer, "Church Policy and the Attitudes of Ministers and Parishioners on Social Issues," *American Sociological Review*, XXI (April, 1956), 156.

and community organizations; (3) *pastor,* or counselor, to those who seek his guidance, visitor to the sick among the parishioners and to prospective members; (4) *preacher,* responsible for preparation and delivery of sermons; (5) *priest,* or liturgist, who leads people in worship and in the church service; (6) *teacher,* or one involved in church school instruction, confirmation classes, study group leadership, and preparation for teaching.

Of these, the roles of preacher, priest, and teacher are those which the Protestant clergyman traditionally performs; the pastoral role is *neotraditional* in that it has a biblical definition, but new developments in clinical psychology and counseling procedures give new direction to this role. The administrator and organizer roles are contemporary, but Blizzard's study found there is little agreement on the legitimate behavior of these roles.

When asked which of the six roles were most important, the clergyman rated them in order of importance as follows: preacher, pastor, priest, teacher, organizer, administrator. They felt most effective in these roles in the following order: preacher, pastor, teacher, priest, administrator, organizer. When asked to assess their feelings of enjoyment in performing the roles they rated them as follows: pastor, preacher, teacher, priest, organizer, and administrator.

The minister's dilemma, according to Professor Blizzard, stems from the fact that he feels best qualified for and most interested in the traditional roles, and the roles that he finds most troublesome are those that are neotraditional or contemporary. "The roles a minister performs in present-day American society are basically equivocal. On the one hand, the church has a traditional set of norms by which he is expected to be guided. On the other hand, the parishioner has a set of functional expectations by which the minister's professional service is judged. This is the minister's dilemma. He faces basic ambiguities in performing the practitioner roles.[14] Joseph H. Fichter, though not analyzing the problem in terms of dilemmas or ambiguities, has indicated the complexity faced by the Catholic clergy in their administration of an urban parish (10).

From the problems of the clergy it is but a short step to the problems of religion as a social system within a community, particularly in an age when secular society is rapidly changing.

The Religious System and the Changing Community. In his thoroughgoing analysis of life in South Dakota, W. F. Kumlien has

[14] Samuel W. Blizzard, "The Minister's Dilemma," *Christian Century* (April 25, 1956), p. 509.

listed five major conclusions regarding social change and the church in that particular state. Although these were published in 1941 they reveal the historical forces at work more than fifteen years ago which continue to have considerable influence in some regions of the United States today:

1. In keeping with other social institutions the church has fewer, but larger and more active units in the state. A number of factors have contributed to this end.
   a. There are more native-born South Dakotans who have been reared here and have learned to work together since childhood.
   b. There are more socially unifying than divisive factors at work in the state. For example, nationality is growing less important as the number of foreign-born decreases.
   c. The importance of the village and town has increased enormously and these now constitute little economic and social capitals around which farm trade and service territory revolves.
   d. The increased proportion of village, town and city population together with more frequent contacts with farm people has helped to break down many of the prejudices and cliques of farm people.
   e. Good roads and faster means of transportation have made it possible for many people to go much farther to church. This has eliminated the necessity for a number of small churches.
2. Certain functions have been transferred from the church to other social agencies. For example, social welfare was originally almost exclusively the responsibility of the church. In recent years many other private and public agencies have taken over most of the burden of providing welfare aid. Character education is also shared with other social institutions although formerly the church was practically the only agency responsible for such education.
3. Communities have developed like-mindedness or homogeneity. This is a result of several changes in population and the introductions of new inventions. The proportion of native South Dakotans with like backgrounds is increasing. Social contacts have been greatly increased by the use of automobiles. The wide-spread use of the radio and daily newspapers has also helped to foster like-mindedness.
4. Changes in population have also affected the church. The increase in older persons in the population has led to an increased.proportion of older church members. This may lead to greater conservatism. The increasing proportion of females in the population has given relative importance to the church.
5. The increasing average extent of education has put religion on a higher plane and has tended to integrate it with other phases of living. As a result of this there is an increase in better qualified leadership in the church. This has increased the quality of the church to the community.[15]

Such findings emphasize that religious bodies, like the economy and the family, are operating within a dynamic society with which they

[15] W. F. Kumlien, *Basic Trends of Social Change in South Dakota: Religious Organization* (Agricultural Experiment Station, South Dakota State College, Bulletin 348 (May, 1941), p. 24.

must deal. The cults and some sects may try to remain outside this society, others may try to adjust through assimilation or come to terms through accommodation, but the interaction is present. Changes also affect the relationship between religion and other major systems.

In an earlier section of this chapter the connection between religion and family life was described. Elsewhere attention has been called to the tie-in between socioeconomic status and religious affiliation,[16] indicating that religion and the economy interact at several points. The local government becomes involved in religious disputes when issues arise as to whether children in parochial schools should share in the free transportation provided by the school board for children attending public schools. Such issues frequently move from the school board to the courts. Religious establishments, to mention one other point of interest, pay no property taxes on their holdings. Some courts have ruled recently that taxes must be paid on revenue-producing properties such as office buildings on Main Street even though a church body does have title to them. And the discussion of this issue goes on at a lively pace in many communities, especially where community leaders are worried about a shrinking tax base.

COMMUNITY MORALITY AND MORAL INTEGRATION

The family and religious systems are brought together in this chapter because of the part which they play in the preservation and in the transmission, particularly to the young, of the traditions and values from the past. Furthermore, since they both "give meaning to life," they can serve as integrating forces leading toward community solidarity. The morality of the community affords some clue as to the consensus prevailing about traditional culture traits which are supposed to be providing a common ground for thought and action.

Moral Reform. Within any community, however, there are those people who are dissatisfied with the existing state of affairs. Frequently their dissatisfaction becomes centered upon some issue which in their minds (and often in the minds of others in the community) is a moral or ethical question. As a result they seek to mobilize support for the eradication of this evil, often by drastic or radical

---

[16] As is shown in the study of Plainville, an Ozark community, by James West, the religious subsystems (churches) of a community are ranked by the people on the basis of prestige, indicating a connection between church membership and class standing. See James West, *Plainville, U.S.A.* (New York: Columbia University Press, 1945), pp. 142–45.

means. Such local reformers are often made fun of by others in the community who do not share their views; or they may be openly opposed by those who would be affected adversely if the reform were to be carried through successfully. In any event, the community becomes a scene of lively interaction with protagonists and bystanders alike trying to keep up with each new development (see Chapter 8).

Groups which come into existence to embody these reform programs, should they survive for any long period of time, find it necessary to adapt to changing conditions. One such group is the Woman's Christian Temperance Union, found in many American communities (12). Such organizations frequently stress as a major goal the strengthening of family life or portray the evil they struggle against as the "destroyer of the home," showing their recognition of the connection between the family and the community. Such groups may or may not have the support of organized religious bodies but do frequently speak in the name of religious principles.

In addition to reform movements directed at some particular target, community morality is often viewed in terms of the extent of social problems such as juvenile delinquency and crime. Albert J. Reiss, Jr., has written:

Delinquency results when there is a relative absence of internalized norms and rules governing behavior in conformity with the norms of the social system to which legal penalties are attached, a breakdown in previously established controls, and/or a relative absence of or conflict in social rules of institutions of which the person is a member. Hence delinquency may be seen as a functional consequence of the type of relationship established among the personal and social controls.[17]

Since family, religion, and the school are the chief systems responsible for the internalization of norms and rules governing behavior, one search for an explanation of the existence of extensive juvenile delinquency would lead to a study of these systems. It may be that these systems are presenting the child with conflicting norms and he accepts and "internalizes" the ones that will get him into trouble later on. Or they may be defaulting in their job to such an extent that other influences, instilling deviant values, are proving determinative. The work that E. H. Sutherland did in the study of "white-collar crime" indicates the willingness of some of the so-called "respectable people" to depart from the accepted norms of good conduct when confronted with an opportunity for personal gain or gratification, an indication that some of the expected controls, personal and social, are not at work in their case (23).

[17] Albert J. Reiss, Jr., "Delinquency as the Failure of Personal and Social Controls," *American Sociological Review*, XVI (April, 1951), 196.

The morality of the community, at least as viewed from the standpoint of the larger society of which the community is a part, may be judged according to the way certain "ethical" issues are faced, though these may not be attacked with any zeal of reform. Some communities may not recognize a given issue as "ethical" but consider it primarily as a legal or political matter. However, once the local church bodies take a stand on an issue in the eyes of most people of the community it definitely assumes an ethical tinge, even though they may not agree with the stand of the church groups. Since World War II, for instance, the various religious bodies in their national assemblies have paid a great deal more attention to the problem of racial discrimination, so much so that "the unbiased observer cannot fail to be impressed by the revolutionary changes in pronouncements since the beginning of World War II."[18] It is usually, however, important to note the distinction between a resolution passed by a national religious body and its translation into action by a local church group, although in some communities the local church groups are far in advance of their whole denomination.

Many religious bodies have set up *social action* boards or agencies yet some of these have been denounced by their own churches as being too much out of line with what the church should be concerned about. When Judson T. Landis studied the kind of cooperation the denomination leaders received from six different church groups, he found that in all sizes of denominations the greatest cooperation had come from youth and women's groups, while the least cooperation had come from laymen, state denominational leaders and ministers (18).

But morality, whether individual or social, must exist with reference to a body of principles. Those espousing principles may think they have universal applicability; others may recognize that their own principles hold true for a particular place at a given time under certain conditions. In other words, the former would hold to absolutes and the latter to a relativity in morals. But in the study of a community, since we are usually trying to understand how and why it works as it does, we try to make the interpretations from the standpoint of those who comprise that community.

Moral Integration. However, when comparisons are being made between two communities, some standards outside both communities must be employed. These are frequently drawn up in terms of regional or national value systems. These can best be determined by

---

[18] Frank S. Loescher, "The Protestant Church and the Negro: Recent Pronouncements," *Social Forces,* XXVI (December, 1947), 201.

TABLE 7

MEASURE OF MORAL INTEGRATION, FORTY-THREE CITIES OF MORE THAN
100,000 POPULATION

City	Adjusted Crime Index	Adjusted Welfare Effort Index	Integration Index
Rochester	17.3	22.4	19.0
Syracuse	17.1	16.9	17.0
Worcester	14.8	19.6	16.4
Erie	15.0	18.6	16.2
Milwaukee	18.4	10.5	15.8
Bridgeport	15.6	14.8	15.3
Buffalo	17.8	9.9	15.2
Dayton	13.4	16.1	14.3
Reading	14.2	14.2	14.2
Des Moines	14.5	13.4	14.1
Cleveland	12.3	12.9	13.9
Denver	14.8	12.0	13.9
Peoria	14.4	12.5	13.8
Wichita	15.6	9.7	13.6
Trenton	12.6	13.7	13.0
Grand Rapids	14.5	9.3	12.8
Toledo	11.5	15.0	12.7
San Diego	15.5	6.5	12.5
Baltimore	14.2	7.6	12.0
South Bend	12.7	9.9	11.8
Akron	12.0	9.8	11.3
Detroit	12.4	8.6	11.1
Tacoma	13.3	6.1	10.9
Richmond (Va.)	7.4	16.4	10.4
Houston	9.4	12.0	10.3
Fort Worth	10.4	9.8	10.2
Flint	11.7	6.0	9.8
Oklahoma City	9.8	9.6	9.7
Spokane	9.7	9.4	9.6
Chattanooga	7.2	13.4	9.3
Seattle	8.9	9.2	9.0
Indianapolis	7.5	11.4	8.8
Nashville	8.2	9.5	8.6
Birmingham	7.9	8.7	8.2
Columbus	6.2	11.7	8.0
Dallas	9.4	5.2	8.0
Louisville	4.1	15.0	7.7
Portland (Ore.)	6.7	8.1	7.2
Jacksonville	6.2	5.5	6.0
Memphis	3.8	8.7	5.4
Tulsa	3.7	8.5	5.3
Miami	5.8	3.6	5.1
Atlanta	2.5	7.6	4.2

Source: Robert C. Angell, "The Moral Integration of American Cities," *American Journal of Sociology*, LII (July, 1951), 14.

the investigator, since the communities must operate within this large unit. Robert C. Angell has worked out a method of comparing American cities with populations of over one hundred thousand for which more adequate statistical information is available. He does so in terms of *moral integration*, but his definition is different from some of those often employed. "Moral integration," according to Angell, "is the degree to which there is a set of common ends and values toward which all the members are oriented and in terms of which the life of the group is organized. Another way of saying the same thing might be that moral integration is the degree to which the areas of possible friction or conflict within the group are covered by a set of moral norms that are accepted and implemented by all."[19] In order to set up indices of moral integration Angell makes use of an Adjusted Welfare Effort Index and an Adjusted Crime Index with the Integration Index being a combination of these two. These indices for forty-three cities are shown in Table 7.

An examination of the items that go into the computation of these indices shows that most Americans would consider the welfare items right and desirable and the crime items wrong and undesirable. In this sense they pass moral judgment upon them. Nevertheless, Angell, in framing his research, has set up moral integration as a positive value and ranks cities in keeping with it.

In addition to the ways previously cited in which the family and religion contribute to the operation of the community system, one must list community integration as a possible contribution. At the same time a word of caution must be raised, since the family units may become so individualistic and self-seeking that they no longer nurture the sentiments and rules of conduct of benefit to society; the religious bodies may become so competitive toward each other or so opposed to contemplated action by local government or the economic groups that they prevent the carrying out of programs desired by the majority of the people. Where either the family or religion fail to carry out this function an even heavier burden is placed upon the school as an integrative force, a fact which will prove one of the main concerns in the chapter which follows.

References and Suggested Readings

1. *American Journal of Sociology*, LX (May, 1955), Part Two. Includes six papers on the sociology of religion drawn from earlier issues of the *Journal*.
2. BLIZZARD, SAMUEL W. "The Minister's Dilemma," *Christian Century* (April 25, 1956), 508–9.

[19] Robert C. Angell, "The Moral Integration of American Cities," *American Journal of Sociology*, LII (July, 1951), Part 2, 115.

3. BROWN, JAMES S. "Social Class, Intermarriage, and Church Membership in a Kentucky Community," *American Journal of Sociology*, LII (November, 1951), 232–42.
4. BULTENA, LOUIS. "Church Membership and Church Attendance in Madison, Wisconsin," *American Sociological Review*, XIV (June, 1949), 384–89.
5. BURGESS, ERNEST W., and LOCKE, HARVEY J. *The Family*. New York: American Book Company, 1945, pp. 509–10.
6. DYNES, RUSSELL R. "Church-Sect Typology and Socio-Economic Status," *American Sociological Review*, XX (October, 1955), 555–60.
7. ———. "Rurality, Migration, and Sectarianism," *Rural Sociology*, XXI (March, 1956), 25–28.
8. EISTER, ALLAN W. "Some Aspects of Institutional Behavior with Reference to Churches," *American Sociological Review*, XVII (February, 1952), 64–69.
9. ELLIOTT, MABEL A., and MERRILL, FRANCIS E. *Social Disorganization*. New York: Harper & Brothers, 1950.
10. FICHTER, JOSEPH H. "Conceptualizations of the Urban Parish," *Social Forces*, XXXI (October, 1952), 43–46.
11. GALLAGHER, O. R. "Looseness and Rigidity in Family Structure," *Social Forces*, XXXI (May, 1953), 332–39.
12. GEISFIELD, JOSEPH R. "Social Structure and Moral Reform: A Study of the Woman's Christian Temperance Union," *American Journal of Sociology*, LXI (November, 1955), 221–32.
13. GOODE, WILLIAM J. "Economic Factors and Marital Stability," *American Sociological Review*, XVI (December, 1951), 802–12.
14. INKELES, ALEX. "Social Change and Social Character: The Role of Parental Mediation," *Journal of Social Issues*, XI (1955), 12–23.
15. JOHNSON, BENTON. "A Critical Appraisal of the Church-Sect Typology," *American Sociological Review*, XXII (February, 1957), 88–92.
16. KEPHART, WILLIAM M. "Occupational Level and Marital Disruption," *American Sociological Review*, XX (August, 1955), 456–65.
17. KOLB, WILLIAM L. "Values, Positivism, and the Functional Theory of Religion: The Growth of a Moral Dilemma," *Social Forces*, XXXI (May, 1953).
18. LANDIS, JUDSON T. "Social Action in American Protestant Churches," *American Journal of Sociology*, LII (May, 1947), 517–22.
19. LITWAK, EUGENE. "Group Pressure and Family Breakup: A Study of German Communities," *American Journal of Sociology*, LXI (January, 1956), 345–54.
20. MAYER, ALBERT J., and MARX, SUE. "Social Change, Religion, and Birth Rates," *American Journal of Sociology*, LII (January, 1957), 383–90.
21. OGBURN, WILLIAM F., and NIMKOFF, M. F. *Technology and the Changing Family*. Cambridge: Riverside Press, 1955.
22. SCHNEIDER, LOUIS, and DORNBUSCH, SANFORD M. "Inspirational Literature: From Latent to Manifest Functions of Religion," *American Journal of Sociology*, LXII (March, 1957), 476–81.
23. SUTHERLAND, E. H. *White Collar Crime*. New York: The Dryden Press, Inc., 1949.
24. TAMBIAH, S. J., and RYAN, BRYCE. "Secularization of Family Values in Ceylon," *American Sociological Review*, XXII (June, 1957), 292–99.
25. THOMAS, JOHN L. "Religious Training in the Roman Catholic Family," *American Journal of Sociology*, LVII (September, 1951), 178–83.
26. WILLIAMS, EMILIO. "The Structure of the Brazilian Family," *Social Forces*, XXXI (May, 1953), 339–45.

Chapter 15

EDUCATION

IGNORANCE IN THE COMMUNITY

We ordinarily think of education as being dedicated to the elimination of ignorance and to the development in the "educated" of a rational, sensible approach to life's problems. But, as Wilbert E. Moore and Melvin M. Tumin have pointed out, "perfect knowledge is itself impossible, and an inherently impossible basis of social action and social relations. Put conversely, ignorance is both inescapable and an intrinsic element in social organization generally, although there are marked differences in the specific forms, degrees, and functions of ignorance in known social organizations."[1]

What, then, are some of the structural functions of ignorance, according to these authors? These will be summarized in some detail because by understanding them one can see how they are partly counterbalanced by education as a major community system.

As Preservative of Privileged Position. Ignorance operates to keep the consumer of a specialist's services from knowing how to perform those services for himself and thereby being able to eliminate the need of the specialist. Accordingly, specialists who have a privileged position because their skills are scarce and functionally important find their superior status partially maintained by ignorance, which they sometimes seek to perpetuate by devices such as an esoteric vocabulary or use of instruments and techniques which the public does not comprehend and which may, in fact, have no basic importance in the skill itself. But not only does ignorance keep the consumer from carrying out the services of the specialist; it also keeps down the number of competing specialists so that those in positions of importance can retain their privileged place. The pres-

---

[1] Wilbert E. Moore and Melvin M. Tumin, "Some Social Functions of Ignorance," *American Sociological Review*, XIV (December, 1949), 788.

ence of too many competitors is avoided by guarding the "trade secrets" and controlling the avenues for training new specialists.

Role differentiation and the maintenance of power, related as they are to privileged position, depend upon a differential distribution of knowledge—and correspondingly of ignorance.

In any society internal social order is in part maintained by allocating statuses and differentiating roles along lines of age, sex and generation. These differentials serve as hooks on which differences in life-chances are hung, and the result is that differentials in knowledge also fall along these lines. In non-literate societies, this tends to result in a monopoly of skills on the part of the elders and the consequent monopoly of power in their hands. It also results in sexual division of special skills, providing females with sources of power that their physique would not otherwise give them, and providing males with a source of power that acts as a balance to the power inherent in the female's control of sexual access.

The universal diffusion of age-respect as an organizing principle of social relations in primitive societies is functionally dependent upon and compatible with differential distribution of skills and knowledge along age lines. Since most primitive societies surround these differentials with traditional sanctions, and since knowledge of alternatives is highly limited, the situation is essentially stable.[2]

But in Western society knowledge does not follow so limited a system of distribution. There is more equalization of power as between the sexes and as between the young and the old because of the accessibility of extra-familial sources of knowledge and skill.

Many examples of the functional role of ignorance might be cited. For example, ignorance, as illustrated in the keeping of salaries confidential in a large organization, lessens jealousy over unequal rewards and thus maintains smooth social relations. Even within the family, older members are told about matters that are kept from the younger members, especially when these are fraught with conflict potentials. And, secrecy and security are practiced by a local law-enforcement agency or in international relations when it is thought that certain kinds of knowledge would aid an actual or potential enemy. From the individual standpoint, many people try to keep others ignorant of past personal experiences which might have an adverse effect upon their being selected for a job.

Some of these illustrations of ignorance, one might claim, are different from the ordinary understanding of the term and have little relevance to the educational system of the community. They do show, however, that there is a connection between a privileged position and knowledge and suggest that some resistances to broadening of education may come from those who feel that their su-

[2] *Ibid.*, pp. 789–90.

perior status will be threatened if too much knowledge or the kind which they possess exclusively becomes widely known.

As Reinforcement of Traditional Values. Ignorance reinforces traditional values in three ways: first, the old behavior patterns continue to be practiced when people are not aware of nor interested in other ways in which they might behave; second, people may not know about the actual extent to which others in the community or society are violating the norms, thinking the violations confined to a small group, thereby accepting and tending to support the traditional normative structure; third, "ignorance also serves to reinforce ultimate values and heighten the sense of community through induction of subservience of individual to group interests."[3] In such a case, the individual has no knowledge of what would happen to him if he went against the group and carried out individualistic wishes; since he lacks this knowledge, he "plays it safe" and conforms to the group mandates.

As Preservative of Fair Competition. The idea of a "free competitive market," which is based on the supposition that all competitors will have equal and free access to the market, can operate only if such competitors and the public generally are ignorant of the many exceptions to this rule. Thus there must be an effective range of ignorance if such competitive systems, including stratification, are to remain in force. We assume that social mobility is a part of our American class system and imply that there is an equality of opportunity, but too much knowledge about any existing inequalities that might be found would threaten not only some of these assumptions but the class system itself.

As Preservative of Stereotypes. In communities where each member is not known to everyone, people tend to act toward social units in terms of stereotypes (10). These stereotypes break down if one is too familiar with or has too much knowledge about the individuals or groups to which they refer. Italians, for example, may believe that "all Albanians are so-and-so," but when they get to know several Albanians, say in an American community to which they both migrated from abroad, they find it more difficult to make such a sweeping statement. They know of too many exceptions. Thus knowledge robs them of the "convenience" of speaking and behaving as though all Albanians were of a certain mold. Should such knowledge pervade the whole social structure and all stereotypes

[3] *Ibid.,* p. 791.

tend to be eliminated (which is hardly likely) then the individual would lack these traditional crutches on which to lean in arriving at a decision, and life would be much more complex for him. Of course, some stereotypes have disruptive overtones, since they negate some of the major values of the community or society. In such cases, there are apt to be groups which attack the stereotype by the use of knowledge, although they are often resisted by vested interests which seek to keep the stereotype in force.

As Incentive Appropriate to the System. Ignorance of what the future holds or even of present rating may be a spur to greater activity within a competitive system. One assumption often made is that ignorance of such matters is a spur in the classroom situation, as well as in a bureaucracy. Or, the greater uncertainty as to how some recreational interest will turn out may add to the zest with which that interest is pursued.

It is clear that ignorance, as discussed by Moore and Tumin, means simply "not knowing" or "the absence of empirically valid knowledge" and that ignorance in this sense runs through all aspects of life. Educational systems tend to be selective in the kinds of ignorance that they try to eliminate, with the result that one who has been through the educational system, even though a highly satisfactory product from the standpoint of that system, may still be operating ignorantly in several areas of life because he lacks the correct facts about the actual state of affairs. Communities allow for this and even make use of it in maintaining a semblance of a stable order. Nevertheless, those individuals who gain the most knowledge about crucial matters and put it to use are the ones who are most likely to receive the highest social rewards of the community.

As we turn to a consideration of education as a major community system, it is well to remember that the school is not the only subsystem connected with education. The library subsystem, as well as certain types of adult education programs, carried on at times outside the school, will deserve some attention in a rounded picture of education. Nevertheless, the school is central and will be discussed first.

The School as a Subsystem

The school, like any subsystem, is a network of groups which are functionally interdependent and which are designed to accomplish what might be called "educational ends." Such a subsystem has its own functions, its functionaries, its members, and even an ideology or explanation which justifies the large sums of money devoted to it.

Functions of the School (7). In most American communities some people would answer if asked about the function of their local schools, "The school is there to teach reading, writing and arithmetic." Businessmen who employ the high school graduates to do office work for them become quite exercised over what they consider the inability of the young people to spell or add up a column of figures. And such an employer will sadly shake his head and say, "I don't know what they are teaching there, but they certainly aren't giving the kind of education I had when I was a boy or the kind they ought to be giving." The rub comes, however, when the man making the complaint has to face up to the choice of just what subjects ought to be taught. There can be general agreement that certain skills and a fair amount of knowledge about the past and present should be taught—the first function of the school, one might say—but there is not always much agreement on which skills and what knowledge.

In contrast to the family which has been losing some of its functions, particularly some of the economic ones, the school has been assigned more responsibilities than it has yet been able to handle fully. Howard Y. McClusky, in viewing the past, indicates that the school has historically operated apart from and above the common life of people. He sees three factors responsible for this: first, traditional subject matter abounds in abstractions requiring the manipulation of words, a skill which may be attained only in a cultural climate accessible to few persons; second, the traditional professions require a prolonged and intensive preparation for professional processes that is beyond the grasp of most people; third, the school has been regarded as a social economic ladder by which the individual climbs away from the common condition of mankind to the upper levels of advantage. Because of these factors, leaders of education in the past have tried to maintain the school as a cultural isolate sealed off from the stream of the community.

But with the shift to a different view of the relationship between the school and community, McClusky feels that often too much is expected of the school:

Society is more and more attempting to pass on to the school functions which non-school agencies formerly assumed. However, there is a distinct limit to the assignments which the school can properly undertake, not merely because of the limitations of time, energy, equipment and personnel that would inevitably occur, but because the total educational task of society is by its nature the responsibility of the community as a whole and cannot be accepted by the school or any other single agency. To fasten the whole burden of education on the school is to delegate to a part of society that which only society as a whole can achieve . . .[4]

He then goes on to illustrate his point in the case of guidance, which admittedly is a function of the school today but which he considers to an even greater degree the function of the community. "The home exerts the greatest single influence in the life of a child. The gang is often next in order of potence. The church has an unparalleled opportunity in another sector of human experience . . ."[5] Another case is the prevention of juvenile delinquency. In a sense that is a function of the school but also the responsibility of the whole community. The school can help in organizing community resources, but it cannot take the sole responsibility.

Visitors to the United States from Europe are as perplexed about our educational system as about any feature of American life. In most of their countries the school satisfies the largely traditional functions of imparting skills and passing on knowledge, frequently through drill and rote memory, in much larger amounts than here. There is a tendency to stress what might be called "the intellectual side." It takes most Europeans a long time to learn that the American public educational system today is not concerned merely with the transmittal of the accumulated knowledge of the past but is rather an important agency in the creation of an American society and a popular culture. Therefore, social considerations play an important part, since the elementary and high school become assimilative agencies whereby children who may not speak English in their homes are taught to read and write English and to gain a familiarity with American traditions.

Since complex social skills are required in our society, some of these are taught in the public schools. All societies, of course, require social skills, but in America the stress in the upwardly mobile middle class is so much on group deliberation and the committee process that one who does not know how to participate in such groups or serve as a committee chairman lacks one of the prerequisites for success in middle class activities. Furthermore, in a democracy one should be able to express one's views forcefully and clearly, which explains the attention given to public speaking, debating, and even classroom discussion. Since an American is urged

4 McClusky, Howard Y. "The School in the Community," *The North Central Association Quarterly*, XV (April, 1941), quoted in *Community Service News*, XI (September–October, 1953), 150.
5 *Ibid.*

to learn to get along with all kinds of people, he must develop the kind of conversational approaches which enable him to strike up a conversation and develop an acquaintanceship.

Within any given community different people emphasize different functions. Those parents who want their children to enter colleges which stress classical subjects as entrance requirements will give weight to the college preparatory (traditional) function of the high school. Those who want their children readied for a good job in the community upon graduation from high school lean heavily to vocational subjects. School administrators and others in the community who view education as contributing to the development of the whole personality stress social studies and activities designed to bring out characteristics which would not blossom in the traditional teacher-pupil relationship.

At the conclusion of this chapter more attention will be paid to some of the school-community relationships, but in the beginning of the discussion it is important to see that within the lifetime of many adult Americans there has been a shift in some of the functions of the public school system. As new functions are added, some of the older ones receive less attention. These changes in functions are related to the changing social position of the teacher in American society.

School Functionaries. A very important group of functionaries in the American school system is the *school board members* charged with determining the official policy for the schools in their school district. In the case of the public schools they usually run for office and are supposed to be representatives of the general public. In the case of private schools they may be selected because of their reputation as individuals rather than because they speak for any specific constituency. But it is in the American tradition that such board members, rather than state or federal officials, have a determining voice in the operation of the schools of a community.

A second group of school functionaries is the *administrators,* such as the county or city superintendent of schools, the school principals and other nonteaching staff members who manage some aspect of school life. In many rural areas the superintendent of schools remains an elective office, although in urban areas he is appointed. He, in turn, makes recommendations to the board about the selection of principals and other staff members. The more complicated the school system, the greater the number of administrative positions, since such miscellaneous matters as bus transportation, cafeterias, raising a school bond issue, or the construction of a new elementary school all need careful attention by those who have developed some expertness in those fields. Supervisors, whose duty it is to work with the teachers in the improvement of instruction, are usually considered an arm of the administration, although they may have just recently stepped from the classroom themselves.

A third group of functionaries is the *teachers*, who generally consider theirs the most important job in the school system. In a city like Chicago the career of teaching has some characteristics which differ in degree at least from those in smaller cities. According to Howard S. Becker (2), some of the teachers look forward to an upward rise from the post of teacher to one of the administrative positions, but the majority are more concerned with what might be called horizontal career movement. This involves moving from one teaching position to another in the hope that each move will result in a more advantageous post. The manner of working out these changes indicates a great deal about the Chicago school system itself.

Schools are rated informally by the teachers as to the less desirable and the more desirable. Such rating is tied in with the type of pupil attending the school: a bottom stratum, probably equivalent to the lower class; an upper stratum, probably equivalent to the upper-middle class; and a middle stratum, probably equivalent to the lower-middle and parts of the upper-lower class. Three main problems seem to be identified with teaching children from these strata: (1) the problem of *teaching*, "producing some change in the child's skills and knowledge which can be attributed to one's own efforts; (2) the problem of *discipline*, maintaining order and control over the children's activity; and (3) the problem of what may be termed *moral acceptability*, bringing one's self to bear some traits of the children which one considers immoral and revolting."[6] The teachers found the "slum" children most difficult on all three counts; the upper children from the "better neighborhoods" learned easily but were spoiled and difficult to control, and they lacked the important moral traits of politeness and respect for elders. "The middle group was considered to be hard-working but slow to learn, extremely easy to control and most acceptable on the moral level."[7]

Other factors entering into the determination of desirable teaching posts are the attitudes of the parents in the highest status groups, which can be threatening to the authority of the teacher,

[6] Becker, Howard S., "The Career of the Chicago Public Schoolteacher," *American Journal of Sociology*, LVII (March, 1952), 472.
[7] *Ibid.*

and of principals, who may not adequately support the teacher's authority. Colleagues, too, may undermine it.

When a Chicago teacher feels that he does not have the right combination of factors, he can ask for a transfer to any school on a list of ten that he submits, although he must stay at a school a year before being able to leave. His name is then put on the waiting list for these ten schools, and he can take a position there if he is next in line when an opening occurs in a given school. Since most teachers wish to get out of the "slum" neighborhoods, few of the schools there have waiting lists and, consequently, new teachers are given posts in them without delay. To make a successful move, the teacher must have a good idea of the factors present at a school which he lists as desirable; second, he must not be of an ethnic type or have the personal reputation that would make the school principal suggest that he might not be happy in that school; and third, he must be patient enough to wait for the right kind of opening and not seize any opportunity that comes along.

Some teachers originally assigned to the schools in the poorer neighborhoods, even though disappointed at this post, do in time become adjusted to the problems and decide to settle down there and not ask for transfers. Such teachers revise their expectations as to what they can teach in a year, learn how to handle discipline problems peculiar to that area, and develop "an understanding" that will help accept what they previously interpreted as immoral actions of the children.

The case of the Chicago school teacher has been cited at length to show that in a large school system there is a "world of the teacher," with its own practices, expectations, and methods of control. But the discussion has focused chiefly on what transpires within the school itself. What about the place of the teacher in the community at large? For some leads on this score we turn to a study by Frederic W. Terrien in New London, Connecticut. A random 5 per cent sample was taken of the citizens of this community who were interviewed at their homes or place of business. Table 8 presents some of the results of this survey. Some of the study's findings could not be put in the yes-no categories. For example, there was a widespread belief in the importance of teachers to the community. Also when asked about the pay of teachers, 61 per cent of the respondents thought that teachers were underpaid, 1 per cent that they were overpaid, 32 per cent that they were fairly well paid, while 6 per cent gave no answer.

TABLE 8

OPINIONS ABOUT TEACHERS IN NEW LONDON, CONN.

Question	Yes	No	No Answer
	(Per cent)		
Should teachers coming from minority groups be employed in the schools of New London?	86	12	2
Should the standards of conduct for teachers differ from those of other good citizens?	16	83	1
Do the high school teachers of New London join in the activities of the community?	61	9	30
In your opinion, should teachers join in community activities?	92	2	6
Do you think teachers are justified in unionizing?	69	26	5
May teachers be active politically if they so desire?	80	18	2
Do you consider high school teaching to be one of the professions?	97	2	1

Source: Frederic W. Terrien, "Who Thinks What About Educators?," *American Journal of Sociology*, LIX (September, 1955), 150–58.

It is to be remembered that this study reflects only the opinions of those interviewed and does not relate the questions asked to any measurable criteria. The opinions too reflect to some extent the social milieu of New London and might not apply to other communities of different ethnic and occupational composition. But they are suggestive of the critical role in which American teachers now find themselves.

The Pupils. One of the most important questions about education in a democracy has to do with "Who gets educated?" C. Arnold Anderson has studied this problem using data about white children from the 1940 census made available in 1945. He reminds us that in 1940 the average seventeen-year-old white boy had completed 9.7 and his sister 10.1 years of schooling but that such averages also conceal important regional, community, and social class variations.

Seventeen-year-olds in the western region achieve the highest grade, and those in the north do nearly as well, but the averages for southern children are consistently lowest. Within each region the means for larger communities exceed those for the smaller places, though the three categories of cities are not far apart; villages show up especially poorly.

Differentials in schooling among social classes or rental groups are considerably greater than those between regions or communities . . . In communities of all sizes and in all regions schooling attained is greater in high status than in low status groups . . . Seventeen-year-olds from the upper economic groups average about eleven years of schooling irrespective of region or size of community. The status group differences are especially marked in the South, which more than holds its own in educating children from homes at the higher rental levels. It drops behind the other regions, however, as we descend the income scale, until in the least prosperous families southern children lag one or one-and-a-half grades . . .[8]

When the Negroes are taken into account some of these regional and income-group figures trend downward.

It is tempting to explain the reasons for these differences in educational achievement pointed out by Anderson in terms of educational opportunity. Some young people, particularly in the rural areas, may find it difficult to attend a high school and, therefore, give up the idea early in life.[9]

Or, another explanation advanced (5, 9, 18) is that teachers misunderstand and reject lower-class children, thereby making them resentful and rebellious and more likely to drop out of school earlier than other children. Jackson Toby suggests that the lower-class child brings certain attitudes and experiences to the school situation just as his teacher does. These attitudes may have a great deal to do with his remaining in school. In attempting to answer the question, "Why should middle-class children 'take to' school so much better?" Professor Toby has this to say:

Middle-class parents make it quite clear that school is nothing to be trifled with. They have probably graduated at least from high school, and their child is aware that they *expect* him to do the same or better. If he has difficulty with his studies, they are eager (and competent) to help him. And not only do his *parents* expect him to apply himself to his studies, so do his *friends* and *their*

[8] C. Arnold Anderson, "Social Class Differentials in the Schooling of Youth Within the Regions and Community-Size Groups of the United States," *Social Forces*, XXV (May, 1947), 435.

[9] Ruth Chambers Little and Mildred Thurow Tate in an article entitled "Some Effects of Commuting on the Adjustment of Elementary Students," *Rural Sociology*, XV (December, 1950), show for *one* community that they studied:

a. Students who did not commute made better grades than commuting students of similar mental capacity.

b. The farther the students were from the school and the more time they spent in transit, the lower were their grades relative to their ability.

c. The farther the child commuted and the longer time he spent in transit, the less well adjusted he was in school according to the teachers' records.

d. The noncommuting students were selected more frequently by their classmates for social contacts than the commuting group.

e. The students who commuted had poorer attendance records than did those who lived nearby.

parents. He is caught in a neighborhood pattern of academic achievement in much the same way some lower-class boys are caught in a neighborhood pattern of truancy and delinquency. This concern with education is insurance against the child's fall in social status. Middle-class parents convey to their children subtly or explicitly that they must make good in school if they want to go on being middle-class. This may be phrased in terms of preparation for a "suitable" occupation . . .

Middle-class parents constantly reinforce the authority and prestige of the teacher, encouraging the child to respect her and compete for her approval . . . He learns that scholastic competition is somewhat analogous to the social and economic competition in which his parents participate . . . Of course, it is not competition alone that gives the middle-class child an emotional investment in continued scholastic effort; it is the *position* he achieves in that competition. Apparently his preschool training prepares *him* much better for scholastic competition than his lower-class classmate. His parents mingle with lawyers, accountants, businessmen and others who in their day-to-day activities manipulate symbols . . . He is stimulated . . . by the rewards he receives from his parents when he shows verbal precociousness.[10]

But when one turns to the problem of the lower-class child, it is apparent that some of them fail to develop the kind of orientation which will enable them to submit to school discipline, particularly if their parents do not support the authority of the school as do middle-class parents. Nor are they able to help the child or provide the encouragement and praise which will give him incentives for school accomplishment at the time when he is facing up to the new situation in school. Furthermore, the child may have mechanical ability but lack the necessary verbal facility which a competitive advantage requires. It may also be that he is less familiar with the kinds of situations treated on standard intelligence tests. Thus the social milieu conspires against his educational success. What is notable, however, is the fact that so many young people from all classes do finish high school. Samuel A. Stouffer, in his study of the American soldier (14), has shown that at the time of World War I only 9 per cent of the selectees were high school graduates in contrast to World War II, when 41 per cent had this much schooling. But, according to Professor Toby, those who do drop by the wayside may have developed a "sour grapes" attitude. The lower class boy may rationalize the situation by stating that he never wanted to improve himself, that is, achieve a higher socioeconomic status, for to do so he would have had to use the school as a channel of mobility.

Such considerations as these do not necessarily answer as many questions as they raise, but they do show the effect of class sub-

[10] Toby, Jackson, "Orientation to Education as a Factor in the School Maladjustment of Lower-Class Children," *Social Forces*, XXXV (March, 1957), 262–63.

cultures upon social relationships within the school, not only upon the student-teacher relationship but upon the student-student relationship as well.

Groups Connected with Education. Probably no professional segment of our population is as gregarious as educators, who have set up an association to deal with every phase of education and who frequently meet to discuss problems of mutual interest. Furthermore, proceedings of almost every meeting are published so that there is a tremendous accumulation of materials about education, much of it dealing with school-community relationships. Thus in any large city one can expect to find formal organizations designed to bring together those connected with the school system, not only to make plans for the coming year, and "talk shop," but also for the purposes of "self-improvement." Educators, no less than the general public, are aware that the school system can be geared more satisfactorily to meet the needs of present-day America.

In addition to the official groups, such as school boards, there are often special committees set up by the school board or organized by interested citizens to study building needs, methods of raising educational standards, and whatever issue seems particularly important at the time (12). Karl Thomas Hereford has surveyed the work of these citizens' committees and begins his report as follows:

Lay participation in and for the public schools is as old as the schools themselves. Early school trustees, the lyceums of the early nineteenth century, parent-teacher organizations, numerous and varied peculiarly local organizations, such as band boosters clubs, athletic alumni associations, as well as certain anti-public education groups, are merely different manifestations of this interest and participation. Boards of education and school administrators have grown accustomed to working in the company of such groups.

Nothing in the past, however, quite prepares the modern school administrator or board member for the rapid extension of lay interest and participation of today. *An estimated ten thousand local citizens committees* with a direct interest in public schools have come into being since World War II. Every state, The District of Columbia, Puerto Rico and Alaska report at least one such committee. All of these committees are extra-legal in that they do not share directly in the legal responsibility for the conduct of the public schools.[11]

Since these groups often play a significant role in the kind of schools that a given community has, it is worthwhile noting the findings of Hereford's study of 109 such groups scattered throughout the United States. For example, they strive to be *representative* of their supporting school districts; they provide opportunities for

[11] Hereford, Karl Thomas, "Citizens Committee for Public Schools," *Bulletin* of the Bureau of School Service, University of Kentucky, XXVII (September, 1954), 9.

citizen participation and at the same time are a channel through which policies and programs initiated by the school can gain wider community support and acceptance; and through their own fact-finding, study, and deliberation, they formulate and recommend policies and programs to the board of education.

It appears that such committees are less competent to deal with the instructional programs than other matters connected with the school. Also, the superintendents of schools and the committee chairmen, although agreeing on goals of the committees, have considerably different ideas about how such committees should organize and proceed to these goals. In the Northeast the committees tend to be highly independent, perhaps a trait associated with the town-meeting form of local government; in the West they tend to be small committees initiated by the school board.

There seemed to be four factors which were most closely associated with effective community activity:

1. A desire to operate at a high level of maturity with respect to all types of committee activities.
2. An atmosphere of freedom and cooperation with the school, the board of education and with the supporting school district.
3. Sufficient time in which to bring the talents of the committee to bear on problems and issues which it believes to be important.
4. An intelligent use of resources, both within and without the committee in organizing for and proceeding to carry out various tasks.[12]

It should be pointed out that much of the impetus to these lay committees was given by the National Citizens Commission for the Public Schools, a national body under the presidency of Roy E. Larson, editor of *Time* magazine, which gained the support of the National Advertising Council in publicizing the idea and which also received sufficient funds to set up state offices to promote such groups in at least twenty-six states. This national effort to arouse citizen interest in the local educational problems has come to be known by the more easily remembered name of *Better Schools*.

These advisory citizens councils, or committees, differ, of course, from the Parent-Teacher Associations, founded in 1897, and united nationally in the National Congress of Parents and Teachers. There are approximately twenty-eight thousand such local units which work closely with the school administration to improve the facilities of the school (e.g., providing lunchroom equipment), to give the parents a clearer conception of what it is the school is trying to do, and to promote the welfare of children generally in the community. School administrators vary in their attitudes toward the P.-T.A.

[12] *Ibid.*, p. 90.

Those that want to run the school with a minimum of outside interference do not appreciate the parents' efforts to participate actively in the affairs of the school; others, who see the P.-T.A. as an effective bridge of communication with the community, as well as a means of financial support, welcome the group and do all that they can to make it successful.

Many other organizations in the community take an interest in the schools and frequently contribute money to some specified activity, such as the annual trip of the high school Senior class to Washington, D. C., better sight for school children, new instruments for the band, or automobiles for a driver-training program. But these contributions often represent peripheral rather than central interests of these groups.

ADULT EDUCATION AS A COMMUNITY SUBSYSTEM

Although adult education operates primarily through the school, it nevertheless has some characteristics of its own which deserve special consideration. Since the time, a quarter of a century ago, when California and Pennsylvania incorporated the instruction of adults and out-of-school youth into the system of free general education, the movement has rapidly grown. Today between four and five million Americans are enrolled in adult education programs conducted by the schools in the United States (16). Since one-fourth of these are found in California, it is only fitting that some attention be given to the California experience, which has been studied in considerable detail by Burton R. Clark, as a case in changing values. He writes:

> Adult education emerged as a movement in the United States in the 1920's with newly-acquired organizations and a corps of spokesmen. Within the public schools the movement meant a changed conception of adult participation. Before 1925 "night school" was emphasized, with programs restricted mainly to elementary and high school work, vocational training and Americanization-Citizenship classes.[13]

Such courses were designed to help individuals make up for educational deficiencies and move on up the educational ladder to a high school diploma. Also, the school authorities told these mature students what was good for them. But changes have occurred which have profoundly modified the original conception. These are related to three main points.

1. Changing purposes and objectives. Professor Clark calls these the "manifest ends of action" and shows that in California there has

[13] Clark, Burton R., "Organizational Adaptation and Precarious Values: A Case Study," *American Sociological Review*, XXI (June, 1956), 329.

been a shift from specific purposes committed to liberal education and a sense of educational mission (such as Americanization) to one so general in purpose that it embraces all "adult learning." This leaves the administrator without educational criteria for determining the most important subjects to be taught. Thus, *purpose* may be replaced by *response,* and those courses offered for which there is the greatest demand, with any one course considered equal in educational value to any other course. When this happens, a qualitative shift in values occurs, and "leadership" comes to mean the administering of a service facility.

2. Organizational marginality. The difficult position of the adult educator is shown in the fact that the public schools concentrate upon the training of the young and are accepted (legitimized) to the extent that they carry out this major concern. But adult education must compete with this recognized pattern for "position, budget and support." Furthermore, it is separated from the primary endeavor and is "not a part of the sequence of grades, [rather] its 'students' exist completely outside of the range of compulsory attendance and have other occupations. These attributes leave adult education as a peripheral, nonmandatory effort of the schools, and its officials find themselves organizationally marginal."[14] Consequently, administrators must constantly "sell the program" to the public and to other school officials, indicating a basic insecurity both in their own positions and in the adult education administrative units. Yet the fact remains that when financial support runs low, they are the first in the school system to feel the cuts.

3. Operating pressures. Granted this diffuseness of purpose and the marginal position in the school system, what complications follow? The most obvious is that of the *enrollment economy.* The school budget is largely set by student attendance, and hence everything is staked on the search for clientele. But when students are found, they have only a tenuous tie to the student body: their attendance is voluntary, casual, and easily terminated. So, not only must students be attracted but they must be kept interested. More and more, therefore, adult education becomes a service enterprise— something quite different from the sense of mission that inspired the pioneers in this field.

Despite the fact that adult education operates precariously, with the public school as a base, it is nevertheless becoming more and more a permanent feature of the American scene. Shorter work weeks, increased longevity, an increasing curiosity about the rest

[14] *Ibid.*, p. 331.

of the world and the individual's desire to learn new vocational skills are some of the reasons behind its growing popularity. For example, Wayne C. Rohrer and F. Donald Laws in interpreting the effects of the changing age composition of Maryland's population write:

> Public school educators and librarians will find their programs have increasingly larger potential adult clientele . . . Apart from the aging trend of our population, another rationale for expanding adult education lies in our increasing urban character. With advancing urbanization, level of education rises, and correlatively the span of years of participation in the labor force shortens. Some factors impinging on this relationship are the level of education demanded of employees of industrial and commercial enterprises, compulsory retirement of personnel in many urban enterprises and the selective migration of the better-educated to urban areas. These factors indicate that with urbanization, vocational and non-vocational adult education may, especially for the aged segment, fill the void created by retirement from work . . . [15]

They correctly point out that farm people have in the Agricultural Extension Service a well-established system of adult education, but no similar counterpart for urban people exists in most states (with a few exceptions such as California), although a program of general extension work (including correspondence courses) is a regular feature of most state universities.

As a part of the adult education activities within any community, one must include the various study groups which meet to learn about any one of a thousand subjects as well as the forum and lecture series, which are informative and educational in character. Educational radio and television programs are also assuming increasing importance here. When the community itself becomes the subject of study, adult education and community development merge into a common identity—a fact fully recognized by the Adult Education Association. The Association is a nation-wide organization, which also publishes an attractive magazine called *Adult Leadership*.

American public libraries have long been active in the adult education field. The American Library Association has sponsored several nation-wide adult education programs and is currently (1958) sponsoring the Library-Community Project under a grant from the Fund for Adult Education. Grants have been made to six states (Kansas, Maryland, Michigan, Nebraska, Tennessee, and Wisconsin). The first task is to involve the communities in the program,

[15] Wayne C. Rohrer and F. Donald Laws, *The Population of Maryland: Growth, Composition and Distribution for 1900–1950 and 1940–1950, Characteristics in 1950* (Univ. of Maryland, Agricultural Experiment Station, Misc. Publication, No. 240, July, 1955), p. 42.

then to gather and interpret data about the cooperating communities and the role of the libraries there, and, as a third stage, to determine educational needs. One of the pilot libraries is the Ottawa Public Library in Ottawa, Kansas, a town of ten thousand people. The library there has fifteen thousand volumes with one professional staff member and one full-time and one part-time nonprofessional staff members. Here is a record of the activities in which this library was involved:

At the pilot library level the following selected activities have been undertaken:

To determine the extent and nature of the adult use of the library for educational purposes:

An analysis of registration by age, residence, and occupation of adult registrants.

Plotting of registration on a map, and interpretation of distribution of registrants in relation to the delineation of community by economic levels, national and racial concentrations, and the location of schools, colleges and industries.

The analysis of circulation of materials by weights and types of fiction, and subject content of non-fiction.

A tabulation of the circulation of materials in each category by the occupation of the borrower over a thirty-day period.

The analysis of materials collection by subject matter in relation to percentage of use in each subject classification.

To determine the educational needs of adults as revealed by a study of the history, structure, and institutions of the community:

Interviews with public and voluntary agency heads, and other key people.

The collection and analysis of community studies done by U. S. Bureau of Census, Agricultural Extension Service and Chamber of Commerce.

Study of the local newspaper.

A postcard questionnaire to leaders of clubs and organizations concerning one area of need—education on the problems of the aging—revealed by other sources.

The formation of a citizens' committee to continue the study of education on the problems of the aging.

Meetings of the citizens' committee to learn discussion techniques in order to enable them to conduct group meetings with other citizens concerned with this area of need.

The staff of the Project in Kansas has been assisted by a State Advisory Committee.[16]

EDUCATION AND OTHER COMMUNITY SYSTEMS

Education can best be appreciated when it is seen interacting with the other major systems of the community and when it is placed

[16] *News,* American Library Association, Library-Community Project, January, 1957, p. 2.

in the context of a rapidly changing society. Each of these topics will be taken up in turn, after which some attention will be devoted to two or three special problems of community-wide concern involving education.

Education, Family and Religion. One of the most detailed studies of suburban life yet to appear, *Crestwood Heights*, was made after its three authors had spent five years analyzing every aspect of daily living in the community studied—"from P.T.A. participation and wage-earning to dating and child-rearing." The community is located "somewhere in central Canada" on the outskirts of "Big City," but is typical of suburbia throughout North America. In Crestwood Heights the school is synonymous with the community for the two grew up together; also, the "massive centrality" of the school buildings makes the most immediate impact on any outside observer coming into the Heights. No attempt will be made here to summarize the kinds of education which go on in this community, which the authors discuss in detail; rather attention will be given the analysis of the relationships between education and other systems found in Crestwood Heights. The authors write:

In the area of social development, the school finds itself partly co-operating, partly competing with other institutions: the church and its sponsored recreation programs, the community center and the program under its jurisdiction, and the families and their wishes . . . The school, while it seems to view its recreational program as necessary to its aims—the inculcation of loyalty has a bearing on learning—still feels it proper to confer with church, community center, and family in any plans for extra-curricular activities . . . The parents, imbued with the belief that it is their responsibility to provide recreational outlets for their children, and baffled as to the means for accomplishing their ends, turn, as usual, primarily to the school for help. Since the school, as a publicly supported institution, is in a more favorable financial and official position to initiate extra-curricular activities, it tends progressively to diminish the need for church and community center programs, which are supported more precariously by voluntary contributions and leadership . . . The school, willing or unwilling, ready or unready, appears also, then, to be moving steadily into a position of dominance where the social development of the child is concerned.[17]

In Crestwood Heights the sphere of ethical and religious training, according to the authors, is not clearly assigned territory.

As the institution invested with the major responsibility for transmitting the dominant cultural values, it (the school) is also expected to transmit a "religious heritage," without, however, espousing the position of any one of the competing "religions" or forms of religion. This necessity, together with the

[17] John R. Seeley, R. Alexander Sim, and Elizabeth W. Loosley, *Crestwood Heights: A Study of the Culture of Suburban Life* (New York: Basic Books, Inc., 1956), pp. 238–39.

special care inevitably enjoined upon a school system encompassing two religious groups supposedly as widely divergent as Jew and Gentile, accounts for something of whatever may be peculiar in the religious instruction of the schools of Crestwood Heights.[18]

Religion in this suburban community is characterized as a guide to a style of behavior rather than to any routine of conduct. It is against aggression and in favor of love and sympathy. It is not preoccupied with *ultimate values,* but teachers and parents alike view it as a *means* to other and much more important ends such as "happiness," peace of mind, or mental health.

If the relationship of the school to the church is considered in this context, an interesting reversal may be observed. Formerly the views of the church dominated the parent who, in turn, dominated the child and the teacher directly—and the child again indirectly through the teacher. The existing configuration would suggest that the teacher now influences child and parent, who mutually influence each other, and these, in turn, unite to influence the church. The school, supported by the human relations experts and their institutions, has largely replaced the church as an ideological source, as the figure below suggests.[19]

Fig. 23. Pattern of dominance about 1850 (left) and 1950 (right) in Crestwood Heights.

Such a complete reversal of traditional relationships may not be characteristic of most communities, but Crestwood Heights certainly reveals one direction in which the pendulum can swing. The writers also point out that the school is more and more being entrusted with the task of developing in the child an adherence to the emerging value system of health, happiness, and success, as well as the responsibility for his emotional well-being.

Education and the Economy. But education, chiefly as embodied in the school, is not only interacting with religion and the family; it is closely tied in with economic life as well (6). Since the employment picture grows more complicated all the time with increasing specialization, schools find it appropriate to conduct some activities and services, as the following quotation shows.

19 *Ibid.,* p. 241.
18 *Ibid.,* p. 239.

Practical arts courses are provided in junior and senior high schools covering general career areas, such as commercial, homemaking and industrial. Among the purposes of these courses is the development of appreciation of the types and standards of work in these fields . . .

Guidance services for youth are also provided in junior and senior high schools and include attention to the selection of courses that provide a foundation for adult life, keeping in mind both cultural and economic needs . . .

When the boy or girl is faced with the necessity of choosing a definite occupational aim, a course in occupations is often available . . . Vocational preparatory courses are offered in many senior high schools and special vocational high schools.[20]

Once the young person has had this instruction and guidance, many schools help him register with the local employment service, or his instructors in shop or laboratory may keep him in mind in their contacts with prospective employers. Some schools even have developed an after-employment follow-up scheme, which keeps the former student in touch with the school and also helps the school officials learn about the effects of their training.

Education and Government. In a discussion of the need for coordination between government and education, Eldon L. Johnson writes:

. . . No evil flows from the separation of school and government when they have no, or few, problems in common. But that time is past. The barricades will have to come down, somehow. The trouble arises when problems are common, but the attack is separate, if not, indeed, rival or competitive or possessively exclusive. Common problems call for common solutions, although the co-operators need not in any sense lose their identity. The evil of separation is the propensity to build rival power structures and to thwart the emergence, recognition and service of the community of interest.[21]

Johnson cogently argues that there needs to be a more realistic appreciation of the schools as a related part of the public enterprises of the community, for they are not a unique entity, existing apart. He points out that it is a basic misconception to assume that school boards and districts, being creatures of the state government, are somehow fundamentally different from all other civil government at the local level. Johnson contends that coordination will prove more likely if school administrators are trained more realistically in the political processes and the nature of "the public" and its controls. He advocates graduate training in the social sciences for school administrators and hopes that acquaintance with these sub-

[20] William P. Loomis and Louise Moore, "Occupational Education in the Schools," *The Annals,* CCCII (November, 1955), 68–69.

[21] Eldon L. Johnson, "Co-ordination: The Viewpoint of a Political Scientist," *The Annals,* CCCII (November, 1955), 136.

jects "will enable the superintendent to see the problems of youth and schools as they spin in their specialized orbits, held in place by all the forces of the community; in other words, to see the schools in the context of the community."[22]

Meanwhile, teachers are doing what they can to teach civics and the ways in which local government operates, frequently taking their classes to various agencies of local government in this process. Although attitudes toward government and citizen participation may not actually be formed in school, much information on which future action will be based may be gained there.

These comments and examples of how education interacts with other community systems are merely suggestive of the approach that could be used in any particular community. Much more detail than can be touched upon here is required if one is to follow the connections of even two of these systems. But these can be analyzed if one has the concepts within which to work out a research design and energy enough to collect and analyze pertinent data.

EDUCATION AND THE SENSE OF COMMUNITY

The Corning Glass Company, in commemoration of its centennial, held a conference in 1951 to which leading businessmen and educators were invited to discuss what had happened to human beings during the past hundred years. Four groups each took up a different topic: what has happend to man in (1) his use of leisure, (2) his job, (3) his world of values, and (4) his sense of community. Those considering the last topic unanimously agreed that community life had changed greatly in the past hundred years. In the discussion some contended that the place where a man worked had become his community; others believed that where a man dwelt with his family was still the locale of his community; and still others, residents of a large city, claimed that they did not want to be hemmed in by any "nosy," controlling community and were glad they could be anonymous in their urban apartments (13). But underlying the whole discussion was a recognition that if any nation or culture is to survive, its members must have a sense of community that will hold them together at least enough to make some common life possible. However, prescriptions as to how this may be achieved vary greatly. Also, the part the school is to play is viewed differently by different people.

Robert M. Hutchins, though devoting most of his remarks to higher education, has reacted sharply against the view that since

22 *Ibid.*, p. 140.

there is an infinite variety of individual differences, there must be an infinite variety of educational offerings. He contends:

There is no doubt that men are different. But they are also the same. One trouble with education in the West is that it has emphasized those respects in which men are different; this is what excessive specialization means. The purpose of basic education is to bring out our common humanity, a consummation more urgently needed today than at any time in the last five hundred years. To confuse at every point . . . the education of our common humanity, which is primary and indispensable, with the education of our individual differences, which is secondary and in many cases unnecessary, is to get bad education at every point. What we have here is a prescription for the disintegration of society through the disintegration of the educational system. This process is now going on in the United States.[23]

Whether or not educators today are ready to accept Hutchins' proposed remedies, they nevertheless recognize most of the problems to which he so forcefully addresses himself (7).

One point of view, while not dismissing other approaches as unimportant or irrelevant, is that school consolidation has often been done without any regard for existing community loyalties and that little guidance is frequently given toward the creation of a new community. The proponents of this view would hold that school consolidation frequently destroys the sense of community, although they recognize that "time marches on" and that the one-room school faces a different world today from that of fifty years ago.

Another approach to current educational problems goes under the name of "Moral and Spiritual Values in Education" and suggests to teachers that any subject or any school activity can prove a vehicle for inculcating values, reverence, and spiritual insight. This does not mean preaching a given theology or recruiting for a particular denomination, but it does call for carrying the student beyond the immediate and the present to a larger view of the universe and his part in it; it helps him see that he is practicing religion and ethics, for example, in the way he treats his schoolmates. Critics of this approach rebel at the idea of "inculcating" values in such a formal way. They admit that this approach is probably better than direct instruction in values but argue that a teacher gets across values not so much by precept as by example. But values of one sort or another are imparted by the school experience, whether teachers and administrators openly recognize them or not. Some of these contribute greatly toward a "sense of community," while others do not. But even in this realm of life, as earlier sections have

[23] Robert M. Hutchins, *The Conflict in Education in a Democratic Society* (New York: Harper & Brothers, 1953), pp. 59–60.

indicated, the school can only do so much, since it is a part of the whole community and can function only as a part of the whole.

REFERENCES AND SUGGESTED READINGS

1. ANDERSON, C. ARNOLD. "Social Class Differentials in the Schooling of Youth Within the Regions and Community-Size Groups of the United States," *Social Forces,* XXV (May, 1947), 434–40.
2. BECKER, HOWARD S. "The Career of the Chicago Public Schoolteacher," *American Journal of Sociology,* LVII (March, 1952), 470–77.
3. CLARK, BURTON R. "Organizational Adaptation and Precarious Values: A Case Study," *American Sociological Review,* XXI (June, 1956), 327–36.
4. *Community Service News,* IX (May–June, 1953), "School Consolidation—A Process Calling for Social As Well As Educational Insight." Also see Volume X (September–October, 1953), which is devoted entirely to the community.
5. DAVIS, ALLISON, and HAVIGHURST, ROBERT J. *Father of the Man.* Boston: Houghton Mifflin Company, 1947.
6. GLICK, PAUL C., and MILLER, HERMAN P. "Educational Level and Potential Income," *American Sociological Review,* XXI (June, 1956), 307–12.
7. HART, JOSEPH K. *Education in the Humane Community.* New York: Harper & Brothers, 1951.
8. HARTFORD, ELLIS F. "Emphasizing Values in Five Kentucky Schools," *Bulletin* of the Bureau of School Service, XXVI (University of Kentucky, June, 1954).
9. HOLLINGSHEAD, AUGUST B. *Elmtown's Youth.* New York: John Wiley & Sons, Inc., 1949.
10. LA VIOLETTE, FORREST, and SILVERT, K. H. "A Theory of Stereotypes," *Social Forces,* XXIX (March, 1951), 257–62.
11. RELLER, THEODORE L. (ed.) "The Public School and Other Community Services," *The Annals,* CCCII (November, 1955), entire issue.
12. *The School Executive,* (January, 1952). Entire issue devoted to "Citizens Organize for Better Schools."
13. STALEY, EUGENE. *Creating an Industrial Civilization.* New York: Harper & Brothers, 1952.
14. STOUFFER, SAMUEL A., *et al. The American Soldier.* Princeton: Princeton University Press, 1949, I, p. 59.
15. TERRIEN, FREDERIC W. "Who Thinks What About Education?" *American Journal of Sociology,* LIX (September, 1953), 150–58.
16. THADEN, JOHN F., LOOMIS, C. P., *et al.* "Adult Education in the Public School and the Community," in *Rural Social Systems and Adult Education.* East Lansing: Michigan State College Press, 1953.
17. THADEN, JOHN F. *Equalizing Educational Opportunity Through Community School Districts,* Special Bulletin CDX, January, 1957. East Lansing: Michigan State University Press.
18. WARNER, W. L., HAVIGHURST, R. J., and LOEB, M. B. *Who Shall Be Educated?* New York: Harper & Brothers, 1944.

Chapter **16**

HEALTH AND SOCIAL WELFARE

The modern American community has a well-defined system of medical care and another system which deals with problems of poverty and dependency. Each of these will be taken up in turn, since no picture of community life in the United States would be complete without some knowledge of how these systems work. After a brief mention of the components of the medical system, a fuller treatment will be given to the major statuses connected with it. Following that, some of the community problems involving health will be indicated.

THE SYSTEM OF PUBLIC HEALTH AND MEDICAL CARE

Components of the System. The social complex of relationships centering around health and physical well-being is as much a national as a community development. Each community, however, has its own adaptation of the national pattern. Central to this system is the physician who today relies a great deal upon highly developed laboratory tests and diagnostic equipment, such as X-ray machines and electrocardiographs, although the old general practitioners' skills of using history and physical examination to guide in both diagnosis and treatment are still of primary importance. Whether he works in a clinic, which is cooperatively owned and operated by other doctors, or in his own private office, he is, nevertheless, the pivotal figure in medical care.

Local hospitals, each with their own internal social structure, provide the doctor a place to treat patients needing such specialized care. There, nurses and occupational and physical therapists assist the doctor, whether in the operating room or in physical therapy for someone recovering from polio. Patients' fees are but a fraction of the total costs of the operation of hospitals, whether privately endowed or publicly supported. Today the governing boards of hospitals in every community are increasingly plagued by the problem of rising expenses in the face of fixed endowments, a problem necessitating the search for additional revenues from other sources.

Another component in this system centering around health is the druggist who compounds the doctors' prescriptions and who sells a variety of "patent" medicines requiring no prescription. Behind the druggist are the large drug firms spending millions of dollars annually on research in an effort to discover new ways to cure or alleviate different diseases. These firms make an impact on the community, not only through the products on the druggists' shelves, but because of the nation-wide advertising that finds its way into every community.

The component of the medical system that is least heralded and praised, although in many ways just as deserving, is the public health staff. Members of the public health staff are interested in preventive medicine as well as in providing medical treatment. The sanitation officials who inspect restaurants and other public places where food and drinks are served and who see that regulations regarding milk are carried out, the public health doctor and public health nurse who are ready to give mass immunizations when an epidemic threatens, as well as routine immunizations (e.g., against diphtheria, tetanus, whooping cough, and smallpox), who examine school children periodically to discover defects that should be called to the attention of the family physician—to mention only some of their duties—have done more to improve the health of the American people than some of the more highly dramatized medical discoveries. Ordinarily, the public health workers do their job in keeping with standards set up by the state health board and are interested in developing a profession of public health, or preventive medicine which, though allied with other types of medicine, is a recognized field of its own.

Another component in any community is the well-organized health and hospital insurance plan which is designed to relieve the policyholder from some of the financial uncertainties connected with unexpected major illnesses. The companies which have such policies to sell are often very vigorous in promoting health and safety education, which is an important assistance in a sound program of public health.

Thus, every community will have its own combination of doctors, hospitals, nurses, druggists, dentists, optometrists, public health workers, and health insurance salesmen. Their combined activity, along with various organizations dealing with health, comprises the system of public health and medical care of the community. A study of a few of these components will show much about the operation of this particular system.

Selected Statuses within the System. The doctor. One of the investigators who has best characterized the professional roles of the doctor is Oswald Hall. In one of his articles he sets forth the stages of a medical career as noted in an eastern American city (6). The first stage is that of *generating an ambition* which, in the case of a medical career, is supposed to be great and of the rigorous sort. Such ambition is social in character, being nourished by family or friends, who help establish the appropriate routines, arrange the necessary privacy, and define the day-to-day rewards. This is why doctors tend to be recruited from the families of professional workers, for they possess the mechanisms for generating and nurturing the medical ambitions.

A second stage in the medical career is the *incorporation into or the becoming a part of the institutions of medicine.* For example, the direction of a doctor's career depends to a great degree upon the character of teaching in the medical school he enters, the hospital where he interns, and the hospital in which he gets a staff appointment once he begins his practice, for without such a connection the doctor is seriously handicapped. In a hospital there is a well-established hierarchy which the person beginning his medical career must try to penetrate. The doctors of a given department are arranged in strata, such as extern (medical student in a teaching hospital), intern, resident (junior, senior, chief), staff member (at various levels of seniority), and the like. Within these strata there are finer gradations through which a new member of the profession can advance. In such a status structure the various positions represent a wide range of rewards to be conferred on the doctors attached to the hospital. Since hospitals are often controlled by religious groups, ethnic and religious differentiation plays some part in the selection and advancement of interns. As a matter of fact, the hospital with which a doctor is associated, along with other related institutions, constitutes a sifting device which tends to establish his status in the community, thus markedly influencing his career.

The third stage is that of *acquiring a clientele.* Not only must the doctor attract patients, he must use the type of strategy which will retain them, especially those who are the type who fit into his pattern of practice. The specialists, although conscious of their superior status over the general practitioner, are, nevertheless, dependent upon other colleagues who refer patients to them. Medical practice is carried on in a competitive milieu and is controlled by a code of ethics, although—as Professor Hall points out—this code is superseded in a community where the profession is well organized by a set of expectations and understandings deeply imbedded in the personalities of the doctors. Such understandings may go so far as to control the entry of new practitioners into the community, allocate them to posts in the various medical institutions, and incorporate them into the established office practices. This is often fairly rigidly controlled by the county medical association.

A fourth stage is that of *developing a set of informal relationships with colleagues.* There is a central core of the profession which exercises the controls and allocation just mentioned. This central core has access to and dominates the main hospital posts. It constitutes "an inner fraternity," or a primary social group whose members have similar social backgrounds and daily working relationships and is small enough so that it is a "democracy of first names." Therefore, from the standpoint of a medical career, acceptance by this inner core is of great importance. This is usually achieved by becoming a protégé of some member of the inner core who insists that the protégé "deliver the goods" and who vouches for him at every step up the ladder of advancement in the profession.

It may seem on first glance a far cry from the study of the community, which is wide and all-embracing, to the study of the social controls within any one profession, such as medicine. But without understanding these controls, one does not see how the system of public health and medical care works and how its fits into the general functioning of the community as a whole.

In addition to being a member of a profession, the doctor, like the lawyer, has extra-professional roles. Harry W. Martin studied these roles in a New England community of about forty-two thousand persons where he interviewed 90 per cent of the physicians. Some of his findings, which support many of Professor Hall's findings about the medical profession, are the following:

The physicians averaged a total of eight memberships in all associations, a very high figure in comparison with other groups where data were available. Fifty per cent of these were professional affiliations.

In the non-professional and non-religious groups to which they belonged the physicians held few offices unless the group had health interests, for then their specialized knowledge could be used. They are not generally expected to hold offices in associations not having health concerns.[1]

---

[1] Harry W. Martin, "Physician Role Conflict in Community Participation," *Research Previews,* V (March, 1957), Institute for Research in Social Science, University of North Carolina, 14–15.

Up until some fifteen years ago, non-Yankee physicians had been effectively excluded from the community's sole hospital, but even today the Yankee physicians—though outnumbered by the Irish, Jewish, French, Polish physicians —hold most of the key staff positions. This pattern also prevails in the business and industrial life of the community.[2]

In this New England community some hypotheses might be made about the physicians' political behavior and sentiments: (1) Physicians have a high level of political interest and a low degree of active individual participation. (2) Induction into this high status profession re-inforces Republican Party sentiments and weakens Democratic Party allegiance. (3) Their perceptions of their professional role and the nature of politics limits direct participation in the frequently emotionally-laden area of partisan politics. (4) Physicians, unlike lawyers, are not expected by the community to participate in politics.[3]

This study also showed that the physicians' participation was affected by the belief that they were too busy to take part in community life, that "people can't depend on them in planning their programs," that it is unethical for a physician to appear to advertise, and he must not let his name or picture appear in the paper too frequently." Another aspect of the extra-professional role is shown in the remark of a physician:

"I can't go out and take part in the activities of these groups. The first thing I knew they would be calling me 'Doc' or by my first name, and when they need a doctor, they wouldn't think of me as one, and they would call in someone else."[4]

Thus, according to Martin, the physician may be compelled to behave in terms of his professional role even outside the professional context so that he will not be thought of as something less than a physician.

The nurse. A second important functionary in the system of public health and medical care is the nurse (22). Although her activity may take place in a clinic, as a visiting nurse in the community, or as a special nurse in a private home, most nurses are employed in hospitals, which they look upon as their natural professional habitat. The nurse's place in the hospital hierarchy is somewhat indeterminate, "being often not a direct consequence of her profession but of her years of service."[5] This results frequently in the display of an excessively professional attitude, in a zeal for not losing one's dignity as a "professional." In brief, what "'respectability' as a badge of membership in the middle classes means to the lower-

[2] *Ibid.*, p. 16.
[3] *Ibid.*, pp. 17–18.
[4] *Ibid.*
[5] George Devereux, and Florence R. Weiner, "The Occupational Status of Nurses," *American Sociological Review*, XV (October, 1950), 633.

middle-classes, a professional attitude means to the nurse."[6] In this country a nurse's responsibility is almost completely subordinate to a physician's and she, therefore, feels markedly her lack of genuine responsibility. She has lost the devotion of rugged service exemplified in Florence Nightingale and Clara Barton but does not have sufficient professional training for major responsibility. The emergence of the practical nurse to provide the bedside comforts is filling the gap left by the professional nurse's desire to avoid menial training and attain greater status.

Within nursing itself there is a conflict between those who stress the professional goals of specialization and advanced education and those who stress the humanitarian values of bedside nursing. According to Irwin Deutscher and Ann Montague:

> It is probably true of many service occupations that, as they attempt to achieve and maintain a professional status, the traditional humanitarian values are sacrificed. This does not mean that the more-or-less intimate type of personal relationship need disappear. When in the process of professionalization an occupation garners new functions and loses old ones, new occupational groups may arise to fill the gap. In nursing we have the appearance of practical nurses and nurses' aides. In some parts of the United States, the vacancy left by the old country doctor is being filled by the osteopath.[7]

The shortage of nurses is spectacularly dramatized when some hospital board announces that it must close a whole ward or wing of their institution because they cannot find enough nurses to staff it.

The druggist. The pharmacist, or druggist, tends to see his occupation as one of the medical-scientific occupations. However, it is a marginal occupation, since it seeks to incorporate the conflicting goals of business and profession. Although these cross-pressures of the business and professional worlds are not unique to pharmacy, they are particularly acute there. With the growth of large-scale retail enterprise, according to Thelma H. McCormack, the businessman status of the pharmacist is threatened because of the growth of chainstores and other economic forces, so he turns to professionalization as a counteracting force. As a consequence, the training for a pharmacist has been lengthened to four years beyond high school and may even extend to five or six years in some states. In concluding her study Dr. McCormack writes:

> The young pharmacist today is trained as a professional; his interests and ability for scientific research are carefully developed, preparing him for the

[6] *Ibid.*

[7] Irwin Deutscher and Ann Montague, "Professional Education and Conflicting Value Systems: The Role of the Religious Schools in the Educational Aspirations of Nursing Students," *Social Forces*, XXXV (December, 1956), 131.

laboratory work required by hospitals, schools and pharmaceutical companies. Yet few pharmacists see themselves in this position. Most expect to become proprietors, with the status of independent professionals, thus fusing the two systems and avoiding a final choice. In this process the entrepreneurial drive is modified by criticism of big business and by retreat from highly competitive circumstances; the professional drive is blunted by subordinating a service goal to individual achievement for its own sake.[8]

Although the druggists' occupation is marginal—neither wholly a business nor yet a profession—it is an important link in the treatment of illness. He has a major responsibility as a check on the physician, who in the pressure of work occasionally makes an error in a prescription which should be counterchecked by the druggist.

The public health worker (preventive medicine). Within any local department of health there is a division of labor leading to differences in status, but it will be sufficient here to outline the six basic local public health functions with the understanding that specialists with their own titles have charge of each function. Four of these functions, as described by Haven Emerson, are as follows:

The statistical function consists of the collection, verification, tabulation, analysis, interpretation, publication and practical use of the facts of births, of certain notifiable diseases of communicable, occupational, nutritional, or other important categories, and of deaths.

Control of communicable diseases is a second function. Diseases which spread from the sick to the well, directly or by intermediate means, carriers, insect and other vectors, or by contamination of foods and fluids used by man, are all, theoretically at least, preventable . . . This was the first field of direct attack by health departments.

The third function of a local health department is to control conditions of the physical and biological environment of man. It includes the protection of the source, processing and distribution of water and foods, especially milk and milk products, against contamination or pollution; the disposal of man's personal and industrial wastes, insects, vermin, and animals capable of causing or spreading disease in the human being; the cleanliness of air; the occupancy of living and working quarters; the conditions of employment, particularly such as permit dusts, fumes, smoke and contact with irritating or poisonous materials in the course of manufacture. Concern with housing standards, with noise as an annoyance bearing upon rest and comfort, and with the abatement of public nuisances . . . accident prevention . . . fall within the scope of environmental sanitation. The public health or sanitary engineer is a professionally qualified associate of the medical officer of health . . .

The fourth function . . . is the operation of the public health laboratory . . . [which offers] a wide variety of diagnostic and analytical tests of biological, chemical and physical character, serving the needs of physicians, the general public and the technical purposes of the various bureaus and divisions of the local department of health . . . Most state laws require blood sero-

[8] Thelma Herman McCormack, "The Druggists' Dilemma: Problems of a Marginal Occupation," *American Journal of Sociology,* LXI (January, 1956), 315.

logical tests of applicants for marriage licenses and also of the expectant mother to make possible the easy prevention of marital and congenital syphilis . . .[9]

The fifth function has to do with "maternity, infancy and child hygiene," considered broadly enough to cover "genetics, eugenics, marriage counseling, prenatal guidance and the whole range of bodily, mental and emotional growth and development of the child from birth until it has completed the years of required school attendance and enters upon self-support."[10] The sixth function, which, like the fifth, has been more recently recognized as necessary, is that of public health education, which provides "program, plan and performance to promote by an informed and understanding public the development of healthful habits of living and a conscious desire to avoid preventable disease."[11]

Dr. Emerson, long a student of public health practice, points out that a population of not less than fifty thousand is needed to give tax support and to justify the employment of the sixteen persons required to conduct a good local health department. These sixteen include a medical health officer, educationally qualified; ten public health nurses (one for each five thousand people); a sanitary or public health engineer; a nonprofessional assistant; and three clerks. He makes a strong plea for consolidation of local health jurisdiction so that more efficient service can be rendered, estimating that twelve hundred local health departments would satisfactorily cover the entire continental United States.

Health insurance salesmen. Throughout America there is a variety of health insurance programs. In some cases physicians themselves band together and offer their services for a fixed rate during the year to families in their area; in other cases labor unions or industrial concerns may provide workers and their dependents with good health care as a part of the condition of employment. Much effort, however, goes into the selling of participation in such voluntary insurance plans as the Blue Cross or the Blue Shield, the first of which covers hospital expenses up to a certain point, and the second, in-hospital, surgical, and certain other fees which physicians might charge. A number of private insurance companies also offer individuals policies which give a certain degree of protection when hospitalization is necessary. But one study (1) has shown that costs outside the hospital (physicians' home and office calls, drugs, dental services, etc.) frequently exceed the costs of in-hospital services

[9] Haven Emerson, "Essential Local Public Health Services," *The Annals of the American Academy*, CCLXXIII (January, 1951), 20–22.

[10] *Ibid.*, p. 22.

[11] *Ibid.*

when totaled over a year. Even the cost of straightening a child's crooked teeth (orthodontics) is a prolonged drain on many family budgets.

For any voluntary health program to be financially sound, enough participants must be enrolled to provide broad support. That is why one of the functionaries in the health field today is the man with a voluntary plan to sell. In 1956 voluntary health insurance benefits totaled almost three billion dollars, or over 25 per cent of the total bill for personal health services. In that year also about 70 per cent of the population carried some form of voluntary health insurance, with these policies centering chiefly around hospital and surgical fees. One of the most interesting features of these insurance schemes from a community standpoint is the stable source of income guaranteed to the individuals and institutions who must provide medical care (1).

Leaders of various health campaigns. The system of public health and medical care consists of more than the medical personnel and the organizations which they create; more and more lay people are involved in raising the funds that must underwrite much of the very expensive medical research now being carried on to find the cause and cure of some of the most dreaded diseases. In every community there are periodic drives to collect money for associations dealing with poliomyelitis, multiple sclerosis, heart disease, cancer, tuberculosis—to mention some of the best-advertised. Such drives not only give a selected group of local people a chance to participate but also educate the public more fully about the nature of some of the diseases being combatted. Each of these associations has its paid staff located most often in some metropolitan center and concerns itself with organizing the drives with the help of local civic clubs or women's organizations. This lay participation in health campaigns on a big scale is one of the most interesting recent developments in this area.

To catalog fully all of those who are concerned with health would extend this discussion to much greater length because no attention has thus far been devoted to dentistry or optometry, to mention but two specialties which play an important part in safeguarding health and promoting physical fitness. But this brief treatment of a few of the statuses, together with some of their problems, can serve to indicate the complex nature of this whole system and the increased efforts being made to help the individual citizen meet the costs which must be paid if he is to get continually better service based on more and more expensive techniques.

The Community and Health. The question of the existence of health facilities and their use was taken up in Chapter 3, since these constitute an important feature of the community as a service center. What continues to call for further study in every community is the degree to which these facilities are available to different income groups. Many people in the low-income groups who depend upon free clinics or general hospitals supported by public funds lose confidence in medicine when they find that each time they go for a regular treatment they are met by a different doctor. This lack of continuity does not lead to the development of the type of patient-doctor relationship which the American medical profession insists is necessary in good practice. Those in the middle-income groups, many barely living within their income, find that one serious illness can wipe away the total savings of the family unless they have relied upon some type of health insurance to meet some of the most pressing expenses.

However, the problem which is deservedly getting much greater attention nowadays is that of mental health and the community. A study of this problem was done in 1951 in Louisville, Kentucky, during which the attitudes of citizens there on the general subject of mental health were noted. Julian L. Woodward summarizes the findings as follows:

1. The public has come a considerable distance in giving up old beliefs and superstitions about mental illness and in adopting more modern, scientific viewpoints.
2. There is still a gross failure to recognize serious mental symptoms, at least when they are described in words. The story may, of course, be different when the people themselves are under observation.
3. There is considerable loss of faith in repressive and punitive techniques, especially in dealing with juveniles.
4. There seems to be no strong negative reaction to the psychiatrist, and he is coming to be regarded as the logical person to handle clearly identifiable cases of mental disorder. He is also beginning to be regarded as a useful resource in dealing with less serious personality problems, although here he is still handicapped because of a certain stigma that attaches to his subjects.
5. The lawyers represent a minor stronghold of reaction against psychiatry and against modern ideas of how to treat juvenile delinquency.[12]

More and more those working in the mental health field are noting the importance of interpersonal relations in what might be called "personality health." A. R. Mangus has devoted much attention to the connection between community factors and mental

[12] Julian L. Woodward, "Changing Ideas on Mental Illness and Its Treatment," *American Sociological Review,* XVI (August, 1951), 454.

health and has listed a few illustrative propositions, many of which tie in with observations already made in early parts of this book:

1. The level of personality health, as measured by the adopted criteria, is a function of position in the social class structure.

2. The level of personality health is depressed by attempts at upward mobility in the class system.

3. Migration from the community is selective with respect to personality health.

4. Being reared in a happy family has a positive influence on personality health.

5. School programs adapted to the needs of individual children have a positive influence on their health.

6. Majority-minority group conflict adversely affects the personality health of both groups involved.

7. The clarity with which social roles are defined is related to the level of personality health.

8. Occupational dissatisfaction exerts a depressing influence on the health of those involved.

9. Level of personality health is positively correlated with levels of marital happiness.

10. Cultural diversity in the community is functionally related to personality health.[13]

Such propositions are listed for further testing and may be modified as later research shows that they need to be rephrased, qualified, or discarded altogether. In the present state of our knowledge, however, these seem tenable enough to be used as starting points in research.

Before looking at the interaction of the system of public health and medical care with other community systems, it would be helpful to get an understanding of the system of social welfare, which is related to health at many points.

SOCIAL WELFARE AS A COMMUNITY SYSTEM

For a comprehensive coverage of social welfare, one needs to turn to the writings of social workers, who have delineated their field with great care, taking pains to distinguish between case work, group work, and what they term "community organization." No effort will be made here, however, to look at welfare in social work terms, but rather to look at social work in sociological terms, since the former approach is that of a profession and the latter that of the social scientist trying to understand some facet of human behavior which in this case is occurring in the local community. After a few words about the development of the social welfare system, atten-

[13] A. R. Mangus, "Perspectives for Social Science Research in Mental Health," *Rural Sociology*, XXI (March, 1956), 20. See article for bibliography of fifty-eight references.

tion will be directed to its components, then to the interaction among these components.

A Developing System. An interesting way of tracing the emergence of social welfare as a system is to see how it is tied in with changing American values (25). This is the theme of an article by Mary B. Treudley. Social work is the coalescing core of the social welfare system as she views it:

> The basis for social work is the conviction that there is a way out of an individual's or a family's difficulties. No situation is so bad that it cannot be bettered. To a certain extent improvement is brought about by the manipulation of the environment, but increasing emphasis is laid upon the client's active participation in his own salvation. Social workers, however, part company with those who believe that any American can solve all his problems by his own unaided effort. They offer their expert assistance in getting people out of troubles too great for them to manage alone, and their help is accepted by a steadily growing proportion of the population. Also in contradiction to the stereotypes of our culture, social workers are not possessed by a boundless optimism which they communicate to their clients. They promise only improvement, not ideal solutions. They urge those who come to them to make the best possible compromise with reality. They hold out no hope of miracles, but only limited rewards for renewed effort.[14]

As she sets forth the connection between cultural values and social work, Dr. Treudley finds that American people in general are becoming more interested in personality development and not merely with getting things done, a trend definitely in keeping with the basic emphasis of the social worker. There also seems to be shift from the harsh, puritan ethic, which stressed industry, thrift, and gratitude, to ways in which a troubled personality can use his own initiative in working out a more satisfying adjustment to reality. A manifestation of this is the growing interest in parent guidance which helps promote the social work approach. The social worker, like most Americans, subscribes to the belief, publicly at least, that all people are capable of goal-directed behavior; therefore, he tries to combat—according to Dr. Treudley—the depersonalization of human beings by modern industry and urban anonymity and to increase the active, rational participation of his clients.

More people are seeking the services of social workers than can be cared for with the limited personnel available. This is some indication of professional success. The social worker, because most of his clientele is neither distinguished nor successful, often acquires a more profound faith than the ordinary citizen in the worth of the

[14] Mary Bosworth Treudley, "American Cultural Themes and Social Work," *Social Forces*, XXVIII (March, 1950), 290.

common man and in his ability to help himself. This explains the divergence in views which sometimes exists between the social worker and members of the board of his agency who come from the upper strata of the community.

Dr. Treudley indicates that social work in one sense opposes change, for it urges people to adjust to things as they are, and yet promotes change, for social workers are themselves in the forefront of social movements; also that social workers over the past twenty-five years have helped remove the sense of guilt on the part of those who accept relief. She then takes up several other themes, such as humor, generosity, expertness, and associationism, showing how they mitigate against or aid social work practice today, and closes with these comments:

In conclusion, social work reflects to some extent the older culture of America. It responds in part to the far-reaching changes that are remaking both our behavioral patterns and our social structure. Through its own development, it contributes in large measure to the process of peaceful evolution, and through its clients it helps to domesticate a mass of new ideas and attitudes. It also serves to ease the tensions caused by social dynamism at the points where they are most keenly felt.[15]

Along with shifts in values there have been organizational changes. Tax-supported agencies, which stem from those patterned after English laws in colonial times, now seek to do more than merely administer aid or assign people to county farms or almshouses. Also, instead of putting large numbers of dependent children into orphanages, they try to keep the child with the parents, if this is possible and the home is desirable, or put the child in a boarding home where he will have something more closely resembling family life. Furthermore, specialized agencies have been organized to care for most welfare needs and for most people with certain types of defects. The development of these agencies was given a great impetus by the passage of the federal Social Security Act in 1935 and the implementation of its programs, administered by the several states, in connection with the needy aged, the needy blind, and dependent children. The Act also contains provisions for unemployment compensation, old age pensions, care for the crippled, maternal and child welfare services, venereal disease control, and other activities required in the full development of the social welfare field. In 1956 this Act was amended to raise the proportion of the federal contribution to the states in programs affecting the needy, to provide dollar-for-dollar matching of federal with state funds to cover

[15] *Ibid.*, p. 297.

cost of medical care to needy persons, and to stress rehabilitation and prevention as a major objective.

In addition to the public- or tax-supported agencies a large number of private welfare agencies have grown up, many of them having their start in religious groups, in settlement houses, or in efforts by citizens to deal with the mass immigration of the past. The last fifteen or twenty years have witnessed a growing coordination of all of these efforts, so much so that one can speak more correctly of a system of social welfare than one could have a generation ago. The growth of the profession of social work has been intimately connected with this coordination, as has the imperative need to go to the general public for contributions to support the agencies which many years ago were sponsored by a relatively few large-scale contributors who took them on as a pet project. In examining the components of the social welfare system today, the fact that it is still in the stage of rapid development must constantly be borne in mind.

Major Components of the Social Welfare System. The chief unit of the system is the "agency," which can cover a wide variety of organizational patterns dealing with many different kinds of problems. The definition of a welfare agency, not always the same in every community, may include the juvenile court and the Y. M. C. A., the Family Service Society and the Florence Crittenton Home for unmarried mothers, the county child welfare department and a day camp for underprivileged children, the Travelers' Aid Society, the Salvation Army and the Girl Scouts. All these units are staffed with professional people who think of themselves either as social workers or as closely allied to welfare work; each group has a board of directors which determines policies for the agency; and each (unless heavily endowed) must depend upon the public for funds, either in the form of taxation or as contributions to some financial drive. Such organizations all seem to share the philosophy of rehabilitation and personal enrichment of those with whom they work and usually think of themselves as acting in behalf of the community as a whole in offering their services.

One type of agency does what is known as *case work*. Its staff members seek to help individuals overcome their personal, family, or employment problems through counseling and through providing physical resources when these seem an important aid in making the individual independent again. One pilot project designed to find out how dependency can best be dealt with in a community has been carried on by Community Research Associates, Inc., in Winona, Minnesota (16). The county numbers forty thousand people, with twenty-five thousand of these living in the city of Winona, the county seat. Those in charge of the project set up a Family Center, to which all regular agencies reported family data which they collected. This center, with its staff of experienced, professional caseworkers and other consultants, first surveyed the welfare needs of Winona County. It found that (1) out of every 1,000 families in the county, 118 received services to meet health and welfare needs in the given month of the initial study; (2) in the same year $33.57 per capita was spent on these families requiring community help; (3) dependency was Winona's top-ranking community problem; (4) there was considerable overlap between dependency and indigent disability; and (5) dependency in Winona was not due primarily to industrial unemployment but to other factors, such as an unusually large family with insufficient income to meet the important needs of all members.

In its effort to find out how problems of dependency can be controlled or reduced through rehabilitation and prevention, those conducting this study devised and tested seven different processes and precise tools as follows:

1. Defined goals, without which prevention planning cannot start nor problems be measured statistically.
2. Community-wide reporting, which seeks to get comparable facts about the social problems from any agencies with diverse professional reporting systems.
3. Family diagnosis, the key process in dealing with individual cases, under which data are structured in terms of the individual members of the family, key relationships between parents and between parents and children, and the identification of problems and factors affecting them.
4. Treatment planning, based on the diagnosis, which specifies particular services needed, what agency should provide them, and identifies responsibility for integrating and coordinating the various services.
5. Prognosis, or a prediction as to whether the family's problem status will improve, deteriorate, or not change.
6. Evaluation, after a period of at least six months, as to the actual problem status to determine the correctness of the prediction.
7. Redeploying staff, or having them concentrate on the cases which are the "best bets" for return to self-support or self-care.

This project is especially significant in its stress upon the seventh point, which leads to better utilization of skilled resources and assists in more recovery than would otherwise take place.

One feature of the casework approach is the preparation of a case record which puts in systematic form pertinent facts about a client's past and provides to the skilled interpreter an insight for current treatment. Much energy and time goes into the preparation of these case records, and this partially explains why such a social worker can only "carry" a small number of cases at any given time.

Another type of agency specializes in *group work* (13). The Boy Scouts and Girl Scouts, the Y. W. C. A. and the Y. M. C. A. are illustrations of this type. These usually have national and international connections and frequently offer a program of activities which are for the most part determined outside the community. The executive directors of such agencies are considered by social workers as part of their number, although they may not be accepted into some of the professional social work organizations if they have not had formal graduate training in social work. The essential skill of the group worker, according to Arthur Hillman (8), is to develop leaders, stimulate participation, maintain a circular response within the group, and constantly keep in mind what the group experience can mean to the individual member.

A third type of agency concerns itself with *community organization for social welfare*. Hertha Kraus makes seven important points about this area of social work:

1. Community organization in social work has developed in a democratic community as an expression of common responsibility for the sum total of all service units and their combined production on all levels of community life. It aims at an increasingly better balance between welfare needs and welfare resources . . .

2. . . . The relationship of all agencies to each other within a given community, the agency's own internal relations with its goal of service, and the area of needs served and the actual output in service are an appropriate matter of concern and action within community organization.

3. Each community service agency requires recurring study and review of its service objectives . . .

4. Social needs should be a determining factor initiating, continuing, modifying or terminating a service program . . .

5. In any classification of needs, the rank of each item will largely be dependent on the culture in which this classification has been developed, and may not necessarily fit another culture. It will also be strongly influenced by the point in time . . .

6. All social needs can be met in a variety of ways. The selection of a certain pattern of response in the form of an organized service implies an important choice . . . In selecting suitable service patterns choices must be made, among others, between providing a temporary or a more lasting solution; a preventive or a curative approach; a common provision for needs recurrent among considerable numbers of people, or an individualized response, to be produced on a case by case basis . . .

7. Community organization as a process, and every one of its instrumentalities—the public and the voluntary service agencies—are subject to economic

laws. They must recognize the principle of economy as basic to their production: the necessity to produce the greatest possible yield in return for a given investment.[16]

In order to carry out these ideas inherent in community organization for social welfare, different types of coordinating or planning councils are set up. They may bring together only those interested in children or may unite the so-called "character-building" agencies, or they may be large enough to encompass all kinds of agencies of whatever type. The Council for Social Planning or a Community Welfare Council is the latter type, since it plans for those groups which are involved in a Community Chest or a United Community Services Campaign and also seeks to draw into its committee work and deliberations representatives of the public agencies. Such Councils also have executive directors who are trained social workers with a specialization in administration rather than in case or group work.

In many communities also there is a Social Service Exchange where the names of individuals and families served in the past by various agencies are kept on file on a confidential basis. Thus when a client approaches an agency for the first time it can find out from this Exchange what other agencies have had dealings with this client. Further coordination is worked out informally by social workers at their professional meetings, since these are often the only opportunities they have to see each other on an unhurried basis.

The components of the social welfare system need not be viewed only in terms of case work, group work, and community organization. A division is frequently made between public and private agencies. The public agency is tax supported and thus restricted as to how its money can be spent; the private agencies theoretically have more flexibility over what they do with their money, but if their funds are raised in a joint community campaign, the finance committee of the campaign organization may have much to say about how budgeted items may or may not be spent. Furthermore, the board members of a private agency may have quite fixed ideas as to how the program should operate, and obstruct any deviation from past procedures. One characteristic feature of the public agency is the basic insecurity many social workers feel in their jobs unless a thoroughgoing system of civil service is in effect. It is a great temptation for a new state administration to try to use the child welfare and parole officer positions as rewards for those to whom they are indebted. The spoils system in politics, therefore, menaces the development of a highly competent and experienced personnel in

[16] Hertha Kraus, "Community Organization in Social Work: A Note on Choices and Steps," *Social Forces*, XXVII (October, 1948), 54–56.

public agencies, particularly when the general public assumes that anyone of good intent and a pleasing personality "can do social work" without realizing the complex nature of the task and the amount of training needed for successfully carrying it through.

In concluding this discussion of the components, it is well to remember that welfare activities are becoming more and more bureaucratized. As Gist and Halbert point out, "A bureaucracy organized as a behavior system of statuses, roles and authority is commonly segmentalized into bureaus, departments, agencies, or divisions of one kind or another, depending on the size and functions of a particular organization . . . If the central feature of bureaucracy is formal organization and a hierarchy of authority and status, within this framework, there is an informal organization in which relationships between personnel tend to be intimate . . ."[17] And then these authors have this to say about welfare bureaucracies:

Public welfare bureaucracies in the United States are rather tightly structured, with a complex hierarchy of functionaries in which the chain of administrative command stretches from the local organization to the state or national level in a gigantic social security system. Private welfare bureaucratic organizations tend to be loosely structured, at least as far as inter-organizational relationships are concerned, many of them being established on the federated principle.[18]

Social Processes at Work within the Welfare System. Once a person has delineated the pattern of the welfare subsystem, he can then observe how the social processes flow within that pattern. In other words, he can apply the type of analysis described in Chapter 8, identifying the cases of cooperation, competition, conflict, or accommodation. He does this not by listening to the reports of the agency executives who may not be entirely objective about their own agency, but by finding out how members of welfare groups interested in a common problem behave toward those in other groups when dealing with that problem.

Where the community has a Social Planning or Welfare Council or a Community Chest agency, or any body made up of representatives in the welfare field, a study of the accomplishments of such a body reveals much about the flow of these processes. How is action initiated? Who rallies to the cause? How is coordination achieved? What representatives (or groups) oppose or lose interest, and for what reasons? A series of questions designed to describe the playing of specific roles shows that the welfare work in any community is

[17] Noel P. Gist and L. A. Halbert, *Urban Society* (4th ed.; New York: The Thomas Crowell Co., 1956), p. 368.
[18] *Ibid.*, p. 377.

not merely a structural setup demanding money simply to keep itself standing still; it is a dynamic field of activity in which individuals, often as representatives of some recognized group, behave toward each other in ways which have frequently become traditional and even predictable.

No one is omniscient enough, even if predisposed to do so, to trace all of the behavior connected with welfare in any one community, since it may range all the way from a neighbor taking care of a sick person next door to a caseworker of the Family Service Society providing enough fuel to tide a family over until the sick breadwinner is able to get back on a job. But if a person uses the types of processes ordinarily treated by the sociologist, he will have a simple scheme for classifying the kinds of behavior that are observed. And when this has been done, he can take an over-all view of the community and reach some judgment as to the degree to which welfare activities are efficient or inefficient as gauged either by the professional standards of welfare workers themselves or by the expectations of the majority of people in the local community.

Cooperation. Cooperation implies that those involved in the interaction have common goals and the willingness to subordinate individual or narrow group interests for the achievement of a purpose or program greater than themselves. In classifying the instances of cooperation, one might use a two-fold scheme: (1) those that seek to avoid duplication and (2) those that combine action in a joint undertaking.

There are many ways in which duplication of effort is avoided. If, for instance, civic groups or church organizations are interested in distributing baskets to the poor at Christmas time, they usually check with the social workers about cases of genuine need and indicate the ones for which they will assume responsibility. Likewise, as already indicated, social workers cooperate in maintaining a social service exchange where the names of all clients are confidentially filed and services reported. This avoids the possibility that two or more agencies may unknowingly be giving help to an indigent family at the same time. Duplication, however, may exist not only with respect to clients or recipients of welfare, since there may be serious duplication of services. Through cooperative discussion, a mutually acceptable division of labor may be worked out, and the community provided with a wider range of welfare activities.

Sometimes community events concerned with welfare programs are scheduled on the same day or too closely together; willingness on the part of the interested groups to space the events at more appropriate times is an example of cooperation. An even more pressing need is that of timing fund campaigns so as not to overlap with those of other welfare groups, since a community can absorb just so many such drives before it is ready to react unfavorably to any and all drives.

Somewhat related to the matter of duplication is the practice of referral of a client from one social work agency to another. This calls for cooperation between the two agencies, since the agency contacted first may not only pass on to the client the necessary information about the second agency but may also send the second agency whatever information it may have collected in its prior dealing with the client. By tone of voice or actual statement the representative of the first agency sets up in the client an expectation of favorable or unfavorable treatment which affects the success with which the second agency can treat the case.

Many instances of cooperation, however, do not relate primarily to the avoiding of duplication but rather to combined action in settling some pressing welfare problem. If juvenile delinquency is a major community concern, no one agency can claim to have all of the answers, nor can any one agency be given the blame. What is called for is an attack on the problem by all agencies having any conceivable contribution to make. Those best equipped to deal with some of the more important aspects of the problem may be given greater responsibility; yet all have some stake. Some communities rely almost automatically upon joint action by groups interested in a social problem; in other communities, each organization continues to go its own way with little effort being made to join forces with other groups concerned with the problem.

Cooperation of this sort need not involve many groups, however. For a program dealing with a deeply rooted problem involving large numbers of people, the multiple approach is usually applied. Nevertheless, there are in every community innumerable examples of cooperation between two or three groups. This is not spectacular in nature or very broad in scope but does add greatly to the quality of community living. For example, the Boy Scouts may collect broken toys from the better residential districts, and the city firemen repair these toys for later distribution by one or more social work agencies to the poorer children of the community. The Travelers' Aid Society may find two young people at the railway station who need shelter but lack funds; the Salvation Army may agree to house them, and the Travelers' Aid Society help them move on to their destination the following day. Such instances could be multiplied hundreds of times, indicating that there is much teamwork in the welfare field.

Competition. Not all welfare groups cooperate all of the time. They are frequently forced by the community situation to compete. This competition may center about four organizational activities: (1) financing, (2) recruiting board members, (3) obtaining clients, and (4) publicity.

1. Financing. Private agencies who are associated in a Community Services organization must justify their budgets and their expenditures before the finance committee of such an over-all group. In order to get additional funds for the following year, the Boy Scouts may have to try to convince the members of this committee that they deserve a greater increase than the Y. M. C. A., although the norms do not permit them publicly to comment adversely upon another welfare organization. A day nursery may try to show that its needs are greater than those of a community-supported baby milk fund. Simply because of the financial mechanism that is set up for these privately supported agencies, each of them must often take a stand against the rest in order to persuade a committee to support its requests. Furthermore, the executives who are most successful in obtaining funds for their agencies often spend much time in keeping the finance committee well informed about the work of the agency, so that when budget time does come the selling job is already half completed.

Public agencies, however, have their problems too. They must get appropriations from local fiscal courts or other local governmental agencies. For instance, if a reduction in the total welfare budget is to be made, should the greatest amount be taken from the local public child welfare agency (such as Children's Bureau), or should it be taken from the local recreation department? In which agency is money being spent most efficiently? Which is serving a greater community need? The mere asking of such questions makes the agencies involved realize that they are in a competitive position even though their programs have nothing in common and may touch entirely different groups of participants.

There are other agencies, such as the Red Cross, which do not affiliate with local community chests and which are not connected with local governmental budgets. They conduct individual drives and are in competition with all other welfare units in their search for contributions. Strategy and tactics of fund-raising campaigns are planned as carefully as those of an army going into battle, and diversionary moves by competitive agencies must be considered as possibilities with which to deal. Many rumors are set in motion in some communities about the unwise use of funds by a particular group, and competing agencies probably do not go out of their way to stop and contradict these rumors.

Thus, the very fact that welfare agencies have to get all of their funds—whether private contributions or appropriations from taxes— from the same community, they are of necessity placed in competition with each other. The greater the difficulty in raising quotas, the greater the competition is apt to be.

2. Recruiting board members. Agencies are also in competition for status and prestige. With private groups, in particular, the social standing of voluntary board members has something to do with the way the agency is viewed by many of the substantial donors of the community. It often happens that some community residents, who embody or symbolize many of the highest values, are asked to serve on three, four, or more boards. Such individuals frequently have to make a choice in order to restrict their activities, thus favoring one or two groups above the others.

Even public agencies operate within the general framework of public commissions on which respected members of the community serve without pay. The individual abilities of these members, as well as their community standing, have much to do with the general approbation given by the community, since they, rather than the agency executive, make official interpretations of policy to the community. The persons most sought after are apt to be involved in other things; even so agencies continue to compete for their services. The same holds true for leaders of fund-raising drives; the choice of one man may be a guarantee of success, while the choice of another may mean that the undertaking is handicapped from the beginning. Most of the leaders of the welfare groups are not always conscious of the existence of this type of competition, but their board members frequently are and tend to maintain a self-perpetuating board which comes to be viewed as a "clique" identified with that particular agency. This leads then to competition between these "cliques," with one seeking to make a given welfare activity more fashionable in the community than that endorsed by a rival "clique." Thus it is that the drama of community life unfolds.

3. Clients. It would at first seem strange that agencies set up to serve the needy would actually compete for clients. In order to justify budget requests, agency executives also have to show heavy case loads. This means more clients, even at the expense of competing with other groups also interested in the same clients. In the case of the character-building agencies, it may mean competition for the support of people to use their facilities or to join their youth groups. Numbers and statistics, like primitive magic, still cast a

charm over many uncritical people who seek to evaluate the accomplishments of any agency. More clients mean high statistics. Such competition is fortunately much less common than the other types, but it must be recognized as intrinsic within the welfare system of most communities.

4. Publicity. A fourth evidence of competition is that for space in the newspapers and time on radio and television. That agency which can tell its story throughout the year in carefully prepared news accounts or dramatic presentations over the air is apt to win the race for funds and board members with much greater ease. Some types of agencies are in a much better competitive position than others, since their activities lend themselves to a warm, human-interest appeal. Others deal with individuals who have made news by some personal misfortune or by some notorious action; agencies to which they are referred are possibly publicized and thereby indirectly thanked for assuming the burden of this problem case in behalf of the community.

Studies continue to show, however, that most social welfare agencies do a very poor job of interpretation, and this is in part due to the fact that the system of welfare itself is in a disadvantaged position when trying to compete with other systems for the attention of mass media.

Conflict. Social agencies are human instruments like any other organization and reflect in their behavior the personality or other differences that grow up between their functionaries. In almost every community with diversified social agencies one can find instances of conflict between some of these agencies. It may originate in friction between the boards of these agencies and the refusal of one to accede, for what it considers good reasons, to the request of the other board. The conflict may grow out of personality differences between the respective directors, who may have a low opinion of the professional competence of the members of another board or who may feel that some wrong has never been righted. The reasons for conflict are numerous, and the official explanation is not necessarily the real reason. Anyone who wishes to work intelligently within the social welfare system of the community needs to know where such strains and stresses exist in order to avoid being drawn into a partisan fight which would seriously affect the program in which one is interested.

Accommodation. But conflict does get resolved. The passage of time often dims the dispute, or the good graces of some interceding third party may be secured. In any case, those who have been involved in conflict work out a modus vivendi without necessarily yielding in principle. As a result, the clients receive better service, and the community is not plagued by a division which carries over into nonwelfare activities as well. Just how accommodation comes about will depend upon the organization of the welfare system and the hierarchy of statuses which it possesses as well as upon the personality of those who fill some of the key statuses. Too few social workers, who spend hours trying to figure out the complex interpersonal relationships of their clients, ever take time to see the network of social relationships in which they are involved and how strains can be eased through the accommodative process.

The Social Control of Philanthropy. The discussion of the welfare system thus far has implied that its control is in the hands of the professional staffs and the agency boards of directors. There is also a community dimension that must not be overlooked. Aileen D. Ross in describing the city-wide campaigns of Wellsville, an eastern Canadian city, shows how the most influential people of the community exercise control over the welfare activities in much the same way as the inner core of doctors guides the fortunes of the individuals in the system of public health and medical care. Anyone interested in the mechanics of control and in the statements of those interviewed should refer to Ross's original article, which concludes as follows:

The controls supporting philanthropy in Wellsville now form a well-established system. This means that, although powerful positive sanctions now induce people to participate in philanthropy, there are also corresponding devices for resisting them when they are resented. Some of the controls of philanthropy are almost universally accepted. Indeed, little conscious thought has been given by most interviewees as to why they actually *did* participate in philanthropic activity.

In Wellsville members of the inner circle may decide the success of a campaign by sponsoring it or withholding sponsorship from it. This is equivalent to saying that they can decide which campaigns shall be held and for what objective. They can control the success of a campaign through the size of their own or company donations of money. They can control the personnel of any campaign through sponsoring individual participants or withholding sponsorship from them. They can control the amount of money raised in any campaign through granting or withholding permission to canvass employees in any corporation which they direct. And yet their total position was never clearly stated or recognized by those participating in leading positions in the different city-wide campaigns, nor were the implications of this control clear to the majority of them.[19]

    [19] Aileen D. Ross, "The Social Control of Philanthropy," *American Journal of Sociology*, LVIII (March, 1953), 460.

INTERACTION AMONG COMMUNITY SYSTEMS

From what has been said, it should be obvious that there is close interaction between the health and welfare systems. For example, in one southern community the board of the Florence Crittenton Home for unmarried mothers was confronted with an acute problem when the hospital where the babies were delivered found it necessary to double its fees—a case of a health institution interacting with a welfare agency. Social workers, too, are trained to call upon the assistance of physicians, psychiatrists, and psychologists when such help is needed; they also have money to distribute to clients for the purchase of medical and dental care, frequently designating to which doctors or to what clinic the clients are to go.

But other community systems are closely tied in with these two. The economy serves both to create and to help solve problems of temporary dependency as its employment cycle goes up or down throughout a given year or over a five- or six-year period. As was pointed out in the description of Wellsville, business interests have much to say about the success or failure of health or welfare appeals in that Canadian city.

Educational institutions not only make use of physicians and nurses, but increasingly many of them are sending problem children to guidance clinics or are actually employing social workers as part of the school system. The truant officer's job is more closely allied with social work than with the job of the policeman.

Religious groups continue to be the inspiration behind much of the idealism which permeates humanitarian appeals in both health and welfare. As the functions have become more specialized, the church has been less actively involved; but through its constituent groups and individual members, it provides the emotional dynamic that keeps many helpful programs going from year to year. From the other standpoint, social work helps religious leaders get a clearer understanding of how the church may better serve in a welfare capacity and how the minister himself can do more effective counseling.

And, finally, government is actively involved in the public programs of health and welfare. Those connected with government usually seem most resistant to changing concepts of welfare, although a healthy skepticism may be of value to the community at large. Nevertheless, the failure of government officials to support modern approaches to rehabilitation and prevention proves a handicap in the long run, since many studies have shown that in welfare, as elsewhere, "an ounce of prevention is worth a pound of cure."

REFERENCES AND SUGGESTED READINGS

1. ANDERSON, ODIN W., and FELDMAN, JACOB J. *Family Medical Costs and Voluntary Health Insurance: A Nationwide Survey.* New York: McGraw-Hill Book Co., Inc., 1956.

2. *The Annals,* CCLXXIII (January, 1951), "Medical Care for Americans." Entire issue.

3. FREEMAN, HOWARD E., and REEDER, LEO G. "Medical Sociology—A Review of the Literature," *American Sociological Review,* XXII (February, 1957), 73–81.

4. FORD, THOMAS R., and STEPHENSON, DIANE D. *Institutional Nurses: Roles, Relationships, and Attitudes in Three Alabama Hospitals.* University: University of Alabama Press, 1954.

5. GALLOWAY, ROBERT E., and KAUFMAN, HAROLD F. "Use of Hospitals in Four Mississippi Counties," *Mississippi Agricultural Bulletin,* CLXXIV (1952), entire issue.

6. HALL, OSWALD. "The Stages of a Medical Career," *American Journal of Sociology,* LIII (March, 1948), 327–36.

7. ———. "Types of Medical Careers," *American Journal of Sociology,* LV (November, 1949), 243–53.

8. HILLMAN, ARTHUR. *Community Organization and Planning.* New York: The Macmillan Co., 1950.

9. HUNTER, FLOYD; SCHAFFER, RUTH CONNOR; and SHEPS, CECIL G. *Community Organization: Action and Inaction.* Chapel Hill: The University of North Carolina Press, 1956.

10. *Journal of Social Issues,* "Socio-Cultural Approaches to Medical Care," VIII (October, 1952), entire issue.

11. KIMBALL, SOLON T., and PEARSALL, MARION. *The Talladega Story: A Study in Community Process.* University, Ala.: University of Alabama Press, 1954.

12. LEE, ALFRED McCLUNG. "The Social Dynamics of the Physician's Status," *Psychiatry,* VII (November, 1944), 371–77.

13. McMILLEN, WAYNE. *Community Organization for Social Welfare.* Chicago: University of Chicago Press, 1945, pp. 95–99.

14. MELINKOFF, OLIVE. "Occupational Attitudes of the Intern," *Sociology and Social Research,* XXVI (May, 1945), pp. 450–59.

15. MILLER, PAUL A. *Community Health Action.* East Lansing: Michigan State College Press, 1953.

16. PAGE, HARRY O. "Progress Toward Control and Prevention of Dependency," *Public Welfare* (October, 1956).

17. PARSONS, TALCOTT. *The Social System.* Chicago: Free Press, 1951. See Chapter X, "Social Structure and Dynamic Process: The Case of Modern Medical Practice."

18. PAUL, BENJAMIN D. (ed.). *Health, Culture and Community.* New York: Russell Sage Foundation, 1955.

19. ROSS, MURRAY C. *Community Organization: Theory and Principles.* New York: Harper & Brothers, 1955.

20. STANTON, ALFRED H., and SCHWARTZ, MORRIS S. "Medical Opinion and the Social Context in the Mental Hospital," *Psychiatry,* XII (August, 1949), 243–49.

21. STRAUS, ROBERT. "The Nature and Status of Medical Sociology," *American Sociological Review,* XXII (April, 1957), 200–4.

22. THORNER, ISIDOR. "Nursing: The Functional Significance of an Institutional Pattern," *American Sociological Review,* XX (October, 1955), 531–38.

23. TRUSSELL, RAY E.; ELINSON, JACK; and LEVIN, MORTON L. "Comparison of Various Methods of Estimating the Prevalence of Chronic Disease in a Community," *American Journal of Public Health,* XLVI (February, 1956), 173–82.

24. WILSON, ROBERT N. "Teamwork in the Operating Room," *Human Organization,* XII (Winter, 1954), 9–14.

25. YOUNG, KIMBALL. "Social Psychology and Social Casework," *American Sociological Review,* XVI (February, 1951), 54–61.

Chapter 17

RECREATION

As the work week of most Americans has grown shorter, even promising to decrease to less than forty hours for many people, new leisure-time activities have come into being and new recreational services have been provided. *Leisure* has been defined as the time when the individual is not sleeping, eating, or working, although it is recognized that children and young people while attending school are working and not at leisure (17). *Recreation* is the way people spend their leisure time. Those professionally engaged in working with recreational groups often hyphenate the word *re-creation* and make it apply to what they and the community generally might describe as "constructive uses" of leisure, giving it the idea of creativity, refreshment, and renewal of energy for the workaday world.

RECREATION: A SERIES OF SUBSYSTEMS

When a person begins to watch how the people in a given community spend their leisure time, he is greatly impressed by the number of activities pursued. Many people simply like to sit in some comfortable spot and watch the world pass by; others chase a ball on a tennis court or more sedately follow the meanderings of a golf ball; some knit, others build model airplanes, read pulp magazines, hike, fish, or go for a drive. Obviously no purpose would be served here in working out a complete classification of recreational activities; what is more useful is a discussion of the chief recreational subsystems through which the more formalized leisure-time activities are made available and promoted. Such a discussion involves the commercial subsystem, the public subsystem provided under government auspices, and the voluntary associational subsystem.

An analysis of these subsystems will make it quite clear that in most American communities there is no major recreational system in the sense that we can speak of an education, health, or economic system. Recreation is still much too widely split into segments attached to the economy, the government, and the family to be an integrated operating component. This state of affairs may be what most Americans want, for nothing would be as repugnant as a community Commissar of Recreation who tried, through the bureaucracy at his command to guide each individual into the type of leisure-time activity the Commissar and his associates thought most beneficial. The right to "waste" time is as inalienable as the right to "spend" time, although the traditional American value system much more clearly supports the latter.

Therefore, the field of recreation in most communities must be thought of as an agglomeration rather than a social system. For one thing, as pointed out above, it is not differentiated sufficiently from other existing systems to give it an independence of its own; secondly, there are no basic functions which accrue to it alone, even though those who work professionally in the field are developing a philosophy of recreation and are setting down objectives for recreation. These, however, are not widely accepted as socially significant by the majority of members in the average community. These same individuals have answers ready if one asks them why they go to church, to school, or to work. But the community as a whole has not supplied any generally accepted answer to the question, "Why are you going to play? going for a drive? going to see a movie?" The response one would most likely receive would be, "Because I want to." Recreation, therefore, depends upon an individual rather than an institutionalized explanation.

In the third place, there is no established hierarchy of statuses connected with recreation which would correspond to those in most of the other major community systems. Those connected with commercial recreation have little or no connection with those in public recreation, and vice versa. Nor is it yet clear whether recreation as it does develop in complexity and perhaps in some degree of institutionalization will be an independent system or one largely in the social welfare field. Recreational leaders, especially those who stress sports and physical education, do not think of themselves primarily as social workers; but those who guide over-all programs of activities for numerous people may ally themselves with the group workers in the social welfare field.

This point of developing special functionaries is important for the creation and maintenance of any major community system. They become the paid watchdogs of that system, as has been previously pointed out; they do the planning for it and seek to expand the sphere of its influence. Just what the effect will be of a large number of professionally trained recreational leaders upon a given community depends upon the auspices under which they work, and the reasons given to the public for supporting their efforts, whether under private or public funds. Many universities are training people to be professional recreational leaders who, upon graduation, go out to a large assortment of jobs: to work in public recreation departments, to supervise recreation in an industrial concern, to serve as supervisors of commercial recreation at resort hotels or similar places where people have much leisure time at their disposal, or to serve as administrators who, through a community-wide recreational council, try to bring about some coordination among the multitudinous leisure-time activities in a community. Whether or not such training will give such professional people, identified with various kinds of enterprises, enough of a common basis to enable them to function as a new cadre of experts for an emerging community system of recreation remains to be seen. The general tendency may well be that each will become more closely identified with the enterprise employing him than with the general field of recreation as such. This is in contrast to the experience of social work where a professional consciousness has been drilled into the social worker to the point that he feels a major commitment to his profession, a fact that explains the sensitiveness and some of the problems encountered in the welfare field.

Therefore, rather than to try to delineate a major community recreation system, it will suffice to describe the three major kinds of recreational subsystems found in the community. No better introduction can be found than that worked out by Meyer and Brightbill, as quoted below.

COMPARISON AND CONTRAST STUDY OF PUBLIC, PRIVATE AND
COMMERCIAL RECREATION[1]

Philosophy of Recreation

Public   Enrichment of the life of the total community by providing opportunities for the worthy use of leisure time. Non-profit in nature.

Private   Enrichment of the life of participating members by offering opportunities for worthy use of leisure time, frequently with emphasis on the group and the individual. Non-profit in nature.

[1] Harold D. Meyer, and Charles K. Brightbill, *Community Recreation: A Guide to Its Organization*, 2nd Ed., pp. 308–10. Copyright 1948, 1956, by Prentice-Hall, Inc., Englewood Cliffs, N.J.

Commercial   Attempt to satisfy public demands in an effort to produce
               profit. Dollars from, not for, recreation.

Objectives of Recreation

Public   To provide leisure-time opportunities which contribute to the
               social, physical, educational, cultural and general well-being
               of the community and its people.

Private   Similar to public, but limited by membership, race religion,
               age, etc. To provide opportunities for close group association
               with emphasis on citizenship, behavior and life philosophy
               values. To provide activities that appeal to members.

Commercial   To provide activities or programs which will appeal to cus-
               tomers. To meet competition. To net profit.

Administrative Organization

Public   Government agencies (federal, state and local).

Private   Boy Scouts, Settlements, Camp Fire Girls, "Y" Organizations,
               Union Groups, Home, Church, industry, private schools, clubs.

Commercial   Corporations, syndicates, partnerships, private ownerships.
               Examples: motion pictures, resorts, amusement parks, bowling
               alleys, skating rinks, etc.

Finance

Public   By taxes, gifts, grants, trust funds, small charges and fees to
               defray cost.

Private   By gifts, grants, endowments, donations, drives and member-
               ship fees.

Commercial   By the owner or promoters.
               By the user: admission and charges.

Facilities

Public   School facilities, swimming areas, community buildings, parks
               (national, state, local), athletic fields, armories, playgrounds,
               playfields, stadiums, camps, beaches, museums, zoos, etc.

Private   Settlement houses, churches, play areas, clubs, camps, etc.

Commercial   Theaters, bowling, dancing, taverns and night clubs, lounges,
               racing, beaches, pools, pool rooms, amusement parks, sta-
               diums, etc.

Leadership

Public   1. Trained to provide extensive, broad recreation programs
                  for large numbers of people.
               2. Frequently subject to Civil Service regulations.
               3. Uses volunteers as well as professionals.
               4. College training facilities meager but growing.

Private   1. Trained to provide programs on a group-work basis.
               2. Employed at discretion of managing agency.
               3. Uses volunteers as well as professionals.

4. College training facilities meager but more abundant than in public field, growing.

Commercial   1. Employed to secure greatest financial returns.
                  2. Employed by company or corporation.
                  3. Uses only paid employees.
                  4. Training facilities in colleges practically non-existent.

Program

Public   Designed to provide wide variety of activities, year round for all groups, regardless of age, sex, race, creed, social or economic status.

Private   Designed to provide programs of a specialized nature for groups and in keeping with the aims and objectives of the agency.

Commercial   Program designed to tap spending power and in compliance with state and local laws.

Membership

Public   Unlimited—open to all.

Private   Limited by organization restrictions, such as age, race, religion and sometimes personal finance.

Commercial   Limited by:
                  1. Law (local, state and federal).
                  2. Social conception regarding race and color in some places.
                  3. Personal finance.[1]

The Commercial Subsystem. There is nothing modest about the American commercial subsystem specializing in recreational activities. It literally forces its wares upon the attention of a leisured public. The theater marquees, the dine and dance emporia, the skating rinks, the sporting arenas, and the billboards promoting some national magazine, beverage, or televised program all urge the passerby to consider their claims. The commercial subsystem is profit-making; it caters to "what the public wants," as interpreted by the individual businessman risking his capital in the economic venture; since it is competitive, in that a customer has many alternative ways of using his time, each establishment seeks to develop a clientele of regular patrons who return over and over again to enjoy the activity it provides. Often it is seasonal in character, which means that enough profits have to be gained over a few months to assure success for the year; this is particularly true of enterprises having to do with tourist cabins, ski resorts, professional football, outdoor swimming pools, and hunting, to mention but a few cases in point.

But before reaching any hasty conclusions about the pervasiveness and dominance of the commercial subsystem, it is well to note the conclusions reached by Alfred C. Clarke in his study of the use of leisure in Columbus, Ohio. He writes about spectator-type activities (watching television, attending motion pictures, lectures, plays, and musical events, attending various sports events—football, baseball, basketball, boxing, wrestling, and auto racing) as follows:

Although value-judgments differ considerably regarding the desirability of certain forms of amusement, the passive-spectator nature of some leisure pursuits has probably received more widespread criticism than any other facet of contemporary leisure behavior. While few people dispute the merits of participation in physical activities, there are those who seem to consider "spectatoritis" as a new national affliction. The idea is current that most Americans spend most of their spare time in a spectator role.

Information collected in this study, however, does not substantiate this observation. The respondents were asked to indicate the spare-time activities taking up most of their leisure time . . . Most of them devoted most of their leisure time to non-spectator activities . . . These findings appear to cast serious doubts on the validity of current conceptions concerning the allegedly ominous portions of time consumed by such activities.[2]

Of course, one study does not refute the general impression abroad in America about "spectatoritis," any more than one swallow makes a summer, but it certainly does suggest the use of caution in any glib generalizations one might be prone to make when studying the large amounts of money spent by the American public in spectator activities.

Clarke also has some important observations to make about commercialized leisure, or those activities involving the payment of a fee, such as attending plays or motion pictures, playing pool or billiards, spending time in a cafe or tavern, attending a night club, dancing, or attending sports events. In using this category, which includes many of the spectator-type activities just discussed, the investigator is looking at recreation from the commercial-fee angle, rather than from the active-passive participation of the individual. Clarke writes:

Another criticism frequently leveled at the American leisure pattern is an alleged dominance of commercialized amusements. Hollywood movies, night clubs and dance halls are sometimes defined as threatening the "basic values of the society." However, the empirical basis for this observation seems to be indeed limited. The surprisingly small proportion of respondents for whom commercial types of recreation occupied most of their leisure hours . . . (Indicates that) even though commercialized recreation has become one of the na-

2 Alfred C. Clarke, "The Use of Leisure and Its Relation to Levels of Occupational Prestige," *American Sociological Review,* XXI (June, 1956), 304–5.

tion's largest business enterprises, it still does not occupy a large share of the leisure time of the adult population.[3]

Although easy to do, it would perhaps be less profitable to multiply the generalizations about the commercial subsystem than to look at one of its specific aspects in some detail. The one selected for treatment is that of popular music and its related activities.

Popular music. The writing, publication, distribution, and performance of popular music in the United States is a commercial undertaking. Singers are judged according to how many of their records have topped the million mark in sales; top hit tunes are selected on the basis of sales of sheet music or dimes dropped into jukeboxes. Few activities could be more crassly commercial; yet young people in particular are able to identify themselves with a particular song which "sends them" and move to a realm of romance and idealization which is completely without a mercenary taint.

Such songs provide the dialogue of courtship, a phenomenon studied by Donald Horton, who analyzed 235 different lyrics published in June, 1955, in four periodicals devoted to song lyrics. In the following table (Table 9) he not only sets up the stages in the drama of courtship from the Prologue through Act IV, but has shown the distribution of the song lyrics according to these stages.

In commenting on the functions of the song language, Horton points out that the dialogue frequently reflects discordances in the relative positions of the lovers in the "career" of love, which is to be expected in a complex and difficult relationship. "Not only are those involved developing at different rates and often making conflicting demands upon each other, but their mutual adjustment is also subject to environmental difficulties and pressures. However stereotyped and sometimes ludicrous the song may be, it is functionally adapted to this phase of adolescent experience."[4] He also points out that in a society where young people express their love for each other with great difficulty and embarrassment, some "conventional, public, impersonal love poetry may be a useful—indeed, a necessary—alternative. It is not essential that such a language be used in direct discourse, for if two people listen together to the words sung by someone else, they may understand them as a vicarious conversation. By the merest gestures it can be made clear that one is identified with the speaker, and the other with the one addressed. This is undoubtedly one of the chief functions of the

[3] *Ibid.*, p. 305.
[4] Donald Horton, "The Dialogue of Courtship in Popular Songs," *American Journal of Sociology*, LXII (May, 1957), 577.

TABLE 9

DISTRIBUTION OF SONG LYRICS BY CONTENT

	Number	Per cent
Prologue: Wishing and Dreaming	9	3.8
Act I: Courtship	76	32.3
Scene 1 (direct approach)	6	2.6
Scene 2 (sentimental appeal)	13	5.5
Scene 3 (desperation)	21	8.9
Scene 4 (questions and promises)	23	9.8
Scene 5 (impatience and surrender)	13	5.5
Act II: The Honeymoon	19	8.1
Act III: The Downward Course of Love	34	14.5
Scene 1 (temporary separation)	5	2.2
Scene 2 (hostile forces)	11	4.7
Scene 3 (threat of leaving)	9	3.8
Scene 4 (final parting)	9	3.8
Act IV: All Alone	58	24.7
Scene 1 (pleading)	25	10.6
Scene 2 (hopeless love)	29	12.4
Scene 3 (new beginning)	4	1.7
Total love songs in conversational mode	196	83.4
Narrative and descriptive ballads on love themes ...	9	3.8
Religious songs	6	2.6
Other ballads	8	3.4
Comic songs	4	1.7
Dance songs	6	2.5
Tune songs	3	1.3
Miscellaneous	3	1.3
Total other songs	39	16.6
Total all types	235	100.0

Source: Donald Horton, "The Dialogue of Courtship in Popular Songs," *American Journal of Sociology*, LXII (May, 1957), 575.

professional singer, whose audience of lovers finds in him their mutual messenger."[5]

This study of the dialogue of courtship in popular songs also makes clear how a youngster, progressing in age and experience, moves through successive stages of the drama outlined in Table 9, "finding that in each new situation the dialogue once practiced in play now can be said in earnest. At the same time, the songs appropriate to the stages already passed will have acquired the

[5] *Ibid.*, p. 577.

private meanings of a personal history. When the cycle has been completed, the whole of this symbolic universe will have been reinterpreted, its meaning "reduced" from an abstract, conventional possibility to a concrete, completed personal experience."[6] Horton concludes:

. . . The working-out of a socially valid and personally satisfactory conception of himself and his role in relation to the opposite sex is one of his most urgent and difficult tasks, at least in contemporary America, where so much of the responsibility for this phase of development is left to the young people themselves, aided by their cynical and somewhat predatory allies of the mass media. If television, motion pictures and popular literature demonstrate and name the roles he may properly assume, the popular songs provide a language appropriate to such an identity.[7]

But such a study pertains to American culture as a whole, although in each community young people are affected by the national song-writing industry. There are some neighborhood and community differences, however, when it comes to preferences for particular song hits and disk jockeys. This was borne out in an investigation by John Johnstone and Elihu Katz of teen-age girls who were members of eight Hi-Y clubs in two neighborhoods of South Side Chicago. Each neighborhood represented a different "culture area," and the girls from the two areas made a different response when asked to fill in the last word of the following verse:

> You were there in my dreamworld,
> In the dreams which I had
> Last night when I saw you,
> When you made me so . . .[8]

The 111 individuals who responded wrote in one of five responses: "glad" (by 57), "sad" (by 24), "mad" (by 15), "blue" (by 10) and "happy" (by 5). When the neighborhoods were compared, a large majority of the Hyde Park girls responded with "sad" or "mad," while the majority of South Shore girls said "glad." The reasons for this ecological distribution are not altogether clear. Another fact emerging from the study was the greater likelihood that highly popular girls will conform more closely than the less popular to the prevailing neighborhood norms in popular music. There is also some evidence that small groups of friends may play an important role in the development of tastes and preferences for particular songs and disk jockeys.

---

[6] *Ibid.*, p. 577.

[7] *Ibid.*, p. 578.

[8] John Johnstone and Elihu Katz, "Youth and Popular Music: A Study in the Sociology of Taste," *American Journal of Sociology*, LXII (May, 1957), 566.

But the segment of the commercial subsystem represented by popular music consists of more than the song writers and the young people who are the ultimate consumers. A key status is held by the professional dance musician, whose attitudes and way of life were studied by Howard S. Becker. He points out some characteristics of this occupation:

. . . Musicians feel that the only music worth playing is what they call "jazz," a term which can be defined only as that music which is produced without reference to the demands of outsiders. Yet they must endure unceasing interference with their playing by employer and audience. The most distressing problem in the career of the average musician is the necessity of choosing between conventional success and his "artistic" standards. In order to achieve success, he finds it necessary to "go commercial," that is, to play in accord with the wishes of the nonmusicians for whom he works; in so doing he sacrifices the respect of other musicians and thus, in most cases, his self-respect. If he remains true to his standards, he is doomed to failure in the larger society . . .[9]

Musicians, who refer to outsiders as "square," feel that they "are completely different from and better than other kinds of people and, accordingly, ought not to be subject to the control of outsiders in any branch of life, particularly in their artistic activity."[10] Furthermore, the musicians tend to segregate themselves and maintain an isolation in order to avoid establishing contact with the "squares." They develop their own occupational slang, which serves to accentuate their differences from others in the society.

This highly differentiated occupation of the dance musician, then, is only one facet of the commercial subsystem which seeks to provide diversion and amusement at a price for as large a number of people as will avail themselves of it. Many other specialties might be mentioned to illustrate the complexity of the popular music–professional entertainment world which caters not only to young people, but to adults as well.

Other segments of commercial recreation have been studied in detail. The movies (14), television (8), boxing (16), and gambling (1), to mention only a few commercial activities, could each have been discussed as fully as was popular music, since each has not only its promoters who profit financially but its idols and its devotees. Each also has its own jargon, its ritualized procedures, as well as its array of publications devoted to it alone. Even gambling needs its racing forms, in states where betting on horse races is legal.

In understanding any community, therefore, it is important to know first of all what commercial recreational outlets exist, which

[9] Howard S. Becker, "The Professional Dance Musician and His Audience," *American Journal of Sociology*, LVII (September, 1951), 136.
[10] *Ibid.*, p. 138.

ones are popularly supported and by what segments of the community. Also, it is helpful to know what business interests control these outlets and what safeguards exist to keep some of them from proving disintegrative and demoralizing factors in the community. A winning team or some well-known sporting attraction often promotes an identification with the community on the part of those for whom this team or event stands as a symbol. Since the part played by commercial recreation will doubtless increase in our urban society, its impact upon individuals and groups in the community needs to be understood more fully.

The Public Recreation Subsystem. This subsystem can be most completely and quickly summarized by reference to the Meyer and Brightbill comparison quoted in the first part of this chapter. According to them, public recreation, deserving of the name, should help enrich the life of the total community and stress *worthy* use of leisure time. Its objective is to contribute to the general well-being of the community and its members, and it is administered through federal, state, and local governmental agencies. Its costs, like those of any recreational activities, must be met chiefly through taxes, small charges, and fees, although it welcomes gifts, grants, and support from trust funds. Some of the facilities commonly found under public auspices are schools, swimming areas, community buildings, parks, athletic fields, armories, playgrounds, museums, zoos—to mention only some of them. Such facilities are increasingly under the direction of people trained to provide extensive, broad recreation programs for large numbers of people. Furthermore, many of these staff members are under Civil Service regulations, although widespread use is made of volunteer workers wishing to contribute their time and skill to the service of their community. A sound program of public recreation is supposed to provide a wide variety of year-round activities for all groups, regardless of age, sex, race, creed, and social or economic status. It should be open to all.

A community program of recreation, therefore, is usually a public program. At least the county or municipal recreation board, or some other comparable body, takes the lead in trying to formulate a program of the type described above. This frequently assumes the form of a survey to find out what kinds of activities most of the people want to pursue and what types of facilities they would utilize. Any such survey reveals, however, that many of the interests specified lie outside the governmental or public sphere of activity. This, in turn, leads to an effort to involve many elements of the commercial subsystem in the comprehensive planning for recreation. Their coopera tion, particularly in the smaller communities, is almost essential if the public program is to succeed. In one small town, for example, there was an enthusiastically launched public program to promote the lighting of an athletic field so that softball teams could be organized into a league with regularly scheduled games. As the campaign got under way, it became apparent that there was some strong, although silent, opposition. Further inquiry revealed that the manager of the local movie house was threatening to withdraw his advertisement from the local newspaper if the paper continued to support the idea of a night softball league; he was making his influence felt in other ways, too, for he thought that such nighttime activity would seriously cut into attendance at his theater. He had analyzed the short-run consequences correctly. But when the leaders of the campaign told him how such a league would bring many people into the community from the outlying smaller communities, who would be involved in the league, he began to see that his business might not suffer very much if these outsiders developed an identification with his community. After considerable discussion and thought, he agreed to "go along" with the softball league idea and this decision was a sound one, for he continued to do a thriving business.

Commercial interests also need to be brought into the picture when the desired facility is too expensive to be built with taxes or revenues from public bond issues but would be likely to prove a successful business venture. Many communities find, for instance, that many attractions they would like to see never come to their city because a large enough "gate" cannot be guaranteed because of the small size of the available facility. A combination municipal auditorium–sports arena, developed and managed by public and commercial interests together, is one way such a problem is met.

Those in public recreation, however, soon learn to work as well as they can with the facilities that they have at hand. One such resource is the schools and their playgrounds, which are usually not busy when most people have most leisure time. The use of the schools is dependent upon a local arrangement whereby the Board of Education has its own recreational program. One case of such an approach is that of Milwaukee, Wisconsin, described by Jackson M. Anderson, as follows:

Perhaps the best-known example of a municipal recreation program administered by a school agency is that of Milwaukee, Wisconsin, which has long been known as the "City of Lighted Schoolhouses."

The major recreation program in this city is provided by the Department of Municipal Recreation and Adult Education of the Milwaukee Public Schools. The program is headed by an executive of extensive and varied school and recreation experience who has the rank of assistant superintendent of schools. In many instances, playgrounds and other recreation areas are acquired by the city and constructed by the Department of Public Works. When completed, however, these areas are turned over to the Department of Municipal Recreation for maintenance and operation. A supervisor with the title of general field assistant has charge of property maintenance and supervision.

Activities in the "lighted schoolhouses" include classes in many applied arts, group athletic activities, literary activities, dramatics, music and dancing and a variety of civic, social and patriotic events. The indoor centers are open to school-age children after school hours up to 6:30 P.M. and to others during the evening hours. Scout troops and similar groups of children may use the facilities during the evening hours by special permit from the principal. Highly organized sports for youth and adults are conducted on outdoor play areas during the daytime and under lights in the evening.[11]

In Milwaukee, this recreational program, although drawing its financial support from a special fund, is nevertheless integrated with the rest of the school program, creating a strong tie with the general school work and minimizing administrative conflicts between the two programs.

In Long Beach, California, a different plan is followed where there exists a joint administration by schools and other agencies under a recreation commission.

. . . Four of the nine commission members are the City Manager, the Superintendent of Schools, a member of the City Council and a member of the Board of Education. Five citizens are appointed by these four and approved by the City Council. The Supervisor of Health and Physical Education of the Long Beach public schools is also director of Public Recreation.

This coordinated plan brings the recreation resources of the school system and the municipality under central direction, thereby avoiding duplication of costs facilities, services and personnel. The significance of the coordinated plan in enabling the city to meet its increasing needs for recreation has been dramatically demonstrated within the past few years. Modern gymnasiums, swimming pools, school playgrounds, tennis courts, auditoriums and athletic fields are among the school facilities available, when not needed for school purposes, to supplement the city facilities for community recreation. Thirty-five municipal and sixty-eight school areas are now utilized for the varied program of recreational activities for people of all ages.[12]

Oakland, California, provides an example of a program which makes use of the schools under a nonschool agency, the five-member Board of Playground Directors.

This board cooperates closely with the Board of Education and, under provision of the city charter, is responsible for the operation of all recreation areas and facilities in the city parks and other municipal areas. The Recreation Department is headed by a qualified Superintendent of Recreation.

[11] Jackson M. Anderson, "Education and Recreation," *The Annals of the American Academy of Political and Social Science*, CCCII (November, 1955), 29.
[12] *Ibid.*, p. 30.

Because of the climate, the diversified program in Oakland . . . consists for the most part of outdoor activities carried on throughout the year. Thus the core of Oakland's program is its playgrounds. The school playgrounds are operated after school hours, on Saturdays and holidays and during vacation periods . . . Although sports and games make up a major part of the program, especially during the school year, many school playgrounds also provide storytelling, dramatics, folk dancing and simple crafts . . .

Recreation specialists are employed to assist the playground directors in conducting these activities . . . In each district of the city, the children and playground directors join during the summer in observing a special day of social recreation, stunts, games and refreshments.[13]

These three illustrations indicate that there is a definite trend toward wider use of schools, although the leaders of each community must work out what they consider to be the best local arrangement for administering the programs using the school facilities. These cases also show how Americans cooperate to "organize" for better recreational opportunities. Such conscious planning and joint action, in most communities, is best carried through as public programs, open to all, leaving for private groups the task of providing recreational outlets for those wishing highly specialized or exclusive programs.

The Subsystem of Private Recreation. One of the pioneering studies of the use of leisure was made by George A. Lundberg and his associates in Westchester County, New York, during the years 1932 and 1933. Although they did not consider private recreation as such, in contradistinction to public and commercial types, they did provide many interesting facts about the private organizations in which many members of this county spent their leisure time. The tasks of competing for social status were such that many participants in these organizations did not look upon the time spent there as recreation but rather as something they had to do to keep in the social swim. If one can construe a wife's task as partly that of making proper contacts so that her husband can rise in the business or professional world, then oftentimes such club activities and the entertaining involved can be viewed as her work and not as part of her leisure time. On the other hand, most of the formal organizations set up in Westchester County, which is suburban to New York City, were recreational in focus. Back in the early 1930's Lundberg found the following;

Not only are the activities and participants formally organized, but many of the organizations and organizers are further organized into leagues and associations, many of them national in scope. Thus, we find represented such organiza-

[13] *Ibid.*, p. 31.

tions as Westchester County Golf Association, Westchester County Green-
keepers Association, Westchester County Tennis Association, the Eastern Lawn
Tennis Association, Westchester County Board of Approved Basket Ball
Officials, Westchester County Baseball Officials Association, National Rifle
Association, Westchester County Whist Club, American Canoe Association,
Westchester County Horse Show Association, Westchester County Archery
Association, Westchester County Chess League, Westchester County Ping-Pong
Club, and many others. We have, however, not found any local chapters of the
National Horseshoe Pitching Association or the Order of Ex-Pipeorgan Pumpers,
although there are in the county eligible individuals for both organizations.[14]

Despite this long, although incomplete list of associations, less
than half the adult population in Westchester County belonged to
any leisure clubs whatever. And, as indicated above, many of the
officials of these clubs who worked hard at organizing, promoting,
and supervising matches of many kinds maintained that they had
no leisure at all, since the club activities occupied all of their time.

It is safe to say that in many communities there is a rather nebulous network of recreationally oriented clubs, some of which keep in
touch with what the other groups are doing; for certain purposes a
few of them may unite in an actual event. Whatever coordination
exists in this subsystem often originates in interlocking directorates,
particularly in those groups catering to a specific social layer.
Friends or even relatives may be prominent in different kinds of
leisure clubs and, through informal conversations, be aware of what
is going on in the other clubs. This communication tends to break
down, however, when some one organized activity keeps strictly to
class lines or is so highly specialized that its devotees prefer social
isolation in the conduct of that activity (such as sculpting).

But most of the private recreational pursuits are not very highly
formalized, many of them taking place in primary groups. Since so
much attention is given by the local newspapers of many communities to the activities of the hometown bridge clubs, the impression is
often created that one cannot play cards unless one is a member of
such a club, made up of acquaintances who form a secondary, rather
than a primary, group. Irving Crespi, in his survey of card-playing
in Endicott, a city in upper New York state, throws some light on
this activity. He finds that in Endicott 57 per cent of the adult
population plays cards, a figure almost the same as the national
average. He also notes that card-playing is most often an activity
carried on by primary groups rather than by groups specifically
formed for that purpose. In the quotation which follows he then delineates three types of motives that relate to card-playing.

[14] George A. Lundberg, Mirra Komarovsky, and Mary Alice McInerny, *Leisure:
A Suburban Study* (New York: Columbia University Press, 1934), p. 80.

1. Motives directly related to the game itself and to the outcome of the game; the game or the rewards of winning are what attract the player.

2. Motives related to the fact that the group affiliation needs of the individual player can be satisfied while playing cards. What the player wants in these cases is the type of group life that card-playing makes possible.

3. Motives related to the social status values that have become associated with card-playing. What the player seeks here is the social acceptance, recognition and even prestige that card-playing bestows in certain situations.[15]

Associated with the first type of motivation is the gambler who plays for the monetary reward that success brings. In Endicott only a small minority of card-players are gamblers. The great majority of players have the motives of the second type. They play because "it enables them to experience the conviviality that stems from playing a game with people with whom they want to spend their leisure time."[16] They may like the "atmosphere" of the game. Those who share the third type of motives consider card-playing a "social asset," since they have discovered that by playing cards they can participate in the activities of groups that have social status value. Such occasions arise in the case of women's card clubs, public card parties, and the gatherings of married couples in high-class status groups.

Crespi concludes his description of Endicott with this interpretation:

The prevalence of card-playing reflects not moral degeneration, but the struggle of primary groups to maintain their viability in the contemporary scene. Eager for friendliness and easy congeniality, many Americans appear to be incapable of generating such relationships without the artificial stimulation of impersonal, competitive group games.[17]

In some communities, or among some groupings of the population where card-playing is considered socially undesirable, the church often provides, through its organizations, recreational outlets which bring together people on an intimate, face-to-face basis. Where the church leaders do not frown on card-playing, it may be an activity frequently carried on at church functions in the parish house.

But games and sports, and even church suppers, are not the only private alternatives open to one who has leisure time. The movement popular since World War II known as the "do-it-yourself" movement provides constructive outlets to many people who find that they can rent the necessary machinery (such as a floor-sander), too expensive to buy, from a shop for a few hours and create some

---

[15] Irving Crespi, "The Social Significance of Card-Playing as a Leisure-Time Activity," *American Sociological Review*, XXI (December, 1956), 719.

[16] *Ibid.*, p. 720.

[17] *Ibid.*, p. 721.

spot of beauty in the home. The utter fastidiousness with which many suburbanites prune and manicure their lawns may be symptomatic of a desire to control completely a little patch of ground as an antidote to the complexities of the occupational situation where they are driven, rather than in control, and where they are a part of a process without ever seeing or understanding the creativity of the whole process. But even here the commercial world of hardware and paint, of fertilizer and lumber provides the sustaining emphasis that keeps the do-it-yourself movement alive even though the inexperienced householder moves from one imperfectly performed job to the next, all the while deriving satisfaction from having accomplished as much as he has.

Private recreation, rich in variety of its activities, strengthened by public and commercial recreational subsystems, is an important feature of American community life. Centered around the home, or enjoyed far away from the home with one's friends or relatives, occasionally formalized into a group of similar-minded enthusiasts, exclusive in its intimacy and tailored to individual taste, private recreation along with other types can serve the function of re-creating and renewing the individual for life's sterner demands.

RECREATION AND SOCIAL CLASS

Within any community it soon becomes apparent that people with different occupational orientations and different income levels develop different styles of life, which include variations in recreational pursuits. Some activities are definitely associated in the public mind with rich men, others with poor men. R. Clyde White, who made a study of Cuyahoga County, Ohio, has tried to discover the extent to which leisure-time activities are influenced by social class, age, and sex. After presenting his data and findings, he concludes:

> It is clear that the tendency to choose leisure activities on the grounds of membership in a particular social class begins in adolescence and becomes more pronounced in maturity . . . As people get older and settle into the ways of the class to which they belong, they choose leisure activities which are congenial to their class. The growing divergence between the uses of leisure by the middle class and lower classes is clear. Class differences are reflected by young people but are not fixed until maturity.[18]

Further light on this matter is gained if one moves from Cleveland, in Cuyahoga County, to Columbus, Ohio, where the previously cited study by Alfred C. Clarke was carried out. The accompanying table (Table 10), which he uses in his article, gives the relation be-

[18] Clyde R. White, "Social Class Differences in the Uses of Leisure," *American Journal of Sociology*, LXI (September, 1955), 150.

tween specific types of activities and participation by prestige level. The fact that a given activity is assigned to one prestige level does not mean that those in other levels do not enjoy or participate in that activity, but this table represents a statistical way of showing with which level the activity is most closely identified. According

TABLE 10

LEISURE ACTIVITIES BY PRESTIGE LEVEL PARTICIPATING MOST FREQUENTLY
COLUMBUS, OHIO

Activity	Prestige Level Participating Most Frequently				
	I	II	III	IV	V
	Highest				Lowest
Attending theatrical plays	X				
Attending concerts	X				
Attending special lectures	X				
Visiting a museum or art gallery	X				
Attending fraternal organizations	X				
Playing bridge	X				
Attending conventions	X				
Doing community service work	X				
Reading for pleasure	X				
Studying	X				
Entertaining at home	X				
Attending motion pictures	X				
Out-of-town weekend visiting (overnight)		X			
Attending football games		X			
Attending parties		X			
Playing golf			X		
Working on automobile				X	
Watching television					X
Playing with children					X
Fishing					X
Playing card games other than bridge and poker					X
Playing poker					X
Driving or riding in car for pleasure					X
Attending auto theater					X
Spending time in tavern					X
Spending time at zoo					X
Attending baseball games					X

Source: Alfred C. Clarke, "The Use of Leisure and Its Relation to Levels of Occupational Prestige," *American Sociological Review*, XXI (June, 1956), 304.

to Clarke, one of the most interesting findings in this table is the way in which golf "is being transformed from the exclusive pastime of a few wealthy individuals to a popular pastime for many, repre-senting diversified backgrounds in income and social status."[19]

It is of interest to note in the study of recreational pursuits and social class membership how often use is made of recreation in the

[19] Clarke, *op. cit.*, p. 304.

attempt at social mobility. Education is, of course, the major avenue, but recreation also plays its significant part. Social mobility depends upon "contacts" as much as upon skill in a sport or the ability to read Shakespeare; and these contacts, or acquaintanceships, are begun and cultivated in the congenial atmosphere of a recreational situation.

The descriptions of the three recreational subsystems—commercial, public, and associational or private—show that they have many interconnections but that they are not fully integrated into any single system. Recreation, as has already been pointed out, is a matter for individual choice and is not highly institutionalized in most American communities today.

But no matter whether it be public or private, participant or nonparticipant, recreation does serve definite functions in the overall community system. It is an important means of socialization, of incorporating people into social groups and therefore of leading them into a sense of community. Whether this sense becomes extensive enough to correspond to the whole local community will depend upon many factors, not the least of which are the operations of the community system itself.

References and Suggested Readings

1. *The Annals of the American Academy of Political and Social Science,* CCLXIX (March, 1950). Whole issue on gambling.
2. Becker, Howard S. "The Professional Dance Musician and His Audience," *American Journal of Sociology,* LVII (September, 1951), 136–44.
3. Brunner, Edmund deS. and Hallenbeck, Wilbur C., *American Society: Urban and Rural Patterns* (New York: Harper & Brothers, 1955). Chapter 20, "Providing for Recreation."
4. Clarke, Alfred C. "The Use of Leisure and Its Relation to Levels of Occupational Prestige," *American Sociological Review,* XXI (June, 1956), 301–7.
5. Denney, Reuel, and Meyersohn, Mary Lea. "A Preliminary Bibliography on Leisure," *American Journal of Sociology,* LXII (May, 1957), 602–15. An excellent source, classified by topics related to leisure.
6. Hillman, Arthur. *Community Organization and Planning.* New York: The Macmillan Co., 1950, ch. XIII, "Planning Recreation Programs."
7. Horton, Donald. "The Dialogue of Courtship in Popular Songs," *American Journal of Sociology,* LXII (May, 1957), 569–78.
8. Horton, Donald, and Strauss, Anselm, "Interaction in Audience-Participation Shows," *American Journal of Sociology,* LXII (May, 1957), 579–87.
9. Johnstone, John, and Katz, Elihu. "Youth and Popular Music: A Study in the Sociology of Taste," *American Journal of Sociology,* LXII (May, 1957), 563–68.
10. Kinneman, John A. *The Community in American Society.* New York: Appleton-Century-Crofts, Inc., 1947, ch. 15, "Recreation."
11. Lee, Rose Hum. *The City: Urbanism and Urbanization in Major World Regions.* Philadelphia: J. B. Lippincott Company, 1955, ch. 19, "Leisure-Time Activities."
12. Macdonald, Margherita; McGuire, Carson; and Havighurst, Robert J. "Leisure Activities and the Socio-economic Status of Children," *American Journal of Sociology,* LIV (May, 1949), 505–19.

13. NASH, DENNISON, JR. "The Socialization of an Artist: The American Composer," *Social Forces*, XXXV (May, 1957), 307–13.
14. POWDERMAKER, HORTENSE. *Hollywood: The Dream Factory.* Boston: Little Brown & Co., 1950.
15. TODD, ARTHUR J., *et al. The Chicago Recreation Survey*, 1937. 5 vols. Chicago: Chicago Recreation Commission, 1937–1940. See especially vol. II, a 176-page report on "Commercial Recreation" in this metropolitan community.
16. WEINBERG, S. KIRSON, and AROND, HENRY. "The Occupational Culture of the Boxer," *American Journal of Sociology*, LVII (March, 1952), 460–69.
17. WHITE, CLYDE R. "Social Class Differences in the Uses of Leisure," *American Journal of Sociology*, LXI (September, 1955), 145–50.

Chapter 18

THE COMMUNITY AS A SOCIAL SYSTEM: OPERATIONS

INTRODUCTION

In order to understand a community as a social system a person does not have to bear in mind simultaneously all of the thousands of facts about that community. Rather, he needs a conceptual scheme into which these facts can be fitted. This is somewhat like having a "social map" to consult. While concentrating on the northeastern section of an ordinary map, the investigator is aware that there is a southwest and that there are some intermediary points in between the two. Thus on a "social map" of the community anyone examining the area dealing with family-church relationships will at the same time know that this particular topic is also related to education and the economy, as well as to local government. The social map affords this awareness of the existence of the other parts not under immediate examination, but when the scope of the inquiry is broadened, these other areas become involved in an orderly way. The presentation of such a conceptual scheme, or guide to analysis, was the chief theme of Chapter 11, which centered on the setting of the community as a system as well as the components of that system. The emphasis there was largely structural in that the questions raised had to do with the parts of a community and how they were connected.

Following this presentation in Chapter 11 a number of major community systems have been described in Part Two, both in terms of the subsystems of which they are composed and in some cases, of the functions which such systems carry out in the community as a whole. It is when one begins to deal with functions that the analysis becomes dynamic in the sense of trying to observe the operations rather than the structure (4). In addition to asking, "What are the parts?" the student of the community also wants to know "how these parts fit together to make the whole system work."

The main attention in this chapter will be given to this second question, that is, to how the community operates as a system. In a sense this is simply pulling together in summary fashion many points touched upon in earlier chapters. It is important to remember that the study of the operation of a theoretical model of a community as an ideal type differs in some ways from the study of an actual community. In the first case—that of the model—one can define the characteristics of a community and say that "when I use the word 'community' I mean that such properties must be present, such components must exist, and they must be interrelated in these specific ways." Then, anything that does not fit the model can be dismissed as not being a part of the community as defined and therefore not germane to the analysis.

In the other approach—that of studying an actual community as defined by those who live there but who are relatively unconcerned with the analysis of a social system as such—one attempts to see what social order exists in that geographical space, what recurring patterns of interaction can be found, and what clusters or networks of behavior become crystallized around some central activities or interests. The level of description in this book has been more in keeping with the second approach in the hope that the statements made and illustrations used will give the reader a better idea of what to look for and how to systematize what he finds. Nevertheless, even to make this more concrete analysis one must have some kind of theoretical model in mind.

In studying the operations of the community as a social system described in this chapter, it is necessary to keep in mind the material in Chapter 11 as well as the succeeding chapters, which have each in a small way touched upon the topic of the functioning or operation of some particular major system in the community.

PROCESSES AND OPERATIONS OF THE SYSTEM

One of the best ways to begin to think in dynamic rather than static terms is to review some of the processes discussed in earlier chapters, even though this may mean turning back to these chapters and reviewing what was said there. For present purposes the ecological processes (Chapter 1) and demographic processes (Chapter 2) can be omitted, but attention should be directed to the following.

Processes descriptive of types of goals in interaction (Chapter 8):

Conflict	Competition
Accommodation	Cooperation
Assimilation	Amalgamation

Processes descriptive of social change (Chapter 9):

Regimentation	Industrialization
Mechanization	Commercialization
Urbanization	Secularization

Processes descriptive of social control (Chapter 10):

Socialization	Persuasion
Suggestion	Coercion

This list by no means exhausts all of the possibilities but summarizes those processes which proved useful in earlier chapters in the description of a general topic connected with the community.

The *processes* listed above are really descriptive terms for a series of observable acts occurring between components of the system. They sum up and classify streams of interaction looked at from various standpoints (goals, change, control) to which one can attach labels. *Operations,* on the other hand, have to do with the behavior of the whole system and describe the behavior within the system which keeps it going as a system. Urbanization, for example, is a process of change which may occur within a large social system, but it is not to be considered a fundamental operation necessary to the survival of such a system. Rather, it is a method of adaptation which goes on within the system when certain conditions are present. *Processes* are useful in various kinds of analyses, but in the working out of an over-all conceptual scheme they need to be supplemented by certain fundamental systemic *operations.* Such operations are listed and briefly characterized in Figure 24.

Recruitment of New Members. For any system to survive, new components are necessary as replacements for old ones which wear out or die out. In a biological organism, such as the human body, new cells are constantly being formed; or again, anyone owning an automobile two or three years old knows about the need for replacement of parts. These analogies should not be carried too far in their application to a social system such as the community but do at least serve as reminders that a community keeps going only through the recruitment of new members, the most obvious way being through the birth of children into the homes of the community.

A second means of recruitment is in-migration of people from other places. Where these newcomers arrive in family groups there

Operations of the Community System	Characteristics of the Operation	Where They Are Discussed More Fully (Review Chapters 7 and 8)
Recruitment of new members	Through birth and immigration	Ch. 2, 14
Communication	Face-to-face contact through transportation; flow of ideas on which individual decisions are made and public opinion formed	Ch. 4
Differentiation and status allocation	Division of labor and specialization of status-role bundles serving the community; assignment of community members to these statuses	Ch. 3
Allocation of goods and services	Production, exchange from outside, distribution, and consumption of necessary material items and nonmaterial services; special systems worked out for distribution of scarce items	Ch. 13, 15, 16
Socialization	Preparation of new members for full-scale participation in society	Ch. 10, 16, 17
Social control (allocation of power)	Mechanisms for maintaining regularity and order and for control of deviant behavior on the part of those insufficiently "socialized" or "improperly" motivated	Ch. 10, 12
Allocation of prestige	Ranking of community members prestige-wise on the basis of degree to which they embody the major values of the community; differentiation on the basis of social class (horizontally) rather than on occupational, ethnic, and other vertical divisions, though the two are usually interconnected as is this type of allocation with allocation of status, goods and services, and power	Ch. 6
Social mobility	Movement up or down the social scale from one class position to another. Usually intraclass rather than interclass shift. Important motivational factor in an "open" society which provides opportunity for mobility	Ch. 6, 9
Integration through adjustment	The establishment and maintenance of "running equilibrium" between the components, leading to social cohesion and solidarity. Done through internal accommodation and through adjustment to forces outside the system	Ch. 5, 18

FIG. 24. The operations of a community system.

is a replacement of people at all age levels. In general, however, the young adults tend to move to cities in search of work opportunities, which means that an above-average concentration of minor children and elderly people is left in rural communities.

With this replenishment of *persons* there are sufficient members available for the groups which local people consider essential, and these in turn keep the subsystems going.

It is not surprising that community leaders become alarmed when they note a total population decline for their community or watch a heavy out-migration of young people. Although they have never thought about it in social system terms, the community leaders nevertheless recognize the fact that this recruitment of new members and replacement of those leaving or dying are fundamental operations in the survival of the community.

A further problem develops when people who are physically located in a community do not participate in the statuses and roles which are a definite part of that community system. In every community, as Hiller (12) has pointed out, there are guests, or transients; those in transitional status who are temporary residents but not guests; provisional members who are under the test of acceptance or rejection by fellow residents; and permanent members with recognized statuses and roles in the community. How one moves from one of these stages of acceptance to the next is tied in with the recruitment characteristics of the community. The problem of transforming strangers, once they are recruited, into neighbors and loyal residents is obviously related to the communication patterns and the methods of socialization existing in the total community (15).

Communication. Again, if we were to use an organic analogy, solely for illustrative purposes, we could say that communication is to the social system what circulation is to the biological organism. In the case of the community, as Chapter 4 has shown, not only do people need to move about physically but ideas and information need to circulate. These ideas and this information must and do go beyond ordinary news events to include ideas about what is desirable and undesirable for the community. It is only through such interchange that people can arrive at a consensus or agreement about common action.

Communication has even more meaning in that a social system survives only as each significant component performs its particular specialty for the total system. In the social world this is not done by a unit isolating itself and following its own interests but by participating as expected in a network of relationships. This implies that the failure of any component to perform as expected disturbs the whole network. Studies show that where such failures in performance occur the underlying problem often proves to be one of communication or the inability to "read the signals" of interaction correctly. Whenever some committee chairman or some professional leader of a subsystem says, "Oh, but I didn't know we were supposed to do that" (or help out in this way), he is indicating a breakdown in communication.

Community problems therefore arise when various groups keep to themselves without developing a community-wide perspective or fail to realize that much of what they do has a bearing upon what others do. Where there is misunderstanding, it is a rule-of-thumb procedure, long recognized by successful community workers, to get the parties in dispute talking to each other. The mere establishment of communication often tends to clarify issues and lead to better understanding.

Differentiation and Status Allocation. A complex community in today's world needs to do many things which are no longer within the ability or resources of any one or even any small group of individuals. If it is to maintain itself as a properly functioning system, some mechanism must operate in the community to determine what specialties are needed and deserving of reward and then to assign or allocate sufficient members (or groups) to the carrying out of those specialties. In a planned community, such as one run by the leaders of a planned totalitarian society, all of these details are supposedly anticipated in a specific way with formal plans for officials to read and try to follow. In American communities this operation of perpetuating and adding to the wide variety of statuses occurs much more spontaneously, with the result that very few people are aware that such an operation is actually occurring in the community.

There is present in every community, of course, the differentiation of statuses related to differences in age, sex, marital condition (married, unmarried, etc.), kinship, and some occupational specialization. As society grows more complex, the communities, reflecting the larger social changes, become more highly differentiated. Not only is each person called upon to hold a larger number of statuses in his daily routine, but some of these statuses are held by a relatively few people. The result is that any individual member differs from his neighbor according to the varying repertory of statuses-roles held by each. Obviously, this differentiation heightens the difficulty of the communications operation.

But even though a community in a theoretical sense may boast of having many specialties, it is badly crippled if some of the more important specialties are not filled. The part of the operation that accompanies differentiation is status allocation, or the assignment of persons (or groups) to the statuses needing to be filled.

One community had no doctor, a status it considered necessary to its remaining a "good community." Its members got together sufficient funds for a health building, provided living quarters for the doctor in this building, and guaranteed a certain amount of practice with the result that it induced a well-trained doctor to come into that community. Here was one example of allocation. Another example is that of elections, when the allocation of people to public posts is carried out in a formal way. Though less spectacular, the informal ways of persuading people to enter different types of work are very important. Intangibles such as prestige, fringe benefits, and the direction of change in the community enter into the decision by individuals—the fundamental mechanism through which this allocation is achieved—to assume a particular position.

Groups develop specialties too. Where there are recognized community needs, available groups are sorted both formally and informally into the part they are to play. This is revealed by the tendency on the part of a community member to think of a particular group whenever he thinks of the Plug Horse Derby, or again to think of The League of Women Voters, for example, when he thinks of good government, or to think of the Shriners and the hospitals they sponsor when he thinks of crippled children. The picture is of course much more complex than this but does involve groups as well as individuals.

Allocation of Goods and Services. Not only do people have to be allocated to the whole array of statuses within a community, but the existing goods and services have to be allocated to the people in terms of the statuses they hold. Since the acquisition of goods and services in American communities is through the medium of the market place (they are paid for in dollars and cents), those who hold the highest paying positions are in the most advantageous location. There are certain minimum essentials that any community member should receive (food, clothing, shelter, education), although the quality of these essentials will vary with the economic standing of their users. How this allocation works was discussed in the description of the economy as a system in Chapter 13.

Aristotle pointed out long ago that the least stable communities were those consisting of very rich and very poor people. If the allocation of material goods in such communities is too one-sided, there are consequent disruptive social effects. Chapter 3 has already pointed out the limitations on the use of community services (hospitals, playgrounds, etc.) which derive from noneconomic factors such as racial or ethnic background but which are associated with economic discrimination as well.

Socialization. Not only must new members be recruited but they must be trained (5). In this sense, socialization—the process discussed at considerable length in Chapter 10—can also be termed a basic operation of the system. Needless to say, in times of drastic change the community system finds it much more difficult both to select the best methods of training and to agree upon goals so that the young people can be made ready for their adult responsibilities. Socialization, as used here, not only includes the inculcation of values and the recognition of what roles are to be played in keeping with given social statuses in specified situations; it also involves a technical efficiency in the carrying out of these roles. A major status each adult is supposed to hold in the community is that of breadwinner (if a man) or housewife (if a married woman), although in modern times many modifications of these statuses occur. To perform the roles tied in with such statuses the adult male must know some occupation, the housewife must know the mechanics of managing a home. Learning how to do these is a part of the operation of socialization, and a community which fails to teach these economic skills along with a value orientation, etiquette, and the rest is functioning poorly as a system.

Social Control (Allocation of Power). As the discussion of social control in Chapter 10 has shown, every individual exercises some control in the social space which he occupies (19). But the ultimate legitimate control of force is in the hands of those acting in behalf of the governmental institution. In addition, there is often another power structure, largely socioeconomic, which in the case of some communities allocates power to a relatively few individuals who are involved in the most important decisions affecting the community. There is no need to review here the basic points about social control as long as one recognizes that it describes how and to whom power is distributed and the manner in which the power is exercised, particularly with reference to deviant behavior and the introduction of new enterprises or divergent points of view into the community. Reference will again be made to decision-making in the concluding section of this chapter, where the community as a social actor is discussed.

Allocation of Prestige. Although this is most commonly tied in with the other kinds of allocation, such need not be the case. For this reason it deserves treatment as a special operation. The status allocation, mentioned as a third operation of the system, refers to all of the numerous statuses in the community, whether they carry any prestige or not. It is based on the fact that many different kinds of things have to be done, and there are certain types of positions whose occupants are supposed to do these things. From the standpoint of community welfare the status of the garbage collector is highly significant (as would be readily apparent if he or others did not perform his duties for two or three weeks), but this status has little prestige. Status allocation, therefore, is an operation by which essential positions up and down the line are filled. It is also possible in many communities for a man to be able to buy much more than his share of scarce goods and services and yet be lacking in prestige, since in those communities the possession of wealth has only a coordinate position with family background, certain personality traits, and service to the community. On the other hand, in some communities "money talks the loudest," and prestige accrues to those who have the most wealth. In the case of another kind of allocation, the possession of power is not in itself an assurance of prestige, for the community members make a distinction between the kinds of power (economic, political, social, etc.) and ascribe prestige to a considerable extent on the way power is exercised.

The social layers, or class system, of a community are correlated with allocation of prestige (22). As Chapter 6 has shown, this system is based on a number of interconnected factors which vary in importance from community to community. Nevertheless, the sorting out of people into social ranks is an operation which continues quietly but effectively.

Having prestige carries with it certain responsibility toward the community. In an aristocratic-type community, the elite develop a sense of *noblesse oblige* and think it their duty as upper class people to render service to the less fortunate, although such an approach to the problem in a democratic society is apt to be misunderstood. But the leader who enjoys the esteem of others in the community usually realizes that he does exert influence and therefore must be responsible; he also knows that to continue to hold this esteem he must play the roles expected of one in his position. This is why he goes through a round of activities which serve the community, even though as an individual he might prefer to spend time in quite different ways.

Social Mobility. Another community operation describes the movement of people from one stratum to another (14). Since it involves changes related to social class, it is frequently a combination of the various types of allocation mentioned. For example, the leaders of the community know that they will not hold their positions indefinitely; thus many of them try to select protégés who can carry on when the original leaders have retired. This movement within the community class system means that qualified persons from lower rungs can by demonstration of ability and interest rise to higher rungs. At the same time, some people in favored positions may fail to measure up and therefore suffer a mobility downward, since members of the community do not rank them as highly as formerly. Just as a community as a system needs a circulation of ideas (referred to as communication) so it needs a circulation of ability, which is often reflected in the rise of those who are qualified for higher position.

Communities vary in the avenues through which people can rise, but such channels must exist if the community is to survive for long as a social system. This is why sociologists frequently study the origins of the present leaders of any community; they want to trace the extent of social mobility and learn how upward mobility is achieved.

Integration. Werner S. Landecker makes a helpful distinction among four types of integration, each of which has a bearing upon the community as a social system.[1] First, there is a *cultural* integration, or a relationship "among traits which constitute cultural standards in the sense that they require adherence." This takes one back to the cultural factor in Figure 16, on The Setting (Chapter 11). If the values, beliefs, standards, are full of inconsistencies (not integrated) then the social system that shares that culture is beset with difficulties. To illustrate, there may be contradictions in certain standards required of everyone (that is, "universal" traits). People may be expected to be both altruistic and competitive and may have these two standards drilled into them without being shown under what circumstances they are to be one and not the other. Or again, there may be inconsistencies among the standards required of special groupings within the population ("specialties") which have societal reference, such as those shared by labor on the

---

[1] Werner S. Landecker, "Types of Integration and Their Measurement," *American Journal of Sociology,* LVI (January, 1951), 332–40. A main theme of this article, not touched upon here, is the problem of selecting indices whereby these various types of integration can be measured.

one hand and business management on the other as to the proper place of labor in the business enterprise.[2] It is clear that what is being integrated in this cultural type are the traits of culture themselves, a topic touched upon in Chapter 5 as well as in the discussion of the setting (Chapter 11). A community whose members inherit many of these unresolved contradictions in their thoughtways has difficulty in achieving community solidarity.

Although a social scientist can study the consistencies or inconsistencies existing among these cultural traits, such matters only become a part of the community system as people react to them and accept or reject them as norms of conduct. Landecker terms this second type of integration *normative,* for its central question is the extent to which conduct is in accord with the norms (2, 17). There could conceivably be genuine cultural integration but little normative integration if the people failed to abide by the norms supposedly in force. This occurs in those communities of rapidly industrializing societies where old standards no longer seem to apply, at least as they have been customarily interpreted, to the new situation. Some young people in particular are apt to reject most of the traditional traits and seek earnestly for what they would consider more modern substitutes. This normative integration under the name of "moral integration" has been intensively studied by Robert C. Angell in six American cities.[3] Angell believes that communities arrive at societal integration when their members are oriented to common values, and he thinks of moral integration as symptomatic of or a key to this societal integration. That is why he uses crime and welfare indices to gauge the correspondence between the norms and actual behavior on the part of community members. His views were set forth more fully in Chapter 14, in connection with the family, religion, and morality.

A third type of integration is *participative.*[4] As Landecker indicates "the more comprehensive the network of interpersonal com-

[2] Landecker points out that the third of Ralph Linton's type of cultural traits ("alternatives") in terms of which people have a choice and face no moral dilemma, is not as relevant to the problem of integration as are the "universals" and "specialties." See Ralph Linton, *The Study of Man* (New York: Appleton-Century-Crofts, Inc., 1936), p. 282.

[3] Robert C. Angell, "The Moral Integration of American Cities," *American Journal of Sociology,* LVII (July, 1951), Part 2.

[4] The term *participative* integration has been substituted here for Landecker's term *communicative* integration as more nearly descriptive of the type under discussion and as more suitable to the analysis of the community as a social system. After all, what is meant here is the integration of social actors (persons, groups, etc.) into the over-all system and not the integration of symbols used in communication.

munication, the smaller the number of isolated persons" and in his interpretation the degree of isolation is an important clue to breakdown in communication. Isolation can be social as well as physical. Being present with a number of other people does not necessarily imply participation or overt interaction with them. This kind of integration is central to an understanding of the community as a social system, since it deals with the degree to which people are involved actively in community life. As earlier chapters have shown, this interaction is through groups, most of whom at times take on communal characteristics in that something they do or stand for has a community-wide influence. Not only does the study of this type of integration deal with the breakdown of barriers of communication but it also involves the means by which community members are encouraged to express themselves with reference to matters of social concern. Along with this goes the process of identification, which Nelson Foote views as an important element in the understanding of motivation. As people participate, they develop a sense of belonging but at the same time derive a heightened sense of their own identity, for "identification is the process whereby individuals are effectively linked with their fellows in groups."[5]

The fourth type of integration is *functional* interdependence, with special reference to the division of labor in the community. How are the social components of a system dependent upon each other? Who exchanges functions with whom? Many who approach the study of society from the standpoint of ecology (see Figure 16) use this particular type of integration as an important tool for analysis[6] and try to arrive at a community description without using the value system as a guide to the interpretation of community behavior. But no matter what the approach and despite varied preferences for terminology, the fact remains that if a social system is to exist its components must be interrelated—that is, function—for the benefit of the system. This is closely tied in with the operation of differentiation and allocation of status, with the emphasis upon what holds the system together once people have been distributed to many specialties.

In viewing integration as an operation of the community as a system we therefore find it useful to distinguish among the various kinds of integration. But when we have studied each of these by the use of varied indices, we can probably express a net judgment as to

[5] Nelson N. Foote, "Identification as the Basis for a Theory of Motivation," *American Sociological Review*, XVI (February, 1951), 21.

[6] Amos H. Hawley in his *Human Ecology* (New York: The Ronald Press Co., 1950) has proven an effective advocate of this point of view.

whether the community is becoming more or less integrated and can list any obstacles to further integration.

What holds a community together as a system (1, 9, 19)? There is no simple answer which can be described in mechanical or mathematical terms. People, because they live in proximity and share a common past, share the accumulation of that past—their culture. To the extent that they agree about the importance of certain traits in this culture—values, norms, etc.—they have a consensus or agreement that makes community members tend to define the same social situations similarly and behave accordingly; they discourage those who would do things differently unless it becomes evident that the innovation has certain demonstrated superiority over traditional ways. But community members also live in a common geographical setting, which means that they must organize, even if in rudimentary fashion, to overcome space, to use whatever local resources they know how to use, and to develop a division of labor that enables individuals to specialize along lines that they can do best or in which they are most interested. The more individuals specialize, the more interdependent they become and the greater the need for functional integration, as a strike of transportation workers, for example, quickly demonstrates. This means that in addition to a common heritage (culture) there are common needs to be met in the present. But the culture and the personal experience of living members indicate ways in which these needs may or may not be met. To the extent that community members feel involved in the conduct of what is considered essential to the community—to that extent they develop a feeling of social solidarity, of being integrated into the community. There is thus a tendency to stick together, to act corporately and not as hundreds of isolated, disorganized individuals. Some term this "social cohesion," which is only another way of speaking about integration.

In summary, when we speak of integration as an operation of the system, we are using it as a label to describe all of those tendencies within the system to give a common orientation (communication and socialization), a sense of participation and identification, and a smoothing out of obstacles to the performance by each interdependent component of the contributions (functions) it is expected to make to the system.

There is no way to summarize the various operations which have been described, for they do not move progressively from small to more inclusive concepts. Rather, they are ways of describing the kind of behavior that must occur if the community is to continue to exist as a system. All operations are obviously related to each other; recruitment of new members is related to socialization; communication, to integration; one type of allocation to the other types; and social mobility to allocation of prestige, to mention only some of the connections.

The components, whether persons, groups, or subsystems, are the units which are involved in these operations. Some operations refer more specifically to some units than others, as was brought out in the discussion of each of the major community systems taken up in Part Two. To illustrate, socialization is carried out through the family, play group, school, and church; allocation of scarce goods and services through the economy, with the family and the class system also being involved. In other words, to begin to delineate all of the possible interrelationships would prove a tremendous task; yet, one by one, each of these must be individually investigated if scientific knowledge about the community as a system is to be accumulated. The purpose of this chapter, however, has been to show the kind of conceptual scheme in terms of which such testing can be carried out.

The Community as a Changing System

No theoretical scheme of the community as a social system would be complete without indicating the importance of change within the system itself and its adaptation as a social actor to changes from without. At this point a review of Chapter 9 is in order, since it sets forth the basic ideas to be included in this part of the scheme, which need not be repeated here. Suffice it to say that the very fact of interaction induces changes in social relationships. The fact that two business competitors may be seen spending a good deal of time together may lead to the conclusion that they are agreeing on prices to be charged or perhaps contemplating a merger. A third competitor, supposing himself threatened by the behavior of these two, takes the initiative in trying to win over the public by a reduction of prices or trying to join forces with a fourth competitor, who has perhaps not been paying much attention to what is going on. The buying public soon becomes affected by the interaction among these four businessmen and the changes in social relationships occurring among them. Such changes among components within the system are constantly occurring, whether they be representative of education, the family, religion, government, or other major aspects of the community.

Somehow or other the community must manage to maintain, at least in all crucial areas, some balance between too little and too much change. There will never be any constant equilibrium, but for fairly long periods there may be what is called "a running equilibrium," connoting that there are many shifts of position, as among runners in a mile relay, but they all stay on the track. Disequilibrium would be present if some of the runners tried to take a short cut to the finish line without following the set course, or if some started running the wrong way.

Since a community is by definition and by fact a part of the larger society, it is invariably influenced by what happens outside its boundaries. Even if its leaders wished, they could not shut out the outside world. For a while they might condition their members not to pay very much attention to these influences, but minorities of this sort fight a losing battle through time. Any thoroughgoing study of the community should include therefore an analysis of the impacts of the larger society upon the community, the points of receptivity in the system, and the means by which the influences from outside are communicated and translated into changed behavior.

It is often assumed that to think of a community as a social system is to put it into a static, unchanging theoretical strait jacket, which does not allow for a satisfactory description of change. True enough, an effort is frequently made to describe the system at a given point in time and to connect the important components with each other so as to clarify the function that each performs; but the term "system" also implies operation or movement. Some mechanical systems may be considered "closed" in that their parts do not adjust or change, but even here wear and tear produces some accommodation. In the case of biological organisms, however, adjustment or change is an accepted fact of life. So it is with social systems.

Thus, integration is not an effort to bring back into unison what was joined together before some event occurred but rather an operation through which components of the system accommodate to each other as new circumstances arise and as pressures from outside (via the setting) impinge upon the working of the system. To put it in other terms, social change occurs when social units face problems and have to do something about these problems. From the standpoint of the system, integration occurs when these units make decisions which have a favorable rather than an unfavorable effect upon the capability of other components to react to the problems that they face. There exists, therefore, this constant internal accommodation or adjustment, which is the essence of social change and is also the key feature of integration as a systemic operation.

Community Leadership and the Community as an Actor

A community is not merely a passive receiver of influences from outside. It occasionally rises to a state of corporate action in which the people of the community express their sovereign will, their righteous wrath, or their common determination with reference to some issue or emergency. For this to happen requires heightened integration, rapid communication which quickly develops a local consensus about this particular issue or the need for action, strong leadership which can serve as spokesman for the popular feeling, and a willingness on the part of persons and groups to subordinate narrow, private interests for the common good. This state of affairs arises but rarely in the life of most communities, but when it does it is an experience long remembered. Most of the time, self-appointed spokesmen (the leading banker, or newspaper editor, for instance), elected officials (the mayor), or some well-knit group (the Chamber of Commerce) may speak out in behalf of the community. They will vary in the degree to which they are truly representative of all interests, but they will at least make people elsewhere conscious of the existence of this community and aware of some of the ideas of at least some of its members. This is to say that on most occasions some component, perhaps with this as a definite function, represents the community as a whole; seldom are all of the components of the total system involved in an active way.

In bicultural or biracial communities there are apt to be two sets of leaders who may interact for certain well-defined problems but who generally tend to go their separate ways. The leaders of the Spanish-speaking minority of Mountain Town, in a high mountain valley of Southern Colorado, are apt to be weak and ineffectual, for if they prove too successful they are accused by their associates of cooperating with the majority group (the Anglos) and betraying their own group. Consequently, Watson and Samora, who made a study of this community (25), conclude that the only potential leaders who might be qualified to provide the kind of leadership which the minority group needs today are by virtue of their very qualifications absorbed into the larger community and are disqualified in the minds of their own Spanish-speaking fellows.

But if one assumes that the community is not so rigidly divided culturally, even though differentiated on other scores (occupation, religion, education, etc.), one can think of community leadership as serving the whole community. But what is a community leader (26)? Is it one who is *nominally* heading up some so-called community program, such as the drive to annex the built-up areas not included in the present city limits? Or, does community leadership automatically include the functionaries of the important community subsystems, many of them professionally trained for their tasks? Or should the term "community leadership" be reserved for those who have an important enough place in the power structure to make their influence felt when any important community decision is to be made? Paul A. Miller has addressed himself to this problem in his study of the leadership manifested in the establishment of a local hospital by communities located in different parts of the country. He thought of decision-making as "the deployment of authority and influence in social situations of goal-oriented behavior. The decision-making process, within the context of community organization, refers to three phases: (1) the making of decisions, (2) the manner in which they are given approval and made legitimate, and (3) the execution of the decisions in the sense of allocation and/or manipulation of the means at the disposal of the community."[7]

A comparison of findings about communities in the Northeast as compared with those in the Southeast led Paul A. Miller and his associates to the following conclusion:

. . . to understand decision-making and community action in the Southeast one is forced to veer more toward an inquiry into community structure and subsequent offices of constituted authority; while, in the Northeast, more attention to the social psychological components of influence is required. Although both sets of decision-makers had strong positional attachments, it appears from both quantitative and qualitative evidence that the Northeast communities functioned, in decision-making, more squarely on the basis of social property, or resources and proficiencies vested in persons of influence; while the Southeast communities were characterized by a structural setting in which positional elements led to roles of authority.[8]

Such regional differences in emphasis suggest that it is important to view community leadership from the standpoint of the community as a social system. One facet deals with the structural side or the components, as shown in the Southeast; the other facet with the operation of the system as shown in the Northeast.

The starting point for the study of community leadership can be the components: the formal groups have their officers and the informal groups their recognized informal leaders; the various groupings may have their spokesman, many of whom make that a full-time pre-

[7] Paul A. Miller, "The Process of Decision-Making Within the Context of Community Organization," *Rural Sociology*, XVII (June, 1952), 154–55.

[8] *Ibid.*, p. 161. (For fuller details see original article.)

occupation; the subsystems have their functionaries. Whether these officers, informal leaders, spokesman, or functionaries are properly to be considered *community leaders* will depend upon how their particular status and their particular following is viewed by the community. In some communities the president of the woman's club, no matter who she is, is numbered among the community leaders simply because her club is involved in so many community-wide activities; or the chairman of the finance committee of the Community Chest may be so listed by those who know most about how the affairs of the community are run. Likewise, the informal leaders of some of the most influential cliques are recognized as community leaders, as for example the clique of a prominent banker, a leading corporation lawyer, a city commissioner, and an industrialist who have lunch together almost every day with a few others whom they invite to join them from time to time.

Spokesmen for various interests such as labor, Negroes, the Jewish minority, veterans, or residents of the West End may qualify as community leaders if they are successful in seeing that the wishes of those for whom they speak are taken into account when community decisions are made. If, on the other hand, the grouping in question is given no consideration and exerts no influence in decisions taken by the community, the spokesman, whether self-appointed or urged on by his followers, is not to be thought of as a community leader—at least as long as that situation prevails.

Functionaries, too, vary with respect to the part they play in the whole community. Some are assigned very specific roles with little community-wide significance. Others, such as the mayor of a city or a county judge, may wield such power that they are involved in many decisions irrespective of whether they have a persuasive personality or not. In some communities clergymen are expected to exert considerable influence in the community at large, whereas in other communities they would be considered meddlesome or troublesome if they concerned themselves with nonreligious matters. As has been noted earlier, lawyers are expected to assume extra-professional roles of community-wide import, while doctors are not usually included in such positions. Whether functionaries are important depends to a great degree upon the prestige and the value placed upon the subsystem which they supposedly serve.

One cannot predetermine in advance, therefore, just which leaders of which components (groups, groupings, subsystems) will be community leaders, since this awaits more intimate knowledge of local community expectations and the value system. Then, too, some communities prefer to let personality considerations play a leading role in accepting individuals as community leaders, because they play down the group or institutional affiliations.

But looking at community leadership in terms of components is only half the story. The community is an operating social system. As Miller points out, decision-making involves, in addition to making the decision and getting it legitimized, the third element of allocation and/or the manipulation of the means at the disposal of the community. This is another way of saying that those who are in a position to affect the operations of the community system are in a decision-making role and therefore can influence others in goal-oriented activities.

A review of some of the operations described in this chapter indicates how this comes about. For example, anyone such as a newspaper editor who is able to affect communication of ideas or information to any considerable degree is dealing with one of the key operations; anyone such as the plant manager in a one-factory town who can allocate jobs exerts influence in the community; those arbiters of social position whose acceptance helps one up the ladder of success are affecting a systemic operation; those—quite apart from the groups of which they are members—who make economic or political decisions with community-wide implications may also be thought of as exercising leadership of a sort. Likewise, the innovators, the coordinators, the boosters who recruit new members for the community, the patriots who Americanize the new arrivals from abroad, are dealing significantly with systemic processes. Since not all of these individuals will be recognized widely within the community, the members there will tend to select for recognition those who in their opinion contribute most to those operations which they consider most necessary for the survival of the community.

This approach to community leadership takes into account the fact that it is primarily a matter of local definition. Frequently an outsider will recognize that some unsung public servant or private individual is contributing far more to the general community welfare than some others to whom local people are paying greater honor; but the latter have the necessary following and the former does not. Furthermore, the only way of interpreting such broad descriptive terms as "community-wide" "significant" and "crucial" must be in terms of local attitudes. In the study of any one or two communities these terms can be given specific meaning but only after the definitions assigned them have been tested with a sample of the residents who know their community fairly well. This treatment of community leadership also takes into account the fact brought out in a number of studies that many community leaders do not have a mass following but rather lead the subleaders of the community, thereby multiplying their own influence greatly (8). It is in this sense that many economic decisions are reached by a few leaders, although the making and legitimizing of the decision are given little general publicity.

In other words, instead of viewing the community from many varied standpoints, without relating one part to the rest, it is important in the case of leadership as in other matters to think first of all of the community as a system. When this is done, the analysis of leadership flows much more meaningfully, and what may have seemed an isolated decision one July day may be seen in conjunction with another isolated decision on a September day, and some new insight is gained as to how this community actually operates.

REFERENCES AND SUGGESTED READINGS

1. ALBERT, ROBERT S. "Comments on the Scientific Function of the Concept of Cohesiveness," *The American Journal of Sociology,* LIX (November, 1953), 231–34.
2. ANDERSON, ALAN ROSS, and MOORE, OMAR KHAYYAM. "The Formal Analysis of Normative Concepts," *American Sociological Review,* XXII (February, 1957), 9–16.
3. ANGELL, ROBERT C. "Moral Integration and Interpersonal Integration in American Cities," *American Sociological Review,* XIV (April, 1949), 245–50.
4. BARBER, BERNARD. "Structural-Functional Analysis: Some Problems and Misunderstandings," *American Sociological Review,* XXI (April, 1956), 129–34.
5. BECKER, HOWARD S., and STRAUSS, ANSELM L. "Careers, Personality, and Adult Socialization," *The American Journal of Sociology,* LXII (November, 1956), 253–63.
6. BIDDLE, WILLIAM. *The Cultivation of Community Leaders.* New York: Harper & Brothers.
7. EISENSTADT, S. M. "Reference Group Behavior and Social Integration: An Explorative Study," *American Sociological Review,* XIX (April, 1954), 175–85.
8. FANELLI, A. ALEXANDER. "A Typology of Community Leadership Based on Influence and Interaction within the Leader Subsystem," *Social Forces,* XXXIV (May, 1956), 332–38.
9. FESSLER, DONALD R. "The Development of a Scale for Measuring Community Solidarity," *Rural Sociology,* XVII (June, 1952), 144–52.
10. FOOTE, NELSON N. "Identification as the Basis for a Theory of Motivation," *American Sociological Review,* XVI (February, 1951), 14–21.
11. GROSS, NEAL, and MARTIN, WILLIAM E. "On Group Cohesiveness," *The American Journal of Sociology,* LVII (May, 1952), 546–53.
12. HILLER, E. T. "The Community as a Social Group," *American Sociological Review,* VI (April, 1941), 189–202.
13. LANDECKER, WERNER S. "Types of Integration and Their Measurement," *The American Journal of Sociology,* LVI (January, 1951), 332–40.
14. LIPSET, SEYMOUR MARTIN. "Social Mobility and Urbanization," *Rural Sociology,* XX (September–December, 1955), 220–28.
15. MEYER, JULIE. "The Stranger and the City," *American Journal of Sociology,* LVI (March, 1951), 476–83.

16. MILLER, PAUL A. "The Process of Decision-Making within the Context of Community Organization," *Rural Sociology*, XVII (June, 1952), 153–60.
17. MORRIS, RICHARD T. "A Typology of Norms," *American Sociological Review*, XXI (October, 1956), 610–13.
18. MORRIS, RICHARD T., and SEEMAN, MELVIN. "The Problem of Leadership: An Interdisciplinary Approach," *American Journal of Sociology*, LVI (September, 1950), 149–55.
19. NADEL, S. F. "Social Control and Self-Regulation," *Social Forces*, XXXI (March, 1953), 265–73.
20. RILEY, MATILDA WHITE and JOHN W., JR., and TOBY, MARCIA L. "The Measurement of Consensus," *Social Forces*, XXXI (December, 1952), 97–105.
21. ROBINSON, W. S. "The Statistical Measurement of Agreement," *American Sociological Review*, XXII (February, 1957), 17–25.
22. SIMPSON, RICHARD L. "A Modification of the Functional Theory of Social Stratification," *Social Forces*, XXXV (December, 1956), 132–37.
23. STARR, BETTY W. "Levels of Communal Relations," *The American Journal of Sociology*, LX (September, 1954), 123–35.
24. TUMIN, MELVIN M. "The Dynamics of Cultural Discontinuity in a Peasant Society," *Social Forces*, XXIX (December, 1950), 135–40.
25. WATSON, JAMES B., and SAMORA, JULIAN. "Subordinate Leadership in a bicultural Community: An analysis," *American Sociological Review*, XIX (August, 1954), 413–21.
26. WHITE, JAMES E. "Theory and Method for Research in Community Leadership," *American Sociological Review*, XV (February, 1950), 50–60.

PART III

Community Action

INTRODUCTION TO PART THREE

People imbued with the spirit of progress are not content to live in a community that seems to lag behind the times; if they are also filled with a competitive spirit, they want their community to have what neighboring communities have; if, in addition, they believe that men should face up to and do something about their common problems, they will try to work out ways and means of doing so.

There are several avenues of community action open to interested citizens who wish to do something about making their community a better place in which to live. These might be classed under two main headings for convenience of treatment. The first is that kind of action which can best be carried out through local government, either through the municipal council and county court or through some quasi-legal body, such as a planning and zoning commission. For such planned change, public funds can be spent and legal sanctions can be brought to bear to force individuals to give up some individual plan for the sake of the good of the whole community. Such an approach will be discussed in Chapter 19.

Another type of action program is that which is nongovernmental and, therefore, based on private initiative and effort. It works for the most part on a voluntary rather than a forced basis. It can be much more comprehensive than that based on government alone if it pools the wide variety of talents and resources represented by the numerous components of the community; or it can base its approach on much less ambitious projects than those called for in present-day planning and zoning. This type of action is discussed in Chapter 20.

Many readers who have gone carefully through the preceding chapters of this book may at times have been impatient with some of the detailed analysis which has been set forth. They are anxious to do something about a local community problem, or they want to prepare themselves for some particular profession and desire guidance as to ways in which they can be most successful in the practice of that profession in a given community. For either of these purposes there is no substitute for a clear understanding of how the social system, called a community, operates. Action, whether pursued for the purpose of disinterestedly helping one's community or consciously followed to gain an individual objective should be based on knowledge and a sense of the factors that influence the successful outcome of that action. Human behavior is complex in nature, a fact which discourages some who, because they cannot master all of the facts, prefer to play their community roles "by ear." Others, realizing the complexity of social phenomena, admit that they cannot control or understand all of the important influences; yet they recognize that to the extent they do increase their knowledge, they are more likely to succeed in their endeavors. So we turn again to the question raised in the Introduction of the book: Why Study the Community? If the analysis thus far has provided even a few new insights into the nature of community life this question has been answered satisfactorily.

The two chapters which conclude this book are not intended as a substitute for the rich literature on community action which has been accumulating in the last ten years. Such works are written primarily to give one the techniques of conducting a community project, of organizing a community council, of getting new industry for the community. These "how-to-do-it" books prove a useful sequel to the kind of analysis taken up in earlier chapters, but without some of this analysis, the mere stress upon techniques can prove barren, both to the individual leaders and to the community. For community action is really a process rather than a bag of tricks; it calls for adjustment in the light of changing circumstances and cannot be woodenly followed according to some blueprint; it involves people and their willing participation much more than rules of procedure. On the other hand, analysis itself is not enough. It must be translated into programs of action if it is to prove serviceable to those who wanted the analysis made in the first place. Thus community action consists of analysis and the techniques of putting to work the knowledge gained by the analysis, a fact demonstrated over and over again by the successes (and failures) of bodies concerned with planning and zoning.

The sociologist often has to play the dual role of analyst (scientifically studying the community) and social engineer (applying the findings of science to the solving of human problems). Sociologist Louis Wirth recognized the importance of the connection between the two roles. Reinhard Bendix, in describing the contributions of Wirth to sociology, deals with this subject:

Now as sociologist, we know a good bit about what ails modern society, knowledge to which Wirth himself made important contributions. But we know next to nothing concerning the conditions which will build consensus within a democratic framework. Recognizing the dilemma, Wirth emphasized time and again that sociologists should become versed in the art of social engineering. The modern world needs a new consensus appropriate to its complexities. This, he argued, can only be achieved if we combine our scientific knowledge of the conditions militating against consensus with intimate experience of social action and social reform: knowledge of the elements of social action will eventually be indispensable for the engineering of public consent. Hence, Wirth called upon sociologists to improve their knowledge as rapidly as possible, even if for the time being it were to be confined to the conditions, making for dissension. But, at the same time, he urged them to participate in social action, partly in order to gain the necessary intimate knowledge and partly also in order to help maintain the conditions necessary alike for the preservation of individual freedom and for the continued pursuit of social science.[1]

Parts One and Two have dealt primarily with sociological analysis; Part Three turns briefly to social action.

[1] Reinhard Bendix, "Social Theory and Social Action in the Sociology of Louis Wirth," *American Journal of Sociology*, LIX (May, 1954), 529.

Chapter 19

PHYSICAL PLANNING AND ZONING

Many action programs in American communities seek to make the local community a more efficient and a more beautiful place in which to live, work, and play. Such problems are connected with *space* and physical appearance. Since these problems have persisted for many years, a number of specialized agencies and organizations, manned by carefully trained personnel, have been invented and developed to cope with them. The purposes of this chapter are: (1) to discuss three of these problems; (2) to present a quick summary of the nature of the work of planning commissions; and (3) to consider some of the sociological aspects of physical planning.

SOME PERSISTENT PROBLEMS

One of the major problem areas of physical planning—that of providing utilities (electricity, water, gas, and the disposal of sewage and garbage)—has already been treated at some length in the discussion of local government in Chapter 12. Three other problems deserve special consideration if one is to see how the community, through a specialized planning agency, tries to anticipate and meet some of its pressing needs. These problems, which are only too evident to any observant person who rides through an American town or city today, are traffic congestion, deterioration of neighborhoods, and the need for town beautification.

Congestion. All towns experience some congestion which may occur only on important occasions, such as a high school basketball tournament, an annual fair or community celebration, the arrival of a circus, a political rally, or some tragedy whose aftermath people drive many miles to witness. There is too much traffic for the local streets to handle and too much demand placed upon local restaurants, drug stores, and hotels to satisfy the needs of outsiders.

In other communities, such as county seat or service center towns, the congestion may occur weekly when people from the rural areas arrive to shop, attend a movie, or talk with friends whom they meet on the street. Since few homes in the town are open to these visitors, they have to congregate on the main street, around the courthouse, or at some other central point where they can see and be seen. Rival communities frequently compete for the trade of these rural people and do much to encourage this weekly congestion, since the businessmen assume that the greater the number of people around, the greater the trade. From time to time, the regular residents of the community seem to resent this weekly influx and may react by staying away from the business section on that particular day.

Congestion in its most acute form, however, occurs on the normal working day in the larger centers where many thousands pour into a comparatively small area to work in the offices, to man the stores and banks, and to provide the services that are a part of urban living (9, 10, 17, 19). As space becomes scarce, skyscrapers rise to create more room; as streets become clogged, subways or elevated expressways carry people or automobiles to their destinations. An interesting case is Washington, D. C., where city and regional planners have worked out a comprehensive plan for the national capital and its environs. They consider a major aim of their plan that of moving two million people, their supplies, and other goods, wherever they need to go, quickly, safely, and economically. Here is their description of the problem and their proposed solutions:

It is to the downtown business district and the Government centers nearby that most people want to go. Of every six people entering that area, one now walks, two come in a car or taxi, and three ride public transportation. But more and more people are trying to use private autos. From three miles out and beyond, people entering downtown use cars more than walking or public transit. In the District, there is one auto for every 6.3 persons. The trend is toward a higher ratio of cars to people. In the years ahead, there will be not only more people, but probably more cars in relation to the number of people.

In addition, truck traffic is an increasingly important part of the lifeblood of American cities. Traffic jams that delay Washington's trucks are a real factor in raising prices and the cost of living. Congestion is not only inconvenient, it is wasteful and costly.

There are three attacks on the problem, which must all be used at once. Most basic: Cut down on the amount of travel needed, by getting home and work closer together. This is one of the major purposes of the comprehensive plan, to be attained by spreading Federal employment centers throughout the metropolitan region. Second, and cheapest, but possibly only as the third step is undertaken: Make public transportation so quick and convenient that more people will use it to go to work and fewer will drive. Third, most costly, but also necessary in spite of what can be done through the first and second: Create a system of collector and distributor roads, both radial and circumferential in function, that will redistribute traffic through the region and diminish the volume demand within the central area. This will entail cutting through modern highways, widening certain old ones, building some new bridges and providing new parking facilities.[1]

Obviously, two important aspects of congestion are the flow of traffic through the streets and the parking of automobiles at or near downtown destinations. Many cities labor under serious handicaps in that some of the leading business streets were originally lanes or narrow roads never designed to accommodate the present traffic load. Weybosset Street in Providence, Rhode Island, is said to have been a cowpath where Bossie, the cow, would have felt very much at home in pre-Revolutionary times. Even more recently established cities, whose newer thoroughfares were intended to serve the automobile age, have difficulties too at the peak traffic periods during the day. Those responsible for physical planning in the community have given much study to the problems of traffic flow. One recent report suggests that the automobile and its highways be viewed as a unified system in much the same way as the railroads which keep under central control everything from the tracks and rolling stock to the terminals and control devices.

In such a system, roadways are a principal element and, in the larger cities, the roadways fall into three general classifications.

Expressways

To carry concentrated volumes of traffic for relatively long distances.

To move this traffic at relatively high speeds (35 to 45 mph) with safety, the design being such as to eliminate cross traffic and head-on conflicts.

To relieve surface streets of a part of the burden of through traffic.

Major Traffic Routes

To distribute traffic moving to and from the expressways.

To carry the through traffic which, because of the location of its trip, cannot save sufficient time to justify detouring via the expressway.

To carry through traffic in the sections of the city where expressways are not yet warranted.

To serve through traffic during the years required to secure right-of-way and to construct expressways.

Land Surface Streets

To carry, at low speed, the traffic destined on those streets.

To provide for stopping, parking and similar activities essential to local business or industry.

To allow a high priority to pedestrian movements, as in residential areas.[2]

[1] U.S. National Capital Park and Planning Commission, *Washington, Present and Future: A General Summary of the Comprehensive Plan for the National Capital and Its Environs* (Monograph No. 1, Washington, D.C., April, 1950).

[2] *Street Traffic Plan, Louisville, Kentucky: Street Traffic Routes* (Louisville, Kentucky, City Planning Commission, 1950).

It is small comfort, however, to a motorist to move smoothly to his destination over major traffic routes if he cannot find a parking place when he arrives. This holds true for a farmer coming into the county seat on a Saturday, a tourist wishing to stop for the night, or an urban resident hoping to patronize a large downtown department store. Communities go about providing parking facilities in different ways. Indeed, there are five broad administrative patterns in practice throughout the country, based on whether private enterprise or local government accepts the full or partial responsibility. The average motorist is less concerned about who provides the facilities but more concerned about their convenience and cost.

1. Private enterprise ownership and management, with only incidental regulation by public authority in a few cities;

2. Private enterprise and public authority in partnership, each making designated contributions to and each having prescribed responsibilities with the provision of off-street parking facilities;

3. Public Parking agencies, the functions of which are exclusively concerned with parking facilities;

4. Special public agencies, which provide parking facilities only as incidental to some other principal function;

5. Regular municipal officials, who provide parking accommodations in the same manner as they establish other public improvements, with no particular administrative organization specially designed for dealing with the parking problem.[3]

Just which of these plans or their modifications will be followed in any community is often the subject of considerable debate, which is well described below:

. . . Opponents of municipal operation argue that while the powers of municipal government may be desirable in the planning and land assembly operations for parking facilities, and even in their construction, the operation should be left to private enterprise, which over the years has developed a know-how that is essential to the successful operation of the facilities. Proponents point out that the operation of municipal facilities is merely an activity incidental to the establishment of such facilities and that this function should not differ, on the merits, in the case of parking facilities from that for any other kind of public improvement.

When well operated, privately-owned, off-street parking facilities are available, there is usually little need for any control and, generally, such facilities are to be preferred. In many cities groups of merchants, largely in their own interest, have formed associations to provide parking facilities for shoppers. The type of facility so provided has varied widely, but generally such ventures have been quite successful.

However, if private capital does not provide sufficient off-street parking facilities to meet parking demand, then it must be recognized that parking is as

[3] Kentucky Department of Highways, Kentucky State Highway Department Statewide Highway Planning Survey in cooperation with the United States Department of Commerce, Bureau of Public Roads. *Lexington Parking Survey,* 1953, 89.

essential to the economic well-being of the central business district as are streets, and that the parking facilities must be provided regardless of the source or control.

In any particular city the methods of financing public parking facilities are limited by municipal action, by the specifications of the state statute or by the provisions of the city's charter. Within these limitations the methods that have been developed are numerous and ingenious. A city which plans to embark upon a program of financing the acquisition of land, its improvement and the operation and construction of a parking facility must look not only to its state enabling legislation, but also to its own financial policy. It must analyze the parking need, not only in quantitative terms, but also in terms of existing private facilities and their current contribution of the supply of off-street parking space. With the counsel of downtown merchants, it must decide to what extent the public as a whole will benefit from the newly furnished parking facilities and to what extent that part of the public patronizing a particular group of businesses will benefit. In other words, the city must decide whether the public as a whole should pay for the off-street parking facility or whether special beneficiaries should pay for it. These decisions will, in part, determine the financing methods, or combination of methods, to be used.[4]

Any approach which may be taken toward alleviating the congestion is apt to be costly in view of the value of property in and around the most congested areas. To cut through or widen a street, to convert areas to parking facilities, or even to redistribute, as in the case of Washington, D. C., agencies and other large employers from the downtown area means spending large sums of money. Since no one person or even a small group is usually in position to finance these changes, coordinated action by businessmen, governmental bodies, or both is necessary. Such steps should concentrate on more than just the present emergencies: they must take into account future needs. This is why comprehensive physical planning is usually advocated to avoid the piecemeal remedies of the past.

Deterioration of Urban Neighborhoods. The ecological processes described in connection with the community as a place (Chapter 1) afford much insight into the past growth of blighted areas in cities. As was noted, there is competition for space in the downtown center, which is constantly expanding. As the center grows, it invades former residential zones which are no longer desired as family dwelling areas but rather for rooming houses and cheap apartments. According to this theory, such areas become transitional and run-down. Before being entirely taken over by business or some other land use, which may eventually happen, these areas are problem areas.

Elsewhere in the community we find sections where real estate men or builders have put up large numbers of very cheap houses

4 *Ibid.,* p. 90.

for the lowest income groups. The houses are not provided with the ordinary conveniences, are not kept in repair, either by the tenant or owner, and are in the parts of town many residents try to avoid. But these areas do exist and constitute a problem. Although city revenues from residential areas in general do not fully cover the cost of public services to these areas, we do know that a disproportionate amount of public funds is spent in policing and giving fire and public health protection to the blighted areas. In other words, those who are making quick profits on a relatively small investment in such low-cost dwellings are actually making these profits at the expense of the other taxpayers of the community. Many cases, such as the following, could be cited:

In Hartford, Connecticut—according to a study of 1935—a slum area there with 25% of the city's population had

51% of the tuberculosis cases
55% of the illegitimate births
57% of the juvenile delinquency
62% of the adult arrests
38% of the commitments to state mental institutions
68% of the relief cases

In Cleveland, Ohio—according to a 1934 study—a small slum area, occupied by 2.5% of the city's population, had

10% of the city's illegitimate births
12% of the city's tuberculosis deaths
26% of the city's vice centers
8% of the city's juvenile delinquency
21% of the city's murders

In addition, this area with only 2.5% of the city's population took

14% of the city's expenditures for fire protection
6% of the city's expenditures for police protection
8% of the city's expenditures for public health
8% of the county's expenditures for relief[5]

The purpose of such studies, much more popular in the 1930's than today, was to show the savings that would be effected by sound investment in public housing, which did become widely accepted as a partial solution to urban deterioration. The development has been described as follows:

. . . Almost two decades ago the Federal Government financed public housing projects in thirty-seven cities as a part of a depression work recovery program. A little later, the Housing Act of 1937 established a decentralized public housing

[5] Jay Rumney and Sara Shuman, *Cost of Slums*, Part III (Newark: Prepared for the Housing Authority of the City of Newark, N.J., 1953).

program which limited the Federal Government's participation to one of financial aid and technical assistance, and gave the local community front-line responsibility for all future public housing. A total of 191,700 low-rent housing units are being operated under provisions of the Housing Act of 1937 in thirty-seven states, the District of Columbia, Hawaii, Puerto Rico and the Virgin Islands. These are located in 268 localities, including both large and small communities.[6]

The Housing Act of 1949 provided for the building of 810,000 low-rent, public dwelling units over a period of six years. Local housing authorities must first be set up and are assisted by the Federal Government by loans and annual contributions. An effort is made to ensure the occupation of these low-rent housing units only by families of low income and to destroy unsafe or unsanitary dwellings equal in number to the number of newly constructed units. After the local housing authority has determined the need for low-rent housing, selected the site, appraised it, planned for the project through use of private architects, and estimated the costs of building and operation—after this has been done, the authority turns to private builders to get the work done. Once the projects are built and occupied, the local housing authority seeks, through tenant and neighborhood councils, to draw the occupants into the mainstream of community life (6, 21).

Another answer to neighborhood deterioration is found in the enforcement of city ordinances governing hygiene and sanitation, fire safety and building maintenance codes (14). Baltimore, Maryland, and Milwaukee, Wisconsin, provide good examples of concerted action by local authorities to enforce through court action the standards set up. In this manner landlords in blighted areas have to improve their property if they wish to rent it and stay clear of the law. By a process of education and strict enforcement, with specially designated "sanitarians" holding police powers, a remarkable improvement has been noted. In Baltimore the tendency has been to go into the worst areas and block by block try to raise housing standards to minimum levels; in Milwaukee the effort has been centered on chiefly those areas where blight is beginning and where proper measures now will prevent further deterioration (5).

A number of national agencies and organizations have been actively interested in the problem of revitalizing our cities in both the physical and the social sense. With the tendency for the center

[6] *Bulletin*, U. S. Housing and Home Finance Agency, Sept., 1949, quoted in Theodore Caplow (ed.), *City Planning: A Selection of Readings in Its Theory and Practice* (Minneapolis: Burgess Publishing Company, 1950), p. 216.

of the city to suffer in competition with many of the newly created suburban centers, there is serious likelihood that some buildings will become vacant for a period of time, the surrounding property will decline in value, and the whole block or cluster of blocks will become a liability to the community. The American Public Health Association, through its Committee on the Hygiene of Housing, is doing what it can to promote interest in neighborhood planning (2). It defines the neighborhood as the area served by the elementary school, a definition used in the Neighborhood Unit Formula, which is said to be the most widely known standard in American city planning (7, 16). ACTION (American Council To Improve Our Neighborhood) is another group that is seeking to fight urban deterioration.

The illustrations which have been used in this discussion of blighted areas have dealt chiefly with large cities. Those living in the middle-sized city have no reason to feel smug, for any resident willing to look will discover that there are areas which for a variety of reasons are becoming more run-down every day. The community may not have proper ordinances to deal with this condition, or the local authorities may not be courageous enough to enforce the ordinances. In any event, if the community is to be a pleasant and attractive place in which to live, there is likely to be the need for some comprehensive planning for all of the physical needs.

Beautification. A beautiful city or town does not simply happen by accident; it is the result of much thought, cooperation, and hard work. As already noted, many communities have eyesores which impress newcomers unfavorably but to which local people become so accustomed that these ugly features are accepted as a normal part of the physical environment. Lack of zoning may have resulted in the motley mixture of two or three types of land use in close proximity; junk yards may be the first landmarks which catch the attention of those approaching the town; certain blighted areas may be so neglected that they give the whole community a black eye. Citizens who travel around their home town with the idea of locating the unattractive spots, particularly if they should be accompanied by a critical visitor from outside, become acutely aware of this problem of "the city beautiful."

Town beautification results from the cooperative efforts of the local government, individual businessmen and home owners, and organized private groups, such as civic and garden clubs. The local government has the responsibility of keeping the streets and sidewalks clean and in repair, of removing rubbish and litter, of seeing that ordinances governing control of weeds in vacant lots are enforced, and of giving assistance to groups wishing to sponsor worthy projects, such as the sale at cost of thousands of young trees to be planted around the community. Local government also becomes involved in the attack on slums and in providing low-cost housing, in enforcing the zoning provisions, and in aiding in smoke abatement campaigns. The mayor, through official action, can give impetus to an annual Paint-up Day, and the city council may even make public vehicles available to those needing them in the clean-up job.

No local government, however, can make a town beautiful simply through its own efforts. The residents of the community must have enough local pride to accept responsibility for their own places of business and yards and homes. There must also be a sufficient economic base to pay the costs of proper maintenance, landscaping, and periodic painting.

Private group action also has an important part to play. The local Chamber of Commerce may decide to urge the businessman to take down the neon signs that jut over the sidewalk and to rely for identification and advertisement on the signs painted flat against the building; the Garden Club may agree to put up a protective screen of shrubs of young trees to hide the eyesores from public view; the Junior Chamber of Commerce may undertake to repaint all of the street signs, while the Woman's Club may seek to beautify a local park.

For anything to be beautiful over a long period of time, its basic structure must be sound. This is true of the community as well. If the growth of the town is unplanned, if it grows like Topsy, then numerous efforts to beautify it will seem patchy and relatively ineffective. In other words, relieving congestion, providing good public utilities and services, slum clearance and town beautification are all tied in together. This becomes abundantly clear as we examine in greater detail the meaning of town planning and zoning.

THE NATURE OF PLANNING

Prudent individuals are accustomed to plan. They work out financial, recreational, or educational plans for themselves or members of their families. Similarly, business firms plan for their future and try to gauge building requirements a few years hence, type and quantity of merchandise needed several months in advance, as well as selection of promising young executives who will in time succeed the present top management. In much the same way, communities are learning to plan. In doing so, they seek to avoid the regimentation that planning sometimes connotes, even though it does mean that a few persons must occasionally alter their individual plans to fit in with the general good of the community.

Types of Planning. If one forgets for a moment the technical definitions used by the specialists in various fields, one can divide the planning for the community into three types: physical, economic, and welfare. Each of these can be characterized as follows: *Physical planning* has to do with the spatial and material aspects of the community primarily. It deals with, among others, the problems we just discussed, which range from congestion to town beautification. *Economic planning* has to do with the improvement of commerce and industry, with raising of economic opportunity, with provision of more stable employment, with training a skilled labor supply, and with increasing the range of services, including professional services, available to the people of the community. It overlaps at many points with physical planning but is usually the concern of a different group (Chamber of Commerce, Area Industrial Development Association, etc.) from that concerned with physical planning. *Welfare planning* deals with problems of the indigent, the handicapped, the delinquent and also with the more positive problems of increased recreational opportunity. Its concern is with the human resources not viewed merely as economic assets. Many communities have welfare councils, bearing quite different names, which consist of representatives from all of the social work and character-building agencies, as well as from other groups actively interested, as laymen and not professionals, in the welfare field.

As one goes through the literature on planning, one finds many definitions which vary in details from the above. For instance, *public planning* is a comprehensive term that would include elements of physical, economic, and welfare planning, but its chief trait is that it is carried out under *governmental* auspices (3). On the other hand, social planning[7] may or may not be through the government, since it describes a general attack on social problems, no matter who seeks to carry it out. It is in essence what was formerly called "social reform." In some communities social planning and welfare planning are considered the same, but one is on safer ground to use "social planning" as the more general term which would include physical, economic, or welfare planning, since what might be called "social problems" exist in all three of these types as defined here.

[7] Svend Riemer, "Social Planning and Social Organization," *American Journal of Sociology*, LII (May, 1947). Views social planning as a new principle of social organization that penetrates our society with a maze of "unorthodox" procedures in the economic and social field.

For instance, slum clearance is a social problem and is of just as much interest to the physical planner as to the welfare expert; unemployment is a social problem but certainly one of interest to the economic planner. Social planning would, therefore, be the over-all planning for the *people* of the whole community, including all facets of their lives. It would insist that there be coordination between the physical, economic, and welfare planners, who are frequently not sufficiently in touch with each other.

What is ordinarily called *city* or *urban planning* is claimed by its supporters to be over-all social planning, a meeting of the needs of the whole community. Yet, when one looks closely at what city planners actually do and at the organizations through which they work, one must conclude that, despite their profession of interest in the broad picture, they concentrate chiefly on physical planning. Thus from the functional point of view, from the standpoint of the way American communities are organized, there is a fairly clear-cut distinction between physical planning (which we are discussing in this chapter), economic planning, and welfare planning.

According to one source, planning for a community has the following four steps:

1. Definition of the community's goals and values. A community's goals and values are merely the sum total of the goals and values of the individuals who make up any community. This is not an easy task since the desires of individuals are often diametrically opposed. Nevertheless, this definition is the starting point of good planning, and if it is passed over, this program will almost certainly fail from lack of community support.

2. Survey of physical and economic resources and future possibilities. The second step is the collection of information about the physical, economic and human resources of the community. If a community doesn't know what resources it has—population, business and industry, physical plant and financial resources—it cannot possibly formulate intelligent plans for present or future development.

3. Formulation of a master plan. The third step is the formulation of a master plan in two major parts—a future land use plan and a community facilities plan. By fixing the location of industrial, commercial, residential and recreational areas for future use, it is possible to determine in an orderly, attractive and efficient manner where people will work, live, shop and play. The second part of the plan, a community facilities plan, is concerned with services provided by public agencies. It should include a capital improvements program setting forth the order in which public projects should be undertaken.

4. Administrative machinery and controls to carry out the plan . . . The desirability of having a special agency undertake planning functions is unquestioned . . .[8]

[8] *A Report of the Greater Lexington Committee,* A Citizens' Committee of Lexington and Fayette County, Kentucky, April, 1955, pp. 118–19.

Needless to say, those engaged in any type of planning for the community would need to go through the first two steps, of determining the goals and values of the community and in assessing its material and human resources. Some of them might part company at the third and fourth steps, preferring to leave to the physical planner the preparation of a master plan and ways of implementing it. Yet, every thinking person in the community should be seriously concerned about the nature of the plan and the steps proposed to put it into effect. Businessmen need to know about the zoning for land use, recreational specialists about the area set aside for parks and playgrounds, welfare workers about the institutional facilities as well as about projects for slum clearance.

The tasks of preparing the master plan, keeping it up to date, and enforcing it call for people with specialized skills. Some cities prefer to employ those who have studied all aspects of physical planning and are generalists at this task; other cities, such as Indianapolis, Indiana, prefer to get individual specialists in population, economic development, law, traffic control, and the like to work together as a team, with no one individual claiming greater proficiency in the field of the other. But no matter how the work gets done, it calls for technical competence. To understand more clearly the nature of physical planning, it is important to know about the legal authority on which it is based, how a master plan is prepared, and what organized body is responsible for the carrying out and enforcement of the plan.

The Legal Authority for Physical Planning. One of the interesting ways to trace the history of physical planning is to follow the steps by which men have agreed to surrender what would seem at first to be basic property rights in the interest of the common good. Arthur B. Gallion has told the story briefly and clearly, showing that with the growth of cities and the growth of population, land took on other values than that attached to agricultural use (11, 15). As he points out, special places were set aside for the storage of explosives, for the slaughter of animals, and for the residential developments of the aristocracy. King Philip of Spain outlined procedures for establishing communities in the New World to the explorers before their departure in the sixteenth century, counseling them to lay out the streets in such ways that they would not be windswept. One of America's first recorded acts of zoning occurred in Boston when a ban was placed on storing gunpowder in the center of the city. Thus these and later measures relative to land use were the legal forerunners of the physical planning of today.

In the ancient cities the ruling group enforced their wishes by the use of police power. Today we accept the principle that the source of all power lies in the hands of the people and that the people, or their representatives, have the power to pass laws to protect the welfare of all the people. This exercise of police power must be for a worthy purpose and with definitely stated objectives.

Legal action on zoning affairs passed through two states of development before it arrived at the place it enjoys today. The first stage included a group of court cases which actually preceded zoning and served to establish the base for zoning law and gained its recognition as a legal use of the police power. These cases dealt with "nuisance uses" which the courts treated as separate and individual matters, the court deciding in each specific case whether the courts required more evidence as a base for reference, evidence "indicating the character of a community" before it was willing to rule upon the validity of a use. This call by the courts for a comprehensive city plan is now answered in the Master Plan of land use.[9]

Thus, if a resident feels that a junk yard burning rubber is a nuisance, he could bring suit and try to have the objectionable practice stopped. If the local government passes an ordinance, in keeping with the authority given to it in the state constitution or in state-enabling legislation, prohibiting the building of stores in certain residential areas, then action can be brought against any individual violating that ordinance. Not to be confused with this police power, however, is the right of *eminent domain*, which means that land can be taken for a public purpose even when the owner does not want to sell. Under eminent domain the property is condemned; the courts then establish a fair price to be paid to the owner.

More and more, the interpretation of physical planning has shifted away from merely the simple desire to eliminate nuisances and to protect the value of property that would deteriorate if undesirable invasion occurred. It has taken a much more positive view in its efforts to promote public health, safety, and general welfare and has even extended to such matters as "public convenience and comfort." This last interpretation, supported by Supreme Court decision, is the basis of our traffic laws which prohibit parking on certain streets where it would seriously impede the flow of traffic.

The Master Plan and Zoning. The Master Plan, as we have already noted, is the third step in the planning process. It consists of two major parts: a future land use plan and a community facilities plan. Such a plan must be based on intensive research. Although the planner gives much attention to *space* and works out numerous maps,

[9] Arthur B. Gallion, *The Urban Pattern: City Planning and Design* (Princeton: D. Van Nostrand Company, Inc., 1950), p. 229.

he must also be aware of *time* and estimate possible trends as accurately as possible.

For example, he not only must know the actual population count and composition of his community, but he must have some clear ideas of likely growth over the next ten or fifteen years, or even farther into the future, if that be possible. Likewise, he must try to calculate the direction in which the expansion is apt to move and the utilities that will be demanded, as well as the types of subdivisions that will be created. In addition, he must have a detailed map showing the use of every plot of land in the area for which the planning is being done, whether it be a city, county, or a wider unit. Then, in terms of expected growth, he must seek to work out, with the help of others, the kind of land use pattern he wants to see develop. The ideal that he will draw up will of necessity differ from real conditions, since in the movement toward a better-planned town, some areas now partly business, partly residential may be set aside exclusively for business. This means that in the course of time the residences will no longer be occupied as dwellings, and no new residences may be built. The same will hold true for other types of zones where present land uses are considered undesirable.

The complexity of the city plan is shown in the following description of what it includes:

In one sense, the city plan has been limited to those features that can be drawn on paper in the form of a map, such as streets, parks and public building sites. But the plan and its various projects must be supported by factual data justifying them and by figures as to their cost. Other elements of the plan, such as proposals for water supply and sewage disposal, can be shown only partially on a map. They must be accompanied by exhaustive reports and by tabulated data. Certain phases of the plan, such as zoning, are expressed, at least in part, by a written ordinance. Finally, improvement programs and budgets are essential to most city plans for completion of the operating machinery. These several elements properly related, broadly-speaking, may properly be called the city plan.

The city plan is ordinarily composed of three principal elements: Projects to be carried out by the municipality; things to be done by private corporations under more or less public control; and improvements to be made by the individual property owner. The first may be accomplished directly with public funds. The second must be approached through suggestion, cooperation and legislation. The third is largely a matter of guidance and education and, to an extent, legislation as illustrated by the zoning ordinance and by control of land subdivision.[10]

Zoning, as is apparent from the above, is only one aspect of planning, and the land use districts are only one part of the over-all city plan. Yet, the ordinary citizen comes face to face with planning

[10] Russell Van Nest Black and Mary Hedges Black, *Planning for the Small American City* (Chicago: Public Administration Service, 1948).

usually in terms of zoning. He learns that he can or cannot erect a certain kind of building on his property or that his neighbor recently had his plans for a new subdivision on the edge of the city turned down by the planning commission because he wanted to develop a residential subdivision in an area which was zoned for industrial use only.

The Planning Commission. But what is this planning commission that acts on these requests from citizens? Perhaps we can understand it best if we take an actual case of a city-county commission that serves an area of about one hundred thousand people. This particular illustration differs little from the general pattern. The larger cities will have larger staffs or may divide the planning from the zoning functions by setting up a separate zoning administrator and board of appeals, but essentially they are the same. Here is an excerpt from the planning report mentioned above:

The Commission

The law requires that a planning and zoning commission and a board of adjustment be established. The present Commission is composed of seven non-paid members appointed for four-year terms. Three City members are appointed by the Mayor. One member who resides outside the City limits is appointed by the Fiscal Court, and the Mayor, City Engineer and County Engineer are members ex-officio.

Powers of the Commission

The Planning and Zoning Commission is empowered to adopt plans and maps of the land within the "municipal area" for the purpose of regulating all traffic, transportation, communication and public utilities. It may remove, relocate, widen, narrow or extend any public way with a view toward the systematic planning of the City and its environs. The Commission may establish zones in which it is allowed to regulate or restrict the construction, repair or alteration of buildings, structures or land. This power includes the regulation of building size, number of stories, lot size, density of population, use of buildings, and so on. In addition, all plots of subdivisions within the City or within three miles of its limits must be submitted to the Commission. Without a vote of two-thirds of the City council, no street can be accepted by the City until the plot and location have been approved by the Commission.

Subject to Veto

The Planning and Zoning Commission, though it appears to have great power, is actually only an advisory body to the Board of City Commissioners and the Fayette County Fiscal Court. Zoning regulations by the Commission have the force of law only after their adoption by the governing body or the areas affected. The Fiscal Court and/or the Lexington City Commissioners must either accept or reject—they cannot alter—recommendations from the Planning and Zoning Commission.

Public Hearings—Individual Petitions

State law requires the Planning and Zoning Commission to hold public hearings *only* before it adopts its *final report* on a zone change. The Commission is *not* required to hold hearings on petitions for zone changes submitted by individuals, although it has made a practice of doing so. Public or private bodies or persons may petition the Commission for specific changes in the zoning ordinance, and such requests are passed along to the appropriate governing body, with the Commission's recommendation for action.

Commission Staff

The staff of the Planning and Zoning Commission is presently composed of a City-County planning director, a City-County community planner, an Administrative assistant and a part-time draftsman . . .

Board of Adjustment

Obviously, no single zoning law could possibly take into consideration each individual case and deal completely and justly with it. To compensate for this fact, the law requires that a five-member board of adjustment be established to examine individual cases where provisions of the zoning ordinance seem to be unjust or inappropriate. Four members of the Board of Adjustment are City residents appointed by the Mayor. The remaining member is appointed by the Fiscal Court and must reside outside the City. All are unpaid.

Powers of the Board of Adjustment

The Board has the power to make adjustments in cases where the zoning ordinance imposes an undue hardship on an owner or lessee of property. The Board may also settle disputes arising out of varying interpretations of the zoning ordinance. Contrary to popular belief, the Board does not hear appeals from decisions of the Planning and Zoning Commission. It does, however, hear appeals from rulings of the building inspector who is charged with enforcement of planning and zoning ordinances.

A glance at the Board's agenda of June 25, 1954, will illustrate the type of cases it deals with—not always wisely. Eight exceptions to zoning restrictions were requested and granted. Six are as follows:

1. Operate a real estate office in a residential district.
2. Operate a beauty shop in a residential district.
3. Operate a photographic studio in a residential district.
4. Erect a duplex in a one-family-dwelling residential area.
5. Operate a parking lot within 1,000 feet of a school.
6. Build a sanatorium within 30 feet of side lot lines.

These examples of spot zoning are but a few of many examples that could be cited. Good city planning is impossible when exceptions to zoning laws are made on the basis of expediency or pressure. In fact, the Board by granting exceptions in wholesale lots merely advertises the fact that it not only condones the practice but encourages it.[11]

PHYSICAL PLANNING AND THE COMMUNITY

Physical planning for any community may be carefully drawn up in keeping with the best scientific procedures, the recommendations may take into account the experience of many other cities, and the predictions about population growth may prove to be almost 100 per

[11] *A Report of the Greater Lexington Committee, op. cit.,* pp. 119–24.

cent correct, yet the plan may prove a failure if it never receives social acceptance. To accomplish even the least important purpose for which the plan was prepared, private citizens must be willing to guide many of their actions by it. Earlier chapters in this book have taken up those elements of community life that have a decided bearing on such a question. Two of these can be reviewed with planning specifically in mind.

Social Values, Norms and Public Opinion. The first step in planning, as we have seen, is to define the community's goals and values. What do the people of this community want most in life? What are they willing to pay for both in terms of taxes and of time? City planners are quick to recognize that various communities differ greatly in the way they respond to physical planning proposals. This individuality among communities is thus a well-attested fact but one that is apt to be overlooked in the hurry to get on with the preparation of the more tangible aspects of planning, such as the graphs showing occupational distribution or the maps locating the recreational facilities.

Communities also differ in the way they permit the citizens to go about the realization of their goals. These norms, as they are called, are the limits set upon the roles people can play. Take for instance the planner. What norms govern him? In some communities people prefer not to be bothered with the details or even the processes of physical planning. They are willing to leave the whole matter up to the experts and wait for them to solve their traffic, sewage, or other problems related to space. The citizens appointed to the planning commission passively accept the recommendations made to them and then walk out of the meeting feeling that they have performed their job in a satisfactory fashion.

It is very different in other communities where the expert is suspect to begin with and where the leading citizens want to know exactly what is going on. Their representatives on the planning commission ask a hundred questions and occasionally vote down a recommendation they do not feel is wise for their community. Here the norms require the planner to be the advisor only, and not the one who, as a lone hand, runs the commission.

Communities differ, too, in the means that they will accept for the remedying of some problem. Some will accept the direct approach. If a slum is to be torn down, the bulldozers are sent in to destroy the hovels or old tenements so that new structures may be erected or the place turned into a parking lot. It is not so with other communities. Some of the leading citizens there are sure to ask, "What is going to happen to those families whose homes are being demolished? Have you made provision for them before you move into action?" Once assurance can be given that each family is satisfactorily resettled, the task of clearance can proceed.

Some communities expect businessmen to be hard-boiled and respect those who can drive a hard bargain, even at the expense of the planning commission. Other communities require that their businessmen give at least a semblance of respect for the general welfare of the community and support the worthwhile undertakings that are periodically sponsored by local groups. Should the work of the planning commission be generally approved in the community, then those individuals who want community recognition must cooperate with the work of the commission. In other words, understanding what the norms are which govern the behavior of the planner, the planning commission member, as well as others in the community, is necessary for effective work in that community.

The third consideration, in addition to social values and norms, is that of public opinion. In 1942 the Bureau of Urban Research at Princeton University made a study of *Urban Planning and Public Opinion.* Their study shows:

> In terms of public opinion, it would seem that the aims of City Planning have often been at the same time too high and too low. On the one hand, grand schemes for reorganization have presupposed a public momentum which does not exist and social means of accomplishment which have been far from realized. On the other hand, many programs have been concerned principally with three-dimensional patterns of physical improvement which have not reflected sufficient consideration of the social, economic and governmental mechanisms comprising the core and essence of the planning problem.[12]

We must remember that physical planning is usually public planning, which means that it is connected with the governmental bodies dependent upon public acceptance and approval. If the community gets aroused over too little planning or too much planning, it may change its local government at election time. This is why those who are involved in physical planning have a definite responsibility for seeking to keep the public informed about the nature of the problem and the possible means of alleviating the problem, together with pertinent information about cost and the benefits that are to be reaped as a result of positive action. The Princeton study also has this to say:

> This survey provides further evidence to disprove the contention that persons of lower economic and educational status are inured to the environmental disadvantages which they endure. In most instances, less fortunate men and women

[12] Melville C. Branch, Jr. (Princeton: 1942), Research Series No. 1, p. 30.

show the highest dissatisfaction and the most definite desire for remedial action. Their understanding and support will be needed if urban planning is to be the concern of the majority, as well as of minority groups.[13]

Response of Organized Groups. In spite of the existence of what seem to be general community values and norms, there are many individuals in the community who are ready to ignore them if some immediate personal interest is served. Physical planners are required to deal with these special-interest groups, as well as with the rather broad and vague general public. The identification of such groups is an important step in understanding the complexity of planning even in a medium-sized community.

Vested interests. In every community there are some individuals whose business ventures might be curtailed if strict zoning practices were enforced. They may be reaping profits from substandard housing and may have little desire to bring these units up to minimum standards. Or, certain firms, such as banks, or even private individuals may have a great deal of money tied up in scattered real estate and may fear that too rigid enforcement of zoning ordinances might result in a decline in the value of this property.

Other vested interests may involve those homeowners who live in a small area which would be radically changed if the Master Plan were put into effect. They may collect money and employ lawyers to protect the interests which they feel are being violated. If they are successful, their property may prove to be a little enclave which is surrounded by land used for very different purposes.

Not all vested interests are necessarily in opposition. Those who have vested interests in physical planning, such as realtors, banks administering trusts and estates, architects and builders, utility and transportation companies, may be ardent supporters of the physical plan worked out for their communities. Vested interests need not be an opposition group. What their attitudes will be depends upon how the plan is interpreted to them, how much they feel they have to say in its formulation, and upon the essential fairness and common sense used in its preparation and application. The tempo at which it is being put into effect will likewise affect the attitudes of these groups.

One must also realize that these vested interests are often organized. The members may be held together quite informally simply by periodically talking over the situation and deciding what their individual action should be; or they may have their own trade or professional association which becomes the official spokesman of

[13] *Ibid.,* p. 33.

the vested interest. Thus it is important to know the spokesmen for each vested interest, either as informal leaders or as organizational representatives. The city planner who sticks simply to his maps and his statistical tables fails to draw up the kind of reports and recommendations which take into account the feasible steps at a given time. Unless the planner makes a conscious effort to become familiar with these vested interests, he will be aware of only the vocal opposition whose members have no hesitation in expressing their dissent from the decisions of the planning commission; he also needs to know where he can look for support among those whose dollars and cents are likewise tied up in the decision reached.

Groups pressuring for change. Wide-awake communities usually have some individuals and groups pressuring for changes affecting the physical aspects of the city. They may not have much to gain financially from the proposed changes but will be rewarded with the satisfaction of seeing some cause won or in having contributed to what they consider the betterment of their community. These frequently include men's civic groups, women's clubs, church organizations, and a number of other widely diversified types, which for various reasons decide to push some community project. Many of these proposals would fit in excellently with the city plan; others would retard it. For example, residents in one part of a city may wish to have the city buy up a few vacant lots and convert them into a playground; elsewhere, there is a pressure for the construction of a swimming pool, with little thought having been given to the problem of water supply and disposal. Other groups may be joining in a drive for a city auditorium and plan to use a site much better suited for another purpose. Still another group may be seriously and effectively agitating for more adequate public housing and may have gone so far in their plans as to suggest that present slums be replaced on the spot by new units, even though the Master Plan seeks to convert this area into a warehouse district because of its close proximity to the railroad and through highways.

The obvious step, although many planners never consider this to be a part of their job, would be to meet with these groups and try to give them an over-all view of what their community could become if some rational, comprehensive physical plan were followed. It could be pointed out that even the best plan can be changed when better arguments are presented or when experience suggests the wisdom of a change, but that mere pressure for change alone is not sufficient reason for modification.

Resolution of Conflict. The discussion so far shows that physical planning cannot avoid involvement in conflict. The very fact that the planner seeks to help the people of a community move from present conditions to some conditions assumed to be more desirable is an open invitation to difference of opinion, running into vested interests and real conflict. The best planning is that which provides sufficient information to avoid that opposition which arises simply out of misunderstanding. This assumes that the values and norms mentioned above are taken into account and that an expert job of informing the public is carried through. It also means that those responsible for planning are willing to listen to the ideas of the residents of the community, since in this way a better plan is usually brought about. Yet, no public relations program is going to eliminate all conflict in physical planning, since people's pocketbooks are affected at many points. An individual property owner may feel abused and may rightly conclude that the plan would cause major shifts in his personal plans, or groups of taxpayers may rise up in opposition to the bond issues which might be necessary if certain recommendations in the plan are to be put into effect.

Fortunately, communities through the centuries have worked out ways of dealing with conflicts of this sort. Where it is a matter of determining community sentiment on a bond issue or some similar matter which can be put to the vote, the ballot is the means of resolving conflict—at least officially—although personal resentments may still remain. When, however, there is a question of an individual's rights versus the welfare of the community, a court decision resolves the conflict and the losing party must abide by the decision, although it may exercise its right of appeal until it has exhausted this possibility of having a decision in its favor.

These considerations bear out the fact that the community is a very lively arena of action and that the physical planner cannot hope to divorce himself, or his plan, from its influence.

REFERENCES AND SUGGESTED READINGS

1. ADAMS, E. M. "The Logic of Planning," *Social Forces,* XXVIII (May, 1950), 419–23.
2. American Public Health Association, Committee on the Hygiene of Housing. *Planning the Neighborhood.* Chicago: Public Administration Service, 1948.
3. ANDERSON, WILLIAM. "Political Aspects of City Planning," in Theodore Caplow (ed.), *City Planning: A Selection of Readings in Its Theory and Practice.* Minneapolis: Burgess Publishing Company, 1950.
4. BERNARD, JESSIE. *American Community Behavior.* New York: The Dryden Press, 1949, ch. 29.
5. COLEAN, MILES L. *Renewing Our Cities.* New York: Twentieth Century Fund, 1953, pp. 37–88.

6. Dean, John P. "The Myths of Housing Reform," *American Sociological Review,* XIV (April, 1949), 281–88.

7. Dewey, Richard. "The Neighborhood, Urban Ecology, and City Planners," *American Sociological Review,* XV (August, 1950), 502–7. (Critical of neighborhood unit plan.)

8. Erickson, E. Gordon. "The Superhighway and City Planning: Some Ecological Considerations With Reference to Los Angeles," *Social Forces,* XXVIII (May, 1950), 429–34.

9. Foley, Donald L. "The Daily Movement of Populations into Central Business Districts," *American Sociological Review,* XVII (October, 1952), 538–43.

10. ———. "Urban Daytime Population: A Field For Demographic-Ecological Analysis," *Social Forces,* XXXII (May, 1954), 323–30.

11. Gallion, Arthur B. *The Urban Pattern: City Planning and Design.* New York: D. Van Nostrand Co., Inc., 1950, ch. 17: "The Legal Foundation."

12. Hillman, Arthur. *Community Organization and Planning.* New York: The Macmillan Co., 1950, entire book.

13. Kuper, Leo. "Social Science Research and the Planning of Urban Neighborhoods," *Social Forces,* XXIX (March, 1951), 237–43.

14. Loring, William C., Jr. "Housing Characteristics and Social Disorganization," *Social Problems* (January, 1956), 160–68.

15. McDougal, Myres Smith, and Haber, David. *Property, Wealth, Land: Allocation, Planning and Development.* Charlottesville: Michie Casebook Corporation, 1948.

16. Perry, Clarence Arthur. *Housing for the Machine Age.* New York: Russell Sage Foundation, 1939.

17. Reeder, Leo G. "Social Differentials in Mode of Travel, Time and Cost in the Journey to Work," *American Sociological Review,* XXI (February, 1956), 56–63.

18. Riemer, Svend. "Social Planning and Social Organization," *American Journal of Sociology,* LII (May, 1947), 508–16.

19. Schnore, Leo F. "The Separation of Home and Work: A Problem For Human Ecology," *Social Forces,* XXXII (May, 1954), 336–43.

20. Warren, R. L. *Studying Your Community.* New York: Russell Sage Foundation, 1955, chs. V and VI.

21. Wirth, Louis. "Housing As a Field of Sociological Research," *American Sociological Review,* XII (April, 1947), 137–43.

Chapter 20

COMMUNITY DEVELOPMENT

INTRODUCTION

During both world wars many American citizens became heavily involved in community activities devoted to the war effort. Following World War I this interest in the community continued for a short while with an initial burst of enthusiasm and then faded away. At the end of World War II the momentum also continued as people turned from wartime to peacetime activities. Instead of dying out, however, this interest in the community has accelerated to the point that it has become almost a social movement. Of course, between the wars, especially in the thirties, noteworthy community undertakings were being carried out but without the self-conscious and studied procedures now being followed by many community leaders. A contributing factor to the staying power of the community approach after World War II was the knowledge of community structure and processes gained since World War I and the willingness by many people involved in social action to take advantage of some of this knowledge. Then too, many professional social scientists took a deep interest in the growth of community development programs and contributed their skills and insight to those guiding this movement.

One of the best descriptions of this increasing attention to the community just after World War II is found in an article by Wayland J. Hayes, who writes:

The tide or drift of community organization became so impressive that the National Planning Association was urged to call a National Conference on the Community in October 1947. Previous to this Conference a rough estimate of the over-all picture was made and multigraphed under the title, *Community Building in America*. On the basis of this report and other sources, more than half the population of America living in more than one-fourth of the communi-

389

ties seek to develop and control some of their most significant relationships by means of formal community organization other than government.[1]

Gordon W. Blackwell, in a brief survey of the community organization movement, points out:

> The movement of rationally directed community organization, then, has become manifest primarily in two ways: (1) attempts to develop machinery for comprehensive community mobilization, coordination, and planning; and (2) more restricted attempts to apply the philosophy, principles and techniques of community organization in the accomplishment of objectives in a single area of community life, such as health, education, recreation, and the like . . .
>
> Here, then, is an important field for sociological research—first, because community organization represents a significant development in American society and may offer a way of achieving a more satisfying way of life as people continually work out their adjustments to their natural environment and to each other; and second, because research in community organization leads the sociologist directly into the basic elements of social structure and social dynamics.[2]

Before the various approaches to community development can be described by the sociologist or by anyone else, some attention to terminology is necessary. The first term is *social organization,* which refers to the structural side of the community as a social system. As Blackwell has expressed it, social organization "embraces the totality of continuing social relationships which develop in a society."[3] This social organization, for the most part, comes into being "spontaneously rather than by rational design."[4] Chapter 11 has dealt chiefly with the social organization aspect of a community.

But the concept *community organization* has taken quite a different twist. It was the term that those responsible for early efforts at community amelioration gave to their programs. They were consciously mobilizing community resources, refashioning social relationships in such a way as to bring about a desired result. Since there is purpose behind it, it should be based on sound information about the community. Hayes sagely advises:

> Community organization is a means of collective action to achieve some end or purpose assumed to be worth while. Community, then, refers to people who identify themselves with a particular local area and with purposes and actions to control or develop their collective life and interest. Therefore, the community must know itself and know its values and interests if it is to bring about balanced and satisfactory living conditions. It must be this in spite of internal dif-

---

[1] Wayland J. Hayes, "Revolution—Community Style," *Social Forces,* XXVIII (October, 1949), 3–4.

[2] Gordon W. Blackwell, "A Theoretical Framework for Sociological Research in Community Organization," *Social Forces,* XXXIII (October, 1954), 60.

[3] *Ibid.,* p. 57.

[4] *Ibid.,* p. 58.

ferentiation, stratification and mobility of persons and groups. Therefore, for the best interests of the community, it is not sufficient for conditions to be known to a few experts who "devise and sell" the citizens on a program which is good for them. The community must not only know what purpose it wishes to achieve, but it must understand how organization and what organization will serve to achieve the purpose. More important still the community must know the nature of the situation in which it finds itself in order to develop feasible and fundamentally desirable ends. If it enthusiastically embraces the rosy and fantastic proposals of misguided reformers, it may become disillusioned and cynical. If it passively submits to this and that suggestion of its paid professional servants, it will find itself in a confused and defeated state . . .[5]

More and more, people have been speaking of *community development* in preference to *community organization*. There may be two reasons for this: first, the health and welfare field has studied and publicized the techniques and procedures of community organization to the point where this term has taken on a social work connotation with many people. Where this has happened, those who were thinking in broader terms than the social welfare field found some other term more appealing. Second, *development* has a more popular appeal to most Americans than *organization* and certainly ties in much better with the economic approaches whose sponsors think of themselves as being involved in community development.

Many people in adult education and those stressing the community-centered school have been carrying on community organization in the sense that they have helped community members set up discussion groups and councils to improve their own knowledge about many matters and also to act upon items of community concern affecting education. Community development would embrace their work as well. City planners, agricultural extension personnel, and civic club leaders are also engaged in community development but would probably not identify themselves with the field of community organization. Thus community development provides a larger umbrella under which people can gather than does community organization, although anyone who wanted to equate the two terms by citing the standard definitions could make a good case for doing so. But that is the usage adopted here, as a later section discussing national community development programs will show.

ECONOMIC DEVELOPMENT AND COMMUNITY DEVELOPMENT

The City and Economic Development. Because of the growing interest in problems of economic development not only in the United States but abroad, it is well to gain some historical per-

[5] Hayes, *op. cit.*, p. 5.

spective which will reveal the connection between this type of development and community life. It is hard for many people brought up in the western world to realize that 150 years ago their economy and communities resembled quite closely those now found in Asian countries where about 80 per cent of the people live in agricultural villages, and what are termed "cities" are really population agglomerations characterized by relatively simple social organization. But with the rise of the industrial cities a century and a half ago, which, incidentally, sprang from villages or small towns more often than from previously established cities, new social arrangements came into existence. In the Western world these cities, according to Bert F. Hoselitz:

. . . adopted and modified the old institutions, but there was never any question that each of these rapidly growing entities formed a "corporation," a whole of some sort, that the inhabitants of the city were the members of one and the same community and that they had rights and privileges in the community and duties towards it . . . In spite of slums and low housing and sanitary standards in many parts of the industrial cities, the whole city formed a community. It was not merely altruism or beneficent self-interest which made some municipal reformers agitate for slum clearance and municipal improvement; an important role was played by the sentiment of community; i.e., the conception that any blemish in the city's landscape was a matter of concern for all its citizens.[6]

Hoselitz points out two ways in which the sentiment of community was given expression. The first was in the tradition of self-government, of the city's taking care of its own present and evolving needs. The second was the attachment of the city's population to the urban way of life which led to a clearer distinction between the city and the country. It also led to the development of functionally specific areas in the city itself:

The concentric arrangement of modern industrial cities, with their central business districts and their changing belts of industrial and residential areas, the location and function of district shopping centers, the pattern of intracity communications and many other features of a similar kind, show the interdependence of all parts of a city upon one another and are proof of the over-all unity of the urban community in spite of its internal wide diversity.[7]

Another characteristic of industrial cities is the fact that their growth was associated for the most part with the demand for labor; people moved there because employment opportunities existed. A third characteristic of the industrial city in economically advanced countries is the role it plays in the process of cultural change. These

[6] Bert F. Hoselitz, "The City, The Factory and Economic Growth," *The American Economic Review*, XLV (May, 1955), 169.
[7] *Ibid.*, p. 169–70.

points illustrate that the modern industrial city, as we know it to-day, developed sociologically as its economy developed.

The contrast between such cities and those in the underdeveloped countries is striking. For instance, the African is not loyal to the city in which he lives, but to his family, his kin, his tribe, and the village from which he originally came.

One of the great contrasts between the cities of the underdeveloped countries and those of the West is, therefore, the absence of "city-consciousness" in Asia and Africa and perhaps also in Latin America. This implies, at the same time, that the distance between urban and rural styles of life is less pronounced than in Europe; that the loyalties of the urban dwellers are frequently to groups whose center of gravity is outside the city; that sojourn in the city is regarded often as only temporary; that migrants to the city from one village or province not only tend to settle in clusters of their own, but that even when they have become permanent city dwellers they maintain some ties with the region from which they came; and that each district of the city forms a community of its own, often rigorously separated from the others.[8]

Because of this historic sense of community, businessmen and industrialists in the Western world have supported civic enterprises by contributing generously of their time and money. A later and relatively recent development in their thinking, however, has been the realization that by their combined efforts they could do much more than as individuals to promote the physical well-being and economic welfare of their communities. Area development associations were set up at the end of World War II in many metropolitan centers for the purpose of dealing—through private enterprise, where possible—with problems of noise and smoke abatement, traffic control, urban renewal, and the attracting of desirable types of economic enterprises to the community. So successful were these efforts in a number of places that almost every community facing economic difficulties began to look upon "the bringing in of a factory" as a panacea. "If only we had larger payrolls," community leaders argued, "we would sell more merchandise, get more tax revenues, and balance our economy." Such thinking, however, frequently proved a snare and a delusion. A study of the experience of many communities and many industries has led to some sober second thoughts on the matter, as shown below.

Industrial Development. The best starting point for any community organization interested in promoting industrial development is to ask two simple questions: What kind of industry do we want? What are we likely to get in view of the conditions which industrialists take into account? The whole problem of community

[8] *Ibid.,* p. 175.

satisfaction is tied in with the first question and that of factory management satisfaction with the second question.

What a community should seek. Although there are marked regional variations in the United States, the findings of a study made recently in New England should prove of general nation-wide interest. In 1949 a study was conducted of 106 manufacturers who had set up new establishments in New England in the three years following World War II; these same firms were restudied in 1954 and 1955 in order to find what further lessons could be learned from the experience of these concerns. The conclusions indicate that:

1. Branch plants are generally a better bet for communities looking for new manufacturers than entirely new firms or relocations. Branch plants had a lower rate of failure, a larger proportion of firms which increased employment, a higher rate of employment growth and a larger proportion of firms which expected to add workers in the future than the new firms or relocations. Branch plants also tended to have fewer problems than the other types of concerns. In addition, they generally had larger financial and personnel resources than new firms and relocations, which enabled them to more easily solve problems which arise.

2. A community's chances for creating permanent new jobs and attracting entirely new firms also appear to be good, particularly if the new firms are given every assistance possible. A larger proportion of new firms than of branches or relocations were satisfied with their present locations. For smaller communities which don't have a large labor supply or which are seeking only small or medium-sized employers, new firms seem especially desirable.

3. In searching for new business, communities should carefully examine the quality of management, for this was the factor that was most important in determining success or failure. Even if the new management is of excellent quality, the community should appreciate the magnitude of special problems facing a new firm and endeavor to smooth its path to success.

4. Relocations appear to be a poor type of concern for communities to try to attract. Firms which moved their operations from one area to another failed more often and had a larger proportion of concerns with declining employment and a smaller proportion with greater employment than the new firms or branches. Several of the relocations included in this study seemed to bring many problems with them. Many did not appear to consider carefully all aspects of their new location before moving.

5. Communities would also be well-advised to make available more realistic information which presents the short-comings as well as the advantages of their area so that firms considering the community will be able to appraise all factors as they relate to their operations.[9]

What is a community likely to get? It is becoming increasingly clear that communities get the kind of industry that they deserve. If they have been concerned through the years with building up a better school system, if they have pride in their churches, their public

[9] *Monthly Review* (Federal Reserve Bank of Boston, September, 1955), p. 4.

auditorium, their crime and traffic records, then they are apt to receive firms whose management is of a high caliber and a definite asset to the community. If, on the other hand, there has been little evidence of local pride and no great willingness to cooperate for the good of the whole community, the firms which will come are apt to be those looking for a "fast buck" and who know that by insisting on heavy contributions from the community before they come they will be able to leave later on with little cost to themselves. If they are in the highly competitive field of clothing manufacture, for example, they may require that the local community provide them with a building on a tax-free (even rent-free) basis for a period of years. They can ship in their sewing machines by truck and be ready to operate in a very short period of time. But should they later be required to pay taxes or should they have labor problems, they can just as easily load the same machines into trucks and go on into some other community to reap what benefit they can while the honeymoon lasts there.

The solidly based firm wants to become a full-fledged member of the community and is usually willing to pay its share. If it is investing heavily in physical plant facilities and other expenses necessary to open operation, it may ask for tax considerations in the beginning, but it certainly does not expect to be placed forever in an unduly favored position.

Other Types of Economic Development. But the gaining of new industry by no means exhausts the field of economic development in American communities. The dressing up of store fronts, the providing of free parking space for rural people, the promotion of recreational facilities, which attract more people to town, and the insistence on good business practices by the merchants themselves tend to develop the economy to the point where more trade means more income.

Under the sponsorship of state chambers of commerce or of some other large-scale group, the businessmen of many communities have gone into what has been termed "community development" rather than economic development. This broader term is used, since the organization that they call into being may have an education committee, a welfare committee, a labor committee, as well as a tourist attraction committee, an agriculture committee, and the like. As set up, the focus is community-wide. Where the community sponsors are chiefly motivated in economic terms, however, committees dealing with noneconomic matters often consist of people poorly chosen for their tasks, or these committees are neglected for what the officers think are more important matters. Over a period of time, what has started out nobly as a community enterprise ends up as economic development alone, which in itself is a worthwhile and legitimate activity, but one which may have unintentionally and unfortunately misrepresented the true nature of community development. Any one segment which tries to speak for the whole community, no matter how noble its sentiments, is apt to set back the cause of community development. Where business leaders work out a truly cooperative approach with representatives from many segments and parts of the community, they are more likely to advance together in the promotion of activities which benefit the whole community as well as themselves. Economic interests can be welded in with other interests.

COMMUNITY ORGANIZATION FOR HEALTH AND SOCIAL WELFARE

Many people besides businessmen have discovered that the community approach is an effective approach in the furtherance of some campaign or organizational program. They "organize" the community. This has been done to such an extent by state and national organizations that some of the local leaders are beginning to feel that they are being "used" to serve outsiders' interests and not those of the community. One man put it this way: "The representative of the State Health Department came around to ask if I would serve as a member of a Community Health Advisory Committee. I agreed. Then we began to have meetings every month or six weeks, and the representative would spend the whole time telling us about the work of the department and what we were supposed to do to help its program in this community. He never asked us what we thought ought to be done or how it ought to be done, but kept telling us instead."

This same individual also recounted how many organizations to raise money for national programs sent specialists in to assure that all segments of the community were being represented in the drive so that a good showing could be made. According to him, the community was being organized to take money out of the community, not to bring money into the community or to realize objectives of the local people.

This is an aspect of the problem of horizontal and vertical coordination which Roland L. Warren has so well described. "As the schools, churches, social agencies, business establishments and other community facilities multiply and differentiate, there is need for keeping these facilities in some sort of adequate coordination with respect to each other. This coordinating function can be performed within the community, along the *horizontal axis,* through the community welfare council or various types of local planning agencies."[10] Or the coordination can be carried out at what he calls "the supercommunity level." This brings in the *vertical axis.* "Thus the national organization of the labor union, the Red Cross, the Methodist Church or a state department of education can lay down rules and procedures for the structure and function governing its particular community association or agency, thus fitting the community organization into the vertical system of local members, local units, district, regional, state and national organization, and in this way the efforts can be coordinated along the vertical axis of common interest."[11]

Warren then indicates that many of the organizations in the supercommunity may or may not be good "citizens" of the communities where they have representative groups.

The conflict between vertical and horizontal axes of orientation is nowhere more readily apparent in our communities today than in the two competing systems of fund-raising for health and welfare. I am referring, of course, to the all-inclusive community chest campaign, on the one hand, and the special fund-raising campaigns, particularly of the various health groups, on the other. Here is the horizontal orientation of agencies getting together for fund-raising on a locality basis, and the vertical orientation of state and national organizations reaching into the local community through their individualized, task-oriented branches, to carry on fund-raising activities in little relation to what this adds up to on the local community level.[12]

The implications of this state of affairs are clear: at the very time when more horizontal coordination is needed because of the increasing complexity of fund-raising, it becomes more difficult to achieve in the face of the vertical coordination which is being forced upon local groups. The representatives of the supercommunity, such as the official of the State Health Department mentioned at the beginning of this section, may already think they "have all the answers" before they come into the community; they may be paternalistic, but they are also—if successful—a disruptive force in the community. On the other hand, the local community coordinator is permissive; he is the nonspecialist "whose chief concern is with what happens to the interrelated parts of the community in planning, coordinating and changing . . ."[13] He is more interested in

[10] Roland L. Warren, "Toward a Reformulation of Community Theory," *Human Organization,* XV (Summer, 1956), 9.

[11] *Ibid.,* p. 9.

[12] *Ibid.,* p. 9.

[13] *Ibid.,* p. 11.

the process and what happens to the people than in a particular program which he must "sell."

In most communities the field of social welfare provides some of the best illustrations of community coordination and cooperation. As indicated earlier, community organization for social welfare is not community development in the broader sense, but it can very well be fitted into the larger picture. The Community Chest and the social welfare planning council frequently associated with it not only draw upon a larger cross section of the community than do other community efforts, but the very pinch of inadequate financial support often forces economies and coordination where they might not otherwise occur. This will become clear in the discussion of the over-all community council in connection with club and group projects.

COMMUNITY DEVELOPMENT AND GROUP PROJECTS

The experience that most Americans have with community development is through club projects, especially for those who belong to women's clubs, men's service groups, and many other types of associations. Some organization with which they are connected decides singlehandedly or in conjunction with other groups to undertake some enterprise for the community. As a matter of fact, it is hard for an association in many American communities to consider itself wide-awake unless it has one or more committees involved in some activity of a constructive or philanthropic nature. One way of viewing community development would be to think of it as the totality of all of these sporadic projects, occurring over a given period of time, which fire away at problems of the aged, juvenile delinquency, relief to the poor, more support to the schools, or commemoration of some historic event. But these widely diversified activities, when uncoordinated, temporarily alleviate the problem without moving toward any long-run solution. Most of the problems are too big for any one organization to handle alone, and only through concerted, community-wide efforts can some of them be effectively dealt with.

The Community Council. It is correct to speak of community development—as far as club projects are concerned—when some formal body such as a community council has been set up to keep each organization informed about what others are doing, to plan for unmet needs, and to combine resources when this seems to be the best approach. A community council comes into existence in any one of the following several ways.

1. Representatives of all interested organizations come together to work out means of avoiding duplication or otherwise to make the efforts of their organizations in community development more fruitful
2. Representatives of different neighborhoods, various professional and occupational interests may be called together to provide a cross-section of opinion and a bulwark of support for those that have current community programs underway; and
3. A combination of organization representatives and citizens at large, who speak for segments not ordinarily involved in the types of organizations sending spokesmen, may unite in a council.

The mistake is sometimes made of giving this community council the right to dictate, though gently, to member organizations as to what they should or should not do in the way of community activities. Community councils tend to last much longer, however, if they serve as a clearinghouse of information and as a place where those groups who want to cooperate can do so without any over-all authority telling them that they must do so.

A helpful discussion of citizen participation in community development is provided by F. Stuart Chapin, Jr., who uses the following figures to show the difference between unorganized and coordinated community development activities.[14] In Figure 25 every group is on its own, each trying perhaps conscientiously to do a good job but wasting much energy and resources in the process.

In Figure 26 coordination takes place first among those in similar areas of interest and then occurs again at a higher or more inclusive level. Chapin goes into a depth of detail not possible here about organizational procedures as he indicates how this coordination can be achieved and maintained.

Partial Substitutes for a Community Council. Even though a community council may not exist, and its formation may seem to be difficult, there are still ways in which members can express their views and on occasions lead toward some plan of action. These ways are quite different in nature and are each only a partial substitute for a thoroughgoing, active, successful community council.

The presidents' round table. It is obvious to many people that the various service and civic clubs could make a greater contribution if there was some coordination among them. One simple device is to have a meeting of the presidents of these clubs once a month to discuss the projects in which each is interested and to work out any cooperative patterns that might seem desirable. The most im-

[14] F. Stuart Chapin, Jr. "A Plan for Citizen Participation in Community Development," *Social Forces*, XXV (March, 1947), 313–20.

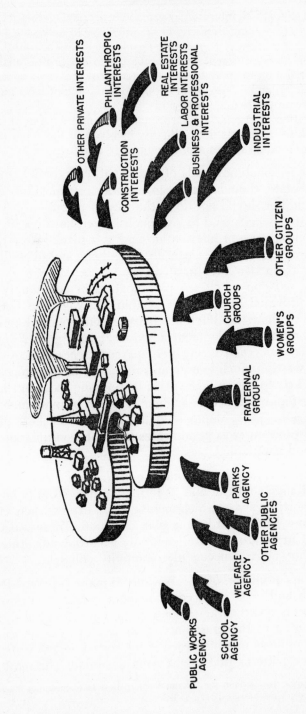

OTHER PRIVATE INTERESTS

PHILANTHROPIC INTERESTS

REAL ESTATE INTERESTS

LABOR INTERESTS

BUSINESS & PROFESSIONAL INTERESTS

CONSTRUCTION INTERESTS

INDUSTRIAL INTERESTS

OTHER CITIZEN GROUPS

CHURCH GROUPS

WOMEN'S GROUPS

FRATERNAL GROUPS

PARKS AGENCY

OTHER PUBLIC AGENCIES

WELFARE AGENCY

SCHOOL AGENCY

PUBLIC WORKS AGENCY

FIG. 25. Unorganized community development activities.

Source: F. Stuart Chapin, Jr., "A Plan for Citizen Participation in Community Development," *Social Forces,* XXV (March, 1947), 314–15.

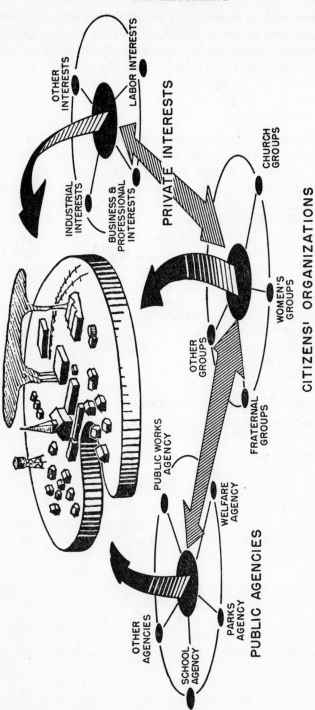

OTHER INTERESTS

LABOR INTERESTS

INDUSTRIAL INTERESTS

BUSINESS & PROFESSIONAL INTERESTS

PRIVATE INTERESTS

CHURCH GROUPS

WOMEN'S GROUPS

OTHER GROUPS

FRATERNAL GROUPS

CITIZENS' ORGANIZATIONS

PUBLIC WORKS AGENCY

WELFARE AGENCY

PARKS AGENCY

SCHOOL AGENCY

OTHER AGENCIES

PUBLIC AGENCIES

Fig. 26. Coordinated community development activities.

Source: F. Stuart Chapin, Jr., "A Plan for Citizen Participation in Community Development," *Social Forces*, XXV (March, 1947), 314–15.

portant purpose such a round table serves is that of providing information, since one group is not likely to start on a project if it knows that another group has already worked out plans to do the same thing. Usually it will turn to something else as a substitute. The presidents of the men's groups may have their own round table, but in some communities the presidents of both the men's and women's groups meet together.

Letters to the editors. Almost every community has a few people, each of whom would like to serve as *vox populi,* or the voice of the people. Some who write letters to the editor may be dismissed as cranks pleading a special cause, but frequently letters from highly respected citizens can have considerable effect in mobilizing opinion relative to a course of action. The social standing of the writer and the organization he represents has much to do with the acceptance of his point of view. Just as an editor has to make a selection from hundreds of news items or write one or two editorials from among a large number of possible topics, so he has to select which letters to publish. Different criteria may determine his selection: reader interest, space limitations, fear of reprisals by subscribers or advertisers, or personal bias. Thus under certain circumstances letters to the editor may partially substitute for the community council but only in the sense of bringing a pressing matter to public attention. There is no follow-up to this public interest, and the issue may again subside and be largely forgotten.

Human relations councils. Many medium and large cities have human relations councils which are designed to reduce race tension, labor-management conflict, and other points of friction among dissimilar groups in the community. For the most part, these are appointed by the city officials and even financed by public funds. They have quasi-official status and may make recommendations to the city council about proper ways to treat disrupted social relationships. Usually such human relations councils are administered by executives trained in psychology and the social sciences who possess an interest in over-all community welfare. For that reason, the council seeks to carry out its program in conjunction with many already-established organizations and performs important tasks of education. In concept and actual operation it is only a partial substitute for a community council, since its focus is more upon problems of racial and group misunderstanding, which may or may not cover a number of other types in which local people are interested. Its inclusion in a community council, along with an area development committee and other special interest types, can give strength to a council and work out advantageously to both parties. But once it seeks to serve as a community council, it is apt to lose some of the force required to deal with the special problems for which it is responsible.

But there is more to organizational projects than coordination. They tend to move through certain well-defined sequences which can be studied and predicted. James W. Green and Selz C. Mayo studied 145 community-needs-oriented actions in ten rural communities in North Carolina varying from the construction of a community meeting house by a community improvement association to the provision of uniforms for the local high school band by the Lions Club. As a result of their study, they posit four stages through which these community actions go, although they point out that sometimes the distinctions between these stages may be hard to recognize. "These stages are: (1) the initiation of action or 'idea'; (2) goal definition and planning for achievement; (3) the implementation of plans; and (4) goal achievement and consequences."[15] Each of these stages may be further broken down into various phases, which need not concern us here. What is important is the recognition that if one is involved in a community project, one can view it as a sequence of actions and determine at any point in time just how far the action (or project) has proceeded. When viewed in such analytically manageable terms, community development becomes not a nebulous but an orderly process concerning which calculations can be made and sound plans drawn up.

NATIONAL PROGRAMS OF COMMUNITY DEVELOPMENT

Few Americans are well informed about the large-scale community development programs operating in many underdeveloped countries of the world. Newspaper headlines play up earthquakes, shifts in political leadership, visits of dignitaries from one country to another, and the relations between the United States and underdeveloped countries, but the general public is unaware of the tremendous drive on the part of the governmental leaders in these countries to press ahead with modernization in every line of human activity, in spite of almost overwhelming handicaps of inadequate finances, insufficient technological training, and a social structure frequently poorly adapted to dynamic change.

In the face of such difficulties the governments of these underdeveloped countries have turned to community development as one means of enlisting the vast human resources of their peoples. They

---

[15] James W. Green and Selz C. Mayo, "A Framework for Research in the Actions of Community Groups," *Social Forces*, XXXI (May, 1953), 323.

have embarked upon nation-wide programs destined, they hope, to reach eventually into every village and to affect the life of every individual citizen. These programs are often complex in character in that they seek in some cases to raise the general level of living as a whole simultaneously; other programs stress some one aspect, such as mass education or public health at a given period of time, but usually the program seeks to coordinate all efforts at village improvement into a unified endeavor.

A general picture of these programs at work may be had by reading the reports of three teams, each consisting of two or three Americans, who studied community development programs in different parts of the world in the summer of 1955. These teams were sent out by the United States International Cooperation Administration, which has contributed to the community development work in many of the countries surveyed. Team 1 prepared a report on India, Pakistan, and the Philippines; Team 2, on India, Iran, Egypt, and the Gold Coast; Team 3, on Jamaica, Puerto Rico, Bolivia, and Peru. A summary paragraph or two about a single country treated in two of the reports will give some idea of the scope of some of these programs:

Community Development in India

With independence, India was faced with the challenge of effective development of her natural and human resources. The "Community Development Programme," initiated October 2, 1952 is a major aspect of the response to this challenge. It is designed to aid the inhabitants of the 558,000 villages that include over 80 per cent of India's population in attaining a higher social and material level of well-being. The program is based on the philosophy of rural development by means of guided self help: villagers are aided in recognizing their needs and potentialities and are given technical, financial and moral backing in programs which help fulfill these needs. "Community development" means particularly improvements in agriculture and animal husbandry, provision for drinking and irrigation water, the building of roads connecting villages with main highways, education, health and sanitation, the stimulation of cottage industries, land reform, rural cooperatives and credit, etc.

. . . Most of the developmental work is done by technicians administratively responsible to established government organizations (e.g., agriculture, public health) and by a new individual, the "multi-purpose village level worker," the VLW, who stimulates much village activity and coordinates the work of specialist technicians on the local level . . .[16]

The report then goes on to describe the administrative and operational levels from the national on down through the block (the basic unit of one hundred villages) to the village, where the multipurpose

[16] Harold S. Adams, George M. Foster, and Paul S. Taylor, *Report on Community Development Programs in India, Pakistan and the Philippines* (Washington, D. C.: International Cooperation Administration, October 5, 1955), pp. 10–11.

village level worker provides the grass-roots stimulation. As of April 1955 there were 718 blocks in operation, covering approximately eighty thousand villages with a population of fifty-three million. This number is to be raised by March, 1961 to cover the entire country with a total of 3,808 blocks. Seldom has there been such planning on so gigantic a scale.

Community Development in Jamaica

Norman Manley, foremost barrister and Rhodes scholar, was one of the first to familiarize himself with the problems of the common people of Jamaica. On their behalf he voiced the situation of the banana laborers and obtained the cooperation of the owners of the United Fruit and Standard Fruit and Steamship Companies. He has remained since 1938 the untiring leader and friend of the Jamaica Welfare Program, continuing its work with government funds when the subsidy from the fruit companies ceased. Volunteer workers in the tiny villages of the bush hills feel free to write him; all seem to have known him personally; from the very beginning he has been engaged intimately in their program.

. . . [In 1953] the director of the Jamaica Social Welfare Commission described "rural welfare as based largely on community development by the people themselves under the guidance of the leaders." Every aspect of the Jamaica welfare program, spreading throughout the island in every city, village and farm community, is based fundamentally on the principle of "make do with what we have; with our own labor and ingenuity we can build a new Jamaica." Or as another leader expressed it, Jamaica has the pieces to build a better place to live in. We use what we have and do not expect manna. The government is ourselves. We must do it."[17]

It is interesting to note that the Jamaica Welfare Society, which began its activities by the cooperative building of community centers, is subsidized by the banana exporters at the rate of one cent for every bunch shipped. The paid professional leaders are called officers of the Jamaica Social Welfare Commission, but the great majority of workers are voluntary. For example, in a typical district of twenty-five villages, there were three paid workers, who could, of course, call upon the services of specialists in cooperatives, nutrition, handicraft, agriculture, etc., but there were from two- to three-hundred volunteer leaders.

Those who prepared the third report pointed out that in Iran there were really three programs going under the name of Community Development; that in Egypt, where government centralization is very strong, the programs being sponsored were paternalistic and not very well coordinated with each other, whereas in the Gold Coast (now independent Ghana), at the district level, the

[17] Verna A. Carley, and Elmer A. Starch, *Report on Community Development Programs in Jamaica, Puerto Rico, Bolivia and Peru* (Washington, D. C.: International Cooperation Administration, November 1, 1955), p. 17.

Mass Education and Community Development Section maintains a district staff headed by a Mass Education Officer, who is assigned to thirty or forty villages with a population of approximately forty thousand persons. Even though he cannot spend much time in each of these villages throughout the year, he does try to work through the District Councils.[18]

A quick round-the-world trip touching on every continent would reveal the rich variety of community development programs and the strong support which many of them receive from the central or federal governments. To those in charge, such programs seem a way toward democratization as well as toward raising the level of living. Few regimes, no matter how unconcerned they may be for the ordinary villager, can consider themselves up to date on the world scene if they are not paying lip service at least to the idea of community development, which forms an important item on the agenda of the Economic and Social Council meetings at the United Nations. In other words, some of the programs and activities taken as commonplace in many American communities have become nation-wide crusades in many parts of the world.

SYSTEMATICS OF COMMUNITY DEVELOPMENT

It should by now be very clear that the term Community Development (often abbreviated as CD) can mean many things to many people. Four ways of viewing it can be seen in Fig. 27, which suggests that some people think of it as a process, some as a method, others as a program, and still others as a movement.

In an effort to promote the systematic study and practice of community development, many people have drawn up series of what they have termed "principles," on the valid assumption that one does not transfer an actual experience from one country to another but rather the principles which that experience reinforced or demonstrated. The United Nations, in a Report on Concepts and Principles of Community Development, set forth ten such principles. These are listed here not because they comprise a final, definitive, or necessarily the best list, but because they illustrate the type of thinking that one finds in the community development field. Remember that these are supposedly applicable to most parts of the world and were not formulated to deal with just a particular community in South Dakota or Ohio.

[18] William C. Gibson, Hugh B. Masters, and Ernest F. Witte, *Report on Community Development Programs in India, Iran, Egypt and Gold Coast* (Washington, D. C.: International Cooperation Administration, December, 1955).

1. As a Process

CD as a process moves by stages from one condition or state to the next. It involves a progression of changes in terms of specified criteria. A neutral, scientific term, subject to fairly precise definition and measurement; expressed chiefly in social relations; e.g., change from condition where one or two people or a small elite within or without local community make decision for rest of the people to condition where people *themselves* make these decisions about matters of common concern; from state of minimum to one of maximum cooperation; from condition where few participate to one where many participate; from condition where all resources and specialists come from outside to one where local people make most use of their own resources, etc. Emphasis is upon what happens to *people*—socially and psychologically.

2. As a Method
(Process and Objective)

CD is a means to an end; a way of working so that some goal is attained. Other methods (such as change by decree or fiat; change by use of differential rewards; change by education) may be supplementary to the CD method which seeks to carry through the stages suggested under *process* in order that the will of those using this method (national government, private welfare, agency or local people themselves) may be carried out. The process is guided for a particular purpose which may prove "harmful" or "helpful" to the local community, depending upon the goal in view and the criteria of the one passing judgment. Emphasis is upon some *end*.

3. As a Program
(Method and Content)

The method is stated as a set of procedures and the content as a list of activities. By carrying out the procedures, the activities are supposedly accomplished. When the program is highly formalized, as in many five-year plans, the focus tends to be upon the program rather than upon what is happening to the people involved in the program.

It is as a *program* that CD comes into contact with subject-matter specialties such as health, welfare, agriculture, industry, recreation.

Emphasis is upon *activities*.

4. As a Movement
(Program and an Emotional Dynamic)

CD is a crusade, a cause to which people become committed. Not neutral (like process) but carries an emotional charge; one is either for it or against it.

It is dedicated to *progress,* a philosophic and not a scientific concept, since progress must be viewed with reference to values and goals which differ under different political and social systems.

CD as a movement tends to become institutionalized, building up its own organizational structure, accepted procedures and professional practitioners.

Stresses and promotes the *idea* of community development.

Fig. 27. Four ways of viewing community development.

Ten Principles Stated in the UN Report on Concepts and Principles as Reported by the Secretary-General, 12 March 1957

Principle 1: Activities undertaken must correspond to the basic needs of the community; the first projects should be initiated in response to the expressed needs of people.

Principle 2: Local improvements may be achieved through unrelated efforts in each substantive field; however, full and balanced community development requires concerted action and the establishment of multi-purpose programmes.

Principle 3: Changed attitudes in people are as important as the material achievements of community projects during the initial stages of development.

Principle 4: Community development aims at increased and better participation of the people in community affairs, revitalization of existing forms of local government and transition towards effective local administration where it is not yet functioning.

Principle 5: The identification, encouragement and training of local leadership should be a basic objective in any programme.

Principle 6: Greater reliance on the participation of women and youth in community development projects invigorates development programmes, establishes them on a wide basis and secures long-range expansion.

Principle 7: To be fully effective, communities' self-help projects require both intensive and extensive assistance from the Government.

Principle 8: Implementation of a community development programme on a national scale requires: adoption of consistent policies, specific administrative arrangements, recruitment and training of personnel, mobilization of local and national resources and organization of research, experimentation and evaluation.

Principle 9: The resources of voluntary non-governmental organizations should be fully utilized in community development programmes at the local, national and international levels.

Principle 10: Economic and social progress at the local level necessitates parallel development on a wider national scale.[19]

These principles, looked at one by one, reveal many of the basic tenets of those who work professionally in community development programs. They have learned that a program cannot be imposed arbitrarily but if it is to take root, must be thought necessary locally. Sometimes the community development worker over a period of time sets in motion the process whereby people learn to feel that something is necessary. Many Americans may find the stress on government help, as expressed in Principle 7, too strong, but they would probably be equally surprised to learn how much help actually comes into their local community from state and federal sources. Nevertheless, the genius of community development as defined and carried out in the United States is the emphasis it gives to the nongovernmental aspects of the program. In a country so rich in economic resources and trained leadership, the private, voluntary approach is feasible, whereas in many underdeveloped countries, much time will have to elapse before physical and human resources are sufficiently developed to the point where the government can assume a more minor role.

[19] United Nations, Economic, and Social Council, *Report on Concepts and Principles of Community Development and Recommendations on Further Practical Measures To Be Taken by International Organizations* (New York: 12 March 1957, mimeographed), p. 13. These are summarized from an earlier UN report entitled, *Social Progress Through Community Development* (New York, 1955).

At the present time much of the thinking, both nationally and internationally, in community development is so *diffuse,* with so many new experiments and approaches being tried, that no one has satisfactorily sifted the evidence to formulate and then demonstrate through controlled experimentation the fundamental hypotheses involved in planned community change. There are many statements, many "principles," many case studies, but as yet little validated social science theory. This represents a challenge to anyone interested in pushing back the frontiers of knowledge and systematizing the accumulated facts about community development—its nature, its operational principles, its successful techniques, the part played by the factors of the setting, which were described early in Chapter 11.

This discussion of community development serves as a fitting conclusion to this book, which has had as its theme the fact that the community is a social system. Not only must one understand the various components of the system as small operating units in their own right, but one must also see how these larger components interact to give the whole community system its unique characteristics or individuality. But the community is part of a larger society and, as a social actor, must deal with the influences brought to bear from outside. It possesses certain operational features which help it in this adjustment, as well as in the integration of its own indigenous components.

The purpose of this analysis has been not simply the enlightenment of the reader or even a passionate search for truth about society; it has been to help provide the understanding with which intelligent, loyal, imaginative community leaders can deal with the intricacies of community life more effectively in their efforts to guide the community toward what its members consider to be desirable changes in their way of life. At times, selfishness will predominate, and some community members will seek to use the community for what are fundamentally antisocial ends. But most of the time the knowledge gained can be made to serve the legitimate interests of individuals who realize that their own personal fortunes and enjoyment are tied in closely with those of the community in which they have put down their stakes. Good schools and good families go hand in hand; a sound economy and efficient local government work together; freedom of religion and freedom from fear are inseparable, as are the right to work and the right to rise in the social scale as the result of that work in the American scheme of things. In a very real sense, therefore, community development is a way of making the intangible values of the social heritage concrete in daily experience, of translating into action what most members of the community profess as noble sentiments, of using a greater measure of reason and less of prejudice in looking toward the future, and of involving more and more people—who become more interested and better informed—in decisions affecting their own welfare.

References and Suggested Readings

1. ALLEN, H. B. *Rural Reconstruction in Action: Experience in the Near and Middle East.* Ithaca: Cornell University Press, 1953.
2. BIDDLE, WILLIAM W. *The Cultivation of Community Leaders.* New York: Harper & Brothers, 1953.
3. BUELL, BRADLEY, and associates. *Community Planning for Human Services.* New York: Columbia University Press, 1952.
4. DAHIR, JAMES. *Communities for Better Living.* New York: Harper & Brothers, 1950.
5. GOODMAN, PERCIVAL and PAUL. *Communitas: Means of Livelihood and Ways of Life.* Chicago: University of Chicago Press, 1947.
6. GOULDNER, ALVIN W. *Studies in Leadership.* New York: Harper & Brothers, 1950.
7. GREER, THOMAS H. *American Social Reform Movements: Their Pattern Since 1865.* New York: Prentice-Hall, Inc., 1949.
8. HAIMAN, FRANKLYN S. *Group Leadership and Democratic Action.* Boston: Houghton Mifflin Company, 1951.
9. HAYES, WAYLAND J. *The Small Community Looks Ahead.* New York: Harcourt, Brace & Company, 1947.
10. HITCH, EARLE. *Rebuilding Rural America.* New York: Harper & Brothers, 1950.
11. KING, CLARENCE. *Organizing for Community Action.* New York: Harper & Brothers, 1948.
12. ———. *Your Committee in Community Action.* New York: Harper & Brothers, 1952.
13. KOOS, EARL LOMON. *The Health of Regionville: What the People Thought and Did About It.* New York: Columbia University Press, 1954.
14. LIPPITT, RONALD. *Training in Community Relations.* New York: Harper & Brothers, 1949.
15. MATTHEWS, MARK S. *Guide to Community Action.* New York: Harper & Brothers, 1954.
16. McKEE, E. M. *The People Act: Stories of How Americans Are Coming Together to Deal with Their Community Problems.* New York: Harper & Brothers, 1955.
17. OGDEN, JEAN and JESS. *Small Communities in Action: Stories of Citizen Programs at Work.* New York: Harper & Brothers, 1946.
18. ———. *These Things We Tried.* Charlottesville: University of Virginia Press, 1947.
19. OLSEN, E. G. *School and Community.* New York: Prentice-Hall, Inc., 1945.
20. POSTON, RICHARD WAVERLY. *Small Town Renaissance.* New York: Harper & Brothers, 1950.
21. SANDERS, IRWIN T. *Making Good Communities Better.* Rev. ed.; Lexington: University of Kentucky Press, 1952.
22. SCHACTER, HARRY W. *Kentucky on the March.* New York: Harper & Brothers, 1949.
23. SPICER, EDWARD H. (ed.) *Human Problems in Technological Change.* New York: Russell Sage Foundation, 1952.
24. STEINER, JESSE F. *The American Community in Action.* New York: Henry Holt & Co., 1928.
25. TATE, H. CLAY. *Building a Better Home Town.* New York: Harper & Brothers, 1954.

NAME INDEX

411

SUBJECT INDEX

The subitems under each heading are so arranged as to assist the reader in reviewing the main concepts treated in this book. When two groups of subitems appear under a term, those which define or state the general nature of the concept (e.g., as subsystem, as type of interaction) are listed first, since they give a quick, comprehensive treatment of the concept. Then follow more specific references which relate the main concept to particular aspects of the community (economy, government, transportation, etc.).